WITHDRAWN

MY LIFE

The Memoirs

of

CLAUDE BOWERS

1962

SIMON AND SCHUSTER

NEW YORK

LIBRARY OF CONGRESS CATALOG CARD NUMBER: 62-14275
MANUFACTURED IN THE UNITED STATES OF AMERICA
BY H. WOLFF BOOK MFG. CO., NEW YORK, N.Y.

Contents

Contents

CHAPTER I

Hoosier Town in the Eighties

THERE HAS ALWAYS BEEN a disposition in some quarters to dismiss the Middle West as drab and uninteresting, and yet I think the Midwesterner especially typifies the American way of life. The early settlers were men of endurance, enterprise and courage. Some left the well-ordered life of the East to seek their fortunes in the wilderness; others came from the South, men of meager means, too proud and independent to accept the status assigned them by the slaveowning aristocracy. These qualities of courage, pride, endurance and independence were the predominant characteristics of the Midwesterner, and I think they still are. Because Gilbert Chesterton was a wise man, when he came to America to learn for himself about American life he did not pitch his tent in crowded cities in the East, but settled down for a sojourn in a small town in Indiana. Fortunate I think the American whose boyhood days are spent in such a community. I was one of the fortunate.

I do not remember Westfield, Hamilton County, Indiana, the place of my birth, since my parents left there in my babyhood, shortly after the death of my only sister a week before I appeared upon the scene. The little town was inhabited mostly by Quakers, whose kindness at the time of the domestic tragedy made an indelible impression on my parents. But Westfield now had sad associations, and they moved to Jolietville soon after I was born. I have no recollection of the short time we spent there, though I am told that it was in Jolietville that I became a Democrat. I was being shown off in my father's store one day during the Presidential campaign of 1880. I was two years old and when the loungers teased me by cheering for Garfield, the Republican candidate,

I at once met the challenge with a "Naw, naw, rah for Hancock." My politics came early and I have been a partisan ever since.

Most of my first ten years were spent in Whitestown, a small town in Boone County, where everyone, including the poorest, lived in abundance. My paternal grandfather, Christopher Bowers, was one of the pioneers who, many years before, had cleared the wilderness, drained the swamps, bridged the streams, felled the forest and given the fields to cultivation. Most of the old pioneers still lived near Whitestown, and my grandfather's farm was on the edge of the town. The only industries in the town were a flour mill and a sawmill; the latter had seen its best days with the passing of the surrounding forests. It was a purely agricultural region. I recall it now as rather primitive, though differing not at all from most small towns of the time and place. The streets were unpaved, as were the sidewalks, and in winter and after rains in summer the pedestrian depended on planks to protect him from the mud. In the night he was fortunate if the plank did not slide in the slime and deposit him in the muck. There were no street lamps of any sort, of course, and a lantern was necessary equipment in every household; he who owned one more ornate than others' was very proud. The only entertainment was found in the Lutheran and Methodist churches. Since my father's people were Lutherans and my mother's Methodists, I attended the Sunday schools of both.

In the winter the stores served as clubs where men fresh from the farms, in work clothes stained by the soil, gathered about the big base-burner stove for gossip and the discussion of controversial political and religious subjects. Always convenient was a tobacco box filled with sawdust to serve as a cuspidor, and it was amazing with what dexterity the tobacco chewer could hit the box from a fantastic distance. As in the old coffeehouses of prejournalism days in London, these loungers about the stove disseminated the news of the town, the birth of babies, the illnesses of old men, the amorous adventures of the young. Everyone knew everybody in town and all about them, and it was the kind of friendly, neighborly community where the women flocked to the aid of the sick.

In these days of telephones, automobiles, radios, television and planes, the isolation of these small towns of the 1880s seems incredible. The people were thrown entirely on their own resources for entertainment. Lebanon, the county seat, was eight miles away and he who made the journey in less than an hour was criticized for cruelty to his horse. Indianapolis, but twenty miles away, seemed remote. Every morning and evening when the train came in the station platform was crowded with curious townsmen, for there was sheer romance in the thought that the passengers peering through the windows were bound for far places. Many met the train to get the Indianapolis papers, which were read literally from the first page to the last, and then the news was discussed with animation about the stove in the stores. Since it was a Democratic community, most people read the Indianapolis *Sentinel*, though a few Republicans slunk away with the *Journal* under their arms. In the evening all read the *News*.

The houses were comfortable but simple. The front room, or parlor, was used on Sundays and special occasions only; the rest of the time it was kept closed and curtained to protect the carpet from the sun. Most houses had an organ and everyone would sing, but the songs, usually from the hymnbooks, were sad and reeked with reminders of the brevity of life. I found them depressing and would escape to the orchard. I have never cared for hymns since, though my father had an excellent voice and I can still remember him singing.

The winters surely were longer in the Eighties. By the first of December the ground was covered with snow, and no one thought of shoveling it into wagons and hauling it away. The wind swept it into drifts, and when the sidewalks were beaten down by the feet of pedestrians one walked along an avenue of snow rising two or three feet high on either side, and thus it remained throughout the winter. In time it hardened and glistened in the sun. Then the people got out their sleighs and I can still hear the tinkling bells on the harness as they drove through the town and out into the country. The boys with their sleds raced boisterously over the white surface, made snowmen, and built forts from which they waged snowball battles for months. Only in April, when the spring thaws began and the snow turned to slush, and rivulets of ice water crept across the sidewalks and into one's shoes, did one realize that snow has its evil side.

The town had its "characters," some vivid in my memory after more than half a century. Dave Trout, the harness maker, who carried a cane because one leg was shorter than the other, amused the townsmen by posing as a Mormon. He knew the Mormon Bible by heart, and he was equally familiar with the Old and New Testaments. He had no vices I know of beyond a tongue that could bite like a viper. He loved polemics and was a natural debater, and he challenged opponents on subjects of their choosing. So wide was his reading, so varied his knowledge, that he invariably prevailed. Many times in early childhood I hovered on the edge of a crowd gathered about him as he sat in front of his shop with his chair tilted against the wall, and marveled at the ease with which he pulverized anyone who challenged him on politics or religion—though he favored religion as a subject. He had a biting wit, a keen sense of humor and a sarcastic tongue. When he was driven into a corner for want of mere facts, he opened his batteries of ridicule on his opponent, while the crowd shouted with laughter and slapped one another on the shoulder in sheer delight. It was he who organized a men's debating society, which met at intervals at night in the schoolhouse. The principal orators were the Lutheran preacher, the harness maker, the doctor and the teacher, and spectators would fill the schoolhouse to enjoy the verbal frolics.

Another town character was an old colonel, of slight build, with a short gray beard, who was never seen out of the faded blue uniform in which he had fought for the preservation of the Union. He had a good mind and considerable education, and I suspect it was his weakness for drink that so lowered his morale that he seemed content to eke out a living by providing meals and furnished rooms for stranded traveling salesmen. Usually he was quiet and seemed sad and morose, but liquor worked a transformation, and it was then that his mind and imagination were most astonishing. Always in his inebriation he relived his fighting days, "fought all his battles o'er again, and thrice he routed all his foes and thrice he slew the slain." He had fought in the battle of Shiloh, and in his cups he relived and refought it, describing it with a vividness and eloquence that would have done credit to Tacitus. These exhibitions were reserved for night, and when he appeared downtown after dark the young rowdies knew they could pull the bung out of the barrel of oratory by merely mentioning Shiloh. Instantly he would launch into a description, his usually sad eyes flashing, his voice ringing, and genuine eloquence would flow like a mountain

4

torrent from his lips. When he seemed on the point of running down, a sepulchral voice would softly murmur from the shadows, "Shiloh," and the orator was off on a fresh start.

Some of my most pleasing memories center in the shoemaker's tiny shop, with its smells of leather, of wood burning in the little stove, and of smoke curling from the corncob pipe that was always in the bearded old shoemaker's mouth when he worked. It was with him that I tried out an eight-year-old's opinions about politics, for the old man was also a Democrat. He would listen with chuckles and inject some pungent observations of his own. Mostly alone, he had time to think and he was well informed. It was in just such a shop that Lloyd George got his training in polemics.

With real affection I recall a very old couple, scarcely ever seen outside their own house, which was level with the street and in the tiny front room of which they sold hard candy to the children. They were seldom seen even in this room until a youngster appeared with his pennies. On the opening of the door a bell rang which summoned one or the other from the interior of the house. Usually it was the old lady, a very sweet old lady in a bonnet, who entered to minister to the needs of the children. She greeted them with an ingratiating smile and waited with infinite patience as they deliberated on their choice of sweets and counted out their pennies. The old couple's profits must have been meager, but they seemed very happy and contented.

Best of all I remember my grandfather, Christopher Bowers, known to the community as "Uncle Chris," who came to America in his very early manhood from the neighborhood of Frankfurt, Germany, more than a century ago, one of the many Germans who at that time abandoned their native land in search of greater freedom and a release from military rule. He landed in Charleston and moved westward to Tennessee, but his resources were limited and he could not submit to the humiliation of the social status of the non-slaveowning farmers; so, having married, he turned north, crossed the Ohio River and proceeded in a covered wagon to Indiana, where he found land and opportunity. He had taken possession of heavily timbered land desperately in need of draining. He and his wife, a woman of strong, even domineering character, had twelve children, but childbearing did not interfere with the near-

5

masculine work that fell to the lot of pioneer women. I heard my grandfather tell of the trials and tribulations of those primitive days. When the men went to the field, with every probability of an attack of malaria because of the swamps, they always carried a pocketful of quinine and, instead of a jug of water, a jug of whiskey, and when they felt the "shakes" coming on they would lick loose quinine from their hands and wash it down with pure whiskey from the jug.

My grandfather's house was burned in my childhood, and I saw it go up in flames. It was a large house, to accommodate twelve children. A wide hall ran through it to permit a free circulation of cooling air. A stairway ascended from the hall, and the many grandchildren amused themselves sliding down the banisters when no one was looking.

On Sundays and holidays the children and grandchildren gathered for a family dinner, which by present standards resembled a barbecue, with chicken, beef, spareribs, pork, all the vegetables in season, hot biscuits, with various spreads, the milk oozing from the butter fresh from the churn, and all topped off with two kinds of pie and cake. Superabundance was not unusual among the Hoosier farmers of the Eighties, but my grandfather was a robust trencherman and probably offered more than most.

He was slender, wiry, his face smooth-shaven, his twinkling eyes denoting a love of fun. He was a just and honest man and so regarded by the entire region. He was a convinced Democrat, but, finding controversy distasteful, he usually kept his politics and religion to himself. It was a bit different during the Civil War (which he always thought would have been prevented if Stephen A. Douglas, for whom he had voted, had been elected); he followed the line of Thomas A. Hendricks and Daniel W. Voorhees, and he did not escape some mild persecution from Indianapolis.

In those days the neighbors came to help when farmers threshed, and my most graphic memories of my grandfather's place is of these threshings. It was then the custom to furnish real banquets for the threshers, and for some days my aunts, who were excellent cooks, were feverishly active in preparation. The tables literally groaned beneath the weight of food. Since the farm was on the edge of the town and my grandfather's hospitality was well known, the merchants closed their stores at noon to join the threshers at the dinner table. The loafers of the town joined the procession and no one resented the intrusion. The consumption of food was enormous and the waste would seem culpable today. We small boys, eager to assist, were kept busy running back and forth to the threshing field with cold water for the workers, our only reward being an invitation to the "second table"—though my aunts hid away enough of the chicken drumsticks for us.

My father, Lewis Bowers, greatly resembled my grandfather in temperament. I have never known in my life a sweeter human being; he was loved by all who knew him. His generosity was extreme, and not a few took advantage of it. The pathetic death of my four-year-old sister, Gertrude, who in her dying moments tried to console him, haunted him throughout his life. He never fully recovered from the blow.

My mother, Juliet Bowers, was perhaps a stronger character, more ambitious, and I am indebted to her for the innumerable sacrifices she made for me in our darker days a little later. She lived into her sixty-second year and died in Washington.

As I have said, the community was overwhelmingly Democratic, and the town seethed and bubbled with politics throughout the year. The few Republicans, forced to unite, made up in fervor and fierceness what they lacked in numbers, as is usual with harassed minorities. I had a narrow escape from contamination once. The Republicans all but seduced me, a nine-year-old boy, with the offer of the tenor drum in the Republican band, but my father heard of the dire conspiracy and yanked me out without ceremony.

I recall clearly the Presidential campaign of 1888, when the Republicans nominated Harrison of Indiana against Cleveland. It was the custom in those days for the two parties to stage great demonstrations in the fairground in Lebanon, with distinguished orators on the platform. In every township and little town in the county the young boys and girls were packed into wagons gaily decorated with flags and bunting for these occasions. The congestion on the roads was such that often the long procession would be forced to stop for several minutes to permit the parking of the wagons in the fairground miles away. The juvenile politicians rejoiced in these delays, since they could count confidently on the farm women of the faith hurrying to the wagons with huge baskets filled with cakes and fruit. That year we sang a song whose meaning is a mystery to me today. All along the line we chanted with hoarse voices:

"Ha, ha, ha, what a fool I see
Standing on the platform of free whiskey."

Cleveland was being attacked as a free-trader, and presumably this was supposed to be a devastating retort to Harrison.

The fairground was always packed with men and women, and Voorhees was usually the orator. And what an orator! Tall, magnificently built, with a handsome head, luminous hazel eyes, a voice of melody, and a marvelous command of language, he lashed the partisans into a frenzy of enthusiasm. Four years earlier, in the first Cleveland campaign, when I was wearing a Cleveland-Hendricks cap, I was introduced to Voorhees by my father, and when he laid his hand on my head I felt I had been anointed.

Strange how some isolated incidents linger vividly in the memory! I recall such an incident in the campaign of 1888, the second Cleveland campaign, when his running mate was the great statesman Senator Allen G. Thurman, who was popularly associated with the red bandana handkerchief. I had joined the relatives on a visit to the farm of an aunt whose husband was going to a rally in Shelbyville, miles away, which Thurman was to address. An excited and enthusiastic group had gathered in the barnyard. The horse was hitched to the buggy, ready for the journey, chickens were clucking, roosters were crowing, and in the pasture cows were mooing. At length my uncle got into the buggy, and when, on driving through the gate, he took out a red bandana and waved it we could see that the country was saved.

For some inexplicable reason, during that campaign both parties in Whitestown conceived the idea of presenting a play with local talent. I even remember the names of the absurd plays, as well as the performances. The Democrats gravely presented *Lula the Pauper*, and the Republicans *All That Glitters Is Not Gold*. I remember it so well because of the distress of the Republicans over the stage fright of one of their artists, the son of a well-to-do

8

farmer, who on the approach of the ordeal of a public appearance became so panic-stricken that he announced his withdrawal a few days before the performance. It would have wrecked the play, but, more distressing, it would have made the Republican minority the laughingstock of the community. The father of the boy remonstrated and gave orders, but the intimidated actor refused to go on. Of course this was common knowledge; it was the sole topic of conversation in the stores, the churches, the streets and the homes, and all the Democrats were laughing and the Republicans cursing. But politics was serious in those days, and when the irate father threatened to disinherit the boy if he failed—and meant it—the unhappy youth screwed his courage to the sticking point and tearfully did his duty.

But my family was politically divided against itself. My mother's family were originally Republicans. Her father had joined the Republican Party on its formation, and in 1860 he was the party's nominee for the State Senate. When he was killed in the battle of Missionary Ridge his was the first body to be taken back for burial in Boone County. He had had a premonition that he would not survive the battle, and I have a letter to this effect written the night before with a pencil on soiled wrapping paper. Because he was ill at the time, his commanding officer had urged him not to go into action, but he wrote that his failure to fight in what threatened to be a fierce engagement would be charged to cowardice by his political enemies at home. Years later, a camp of the Sons of Veterans was named after him. At twilight on the day of his funeral, his oldest son shouldered his father's musket and hurried off down the country road to take his place in the Army. It is not unnatural that my mother's family were strong Republicans.

In summer in the 1880s I usually spent three weeks on my maternal grandfather's farm on the county line between Boone and Hamilton counties, near Big Springs, a tiny place with one general store. There were no children in the immediate neighborhood, and farms in those days were really isolated. Forced on my own resources for amusement, I followed the hired man at the plow, but mostly I relied on the books in the house. Most of these were biographies of Republican leaders, though one was of Thomas A. Hendricks, a concession to a Hoosier Vice-President.

9

It was on one of these visits that I was almost terrorized from my Democratic moorings. I was taken to Eagletown to hear a campaign speech by Corporal Tanner, one of the most obnoxious wavers of the bloody shirt. I was seriously disturbed when I heard him say, "In Michigan, where it's cold, they're almost all Republicans; in Indiana, where it's a little warmer, there are a few more Democrats; in Kentucky, where it's still warmer, there are more Democrats; in Mississippi, where it's very warm, they're almost all Democrats; and in hell, which is hot, they're all Democrats."

I knew my politics well enough to know that the geographical estimate of party strength was correct, and to a small boy it seemed logical that the last might follow. I scarcely slept that night. I was not much worried about myself, for I was young enough to change my politics and escape the eternal fires, but I kept picturing my father and grandfather writhing in the flames. This bloody-shirt variety of speech, a leftover from the worst days of Reconstruction, was heard well into the Nineties; it was thought an adequate substitute for argument.

The farm life of that time would seem unbearably dreary today. Those were not merely the horse-and-buggy days. There were no telephones in the farmhouses, and of course no radios to carry news and entertainment. There was no rural delivery; the only newspapers were the weekly county journal and an edition of a city paper once a week, and few took this. The horses were needed for farm work, and when they were harnessed to a buggy it meant only a visit to some village not far away.

But once a year the residents of the small towns and farms, including all the children, made merry at the county fair in Lebanon. The farm families usually went in large wagons, and great baskets of food were taken along for a feast on the fairground. This meant that for some days the women had been busily engaged in the kitchen, determined that none other could offer more or better food. At noon, white tablecloths were spread on the grass; so general was this custom that it seemed the entire fairground was covered with spotless linen. The families sat on the ground about the cloth and literally stuffed themselves with chicken, hard-boiled eggs, pies and cakes. It was a gala occasion for the youngsters, since peddlers mingled with the throngs offering many-colored balloons, and groups gathered about the taffy vendors, watching them pull the taffy from a hook fastened to a tree. Prizes were offered for the best needlework, the best pies and cakes, and the disgusted children were dragged away by their mothers to see if the blue ribbon had been given to their exhibits. More interesting was the visit with the fathers to the stables to see the horses that were to compete on the track, and if these races were not memorable, all things are relative, and no one was the less excited because no Maud S was on the track that day.

These days of my first decade of life made a lasting impression on me. There, in and around Whitestown, I began to learn something about human nature, to appreciate the dignity of labor in the fields, and to sense the instinctive feelings and prejudices of the average man. About the stores on winter days, when the typical Midwesterners of their time shot the tobacco-box cuspidors from incredible distances and angles, discussed the crops and the varying fortunes of their neighbors, and, with animation and intelligence, debated measures pending in Congress, I came to know a little about America. If sometimes their views were wrong—and frequently, of course, they were—these were at the moment the views of the average American.

It was in these days that I found my two greatest interests in life, politics and history. I read and reread a school history book, which was all the more fascinating because of the biographical sketches in the footnotes. A full-page picture of Calhoun, with his rearing hair, burning eyes and intense look, delighted me, and he entered, and has since remained, in my gallery of the great Americans.

On the day Harrison was inaugurated President we moved to Lebanon for a sojourn of a year and a half. The county seat then had a population of less than four thousand. My interest there centered in the courthouse, an old brick building erected in the time of Franklin Pierce. The courtroom fascinated me, and I haunted it, listening to the verbal combats of the lawyers. The leader of the bar was Samuel M. Ralston, later to become Indiana's much-loved governor and United States Senator and to refuse the Presidential nomination in 1924, as we shall see. I associate him with the first serious biography I ever read, a cheap edition of Jenkins'

11

biography of Calhoun, which I still treasure. My mother thought it too heavy for a boy of eleven, but Ralston urged her to let me have it. He was to become one of my most cherished friends.

The life I have described is a part of the American past that will never return. For me it ended in 1891, when we moved to Indianapolis.

CHAPTER II

The Golden Age in Indianapolis

WHEN WE SETTLED in Indianapolis in 1891 it had a population of from ninety to a hundred thousand. Aside from its size, it differed from the average Indiana county seat mainly in that it had been planned, as was Washington. The streets are arranged in a gridiron pattern, cut diagonally by four long avenues radiating from the Circle, the plaza in the heart of the business district. During the greater part of the 1890s the center of the Circle was enclosed by a high wooden fence, behind which the Soldiers' and Sailors' Monument was slowly rising to its ultimate height of 284 feet. The chairman of the Monument Commission was the father of a friend of mine, and when the shaft was almost completed I was permitted to walk to the top. This was a distinction, since few were allowed behind the fence.

Transportation was by little horse-drawn streetcars, all converging at the transfer station—which was nothing more than an abandoned streetcar—at the corner of Washington and Illinois streets. The cars were without conductors, and the passengers were supposed to drop their fares into a slot inside, which connected with the money box beside the driver up front. Many times I was to see the car stopped between streets for the driver sharply to remind a tricky passenger that he had neglected to deposit his nickel. Around this time the first electric streetcar appeared, going up Massachusetts Avenue to College Avenue. It was the only decent way to travel on Massachusetts Avenue, which was unpaved and often deep in mud.

On the ground floor of Tomlinson's Hall, on Delaware Street, was the market, where the butchers had their stalls and where farmers brought their produce fresh on market mornings. All

13

housewives, from high to low, did their own marketing, the more prosperous driving to the market with a servant to carry their baskets to the carriage. On market mornings one would almost certainly meet most of one's acquaintances there.

The hall above, the largest in the city, was the scene of political rallies and state conventions all through the Nineties. In that hall I heard the greatest American orators of the time. There many times I heard Bryan's moving eloquence, and Bourke Cockran thundering against "free silver" and imperialism with a brilliance that would have been notable in the St. Stephen's of the days of Fox, Pitt and Sheridan. There, too, I listened to the polished periods of William C. P. Breckinridge, the "silver-tongued orator of the Blue Grass," to the wit and humor of Chauncey M. Depew, and to the thrilling oratory of Albert J. Beveridge that could have been set to music.

The city had the charm of a large country town. There was nothing then beyond Sixteenth Street. The three most fashionable streets were Meridian, Pennsylvania and Delaware, all of them tree-lined, with their fine old houses, most of them brick, built in the days when people demanded spaciousness. These homes were usually set back from the street in wide lawns shaded by tall forest trees, and on summer afternoons passers-by could see the members of the households sitting in rocking chairs far back in the grounds, the women with their sewing or knitting, the men with their newspapers. The autonomous community of Woodruff Place had been fantastically conceived twenty years before—eighty suburban acres, with wide drives in the center of which were park strips for flowers, grass, fountains, fancy urns and bad statuary. In this sylvan retreat Booth Tarkington was to place *The Magnificent Ambersons*.

The country-town touch of the proud little capital could be seen especially on Saturday nights, when the stores stayed open and the streets downtown were thronged with people bent on buying, or merely on mingling with their neighbors, and when a band gave concerts from the balcony of the leading store. All in all, it was a comfortable, homey community, with no pushing or shoving, where the people lived normal lives and where businessmen went home for lunch and in the evening found time and inclination to read the *News* and to stroll across velvety lawns to their neighbors' to exchange views on what they read.

In those days it was the custom of the greatest artists of the stage
to close their New York engagements in early spring and gallantly
fare forth across the continent. In my boyhood in Indianapolis I
saw all the great actors and actresses in all the great plays at the
English Theater on the Circle. This had been built in 1880 and had
opened with Lawrence Barrett in *Hamlet*, followed by Sarah Bernhardt in *Camille*. The Indianapolitans were enthusiastic devotees
of the play. When a brilliant artist was to appear, it was usual to
find the play itself on the reading tables of the homes before it
was given on the stage. Outstanding new plays like Rostand's
Cyrano de Bergerac created real excitement. When Mansfield appeared in Indianapolis during his first season in the role, there was
an intense competition for seats. It was winter, but, in spite of sleet,
rain and a biting wind, by late afternoon of the day before the
tickets were to go on sale there was already a line of people stretching from the box office on the Circle to Meridian Street and for a
block up that thoroughfare. Some of those who stood shivering in
the storm throughout that bitter night suffered the penalty of pneumonia, and I know of one who died from the effects of the night's
hardships. We boys went to the gallery, entering through an alley
that was packed back to Meridian Street, and since gallery seats
could not be reserved, the congestion in the alley was dense. All
who availed themselves of the gallery seats were not boys, but I
am sure that the great proportion of the galleryites carried to the
play a finer background for appreciation than was generally found
in the pit and the boxes.

Ours was a churchgoing town, and I am afraid there was something puritanical and prudish in its stern resentment of the coarse
or suggestive, and its definition of the indecent would seem ridiculous today. I recall the reaction when Sadie Martinot, a French
actress, appeared in a comedy called *The Turtle*. It was understood to be immoral, and the press editorially urged the people to
show their disapproval by staying home. Paxton Hibben and I
went to the Circle and, having made sure that no respectable person
saw us, sneaked in and found seats in the pit. But when the theater
began to fill, we noted with amusement that the most staid of the
city's matrons were arriving, looking a bit flustered as they glanced
about and found friends, equally embarrassed. We were delighted

15

when a woman who was a friend of Pax's mother found her seat to be beside him and blushed prettily. When the play was over, we were astonished to find the carriages of the most fashionable in Indianapolis congesting the Circle.

Now, *The Turtle* was really inane and, judged by present standards, positively puritanic. The most "immoral" scene was that in which the naughty lady of the play disrobed behind a screen and hung her lingerie on it in sight of the horrified—and delighted—audience. We observed that the more sedate ladies pretended not to look, but out of the corner of their eyes they missed nothing. But unfortunately for their pose, the boys in the gallery, by their obscene screams, put special emphasis on the dreadful scene.

In Anna Held's first American season she took Indianapolis by storm, though one of our foremost citizens was moved to wrath when the little actress, her protruding breasts none too completely covered, leaned far over into the box where he sat with his wife, and with outstretched arms and languishing looks, sang:

> "Oh, won't you come and play wiz me?
> I've got such a nice little way wiz me!"

It was this appearance of Anna Held's that introduced me to the awesome mysteries of the stage door. Pax Hibben had laboriously wrought a sonnet in French expressing his adoration and asking for an autographed photograph, and had sent it to her private car. That afternoon a messenger with a package from Miss Held appeared at the Hibben home, requesting payment for delivery, but the family was out and a servant refused it. In the evening when Pax learned of the tragedy he was beside himself with rage and demanded the immediate discharge of the servant. To placate him and save the servant, his mother helped him write an explanatory note in French, and Pax and I found our way to the stage door and, by means of a ten-cent cigar, bribed the doorman to deliver it. To our joy he returned with an invitation to go backstage, and we soon found ourselves standing beside the little charmer in the wings, not a little embarrassed by her state of undress. Pale and trembly, the infatuated Pax poured forth his explanation in a French no Frenchwoman could have understood, and the smiling lady replied in an English never before heard on land or sea. We had got nowhere when Miss Held's cue called her to the stage, and the picture never was delivered.

I always remember with affection the gallery of the English Theater, which seems to this day a place of magic. From there I looked down on Bernhardt, on Mansfield, on Irving and Terry in *The Merchant of Venice* and *The Bells*, on Modjeska in *Macbeth* more than once, on Ada Rehan at her best, on Mrs. Fiske in her famous roles. I recall vividly, as though the scene actually were before me, Maude Adams frisking like a sprite over the moonlit stage in *The Little Minister*, Sothern and Julia Marlowe playing their famous Shakespearean roles, and the latter in *When Knighthood Was in Flower*. The thrill of the night I saw Nat Goodwin and Maxine Eliot in *Nathan Hale* abides. John Drew, the perfect gentleman, was always a delight, though I doubt that *Rosemary* would seem so sweet and charming in this scoffing age.

Nothing stands out more impressively in my memory of the Indianapolis of the Nineties than the general appreciation of fine speaking and the respect for political leaders. This was before the totalitarians, fascists and Communists taught the people to sneer at politicians, without whom democracy cannot work.

This was the home of President Harrison. I first saw him emerging from the railroad station with his daughter on his arm, and followed by the members of his Cabinet with their wives, when he brought home for burial the wife of his youth, who had died in the White House. The next time I saw him was on his return after his defeat in 1892, when he was greeted in the rotunda of the State House by his old friends and neighbors. Later I was to have an amusing personal experience with him.

In those days, men of distinction in Indianapolis dressed the part, wearing Prince Albert coats and high silk hats. One of these was Albert G. Porter, who had a distinguished career as governor, as Congressman and as minister to Italy. I remember him after his retirement. He wore a carefully trimmed beard like Harrison's and he had a courtly manner and a friendly twinkle in his eye. I recall my astonishment when I saw him lifting his high hat to a ragged Negro in the street.

But more impressive and thrilling to me was another governor, Isaac Pusey Gray, a really superior person. In 1892 the opposition of the mugwumps of the East to having a "professional politician" on the ticket prevented his nomination for Vice-President. This was strange in the light of his record. He had begun life and held office as a Republican, but in 1872, disgusted with the corruption of the administration of Grant (who was not a "professional politician"), he supported Greeley. He held a commanding position at the bar and practiced before the United States Supreme Court in his early thirties. As president pro tem of the State Senate he played a historic part in securing the ratification of the Fourteenth Amendment, which without the vote of Indiana, the last state to ratify, would have failed. Within two years after he left the Republican Party the Democrats elected him lieutenant governor, and in 1884 he was elected governor.

That he was a man of unusual qualities was evidenced by his refusal of the United States Senatorship in 1887, when he was chosen by the Legislature, because he felt in honor bound to serve out his term as governor. President Cleveland's first diplomatic appointment in his second term was that of Gray as minister to Mexico. There he died two years later, and President Díaz and all his ministers accompanied the casket to the train. I remember his flag-draped casket in the hearse as it was borne from the train to the Capitol, where the body was to lie in state.

Like Harrison and Porter, he invariably wore a Prince Albert coat and a high silk hat; the Democratic club which bore his name made an impressive show parading at rallies in gray uniforms and gray top hats. I saw him often on the street, his demeanor serious and dignified, and once as a boy I had the thrilling experience of finding myself seated beside him at a soda fountain. He had ordered a lemon phosphate and I a chocolate soda, but the near presence of the great man so confused me that when the clerk, by mistake, switched our drinks, I began to drink the phosphate before I could be stopped, and I remember the look of disgust in Gray's eyes.

He was a truly able man, a man of the most positive and rugged character, of unquestioned integrity, of great native ability, and he would have made a strong President. Now that the clamor of the mugwumps is stilled, the *Encyclopedia of American Biography* concludes that he "represented much that was best in the public life of his time."

I always think of the Indianapolis of the Nineties as the spring-time of the city. The Harrisons, Grays and Porters were of the past, but in those years the community had a number of younger men of unusual promise around whose personalities and achievements public interest revolved. None of these intrigued and fascinated me more than two young Republican orators, Albert J. Beveridge and John L. Griffiths, between whom there was a polite rivalry.

Beveridge was the more spectacular and dramatic as an orator, and people enjoyed his rolling periods and brilliant delivery as they would the art of an actor. He was slender, handsome, supremely self-confident and blessed with a memory so retentive that he could prepare long speeches with the infinite care of an artist and commit them in two readings. He once told me that he had a photographic memory. No one in the audience could suspect from his manner that the speech was not spontaneous.

Frequently in those days I was at his house on Delaware Street with his brother-in-law, George Langsdale, one of my school friends. Whenever Beveridge was working on a speech in the upstairs front room he used as a study, we were shushed to silence. I thought I was touching the hem of history when, after his speech against Governor Altgeld in Chicago in 1896, which gave him a national reputation, Langsdale and I scoured the town for Chicago papers.

The night he delivered his imperialistic "March of the Flag" speech in Tomlinsons Hall, during his 1898 campaign for the United States Senatorship, I was there, and I can see and hear him vividly to this day: virile, arrogant in his self-assurance, his voice ringing clear as a bugle to the frenzied applause of the packed auditorium. Years later we were to become close confidential friends, after he left the Senate and had written his great biography of Marshall. It was to fall to me to write his own biography.

In later life I have often meditated on the career of John L. Griffiths, who, with rare gifts, was never to realize his capacities. He was short and corpulent, with a double chin, the complexion of a schoolgirl, mild, amused blue eyes, and the expression of a cherub. His voice was a silvery tenor, and his tone in delivery was just a bit higher than the conversational. He was more intellectual than dramatic, and his speeches had a literary flavor. When at length he

turned his back on Indiana politics, he made a great impression on
Theodore Roosevelt in a speech in Buffalo and was sent as consul
to Liverpool. Soon thereafter he was made consul general in London, where his speeches attracted wide attention. His lecture on
Hawthorne at the University of Liverpool, his speech at the annual Dr. Samuel Johnson dinner in the home town of that gusty
literary tyrant, and that at the unveiling of the Harrison monument in Indianapolis have been preserved in a volume of his
speeches, but, this aside, he has left nothing behind him. Harrison
was fond of his company, and on his death Griffiths was selected to
write his biography. Had he been temperamentally capable of sus-
tained work and some drudgery he could have produced a biography of charm and brilliance. But he did nothing, and years later
I learned that important papers given him for his work had disappeared.

A charming conversationalist, Griffiths numbered among his in-
timates men and women in the political, literary and theatrical circles of London, and he is said to have inspired Lord Charnwood
to write his biography of Lincoln. He was brilliant, he had a genius
for friendship, but nothing availed to command recognition from
his party, whose favors were jealously guarded by rivals. He was
still in London in 1914 when he died from a heart attack while
riding in Hyde Park.

At that time I haunted the criminal court, since there was an
epidemic of murders involving prominent men, mostly crimes of
passion or at least involving women. Two great trial lawyers fascinated me with their forensic eloquence. John S. Duncan and
Henry N. Spaan were masters, and they were usually engaged in
all the most dramatic trials. Duncan was powerful in argument and
in the analysis of evidence, but Spaan knew how to appeal to the
emotions. These murder trials attracted wide attention and the
newspapers reported them at length, including the speeches.

In appearance, Spaan was impressive. Of medium height, slender,
with iron-gray hair worn in a pompadour, a slight grayish mustache and a slender face reflecting every emotion, he so dramatized
himself in the courtroom that the jury followed his every movement with keenest interest. To hear him was like listening to a
great actor. His cross-examinations were penetrating and devastat-

ing to a witness who was lying. His closing argument to the jury was always superb.

Everything was grist that came to Spaan's mill. I recall vividly standing for a day and a half in a courtroom packed to capacity listening to his closing speech in defense of a German immigrant girl charged with having poisoned the wife and children of her employer on the assumption that he might marry her. The husband, to avoid undeserved suspicion of connivance, had employed Duncan as private prosecutor. The accused in cross-examination by Duncan had been asked her movements on All Souls' Day. She said she had gone to the Catholic cemetery to take flowers. Did she know anyone buried in the cemetery? She did not. Then why had she gone? Because she had always done so with her mother in the old country and, being homesick for her mother, she had gone because she felt it would please her. Duncan hastily passed on to another line of questioning.

But the exchange had not been lost on Spaan. In re-examination he asked her how she could afford to buy flowers. Timidly she replied that she had plucked a few wild flowers in the country. None of this had anything to do with the case, but when Spaan made his final appeal to the jury he spoke for twenty minutes on the incident, leaning against the judge's rostrum, speaking in a low, intimate tone choked with compassion, psychologically analyzing the girl's reason and her feeling, and soon from all parts of the crowded room came the sobs of women, and there were tears in the eyes of the jurors. Having created this atmosphere, Spaan stood a moment in silence. One could hear the ticking of the clock on the wall. Then with a startlingly quick change he turned to a denunciation of witnesses for the prosecution, his voice rising shrilly as he advanced slowly on the jury, his slender frame quivering with indignation, and he reached the climax only when he could touch the front row. The effect was electric. Such was his method in desperate cases, and most of his were desperate.

Many years later, when he was growing old, he became an ardent admirer of Woodrow Wilson and supporter of the League of Nations, and he threw himself into the fight with all his eloquence aflame. One time during this period it fell to me as chairman of a political meeting at Fort Wayne to introduce him, and I saw and

21

talked with him for the first time at the hotel before going to the theater. He was amazed when I recalled to him many incidents in his famous trials that he himself had long forgotten. Thereafter we were friends and correspondents until his death, when I was in Spain.

This was a period of literary achievement in Indiana. General Lew Wallace, author of *Ben-Hur* and *The Prince of India*, was still living and a familiar figure on the streets of Indianapolis, though his home was in Crawfordsville. He was a rather small man, invariably dressed with meticulous care, and he walked with a military bearing. Once or twice I had the privilege of a long conversation with him, and my boyish timidity faded instantly in the warmth of his amiability and humor.

But it was James Whitcomb Riley who was really loved and revered. Innumerable times I saw his trim, immaculately garbed figure strolling nonchalantly, leisurely along the street, with all passersby turning back to look at him with smiles of affection. He then lived a life of ease, without hurry or worry, with royalties flowing in beyond his needs. He lived at 522 Lockerbie Street, in a two-and-a-half-story brick house in the best Victorian tradition of architecture. Lockerbie was a short street that gave the impression of standing a little aloof from those around it, and he wrote a charming poem in appreciation of it.

He was happy in his publisher, Bobbs-Merrill. On a balcony in the rear of their retail store on Washington Street a table was reserved for him, hard by the railing. There he was often found bending over his desk, and customers below would look up with something of awe upon the great man in the throes of composition, but I have no doubt that on these visits he was more concerned with the business end of poetry. He is known as the poet of the children, but among these he had decided preferences and prejudices. He did not care for the Little Lord Fauntleroys with scrupulously scrubbed faces so much as for the impudent, dirty-faced street gamins, the newsboys, the bootblacks, and little ruffians bent on mischief.

But even then Wallace and Riley belonged to the past, and I think of the Indianapolis of the Nineties as the literary spring when young trees were budding and leafing, promising to blossom. The young Indianapolitans of my boyhood were especially intrigued by the younger novelists just emerging.

In those days before the publication of *The Gentleman from Indiana* there was much gossip about Booth Tarkington, and it was critical. He had graduated from Princeton and gone home, and to outward seeming he was squandering his talents, if indeed he had any, in frivolous living. Was he not found almost every night at some silly party? Clearly he was doing nothing. He showed no interest in any trade or profession, and the backyard gossips clacked and clucked about the youth without ambition who stayed up late at parties and slept far into the day. It was not until later that it was known that after the parties he sat down to write until dawn. He was writing fiction, sending it to magazines and book publishers, and the rejection slips poured in to the ivy-clad brick Tarkington home on Pennsylvania Street.

Then, too, the gossips were concerned about the young man's morals, for did they not say he drank? We boys, not without some relish and envy, heard of his fantastic friendship with a queer character who drove a horse-drawn cab. The tale was told that once near dawn Tarkington, very high, hailed the cab for the journey home and promptly put his foot through the window. When the irate cabby remonstrated he was told to "think nothing of it," to have the cab repaired and to send in the bill. And thereafter, so the gossips said, the incident was repeated with some regularity, and the cabby, who came to love his passenger, thought nothing of it at all.

At length, toward the end of the Nineties, a publisher discovered Tarkington's talent through the cleverness and devotion of the writer's sister. The gossips heard that the sister, indignant over the monotonous arrival of rejection slips, went to New York and bearded McClure, the publisher, in his den, with the accusation that the manuscript of the rejected novel had not been read. The publisher politely summoned the reader for her. Had he really read the manuscript? she asked. He insisted that he had. The lady quoted a long passage. He did not like it? The smiling reader replied that he did not. The lady quoted another, and still another. Did he remember them? The reply implied that he remembered them too well. Then, turning to the publisher, she said, "I *knew* he hadn't read it. Not one of those passages is in the manuscript.

23

I improvised them as I went along." The publisher ordered the manuscript sent to him personally, and *The Gentleman from Indiana* was accepted, on condition that it be accompanied with another story—and the other story was *Monsieur Beaucaire*, which was to be an even greater success.

The publication of these novels was taken as a triumph for the town. How delightful the spirit of those days when a speech by Beveridge in Chicago and a novel by another young man of the community set all the tongues to enthusiastic wagging! I well remember how everyone glowed with pride, as over a personal triumph, and paid homage to the "indolent young man" who would not take a job. Tarkington was on his way.

Once only, and that was very early, did he momentarily turn aside from his vocation: when, to his neighbors' amusement, he announced his candidacy for the Legislature. Everyone assumed the truth, that he had no political ambition and merely sought experience and color for a political novel. His campaign was directed by Fred Joss, a young political leader. Joss insisted that Tarkington take a buggy ride into the poorer section to meet the People, and he suggested that the nominee take cigars along for distribution. When they started on the drive Joss asked if he had the cigars. He had—under the seat. At length they drew up to the curb beside some disreputable-looking loungers who were basking in the sun, and he was introduced. Tarkington passed out the cigars, and Joss never was so embarrassed in his life. The cigars were slender, and about four inches long. As they drove away, he turned indignantly on the young candidate and cried, "My God, where did you get those cigars? They're awful!" A bit hurt, Tarkington assured him that they were expensive Havanas bought at the University Club. "For God's sake, dump them," said Joss. "They're so tiny these people will think you've cheated them. Get those big long ones that sell for a nickel and make yourself popular."

Thus Tarkington learned about campaigning. He was elected, and he served one term with no other distinction than that of giving the most epicurean dinners his colleagues had ever known. The political novel was written, but it added nothing to his reputation.

About the same time another Indianapolis man published a novel that had a great vogue and became a best seller. Some years later I formed a warm friendship with this author, but at the time he

emerged as a novelist I knew him merely by sight. He was Meredith Nicholson of the Indianapolis *News*, who had written a small volume of verse that I found occasionally on the tables of friends to whom, probably, he had given complimentary copies. He was a handsome young man, tall, slender, graceful, courtly, eager for life, bubbling with humor. There was some astonishment when he flashed upon the town with his novel *The House of a Thousand Candles*. It appealed to the popular taste of the time and had an enormous sale, and again Indianapolis buzzed with acclaim and extended itself with pride. I was one of the many curious who made a pilgrimage to the old-fashioned house—on Central Avenue, I think—which figured in the gossip as the house of the thousand candles.

I was working temporarily in the Bobbs-Merrill publishing house when it issued its first sensationally successful novel, *When Knighthood Was in Flower*. No publisher ever did a more perfect job of publicity, and I had a part, though a purely mechanical one, in this. Before publication, inspired press reports announced that a rare old manuscript had been found and would soon appear. These press stories were clipped by the hundreds and sent to all bookshops. Then followed another news story announcing that the discoverer of the manuscript was Charles Major, a lawyer of Shelbyville. Then followed personality stories about the author. When the book appeared, the enthusiastic reviews were sent in stacks to bookstores everywhere. The demand for the novel reached such proportions that it was difficult to fill the orders, and I, in the law division, volunteered to assist the overburdened packing department, packing thousands of these books in huge boxes, nailing the boxes down, discovering and developing muscles in putting them on trucks and running them up a hand-operated elevator to the alley for the drays. How thrilled we all were when the brilliant and dynamic Bobbs returned from a journey with the announcement that he had arranged for Julia Marlowe to appear in a dramatized version of the story!

Only once did I see Charles Major. He visited the store one day, and all the employees, in awed silence, craned their necks to see the very handsome author—he was tall, well built, with a large, attractive, smooth-shaven pink face—as he walked with the stride of an athlete to the office in the rear.

Meanwhile other Hoosiers, in exile in Chicago, were adding luster to the "Indiana school," for George Ade was convulsing the nation with his humor, and the two McCutcheons, the novelist and the cartoonist, were in full stride.

With Beveridge thrilling metropolitan audiences with his eloquence, with Griffiths charming the home folks with discourses that might have come from Macaulay, with President Harrison's occasional speeches attracting national attention, with Riley's poems issuing from the press regularly for Christmas, with Tarkington delighting an ever increasing number of readers with his style, this was surely a golden age for us in Indianapolis.

And so it came to pass that two boys convinced themselves that the town was ready for a magazine that would be no less ably edited than the old *Edinburgh Review*. But that's another story, which involves a President, two poets and a great Senator.

CHAPTER III

Two Poets, a President and a Senator

To A BOY of eighteen who had read a biography of Lord Brougham, the brilliant founder of the *Edinburgh Review*, nothing seemed more reasonable than the launching of a similar magazine in Indianapolis. I took George Langsdale into my confidence, and blithely we determined to follow in the wake of the great Scottish orator and writer. The lack of a penny of capital seemed inconsequential, since the most distinguished of Americans would surely delight in the honor of being enrolled among the contributors. I have often wondered how we succeeded in getting so many favorable responses to our request for contributions without pay. Years later, when I was ambassador to Spain, the Congressional Library sent me a photostatic copy of my letter to Carl Schurz, which had been found among his papers there, and I blushed at its crudity. Before we had finished our modest solicitations, leading novelists, poets and statesmen had promised contributions, and we had enough to fill a magazine the size of *Harper's* for almost a year—without the expenditure of a penny beyond the cost of postage stamps.

Our one galling experience was with President Harrison. Beveridge had arranged for our interview with the great man, from whom we hoped to get an article, and we walked up Delaware Street to his home a little in awe, but none the less self-confident; we had not yet become acquainted with failure. Harrison lived in a two-story Regency-style brick house with bay windows and stone trimmings. He had built it in 1872, and there he lived continuously except when he was in Washington. The grounds were not enclosed, since the fence had been cut to pieces and carried away by souvenir seekers during the Presidential campaign of 1888.

27

When we arrived at the house, a somber servant who might have been a funeral director ushered us into the drawing room—small, dark, overcrowded with souvenirs, among them a sword hanging over the entrance to another room. We found seats and waited.

After a while we heard quick steps on the stairs, and in a moment the great man appeared, stiff, coldly dignified, without the semblance of a smile of welcome. He was short, stout without being fat, with hair and beard almost white and eyes penetrating and strangely cold and unresponsive. He seemed old but not tired or worn. His face and forehead had a network of tiny wrinkles that were superficial rather than deep.

Harrison shook hands in the businesslike manner of a man with no time to waste. Then he took a chair by a window opening on the grounds and sat looking at us, silent as a Buddha in marble. Clearly it was up to us. It was not an auspicious beginning for two boys.

The moment we submitted our plan, he suggested a difficulty in a very low voice. We were ready with an answer, but he sat as though indifferent to the replies, gazing with brooding eyes out the window. After a while we were convinced that while we were answering one of the objections he was meditating another. Under such treatment, all awe of a former President gave place to resentment, and I am afraid that finally our answers became a bit rude. At length we took our departure, Harrison going with us to the door, but without having made a definite promise.

We stormed down Delaware Street exhausting our puny vocabulary of vituperation upon the great man's head. At the Denison Hotel corner we met Beveridge, who asked how we had made out. We exploded with denunciations. Beveridge seemed puzzled.

"How long were you there?" he asked.

"About forty minutes."

"Then go right back and fall on your knees and thank him," he said. "If you had been United States Senators, he would have given you but five."

Even so his treatment of us rankled. Later, when the poet Joaquin Miller lectured in the interest of our project, James Whitcomb Riley, who managed the event, gave us two tickets with instructions to take them personally to Harrison and invite him to attend. This time we didn't even get into the drawing room, for

Harrison came running down the stairs and met us in the hall. To our amazement, his face was wreathed in smiles. Taking the tickets, he said pointedly, as we were afterward to recall, "I shall be there *if nothing happens.*" When we glanced over the audience that night we were not much surprised, or even annoyed, to note his absence. We expected the worst of Harrison. But the next morning we found in the papers that something had "happened"—that night his daughter Elizabeth was born.

In time we realized that he had been having gentle fun with us in a friendly spirit. Frequently, during the remainder of his life, I met him on Delaware Street walking slowly and leading the baby Elizabeth by the hand, and he always smiled genially in recognition, lifting his high hat in salutation.

I came in time to appreciate his really great qualities, his dignity and integrity, his great intelligence and independence, and to conclude that in sheer brain power no more than five or six Presidents have been his equal. I heard him twice on the platform. His speeches were sound and serious, and his close reasoning was possibly above the appreciation of the multitude. I heard that, cool as he was outwardly, his knees trembled when he rose to speak, and that he had said that if this didn't happen he knew the speech would be a failure. He never sought a Presidential nomination after his defeat in 1892, due partly to the Homestead strike, partly to the disloyalty of Republican leaders who had found him not "amenable to reason" in the matter of patronage and too unyielding where principle was involved. Unquestionably, until his retirement he was cold and aloof.

During the gubernatorial race in 1872, when he was running against "Blue Jeans" Williams, a dirt farmer, his enemies described him as a snobbish aristocrat, and because he wore gloves in driving to his appointments he was called "Kid Glove Harrison." The reputation then given him clung to him to the end of his days. Then, after leaving the Presidency, he did not endear himself to the dominant wing of his party with his speeches on the obligations of great wealth and against the hysteria of imperialism. Unlike other former Presidents, he returned to the practice of law. His most famous case was the boundary dispute between Venezuela and Great Britain, in which he represented Venezuela before the tribunal of arbitration in Paris. He worked on the case for two years, and his argument, consuming twenty-five hours, was so powerful that before it was finished the lawyer for the Crown warned the Prime Minister, Lord Salisbury, to prepare for defeat.

We Americans are always clamoring for a President and leaders capable of withstanding the importunities of petty politicians and with the courage of their convictions regardless of the effect on their personal fortunes. We had such a man in Harrison—and that is one reason he was defeated for re-election.

But the great event of these months of preparation for rivalry with Lord Brougham was the visit of Joaquin Miller, "the Poet of the Sierras." We had written him in California asking for a poem, and he had responded—from Cincinnati, where the letter had followed him—with a stirring poem, "Cuba Libre," and a long, almost indecipherable letter solemnly urging that we call our magazine *The Cornfield.* We were disgusted. Why, in heaven's name, *The Cornfield?* We were reminded that there was a *Cornhill Magazine* in England and that Indiana was the center of the corn belt. But we decided to find some way to spare the magazine this indignity.

More to our satisfaction was his offer to lecture in Indianapolis and contribute the proceeds to the magazine fund. As a youth many years before in the days of the gold rush to California, he had put his pack on his back, turned away from his native Indiana and taken the long trail. In all the intervening years he had never visited his native heath. Now, an old man, he wanted to return, and this lecture would offer the opportunity. He made one condition only—that his friend James Whitcomb Riley preside and introduce him. In due time he would send his secretary, Harr Wagner, to assist with the plans.

Elated that we were to sponsor the homecoming of the poet, we called on all the newspapers for appropriate editorials, and they all responded magnificently. When we asked the Speaker of the Indiana House of Representatives for permission to sell tickets on the floor he said he would do better than that—he would arrange a joint session with the Senate and do the poet the honor of asking him to address it.

Meanwhile we were frequently calling on Riley at his desk on the balcony at Bobbs-Merrill, where we found him working like a schoolboy on his speech of introduction. I can still see the neat, beautiful, tiny writing of the manuscript. We had rented Plymouth Church for the lecture, since this historic edifice was somehow associated with literary and intellectual events. We had obligated ourselves to pay nine dollars for it, and this worried us a bit.

But we heard no more from Miller. Two days before the day of the lecture Harr Wagner arrived with the promise that the poet would appear the following day. But he did not arrive. We went to meet every train that day, but he did not appear. We appealed to Wagner to telegraph him.

"No use," said Wagner. "He wouldn't open the telegram. One night when he was about to lecture he was handed a death telegram and it ruined his lecture and he has paid no attention to telegrams since."

That nine-dollar obligation weighed upon us like the national debt!

The next day Riley joined us in a trudge to the station. He was impeccably attired, as usual, and had a little red flower in his buttonhole. We stood in the door of the station with a sickening fear as the train drew in. At length, in the midst of the crowd emerging from the gate, we saw a very tall, bearded man wearing a slouch hat and waving a carpet bag vigorously, to the evident annoyance of his neighbors. It was the Poet of the Sierras. He was wearing boots which, though his trousers covered them, were clearly outlined beneath, and he looked like a rustic from the ranch country. Impulsively he threw his arms around Riley's neck. The two poets offered a great contrast: Riley short and slight, Miller tall and burly; Riley a veritable fashion plate, Miller almost a caricature of a rustic; Riley cool, quiet, dignified, Miller boisterous as a storm in the mountains.

As we walked our guest up Illinois Street to the Claypool, trudging along without a word, Miller again threw his arms around Riley with the exclamation, "Jim Riley, I love you more than any man on earth!"

This broke the silence, and Wagner announced that the Legislature had invited the poet to address a joint session.

Miller stopped in his tracks, an expression of consternation on his face. "Now, Wagner, you know that all my biled shirts are in the trunk we sent ahead."

"Never mind," said Riley. "It's just barely possible that we may

31

be able to persuade some merchant to take your money for a shirt and collar."

Miller was still in a boisterous mood as we entered the hotel, and he approached the supercilious clerk waving his carpet bag vigorously.

"Do you think you can furnish bed and board for a man like me?" he asked.

The clerk seemed in some doubt as he surveyed the rough man before him, but when his eyes fell on Riley, faultlessly groomed, he softened and agreed to furnish bed and board. We accompanied Miller to his room, where his first act was to open the carpet bag, extract a picture of a beautiful girl and place it on the mantel. It was a portrait of his daughter.

The homecoming lecture of the poet was a brilliant success. The church was packed, with the Governor and the Legislature in attendance. Riley's introduction was a beautiful prose poem. Miller's lecture was really blank verse, and charming. Later when the complete works of Miller were published, Riley's speech was used as the introduction.

But even the success of the lecture failed to save the magazine from burial. We had cautiously guarded our secret, since Harrison's critical attitude had discouraged us as to the wisdom of the venture. We sneaked to a job-printing office to get an estimate on the first issue, and the price appalled us. The idea of soliciting advertisements had not occurred to us, since that would have seemed sordid, commercial, unworthy of the dignity of the project. We asked no advice, and all that was left of this adventure of two foolish boys was the Riley Introduction to the complete works of Joaquin Miller. But we had the consolation of knowing that we had sponsored the homecoming of a Hoosier poet, and that seemed glory enough.

If Harrison had failed us, another statesman to whom we applied for literary alms did not. David Turpie had just retired from the United States Senate after eighteen years and was living quietly on Tennessee Street in a house filled with books, and, unabashed, we knocked on his door. Though we had never seen him, we had heard that he was a great statesman and jurist who spoke a classic English that was scarcely matched in the Senate. We had heard

that when Henry Cabot Lodge entered the Senate a bit preten-
tiously and his colleagues thought a bit of hazing might cut him
down to size, Turpie, a master of satire, had been assigned the task,
because he could do it so beautifully.

The door was opened by Turpie himself, a smiling bearded old
man with a scholar's stoop. We did not know that he suffered from
palsy, and while we were explaining our project we were almost
silenced when his head shook as though he were dismissing our
magazine. But he listened with evident interest and ended by promising to write an article on one of the books of the Bible.

After his defeat in 1898, Turpie was asked to write the memoirs
of his long public service, which began before the Civil War. His
Sketches of My Own Times was written delightfully and condensed with his characteristic modesty into a short book. His
friendship for Voorhees, with whom he served in the Senate, is
expressed in the most beautiful and illuminating tribute ever paid
to that great man, in which he referred especially to Voorhees'
long fight for the building of the Congressional Library.

Turpie was primarily a statesman of the noblest mold. He had
lofty ideas of the dignity and responsibility of the Senate. Later,
as a reporter, I called upon him for his opinion of a Senate action
that we knew he disapproved. He said he preferred to be silent,
because he thought it would be indelicate for him to criticize his
recent colleagues. He seemed to me like a Roman senator of the
best days of the Republic. In these feverish, hurrying days of more
shouting than thinking, one seldom hears him mentioned. Too bad!
He set a Senatorial standard too seldom matched. One of the compensations of the two boys who failed to establish another *Edinburgh Review* was the privilege of talking with Turpie.

CHAPTER IV

Education the Hard Way

MY HAPPIEST MEMORIES of those days cluster around the long brick building on Pennsylvania Street, between Michigan and North, known as the Shortridge High School. It had a faculty of extraordinary men and women, and the student body represented every social and financial station—a thoroughly democratic institution. The daughters of the wealthy passed from Shortridge to Vassar, Smith and Bryn Mawr, and the sons to Harvard, Yale and Princeton.

In one member of the faculty, Laura Donnan, I found one of the greatest women I have ever known, who had a decisive effect on my life. After more than half a century those who came under her influence speak of her with admiration, appreciation and affection. Her specialty was civil government, and everyone but the dullest emerged from her classroom with the keenest and most lasting understanding of the meaning and obligations of citizenship. She did more to make citizens, and to make them fundamentally American, with a reverence for American institutions and the American way of life, than anyone else I have ever known. She adhered to the Jeffersonian theory that the truth is best served in the arbitrament of debate. If she were living today I am sure she would devote less time to showing that the totalitarian philosophy is wrong than to proving that the philosophy of democracy is right —she would give more time to the positives than to the negatives.

She was vigorous and vivid in her teaching, and her voice, though ordinarily warm and pleasant, had at times a booming quality which made her somewhat formidable though not less feminine. One instinctively felt that she was not only a teacher, she was a Personality. In her classes she encouraged argument, and, since she had powerful convictions and some prejudices, the student trying to curry favor and escape her sarcasm by simulating agreement had her contempt. Having stout convictions of my own in opposition to some of hers, I blurted out precisely what I thought, and, to my amazement at first, I could see that she was immensely pleased. She believed in a robust discussion of controversial subjects. She would have despised the now growing trend toward mildness and conformity in thinking. It was this mutual spirit of combat and independence that made us the closest of friends.

Her interests were unusual for a woman of her day. In her girlhood during the Civil War she had frequented the State House, which was a block from her home, and had listened to the impassioned discussions of the wartime legislators. She had read law under the direction of President Harrison, had lectured on constitutional law at the Law School and had written an excellent class book on our fundamental law.

The old family home where she and two unmarried sisters still lived would have seemed quite in place in the Concord of Emerson, Alcott and Hawthorne. A frame house, plainly and comfortably furnished, it had a library rich in the volumes that live on. I recall busts of Emerson and Lincoln, whom she loved. Being an individualist, she refused to measure her conduct by the tape of fashion. Because she did her own marketing and found it irksome to carry the packages, she bought a boy's toy wagon, and her friends smiled and strangers stared when they saw this woman in her plain gray tailored suit nonchalantly drawing it along the sidewalks. In debates and oratorical contests she was our drillmaster and manager, and woe to the boy who caught a cold on the eve of a contest, since she forced him to take her favorite remedy, hot pepper in capsules, standing sternly by to see them down. To this day I never see pepper on the table without thinking of her.

My prospects were dark during my school days, and her faith in me was a torch. Our close friendship continued throughout her life. When I delivered the keynote address at the 1928 Democratic national convention in Houston, a reporter went to this robust Republican for her comment, and she paid me her highest compliment: "He has always had the courage of his convictions, and we can use more like that today."

After her death former students placed a bust of her by Laura

Richards in the new Shortridge High School building as a memorial to a truly great woman who made an indelible impression on the thinking of a great community.

Throughout my Shortridge days I averaged three hours a day in the reading room of the public library in the old building at Pennsylvania and Ohio streets, and later in the one at Meridian and Ohio. This was my university, and I was the sole member of the faculty. I would send for a book, usually a history or biography, and, finding references to other books, I would send for them too, and soon my table would be covered with books, to the clear annoyance of the attendant. I read biographies of almost every American statesman from Jefferson and Hamilton to Blaine and Conkling, and of English statesmen from the days of Walpole down through Chatham, Pitt, Burke, Cobden, Gladstone and Disraeli, and ever since then I have been as keenly interested in English politics as in that of my own country. A desire for firsthand information, especially about the American scene, led me to go through the newspapers of the periods concerned, and thus I formed a proper appreciation of the value of newspapers as a source in history. The greatest ally of the historian is curiosity.

It was at this time that I found hidden away on a back shelf in the public library a copy of Goodrich's *British Eloquence,* with the major speeches of Chatham, Fox, Pitt, Burke and the Irish orators Sheridan, John Philpot Curran and Henry Grattan. These impressed me as literature on fire, and every speech was read and analyzed in an eager search for the art of the orators. In a boyish diary of those days, recently discovered among old papers, are earnest notations on the progress of this study. I was especially fascinated by the oratory of Curran, the incomparable genius of the Irish bar. "Tonight finished John Philpot Curran," records the diary. "How graceful and beautiful are his speeches! How vivid and stirring his word pictures! How much burning indignation he can put into a sentence!" I thought then, and still think, that Curran was one of the supreme orators in the English tongue, perhaps in sheer genius the greatest. Soon I was to have my judgment fortified by that of one of the great masters of the art.

Taking the study of the orators seriously, I sought the advice of the living masters. Robert G. Ingersoll had charmed me with his artistry, and I had the audacity to appeal to him for advice. His reply delighted me, since he pronounced Curran the most finished of the British orators. I have that letter, written from his home on Madison Avenue in New York, before me now. "If you wish to know the English language in its strength and beauty, read Shakespeare," he wrote. "He is the master. All other writers are fragmentary compared with him. Study Shakespeare." And then the sentence that pleased me: "I think Curran was a greater orator than Chatham, Fox or Burke."

When the "Gold Bug" National Democratic Party convention met in Indianapolis in 1896 a friend and I pounced on the orators. The "silver-tongued orator of the Blue Grass," Colonel William C. P. Breckinridge, all courtly grace, received us in his hotel room, apologizing profusely for its disorder, and entertained us for an hour. He thought our own Senator Turpie a master in the use of the English language. "If, fifty years from now," he said, "someone submits to competent critics a speech of Turpie's and one of Henry Cabot Lodge's with the statement that one was by an Eastern literary man and the other by a Western lawyer, they would report the speech of Turpie as that of the Eastern literary man and that of Lodge as by the Western lawyer." Later on his return to Lexington he wrote a long letter of minute advice.

Of more lasting value to me was the call on William Everett, son of the accomplished Edward, educated at Harvard and at Trinity College, Oxford. He had studied law but had abandoned it for the pulpit. Being a natural teacher, he had accepted the direction of the Adams Academy in Quincy, Massachusetts, at the request of a dying friend. When Henry Cabot Lodge was elected to the Senate, Everett succeeded him in the House, though he was a Democrat and not a resident of the district. One term sufficed. Later Champ Clark, who was Speaker of the House for eight years, told me that Everett was the greatest scholar ever to sit in the House and that he amazed his colleagues during drowsy debates by reading the Greek classics in the original. After the meeting in Indianapolis he wrote me frequently and at length on my reading.

In pursuit of an education I found much to my advantage by haunting the law offices of Frank B. Burke and Henry Warrum, men of much brilliance and eloquence. Burke was a rugged character, Irish to his finger tips, with the spontaneous eloquence of his

37

race. Warrum had a brilliant mind and wide culture; the library in his home was a treasure house. During his last twenty years he was the attorney for the United Mine Workers, and in his frequent appearances before Senatorial committees he impressed the Senators as a really great constitutional lawyer.

These men contributed to my education. Their minds were so active that they were in frequent verbal combat in the office over matters remote from their work. One of the most exciting and eloquent debates I have ever heard was between them when I was the sole auditor, my presence overlooked. The dispute grew out of Warrum's assertion that the bloodletting of the French Revolution was unnecessary; Burke disagreed, and the debate was on. Had they been fighting for a client's life they could not have been more excited or intense. They paced the room as they talked. Both had made intensive studies of the French Revolution, and the debate was a historical treat. That day for an hour and a half I listened to passages of eloquence equal to any I have ever heard.

In Irvington, a charming suburb of Indianapolis in my boyhood, I knew an old statesman through whom I felt I contacted Webster, Clay and Prentiss. This was George W. Julian, who had played a conspicuous part in politics many years before. A militant abolitionist, he was the nominee for Vice-President on the Free Soil ticket. During the Civil War he was a member of the House Committee on the Conduct of the War, which was a source of annoyance to Lincoln. Because he was a thoroughly honest man, the corruption during the Grant administration and the inauguration of the system of privilege had driven him to support Greeley in 1872, and this led him ultimately into the Democratic Party, though actually he remained an independent throughout his life.

Occasionally I made pilgrimages to the brick house in Irvington, where I always found the tall old man stretched full length on a sofa in his study. Though he was physically feeble, his mind was as alert, keen and brilliant as ever, and he would talk to me about politics for an hour and more. I found these conversations with Julian always fascinating, because I directed them to the Forties, Fifties and Sixties of the nineteenth century. Being an uncompromising abolitionist, he looked upon Henry Clay as a "trimmer," and, while conceding Webster's eloquence, he had "no admiration for his character." But his pet aversion was Garfield, and the old man, prone on the davenport, grew vehement in discussing him. I was shocked to hear him say that Garfield was responsible for his own death because as a candidate he had lavished promises of preferment right and left, perfectly conscious of his inability to fulfill them all. This, thought Julian, had acted on the sick mind of the assassin and brought on the tragedy. In truth, Julian had an honest man's abhorrence of the politicians of that period of land grabs, the Crédit Mobilier and the system of privilege.

My political education came in the preparation of my speech in a state oratorical contest in which I represented Shortridge. With the paternal and maternal branches of my family sharply divided, I was confused as to my allegiance, but I had formed a great admiration for Alexander Hamilton, whom I took as my subject. As I waded through the ten volumes of his works edited by Henry Cabot Lodge, my consternation grew. It was all too clear that all my instincts were opposed to the philosophy of my hero. I was shocked to find that he scorned democracy and honestly thought that only through a partnership between the moneyed aristocracy and government could governmental stability be assured. Too late to change the subject and make the necessary research on another, I confined my oration on Hamilton to the part he played in bringing about the ratification of the Constitution, in which he had little faith. However, I won the contest. Then, finding myself wandering in the no man's land of politics, I turned desperately to the many volumes of Jefferson's works, and when I finished it was clear to me that I was a Jeffersonian.

Wishing to convince myself of my political conversion by putting my impressions of the clashing philosophies of Jefferson and Hamilton in writing, I wrote two articles for the *Jeffersonian Democrat*, an obscure magazine, assuring the editor that I expected no compensation. I got none. But the articles were printed.

Soon thereafter I was asked to speak for the young Democrats at a political banquet in Lebanon, because my two grandfathers had been pioneers in the county. The speech must have been aggressive, if crude, for when it was finished Governor Ralston, presiding, asked all who thought "the boy" could be elected to Congress from the Indianapolis district to stand, and the audience rose and cheered; of course they all understood the spirit of the suggestion, since they knew I was barely old enough to vote. But the correspondents of Indianapolis papers, knowing that were my age given there would be no story, ignored this detail and gave the incident a sensational play. The party leaders in Indianapolis were astounded, since Ralston was high in the party hierarchy, and they scurried about to learn the identity of the interloper. One reporter appealed to Senator Kern, who said that he had never seen me but that he had read two articles of mine and they were "crackerjacks." It was this boyish speech and this reply of Kern's that introduced me into newspaper work.

At that moment, Jacob Piatt Dunn, the sole editorial writer on the Indianapolis *Sentinel*, the organ of the Indiana Democracy, was much distressed because of his inability to find a substitute to permit of his occasional meandering in the woods beside a stream with hook and line. Reading the interview with Kern, he sent for the magazine, and after he had read the articles he invited the author to his home. He pumped me on politics and history, and while I thought from his whimsical expression, and a disturbing gleam in his eye, that he found much lacking, he ended by asking me to take his place on the paper during his fishing excursions.

Thus in my twenty-first year I became an editorial writer while Dunn sat on the bank of a stream with his pipe in his mouth and his line in the water. Soon thereafter he was appointed city comptroller, and I got his editorial job with the understanding that if the Democrats won the city election I would remain, otherwise he would return.

This was the day of the frankly partisan newspaper. The Indianapolis *Journal*, the Republican organ, was owned and edited by John C. New, who had been American consul general in London during the Harrison administration, and the Democratic *Sentinel* was owned and edited by Samuel M. Morse, who had been consul general in Paris during the second Cleveland administration. These papers did not pretend to political impartiality, and their news stories, while colored, deceived no one. With papers representing both parties, the public had the advantage of a debate, so important in a democracy.

The fact that in most metropolitan centers we now have a one-party press deserves more meditation than it receives. The scrapping of the New York *World* left the nation without a crusading liberal paper with a national circulation. In Indianapolis there have been nothing but papers of one political persuasion since the liquidation of the *Sentinel* at the turn of the century. When I was in Spain I had an interesting conversation with Salvador de Madariaga, the brilliant professor, diplomat and historian, and I was impressed by his pessimism over the future of democracy. It was based on the fact that the mass media of communication were passing into the possession of one school of thought and one economic group.

The *Sentinel* had been a robust party paper for more than sixty years, but in my time its popularity was at a low ebb. Morse was an able man whose powerful editorials on the tariff had attracted the attention of Cleveland. The transformation of his political character began during his stay in Paris, when Americans of wealth and social prestige expressed astonishment that a man of such intelligence and charm should be affiliated with the party of Bryan and the common herd. This tickled his vanity, and he returned to Indianapolis an ultraconservative, if not a reactionary. This, reflected in his paper, was not lost upon the Democrats, who began to doubt the authenticity of his party loyalty. He now seldom wrote an editorial, and when he did it was off key. His vanity was often amusing. One day George Gray Barnard, the sculptor, came to the *Sentinel* with a letter of introduction to Morse, whom, he told me, he had never met. Morse was absent at the time and on his return I was beginning to tell him that Barnard had been to see him when he broke in—"George here? We were great pals in Paris!" I didn't dare mention the letter of introduction.

My sanctum at the *Sentinel* was in a back room with an uninspiring view of an alley, and it seldom felt the touch of the janitor's broom. My editorials were written with a lead pencil and were ardent enough, I'm sure. I would take them to Morse for his approval, and after reading them and chuckling he would usually say, "Well, I don't know exactly what you're trying to say, but they sound all right, so send them down." I was so naïve at the time that I accepted this as a compliment, but when, quite early, he made me a present of a dictionary I was not so sure.

When Bryan, renominated in 1900, was notified in Indianapolis, Morse's interest was so slight that he assigned me, a mere boy, to write the editorial comment in the party organ.

41

My reading of the works of Jefferson and Hamilton had made me a Jeffersonian, but my education in contemporary politics began in 1896. Never had Indianapolis or the nation seethed with such frenzied excitement as during the memorable campaign of that year. That incomparably appealing crusader William Jennings Bryan had appeared in the political firmament, a star of the first magnitude, shedding an unaccustomed light on the political and economic evils of the time, and awakening a drowsing people to the realization that government and its policies are the business of every citizen, that small selfish groups have no divine right to exploit and oppress the masses through the misuse of the instrumentalities of the state, and that democracy, as conceived by Jefferson, was being undermined. From the close of the Civil War men had been Democrats and Republicans pulling for their team, with not much consideration of what it was all about.

The country in 1896 was still steeped in the gloom of the depression of 1893. Grover Cleveland was President for the second time. He had made a valiant though futile fight for tariff reform and had caught the fancy of the reformers by treating the civil service seriously. He was honest, sincere and courageous, within the framework of the economic and political system in vogue for many years. Yet at this time farms redeemed from the wilderness by the sweat of the pioneers were falling under the hammer of the auctioneer because the farmer could not make enough to pay his taxes; the products the farmer bought were artificially raised in price by the tariff, which enriched the manufacturers at his expense, while for his own products he had to take what he could get in the open market. Labor had no rights that the employer was bound to respect. The Pullman strike had been put down by federal troops, and "government by injunction" had become a live issue; the fact that the Attorney General who had advised the use of the federal troops, Richard Olney, was a railroad lawyer did not make the act more acceptable. Millions of workers were idle in the streets, and Coxey with his absurd but pathetic army of the unemployed had marched on Washington. With a Democratic Administration in power, an overwhelming repudiation of the party at the polls in the Presidential election seemed inevitable.

The Democrats met in convention in Chicago in an atmosphere

of black depression. Then came a miracle, when, with something akin to magic, a young man of thirty-six aroused the masses to unprecedented heights of enthusiasm in a speech that was to make history. The "Cross of Gold" oration was an alarm clock, and the common man awoke to the fact that he had a vital interest in the election.

A boy in high school at the time, I remember sitting on the back steps of my house the next morning reading the speech in the *Sentinel*. It thrilled me through and through. I knew nothing about the money question, but this great oration went far beyond any one issue. It was, in its general tone and content, the submission to the people of the paramount issue of democracy and human rights. It marked the beginning of a crusade that was to go on without serious interruption, with minor parts of the program adopted later by Theodore Roosevelt and by Woodrow Wilson, reaching its climax in the policies of Franklin D. Roosevelt. Certainly that speech, followed by Bryan's nomination, put dynamite into the campaign. For the first time since the days of Jackson and Lincoln the partisans began to think in terms of policies and principles, and not so much of the triumph of their team. Party lines were blurred.

On all street corners in the business section of Indianapolis great crowds of excited partisans congested the sidewalks, listening passionately, or with amusement, to the amateur debaters. The excitement had the force of hysteria, and this hysteria reached down to the schoolboys. My friend Langsdale—the brother-in-law of Beveridge—and I rose at four in the morning to carry papers, and since our routes crossed at various points, and we were not in agreement on how to save the country, we always paused to continue the dispute, our voices rising to a shout, as windows flew up and indignant householders in nightshirts leaned out to curse us and order us away.

I can never forget my first view of Bryan. He arrived in Indianapolis in the morning, and it was announced that he would speak from a platform outside the State House in the afternoon. The grounds were packed to suffocation. Then out through a window stepped the young crusader. Nothing could have been more satisfying to the eye. He was remarkably handsome in a virile sense, and his glance over the huge throng was magnetic, his eye piercing and yet warm with emotion. His voice was strong, mellow and expressive of the sincerity of the man, passionately earnest. One could feel the emotional response of the crowd.

That night he spoke in Tomlinson's Hall. Hours before the doors were opened, thousands had gathered in the street, reaching far back. As time passed, with the doors still closed, the pressure of the crowd became almost unbearable. Many women fainted. When the doors finally were thrown open the thousands pressed forward, threatening to crush those nearest the door. I was among these, and had I not worked myself up, held up by my neighbors, my feet not touching the ground, I would have been suffocated; it was thus that I was swept into the hall. Bryan's speech that night was a godsend to the amateur debaters; it munitioned their arguments.

From that hour I thought in terms of politics.

I felt little enthusiasm for the war with Spain, and its aftermath of imperialism shocked me. (That war, as we now know, was unnecessary. The diplomatic correspondence I was to read in the embassy in Madrid bears painful proof that we forced the war. The sinking of the *Maine* certainly was not the work of the Spaniards. Just why we were so insistent on war remains a mystery.) The victory of Dewey in Manila Bay was loudly celebrated in Indianapolis; Richard Harding Davis was thrilling us with a description of Teddy Roosevelt charging up San Juan Hill. Some Democrats were complaining that Bryan and his regiment were not permitted to reach Cuba lest to his glamour as an orator be added that of a soldier, but our easy triumph over an ancient nation had its effect on our national adolescence, and the young, especially, responded jubilantly to Beveridge's thrilling speech in Tomlinson's Hall, lyrical in its call to carry the flag over mountains and seas to the domination of the world.

No other Presidential election has meant so much to me as that of 1900, because of its emotional appeal. I was fresh from the study of Jefferson and the fundamentals of Americanism, and the idea that we should plunge into a career of imperialism seemed treason to our principles. I was young enough to really feel it and be hurt. Bryan was renominated and he made his speech of acceptance in Military Park, Indianapolis, where I joined the throng. It was a hot day and the odor of the sweating multitude was unpleasant, but Bryan never made a greater speech. It was a brilliant and powerful restatement of the elemental principles of the Republic, and parts were beautifully phrased. I recall that when his glasses became moist he turned to a tall, gray-mustached man on the platform and borrowed his. This man was Adlai E. Stevenson, Vice-President under Cleveland and Bryan's running mate that year. Fifty years later, his grandson would delight America and Europe with political speeches of rare eloquence.

But even more impressive to me that year was the tempestuous oration against imperialism that I heard Bourke Cockran deliver in Tomlinson's Hall in support of the Bryan he had opposed four years before. In his generation Bryan alone approached him as an orator. Their methods were entirely different. Bryan's eloquence was primarily of, and to, the heart. It was natural eloquence, like that of Patrick Henry. The phrasing was almost Biblical in its simplicity. But Cockran was the conscious artist. Had he lived in the golden days of parliamentary eloquence in the British House of Commons, he would have yielded nothing to Pitt, Fox, Burke and Sheridan. Indeed, his style was strongly suggestive of that of the greatest orators of that time. In diction and delivery, he was the supreme artist. I can still see him in action that night and hear his rolling golden sentences and their thrilling climaxes as he beat upon his chest or slapped his thigh. In that campaign he spoke from the heart and out of the richness of his brilliant mind.

My first disillusionment came in that campaign. It coincided with my first appearance on the stump—in Neidlinger's Hall in Whitestown, the town where I had spent the first ten years of my life. People packed the hall to see and hear the home-town boy. My talk was confined to the one issue of imperialism, and since I felt all I said, I have no doubt it was unnecessarily vehement. The attention was perfect, the proverbial pin could have been heard to drop, but I was disappointed when my most earnest passages were heard in silence. It was not until afterward when I walked away with the village blacksmith that I began to understand. "It was a good speech," he said timidly (and, I'm sure, with many reservations), "but I think the boys would've liked it better if you'd gone into the price of corn and hogs." Thus my education in campaigning began. I remember my depression at the realiza-

45

tion that perhaps idealism and abstract principles are hard to impress on an average audience, and that even the liberties and independence of peoples mean less to many than the price of corn and hogs. However, I clung tenaciously to the speech and delivered it in a number of small towns.

The second defeat of Bryan and the triumph of imperialism depressed me more. Never had a candidate been received with such continuous ovations from millions from coast to coast, and while cheers are not votes, they bear a relation to them. I still suspect that but for the intimidation, coercion and corruption, Bryan would have won. It was something new, since the days of Andrew Jackson, to threaten workers with the loss of their jobs unless they voted as they were told. Intimidation was commonplace in the campaigns of 1896 and 1900. Slips in the pay envelopes of factory workers informed them that should Bryan be elected they need not return to work; if McKinley won, they would still have their jobs. Under the clever direction of Mark Hanna the greatest campaign fund in history up to that time was raised for McKinley; but the Democrats could raise little money, because they had nothing to sell to the people who had it. It was to take some years of crusading by Bryan to make it clear that, under our form of government, intimidation, coercion and corruption are tantamount to treason.

The plunge into campaigning in 1900 had whetted my appetite for politics and that of my friend Frank P. Baker (who later became a judge), but we observed with dismay that the Democratic leaders were not impressed with our value to the party. Something had to be done about it, so we decided to organize a state banquet at Franklin, to invite the party leaders, and to put ourselves on the program to tickle the ears of breathless listeners with our eloquence. Being on the *Sentinel* at the time, I gave the banquet great publicity. There was much speculation as to its significance, and the politicians flocked from the river to the lake, agog with curiosity. The Taggart organization suspected it to be a trick of the opposition; the opposition was sure it was a scurvy plot of the organization. The result was such an influx of the curious that the hall could not begin to accommodate all those clamoring for admission. We had John W. Kern, the future Senator, and other leaders as background for our appearance, and, more to the point, Baker and I spoke to our own satisfaction.

Encouraged now, we hastily arranged another meeting, in the old Masonic Hall in Indianapolis, and again we summoned the bored leaders to serve as our background. Unhappily, the reporter who covered the meeting had a sense of humor, and in his story we read that Taggart had appeared to "pull the bung out of the barrel of oratory and then made his escape"; that Henry Warrum "shifted his tobacco from one cheek to another and waded in," though in fact he did not chew tobacco; that I was a "dreamy-eyed young man with a soulful look" who "attacked the British Redcoats and the Boer War and administered hatpin jabs at the money power." The young man who spoke for the Law School had been "patterned by nature as a funeral director" and in "a sad sepulchral voice" had "expressed grave fears for the future of the Republic."

Nothing daunted by this rebuff, we took it on ourselves to arrange a great banquet in Tomlinson's Hall with a speaker of some distinction from outside the state, and we selected Mayor David Rose of Milwaukee, who was an excellent orator with some polish. We sent the invitation to Mayor Rose without consulting Taggart or any of the leaders, and, on its acceptance, Taggart, with evident disrelish, was forced to co-operate. It was Rose who made the scandal. Unknown to us, he was hostile to Bryan in a day when Bryan was an idol in Indiana, and his speech left no doubt of his hostility. Seated at one of the tables was the venerable Judge David Gooding, whose life had touched the Jackson period and who had patterned his speeches accordingly throughout his life. He was therefore known for his abuse of the enemy. Soon after Rose began his anti-Bryan discourse every eye was turned on the tall, powerful figure of the venerable Gooding, his face suffused with fury, as he sprang to his feet and stalked down the aisle pounding the floor with his cane and exclaiming loudly, "By God, this is treason!" This did not sweeten the temper of the irritated Taggart, since many would suppose not only that he had selected Rose as the speaker, but that he approved of the anti-Bryan tone of the speech. So our method of forcing recognition from the bosses backfired, and I was definitely on Taggart's blacklist for several years.

But the audacity of the two young men in a hurry did attract attention. At that time I spoke with such rapidity that for some

47

years thereafter I was designated "the Gatling-gun orator of the Wabash"!

To make my prospects in Indianapolis even darker, my economic situation was gloomy. I had set my heart on law as a profession, but I could not afford the necessary study of some years followed by the usual starvation period of the young lawyer. The momentary glamour of my Shortridge days was fading out, most of my friends were now at Yale, Harvard or Princeton, and I was in the depths of depression, ready to abandon all my boyhood ambitions with the sad reflection that "the thoughts of youth are long, long thoughts." Humiliated by my position, I was eager to leave Indianapolis when I noticed an advertisement for a newspaperman on the Terre Haute *Gazette*. In making application I gave John W. Kern as a reference. With such a sponsor a favorable reply was almost certain. It came, but when it did I was more depressed than elated. I had never been in Terre Haute and I knew not a single person there. Had anyone suggested when I took the train for the city on the Wabash in January 1903 that within eighteen months after my arrival I would be nominated for Congress by the Democrats, it would have seemed a bad joke.

CHAPTER V

A Plunge into Politics

I WALKED from the station in Terre Haute that cold January day
with the uncontrollable feeling that I was in a community of
strangers. Nevertheless, the town had many historical associations
for me. Its name, French for "high land," was, I knew, a heritage
from the days when the whole territory had belonged to France;
it was thus that French traders and Jesuit missionaries had referred
to the site in the early eighteenth century. Three miles up the beautiful Wabash, the river lined with sycamore trees and sung so senti-
mentally by Paul Dresser, was the site of the fort built by William
Henry Harrison in 1811 as a protection against the Indians. Terre
Haute had produced more than its share of distinguished men and
women. The house in which Secretary Usher of Lincoln's Cabinet
had lived still stood on Ohio Street. Richard W. Thompson, Secretary of the Navy in the Hayes Cabinet, had died only a little while
before my arrival. But to me the sentimental appeal of the town
was in the fact that it had been the home of Daniel W. Voorhees,
whom I had idolized from early childhood, and I went in search
of the house where he had lived in the days of his early triumphs.
In his day most of the best houses were on the riverfront, and from
the windows one could look across the Wabash to where "the candle lights were gleaming." But fashion had moved from the river
now, and though the solid brick house where Voorhees had lived
was still there, I found that it had been converted into a bawdy-
house.

In a small house on a slight elevation across from the jail Theodore Dreiser and his brother Paul, who by now had become the
songwriter Paul Dresser, had lived in abject poverty in their early
youth. The Dreiser family was still the subject of familiar gossip

49

in my time. Here in Terre Haute lived Eugene V. Debs, and, in girlhood, some famous women—Janet Scudder, the sculptress; Amelia Küssner Coudert, the miniature painter; Alice Fischer, the actress; and Rose Melville, the original "Sis Hopkins" of the plays. Alice Fischer really loved the town, occasionally visiting her family there, and I vividly recall one afternoon when she delighted me with her rollicking reminiscences of her girlhood. In talking she gushed, sparkled, roared with laughter. Her loyalties were of the heart. When a friend of hers referred to Debs as a Socialist, Alice flared. "Don't be stupid," she said. "Gene is not a Socialist. He's from Terre Haute. Am I a Socialist because I come from Terre Haute?" she asked triumphantly. Such was her logic where her loyalties were involved.

If I entered the town a stranger I was not long to remain one, for the Terre Hauteans combined the qualities of the generous West with those of the hospitable South. They had no reticence among strangers, whom they quickly drew in. The big lobby of the old Terre Haute House was a veritable club where any evening one could find a goodly assembly of leading citizens lolling in the big black leather chairs in gossip or disputation. The population included all sorts. There were numerous rich men among the brewers, distillers and coal operators, but they were democratic in their social relations. The large labor population employed in factories and neighboring mines exerted an abiding influence on the social thinking of the community. I was astonished by this at first, having come from Indianapolis, where labor unions were then anathema. I often marveled why a city so ideally situated for industrial purposes as Terre Haute was should not have had a more rapid growth as an industrial center. Here was coal in abundance almost at the furnace door, an ample water supply, and railroads running east and west and north and south. I was told elsewhere that the reputation of the city as a labor union town had tended to divert manufacturers to other fields.

The Terre Haute *Gazette* was a family paper, owned and edited by the Ball brothers, men of sound ability and character. It was an old-fashioned paper with a high ethical standard, but, refusing to unionize, it steadily lost in circulation. When the profits had approached zero it was sold and merged with the *Tribune*, and I left to go to the *Star* as an editorial writer.

It was in these days that I received my education about labor unions. The process of making the periodic contracts between miners and operators was this: The miners met in their convention and decided what they would ask; the operators met in theirs and agreed on what they would concede or refuse; and then miners and operators met together for the struggle. I attended these meetings, and the more I saw the greater my admiration for the miners grew. The operators were no match for them in debate, and eventually the operators had to employ as secretary and spokesman a former head of the United Mine Workers, Phil Penna, a Welshman with great facility in speech who understood the language and the psychology of the coal diggers. Many times I saw an operator so bungle his case that while he was blundering along half a dozen scarred miners were on the edge of their chairs awaiting an opportunity to tear him to pieces. Instantly Penna would spring to the defense and direct the withdrawal. He usually began with a witticism that brought laughter, and then deftly he would cover the retreat. I found that these miners were students of economics, and natural debaters. At these joint meetings the contracts, for stated periods, were made and signed; in those days such contracts were scrupulously observed.

My first year in Terre Haute remains a pleasant memory. It was a new experience. I lived on South Fifth Street, in a little room heated by a small stove, and on winter mornings, I often had to break through ice in the pitcher to wash and shave before tramping ankle deep in snow to Mrs. Collins' boardinghouse on Third Street for breakfast. The meals there were delicious and abundant and cost three dollars a week. Alas, the good old days!

I had put aside all thoughts of politics, cultivated no politicians, and was happy in my isolation. It was then that I yielded to the natural ambition of many honest Hoosier lads to write a novel. At night, by the dim light of a smoking kerosene lamp, hovering close to the stove to keep warm, I sat writing what, of course, was to be the great American novel. Inevitably, it was to be a political yarn. The hero was patterned after Tom Taggart, the heroine after a charming and clever girl I knew in Indianapolis, who, after more than fifty years, is still my friend. The manuscript was sent to Lippincott. To my astonishment, when it was returned it was not with the usual curt rejection slip but with a long letter to the effect that the man in the story was "a distinct creation" but that the woman was not quite real. I was urged to rewrite the story and re-create the lady with more usual traits. Since I had created the fictional lady meticulously after the real one, this puzzled me no end. But before I could sit down to the rewriting of the tale something happened to change the course of my life back to its earlier trend.

The most famous Terre Hautean of the time was Eugene V. Debs, leader of the Socialist Party, and one day I went in search of him for a feature story. Looking for his home, I was confused to find myself in a prosperous neighborhood with large, comfortable houses. I had assumed I would find him living in a shack in some outlying district of vice and squalor, this being my conception of a Socialist. When at length I found myself in front of a two-and-a-half-story frame house set in grounds with well-tended flower beds, I was positive I had made a mistake. I glanced at my memorandum. Yes, this was the address. Still incredulous, I ascended the steps and rang the bell.

I expected to be confronted with a dour-faced, rough, scowling man in shirt sleeves, probably unshaven—since this, again, was my idea of a Socialist. The door opened, and I was facing a tall, slender man in a smoking jacket, with a pipe in one hand and a book in the other, and on his face one of the sweetest smiles I have ever seen. This, I realized, was Debs.

He led me into a library lined with books to the ceiling. I studied this man who was a monster to those who did not know him, and noted his fine head, his long strong neck, his deep-blue eyes that beamed with benevolence and yet were keen and penetrating, and the smile that seemed so childlike and pure in its sincerity. I found it impossible to reconcile what I saw with what I had heard about him from those who had never seen him. He could have been taken for a physician, a lawyer or a professor, for his features had the refinement of the intellectual. One could even imagine him in clerical garb, a parish priest of the more tender sort, and picture him passing in and out of the lowly houses of his flock on errands of kindness and mercy.

For two hours we sat and chatted. My mission was such that I could draw him out on his life and thinking without indelicacy.

In a reminiscent mood, he talked nostalgically of his youth. His parents, revered by him, were Alsatians who had had to struggle for a living when they came to America. His boyish hunger for knowledge had led him into the Occidental Literary Club, before which he read papers and engaged in debates, thus unwittingly preparing himself for the rough-and-tumble of the hustings. He was still a boy when he conceived the idea of introducing James Whitcomb Riley, then at the beginning of his career on the platform, to a Terre Haute audience. The poet was then scarcely known in the community, and I gathered that the boy had been bitterly disappointed by the size of the audience, but captivated by the poet. That was the beginning of a lifelong friendship matched by that between Debs and Eugene Field. It was Riley who said that "God was feelin' mighty good when he made Gene Debs, and he didn't have anything else to do all day." Later Riley was to write:

> Go search the earth from end to end
> And where's a better all-round friend
> Than Eugene Debs?—a man that stands
> And jest holds out in his two hands
> As warm a heart as ever beat
> Betwixt here and the Mercy Seat!

That day Debs recalled with boyish delight and laughter his brief excursion into the drama in early youth. A group of the very young proposed to storm the stage with their own version of *Uncle Tom's Cabin*. It was a disappointment to Debs that his companions thought him especially fitted for the role of advance agent, because of his ingratiating personality. Alice Fischer, later a woman of such imposing stature that it was difficult to find a suitable role for her, appeared as Little Eva, and John E. Lamb (who was to become a brilliant lawyer, orator and political leader), being large and muscular, undertook the unpleasant role of Simon Legree. The play amused the neighbors, and, full of confidence, Debs fared forth among the small towns of eastern Illinois preparing the villagers for an artistic treat. Unhappily the rustics were not amused, and soon, after being stranded in a village, the thespians hilariously found their way back home.

That day Debs also described an experience he had had with a distinguished conservative club in Boston soon after his release from the Woodstock, Illinois, jail, where he had been confined under the tyrannical system of "government by injunction" used to break the Pullman strike. After a speech in Faneuil Hall he had returned to his hotel and found, to his astonishment, a note from the famous editor of a conservative magazine, inviting him to a luncheon at the club, of which the editor was president. No one but the editor knew of the invitation, which Debs accepted, and, since none of the members had compromised themselves by attending the Faneuil Hall meeting, no one suspected the identity of the stranger seated beside the president. At length the latter rose and asked the indulgence of the company in listening to a man he considered misunderstood, and presented Debs. "I shall never forget the expression on their faces when they heard my name," said Debs. "It was just such an expression as one can imagine on the face of a person finding himself looking down on a loathsome snake slimily writhing at his feet." But the members were gentlemen, and they listened in silence for half an hour, and gradually they thawed in the warmth of Debs's smile, and in the end they gave him generous applause. Thereafter, throughout his life, he numbered among his friends some of the most conservative men of Boston.

For Debs was a gentleman. He was no vulgar demagogue, and he did not think that a dirty collar or a ragged coat made one a friend of the people. His dream was of a world in which there would be no dirty collars and ragged coats.

One bitter January day a prosperous businessman looking out his window saw Debs hurrying along, bending against the winter wind, and then stopping at the doorway of a business building to talk with a derelict who evidently was soliciting alms. To the observer's amazement, Debs removed his tailored overcoat, handed it to the beggar and then hurried home at a dogtrot to save himself from a chill. The next day the onlooker took him to task for his improvidence. Debs blushed with embarrassment. "You see," he said, "the beggar was an old railroad man and a good one until drink got the better of him and he lost his job, and I couldn't see him suffer in such weather." "But," remonstrated the businessman, "why didn't you give him a little money to buy a secondhand coat?" Debs smiled sheepishly and confessed it had not occurred to him. I heard of several incidents of this sort in Terre Haute.

Debs's oratory was not that of the soapbox ranter. He spoke conversationally, his model being Wendell Phillips, with whom he corresponded until the latter's death. His diction was good, and many passages of his speeches had a literary flavor. He was a phrase maker, and his humor and gentle irony brought cheers and laughter. His voice was pleasant, and his charm in conversation was transmitted from the platform.

Though his speaking engagements took him out of town most of the time I saw him frequently, and never was I to find a flaw of any consequence in his character. Refusing the fifth nomination of the Socialists for President, he accepted the Congressional nomination in 1916. One raw October day in Bowling Green during the campaign, I had concluded a speech for the Democrats and was leaving when Debs drove into town. Learning that he had been unable to find a hall, I went to his car and offered him the one I had taken for the afternoon. He thanked me with his usual courtly courtesy, his face beaming with appreciation, and as I turned to leave I noticed with surprise that his eyes were moist. Deeply sentimental, he was easily touched by acts of kindness. I shall come back to Debs again.

While it was a privilege to know Debs, my most valuable friendship in Terre Haute was with John E. Lamb, one of the most amusing men and consummate politicians I have ever known. He had a striking personality, political genius, sound judgment and great eloquence. His spectacular rise took him to Congress before he was thirty as the protégé of Voorhees, but in Washington he became a favorite of James G. Blaine, despite political differences. The gossip columns of the times had him engaged to the "plumed knight's" daughter Hattie, who later married Walter Damrosch. In young manhood he was spectacularly handsome, and he was still an imposing figure when I knew him. He had a magnificent head, and his features would have commanded attention in any crowd. His face was large, with a pink complexion; his jaws were firm, his lips full, expressive and sensuous, and his large gray Irish eyes so penetrating that they made liars wilt under his cross-examination in court. In manner he was courtly, but when he was aroused his arrogance was intimidating.

Voorhees once told Lamb that if he had as much genius in making friends as in making enemies he would have been President.

Unhappily his life was a series of battles. His enemies were made in large measure by his intolerance of bores and his impatience with the pretensions of mediocrity. His acid wit and his scorching sarcasm embittered many who would have preferred to be his friends. I am sure he did not realize how deeply he wounded, since often it was his irresistible sense of the ridiculous that led him into ironic comments in a spirit of fun, without realizing the effect on his victims. In social contacts and in conversation he was charming. In his home and in his office on Sunday mornings, when his close friends usually gathered, it was a treat to listen to his observations on people and politics and to hear his chuckle.

As a political leader he was masterful, uncannily resourceful, and unerring in timing and in judgment. He began his professional career as a brilliant criminal lawyer. He was a genius in courtroom strategy. His eloquence was irresistible with most juries. During one bitterly contested and very prolonged murder trial, with a mob clamoring for his client's life, he walked the floor at night without sleep for days, and though the trial ended with the acquittal of his client it resulted in his nervous collapse. Thereafter he abandoned criminal practice to confine himself to civil and corporation law, a field in which he had an equally brilliant career.

In 1903 when I first went to Terre Haute I carried a letter of introduction to Lamb from Kern, but after a glance at the scrawny, unpromising youth that I was he received me with a cold, distant courtesy that discouraged me from seeing him again until a year later, when he sent for me.

This summons had a novel background. The annual Terre Haute Jackson Club banquet was important in state politics. I had been in Terre Haute just one year, remote from politics, when an Indianapolis Democratic leader who declined an invitation to speak at the banquet suggested that there was a young man in Terre Haute who would do "quite as well." My speech made a favorable impression, and the leaders of the Congressional district's seven counties, who followed, proposed my nomination for Congress. No one would have thought of selecting a candidate without the approval of Lamb, who was then in Cuba. When on his return he heard of the suggestion, he arranged to have me speak at the Saint Patrick's Day banquet so that he could hear me. During my speech I noticed with some satisfaction that Lamb seemed moved. The next morning I was summoned to his office.

"How would you like the nomination for Congress?" he asked.

I admitted that I would like it.

"Very well," he said. "There's hardly any possibility of a Democratic victory this fall"—it was the year of the Teddy Roosevelt landslide—"but you're a young man and can afford the sacrifice. By making a speaking campaign in all seven counties you'll help the local tickets and put the party under obligation to you in the future. I suppose you have no money. We'll take care of that."

And so, when scarcely the constitutional age to hold the office if elected, I was nominated for Congress in the courthouse in Martinsville.

It was evident from the beginning that the Democrats had no chance at all in the campaign of 1904. The party bosses had conceived the idea of doing a right-about-face and nominating a pronounced conservative for President—a repudiation of Bryan, still the idol of the rank and file. Alton B. Parker, a New York jurist, able and honest, was nominated at the St. Louis convention over the protest of Bryan, whose moving speech as dawn was breaking was one of the most remarkable of his career. To make matters worse, after his nomination Parker was persuaded by foolish advisers to telegraph the convention that he would refuse if it did not accept his repudiation of Bryan's policies, and the convention acceded to his wishes. In my first speech as a candidate that year, when I mentioned the name of Parker the silence was so impressive that I did not mention it again.

My Congressional district comprised seven counties: Vigo, Vermillion and Clay, which had a large mining and industrial population, and Parke, Putnam, Hendricks and Morgan, which were entirely agricultural. The memory of that campaign is still pleasant and vivid. For seven weeks I spoke every afternoon and evening, going into every township of the seven counties. And since, for financial reasons, I had to keep my newspaper job, I would sit down each night after the last meeting and write—usually beside a kerosene lamp in a country hotel room—nonpolitical editorials for the *Star*.

In those days candidates campaigned in rural areas by horse and buggy. We set out from the county seats in a cavalcade of buggies the first of every week, sleeping wherever the night meeting might be held. During the day the procession would move slowly through the countryside, pausing at each farmhouse to solicit the farmer's vote personally. If he was working in a distant field some of our party would join him at his work and others would talk to the farmer's wife or daughter, and if he was at the churn the candidate would take his turn. The elector would be quizzed discreetly about the other candidates, and the information as to preference and prejudice would be passed on to the person affected. The practical jokers took advantage of this system to play upon the morbid fears of the oversensitive candidate, who would be solemnly warned of imaginary grievances against him, and, smothered in gloom, he would suffer until evening, when his fears would be lifted with the truth.

Nothing could have been more pleasant than these drives through the countryside when the forests were flaming with red and gold and the odors of the fall were sweet. In the evening we could count on a country dinner at the farmhouse of one of the faithful, where we would be surfeited with fried chicken, cream gravy, spareribs, yeast biscuits, pie and cake. After eating we would draw up our chairs before the blazing hearth until time to go to the evening meeting at some neighboring town. When there was no such town, the meeting would be in some country schoolhouse, and as we approached we would see the flaming torches and hear the fife and drum. The room would be packed with farmers in their work clothes, and these meetings were the most intimate of all, since the speaker could reach over and touch the shoulders of those in the front row. Usually the country hotels offered a comfortable bed and good fare, but some of the roosting places were primitive beyond compare. One morning I woke to find my bedcover under three inches of snow that had drifted in through a broken windowpane.

In Hendricks and Morgan counties, both overwhelmingly Republican, little encouragement and scant courtesy could be expected. In these I had to take the week-long journey alone or accompanied only by a driver from the livery stable. In Morgan it was particularly depressing. One evening I drove into a small town in this county and found there were fewer than ten Democrats in the township. I was told that we had been refused a hall for the speech. I suggested a vacant store. No, the owner had indignantly refused its use. I was staying at a pleasant little hotel with a porch in front; when I proposed speaking from the porch mine host protested with such vehemence that he seemed on the verge of a stroke. Thoroughly disgusted and angry, I told the cringing Democrats to have a goods box set in front of the lighted window of a store and I would speak from there. The suggestion clearly alarmed my little flock of the faithful, but it was so arranged. I spoke almost an hour, facing a crowd that extended back into the blackness. When I closed, my audience gave three cheers for my opponent. Later I learned the secret of the fears of my few supporters. Many years before, Thomas A. Hendricks, later Governor, Senator and Vice-President, had been stoned from the town when he attempted to make a Democratic speech, and the threat was made that any Democrat presuming to speak there would be given similar treatment. I had not heard of the incident, but the crowd, assuming that I had, formed a better opinion of my valor than I deserved.

Defeated, as I expected, in the Republican landslide of 1904, I was unanimously renominated in the park at Rockville in 1906, and again for seven weeks I made the rounds. As late as the afternoon after the election, the Republican State Committee conceded my election, the Associated Press announced it, and I was deluged with congratulations. It was fortunate that I opposed the suggestion that we hold a celebration, for I was eventually defeated by returns that came in almost twenty-four hours after the closing of the polls, though there was no convincing reason given for the delay.

The 1906 campaign brought me into personal contact with Bryan, and I had an interesting glimpse of his alertness. He was touring the state in a special train, speaking briefly in numerous towns during the day and closing with a large meeting in some city in the evening. He had spoken early in the day in Brazil, where I joined his train to accompany him to Terre Haute, and then he had retired to his drawing room for a massage and a change of underclothes, as was his custom. Often he slept for ten or fifteen minutes between towns, since he could sleep at will and awaken when he wished. After his rubdown I was sitting beside him with a copy of the Cincinnati *Enquirer* on my lap. Glancing at it, he caught the headline of the report of a speech by Senator Beveridge in which that orator had called him a "dreamer." Bryan smiled and murmured, " 'The dreamer lives forever, but the doer dies in a day.' " Then, taking the paper in his hand, he told me the story of Joseph the dreamer, who went into the land of the stranger and "got the corn." This flashed upon him as a reply to Beveridge's taunt, and he incorporated the Biblical story into his speech that night; it was one of his happiest retorts to his foes.

That campaign was the last in which I was to figure as a candidate, but every two years until I left Indiana I made speeches for a month or so in every campaign.

My next contact with Bryan was in Nebraska in 1908 when, as a delegate, I was en route to the national convention at Denver with Kern and Lamb. We stopped in Lincoln on a rainy morning, and Bryan drove in from his farm to have us to lunch. He was lighthearted and gay. At the convention he was easily nominated.

In the ensuing campaign I learned something more of Bryan's system for preserving his health and conserving his strength. He spoke one afternoon to a huge crowd in the ballpark in Terre Haute for an hour and a half. That evening we were to dine at Lamb's, and I left the meeting with Bryan and Lamb in the latter's little electric runabout, sitting facing the Commoner. As the car was slowly creeping through the throng on the grounds, with fervent partisans crowding about it, Bryan seemed suddenly very tired, and his hands hung limply over the side of the car. When his admirers grasped them there was no responding clasp from him, and he looked old. I was alarmed, for he had the appearance of a man on the verge of a collapse. But the moment we emerged from the grounds, he straightened in his seat; the transformation was astonishing. Then I realized that he had the rare capacity of relaxing utterly in the midst of a crowd. He had been resting!

That night at dinner he was very hoarse, but, because the factory owners had refused permission for their employees to hear the speech in the afternoon, a last-minute plan was made for a fifteen-minute speech from the steps of the courthouse after dinner. Handbills were speedily printed and scattered; it was not thought probable, however, that many people would be reached. But when we emerged on the courthouse steps, having entered the building by another door, we were startled: before us, a huge crowd was packed solidly from the steps to the buildings across the street and for a block in both directions. "I cannot disappoint this crowd," I heard Bryan say, and he began to speak. His voice was husky for a minute; then it became as clear as a clarion and he spoke for almost an hour. But what interested me most was the carrying power of that voice. I was standing beside him and it seemed to me that his tone was entirely conversational, and yet I noticed that every word reached those on the outskirts of the crowd a block away.

It was that year, too, that I learned something about the cunning of Uncle Joe Cannon, Republican Speaker of the House and one of the most picturesque figures of his time. He had incurred the resentment of the temperance people, and for the first time in years he felt it necessary to campaign in his own Illinois district. When I was sent on a speaking tour into the district, I was puzzled to hear Democrats making sympathetic comments on the old warrior and his campaign. With the best opportunity in years to defeat him, this was disconcerting, and I asked the reason for so much compassion. In almost tender tones one of the Democrats replied that Cannon was an old and feeble man and that it was too bad that in his closing days he should be subjected to the rigors of a campaign. I knew that, en route, he had stopped in Indianapolis to attend a dinner at the Marion Club and had stayed till an hour when some of the other diners were just about under the table. I asked why he was thought feeble. "Well," I was told, "when he spoke in this hall last night he was so weak that they had to help him down the aisle, and he asked permission to speak seated." Hoping to overcome this unseasonable sympathy, I suggested that he probably was strong enough to give the Democrats a trouncing. "No, that's the unusual part about it," I was told. This was soon after Bryan had toured Europe and been wined and dined (or, rather, dined, since he did not drink) by the statesmen there. "No doubt," continued the tender Democrat, "being old and feeble, he has lost his wallop. He said in a weak voice that every time he picked up a paper and noticed that a prime minister had accorded Bryan high distinction in Europe, he exclaimed to himself, 'Thank God he's an American.'" I could find no way to combat this, and

I have no doubt that for every temperance Republican vote Cannon lost, he gained a Democratic sympathy vote.

The night of the election, when the Republican triumph was assured, the Elks club in Danville, his home, paraded to the house of the "feeble old man," who placed himself at the head of the procession and did a jig dance all the way to the clubhouse; and at midnight he took the train to New York to attend a dinner in honor of James S. Sherman, the Vice-President-elect. No one knew better when to play the lion and when to play the fox.

That year, 1908, also marked the beginning of my long friendship with Thomas R. Marshall, later Vice-President for eight years through the Wilson regime. While Bryan had lost Indiana, the Democrats had elected a governor and a majority in the Legislature on the local-option issue which injected Prohibition into politics. Thus Marshall entered upon his interesting career. Little known outside his own district, he had been nominated for governor as a compromise candidate when the struggle between the organization and the anti-organization forces threatened to create a feud. Because in the early stages of the state convention few thought his nomination possible, there was no feeling against him in any quarter. When, like most delegates, I called at his headquarters, I found a slightly built man with a big mustache (not closely cropped, as in his Washington days) and humorous eyes who amused callers with his whimsicality and gave the impression of being a modest man capable of poking fun at himself while paying compliments to his opponents. His visitors left his room with a kindly feeling for an old-fashioned Democrat. Thus it was that in the end the organization forces dumped their votes into Marshall's lap.

But the real drama in state politics came after the election: the defeat of Kern for the United States Senatorship. With a Democratic majority in the Legislature, it was assumed by the rank and file that he would be elected. (This was before the Seventeenth Amendment, and Senators were still chosen by the state legislatures.) He had made many sacrifices for the party, and he had just been the Democratic nominee for Vice-President—Bryan's running mate in the 1908 campaign. But the state campaign on the issue of county option had given the brewery and distillery interests a powerful influence in the Legislature, and its obligations, supported by the machine, were elsewhere, so Kern was defeated. When the result was announced and Kern, looking crushed, was leaving the State House, Lamb—who had also been a candidate for the nomination before the Democratic legislators' caucus—said to me, "Lord, how he would enjoy a drink!" Kern had not touched liquor for many years.

Another Senator was to be elected in 1910 (Beveridge's second term was about to expire) and Lamb was again a candidate for the nomination. He was too consummate a politician not to know that in a legislators' caucus, with the organization hostile to him, as it now was, he would inevitably lose. One day he called me to his office and outlined his plan. He proposed that the state convention should make the nomination, pledging all the party's legislative candidates to the election of the nominee. He knew that the resentment of many over the defeat of Kern would rally them to the support of the plan. But, as he knew and said, were it known that the plan originated with a candidate it would make much less of an appeal. Governor Marshall was an excellent governor and was very popular, and Lamb planned to persuade Marshall to sponsor the plan, which would be known as "the Governor's plan." He hoped to convince Marshall that this would attract national attention, as indeed it did, and, if successful, would put him forward conspicuously as the champion of the rank and file against the bosses. He counted on the Governor's pride and ambition, and with reason. Thus "the Governor's plan," in truth Lamb's plan, was announced.

The bitterly hostile reaction of the organization caused Marshall some concern, and he showed signs of wavering. Lamb called me to his office. "Marshall is weakening," he said, "and we must do something to bolster him up. Bryan arrives in New York from South America the first of next week and I want him to telegraph Marshall his enthusiastic endorsement of the plan and give it to the press. I can't go to New York without attracting attention and defeating my purpose. I want you to go and see Bryan, explain the situation, and ask him to send the telegram." I did not go, since another way was found to reach Bryan with the message. His telegram created something of a sensation among the Hoosiers, and the effect on Marshall's morale was excellent.

Thus the Indiana Democratic convention of 1910 made history

and anticipated the popular election of Senators. The excitement was intense and feeling ran high. The opposition, under the clever leadership of Taggart, marshaled its forces for the fight. The lobby of the Denison House buzzed and throbbed. Living and working with Lamb, as I was doing, was a nerve-racking experience. He believed that the one hope of victory would be in rallying the outside counties against the organization in the capital, which he intended to attack. He even proposed to attack Taggart, and I was unable to dissuade him. He expected to be hooted and jeered and he hoped that the mobbing by the Indianapolis delegates would be resented by the outside counties. The moment he mentioned Taggart's name the storm of hisses and jeers broke. Through the pandemonium Lamb stood smiling and silent, getting in a word in the infrequent lulls. Marshall, on the platform, was pale and nervous. But on the roll call the plan carried.

I watched this mad scene with Meredith Nicholson, the novelist, who, indicating an opposite box in which were Mrs. Lamb, Mrs. Kern and Mrs. Marshall, commented, "There's the real drama— more than on the floor." For in the end it was Kern who was chosen as the nominee for Senator.

The sensational triumph of "the Governor's plan" gave Marshall a national reputation as a popular leader of progressive forces and led to his becoming a candidate for the Democratic Presidential nomination at the 1912 convention at Baltimore, which finally chose him as Woodrow Wilson's running mate. (The uncannily clever Taggart assumed the leadership of the Marshall forces at the Baltimore convention and made the most of his candidate's triumph over the bosses of whom Taggart himself had been one.) Thus the net result of Lamb's strategy was that Kern went to the Senate— where he later became the Wilson Administration's floor leader— and Marshall became Vice-President. The sole reward Lamb received was the offer of the embassy in Mexico, which he was not to enjoy, since it was thought wise to postpone his appearance in Mexico until conditions cleared up there, and during the interval he died.

The Senatorial election of 1910 was more than ordinarily exciting, with Kern, a veteran campaigner, pitted against the eloquent Beveridge. While campaigning I found abundant evidence that the Republican enemies of Beveridge banded together for his defeat.

Years later, I was to write biographies of both Beveridge and Kern.

Soon after the election, Kern asked me to serve as his secretary. This offer provided an easy release from a municipal office which did not interest me, and I accepted with the mental reservation that I would serve one year for the experience and then resign. But, for reasons that will appear, I was to continue with Kern throughout his term.

CHAPTER VI

Washington, 1911-1917: Unwritten History

THE WASHINGTON I KNEW from 1911 to 1917, a city of leisurely tradition, has passed into history. The First World War was to change the tone and tempo of the town. During my residence there the people lived rather quietly and moved about as though time were of little consequence. The downtown section was really lonely at night. Pennsylvania Avenue was a drab reminder of the years before the Civil War, the architecture of the buildings commonplace to hideous unless one could visualize the past on which these structures had looked. Strolling along the avenue, one saw the identical buildings that Clay and Webster knew, now worn and shabby with time and weather. The National Hotel, a four-story brick structure painted white and turning yellow, was still open to guests as in the days when Clay died within its walls and Buchanan was a guest the night before his inauguration. Hancock's retained its old quarters in a little two-story brick building, with its sawdust-floored bar that had been a favorite of Clay and Webster. It was still famous for its chicken dinners, Southern style, but anyone wishing to partake had to reserve one of the tables the day before. The colored waiters, old and dignified, might have come down from the 1840s.

Nearer the Treasury, Shoemaker's Bar, also with a sawdust floor, and with old prints and posters on the walls, remained a favorite meeting place for statesmen, as in the days when Stephen A. Douglas spent too much time there. It was also a favorite of newspapermen, and when its ornate and unique beer mugs began to be taken as souvenirs the proprietor took to painting three telltale words on the bottom of the mugs. A story was told that when Prince Henry of Germany was a guest at the White House during the Teddy Roosevelt administration the President thought it would be nice to have a beer party. It was a last-minute thought, and because the party would be a failure without old steins Archie Butt suggested borrowing some from the famous saloon. All would have gone well but for the fact that when the steins were lifted to *hoch* the Kaiser one could read on the bottom that they had been "STOLEN FROM SHOEMAKER'S."

Harvey's was still on Pennsylvania Avenue, where it had been generations before when statesmen in search of a good game or fish dinner with choice wine ate and drank there while planning historic legislation.

To me the most fascinating spot in Washington was Lafayette Square, facing the White House and dominated by Jackson on his rearing stallion, for all around the square were houses associated with many of the great figures and events in our history. The old Arlington Hotel was torn down during my Washington days, and the Belasco Theater stood on the site of the house in which the murderous assault was made on William H. Seward the night of Lincoln's assassination, but otherwise most of the houses of antebellum days remained. The Cosmos Club occupied the house in which Dolley Madison held court years after her husband's death. The Cameron house, where the Taylors had lived and whence on a blustery, rainy day President William Henry Harrison had walked across the park to his death from pneumonia, still stood. Across the square was the house from whose windows the beautiful Italian wife of Daniel E. Sickles gave the signal to her lover, who was shot in the square by her outraged husband, resulting in one of the most sensational murder trials in our history.

But the house that intrigued me most was the Decatur house, where the wife of the naval hero played on the harpsichord and whence at dawn one day her husband sallied forth to his rendezvous with death on the field of honor; in which Fox, the British minister, slept by day that he might be fresh for the card table with our celebrities by night; in which Clay lived, mourning his defeat for the Presidency; and where Martin Van Buren, when in Jackson's Cabinet, had a window cut so that he could see Old Hickory's signals from the White House, and pretty Peggy Eaton came for

67

comfort and advice during her bitter battle with the snobs. Diagonally across the street was the Corcoran house, where Webster lived and at whose table, over wine and walnuts, he and Ashburton negotiated the treaty which bears their names. Alas, this house has been demolished to make way for the uninspiring building of the Chamber of Commerce, and it seemed probable that the Decatur house would suffer the same fate until, years later, it was given to the nation. One wonders why those charged with the planning of the city have not thought it worth while to preserve these historic houses.

When I went to Washington I was engaged to Sybil McCaslin, a beautiful girl from Indianapolis whom I had been earnestly courting for several years. After our marriage our first quarters in Washington were in an apartment on G Street, within a stone's throw of that monstrous mountain of masonry that then housed the State, War and Navy departments. The next year we had more attractive quarters in the Cliffbourne on Calvert Street, in a pleasant neighborhood, with the windows looking out on Rock Creek Park. Though we have always thought of the Cliffbourne as our Washington home, our last year found us in the Prince Karl on K Street, a staid old apartment house without much charm, but convenient. During these years our favorite walks were through the historic streets of old Georgetown, not then fashionable, and through the Virginia and Maryland countryside.

Looking back on my six years in Washington, I am convinced that those years marked the beginning of a new and more progressive period in our history. There had been a break in the long sordid tradition during Theodore Roosevelt's administration, but that of his successor, Taft, returned to the old policies and principles on which we had operated since the middle of the 1860s. The high tide of privilege was reached with the Payne-Aldrich Tariff of 1909. In the dissension that it stirred up, the domination of the Republican Party by Senator Nelson W. Aldrich of Rhode Island and the big-corporation interests was challenged and the old order began to creak and crack. Then came the break between Roosevelt and Taft; later, in 1911, there was even a rift between Taft and the Republican Old Guard, over his support of the Canadian reciprocity agreement, which they opposed bitterly. Meanwhile the electorate had been aroused by the tariff and by some investigations through which the Democrats were beginning to pry into dark government recesses. In the elections of 1910 some of the stoutest champions of reaction in the Senate had been retired and replaced by more progressive men, and the Republicans had lost the House. In 1912, with the Republicans split wide open, Woodrow Wilson was elected President and the Democrats gained control of the Senate. And, to add immeasurably to the advantage of the Democrats, they had an enormous superiority in the caliber of their Senate leaders and in their notable effectiveness in debate.

I spent much time in the Senate studying my favorites. For some years Senator Joseph W. Bailey of Texas had dominated the Democratic minority like an overseer. It had been an ultraconservative and reactionary minority, easily impressed by the domineering, extraordinarily able and eloquent Bailey. They followed him as meekly as the bull follows the steer. He even looked the part of the overseer. Tall, powerfully built, with a handsome head and features, he carried himself like a conqueror. His eloquence was both powerful and persuasive. His speeches were phrased in the best English and were fairly well knit in logic, though he was prone to draw on his imagination for history when required to make his point. His voice was melodious, and when he finished his peroration his tones lingered in the chamber like the echo of chimes in a cathedral.

The election of 1910 introduced new faces on the Democratic side, and most of these were able men of strong liberal and progressive tendencies. No longer was Bailey able to speak *ex cathedra*, without a challenge. I am sure I was present when he suffered the humiliation that made private life more attractive to him than his seat in the Senate.

Bailey was contending, in a tariff debate, that no Democratic statesman had ever favored free imports on raw materials. He spoke with great force and confidence, due to his previous successes in substituting stout assertions for history. He challenged anyone to produce a name in contradiction. He paused. Silence, as usual. He reiterated his challenge and sat down.

A small man, slightly stooped, rose slowly and began speaking in a soft Southern drawl: John Sharp Williams of Mississippi. Williams had certain cultural advantages over even Henry Cabot

69

Lodge, habitually referred to as "the scholar in politics." In youth he had taken the grand tour, studying in Germany, lingering long and understandingly in France and England. His clothes sometimes suggested the need of a valet, but his English never the need of a grammarian or rhetorician. There was nothing pretentious in his eloquence. He offered no purple patches, but when his emotions were aroused he was movingly eloquent. His wit was biting and his humor irresistible. He could cripple an opponent with a sentence.

Williams began his reply to Bailey with an expression of his profound admiration and affection for the Texan. Then he accepted Bailey's challenge. Citing dates and occasions, he called the roll of a string of Democratic statesmen who had favored free imports of raw materials. Bailey flushed and was clearly flustered. When Williams sat down the Texan sprang to his feet and angrily replied with more "facts" from history. Observing that the Mississippian was taking notes, he became angrier and laid himself wide open by more loose assertions. Up rose Williams nonchalantly to reiterate his admiration and affection, and then in a bored drawl to pulverize the object of his adoration. Bailey, red in the face, rose again, so infuriated by this mutiny that he said the opposite of what he meant, despite his mastery of the language; Williams, saying in his sweetest tones that he loved his colleague too dearly to permit the mistake to go into the record, corrected him. This exchange lasted for a long time. When it finally ended, everyone in the crowded chamber was persuaded that Bailey had lost his control of the minority.

And when, after the election of 1912, the militantly progressive Senator Kern displaced Senator Tom Martin, the ultraconservative Virginian, from his long-held position of Democratic floor leader, it became crystal clear that the Democratic Party—now the majority party in the Senate—was experiencing a rebirth and rejuvenation.

The new Democratic Senators of 1910 and 1912 greatly surpassed the Old Guard Republicans as orators and debaters. There was no one among the Old Guard comparable in debate to Ollie James of Kentucky, Thomas J. Walsh of Montana, James A. Reed of Missouri and James Hamilton Lewis of Illinois. I never missed an opportunity to hear these men. The most precise mind was that of Walsh, the most devastating debaters and orators were Reed and James, the most finished artist was Lewis.

I had heard of Walsh before his election to the Senate. On the homeward journey from the Denver convention, John E. Lamb, who had served on the platform committee, told me he had just met on that committee the keenest mind he had ever known. "His name is Tom Walsh," he said. "Keep your eye on him." With this in mind I observed Walsh closely. There was little in the appearance of this smallish man with the heavy, drooping mustache of a poker player of Bloody Gulch—for it was of this variety when he entered the Senate—to arouse high expectations. He was on the Committee on Privileges and Elections, which numbered among its members some of the greatest lawyers in the Senate. I was secretary of the committee, and in its meetings I caught the meaning of what Lamb had said. The members would be mulling over a measure that involved some intricate legal difficulty, talking incessantly without reaching a solution, and Walsh would sit in silence, looking down. At length he would straighten in his chair, lean forward, fix his gimletlike eyes on his colleagues and in one or two precisely spoken sentences suggest the wording that ended the discussion. His masterful conduct of the Teapot Dome investigation rendered a historic public service. In time I came to know him well and to find that despite his cold exterior he had a warm heart and no little sentiment.

Senator Reed was also a great lawyer, a master of courtroom strategy. Tall, powerfully built, with the features of a natural commander, the voice of a trained orator, the art of a consummate actor, he was tremendous in debate, and few cared to cross swords with him. He aroused the emotions with the greatest ease. His vituperative force was incomparable. He lived on combat. He loved controversy, and his mind worked with magical rapidity.

Ollie James was more the popular tribune. More than six feet tall and large in proportion, with an immense head and a smoothly shaven face that reflected every feeling, and with a powerful voice that could absorb all other sounds, he would have been a commanding figure in any legislative assembly. In cold print his speeches lacked finish, but he relied on force, and his delivery accentuated the power of his argument. In debate he rode the whirlwind to direct the storm, overwhelming his opponent with ridicule when unable to combat him with logic. I always felt sorry for his victims.

James Hamilton Lewis was the opposite of Ollie James. He was a small man with a reddish beard, and he was always impeccably dressed. Scarcely a vest-pocket edition of the monumental Kentuckian in size, he was even more dangerous than the other in combat. He was a master of subtle irony and a brilliant rhetorician; he could astonish and fascinate with the beauty of his phrasing. Ever and anon a deadly witticism would flash like a sword, leaving his victim bleeding. In many ways he approached genius. During the long filibuster on the shipping bill of the Wilson Administration, when one vote or two would determine its fate, Senator Kern was on the anxious seat lest some Democrat be absent when needed. When he received a note from Lewis announcing he was on his way south on the orders of his physician, Kern, doubting the truth of the excuse, wired him to return or he would be denounced in the party caucus. A day later, when Elihu Root was making his farewell Tory speech, the door opened and Lewis entered. It was evident that he was really ill. Kern, wanting to make amends and recalling that Lewis was always eager to cross swords with Root, whispered to him that he might make a short reply. Lewis had no opportunity to consult sources or to make notes, but he rose the moment Root sat down, and never have I heard a more clever speech or one more beautiful in phrasing. The peroration particularly impressed me, for it was inspired by an incident in the chamber after Lewis rose, and yet its literary flavor was such that it was difficult to believe that it had not been carefully written and polished beforehand. No other member of the Senate could have approached it. His was almost a freak mind. Men smiled at his foppishness and his vanity, but no one doubted his ability, and if he was a prima donna he belonged in the front rank of the artists.

There were able men on the Republican side of the Senate, but, unhappily for the Old Guard, the ablest of their speakers and debaters were the progressives with more in common with the Democrats on fundamental issues. These had split the party on the Payne-Aldrich bill a short time before. For years, Senator Robert M. La Follette had been a thorn in the side of the faithful. He was a great statesman, a tireless crusader, a militant liberal, an enemy of privilege. His speeches were treatises crammed with indisputable facts. The Old Guard usually manifested its contempt by marching like sulking schoolboys into the cloakrooms when he spoke, but this only amused him, since he was speaking primarily to people outside the chamber. Many times when some Senator was taking liberties with the truth I saw the expression of mingled amusement and distaste on the face of La Follette as he sat with his hands on the arms of his chair as though about to spring to his feet. Jo Davidson caught him thus in the statue now in Statuary Hall in the Capitol. I had the honor of speaking at its unveiling some years later. La Follette was a crusader for the common man, and he fought with a battle ax. No bosses could deter or divert him and all hell could not intimidate him.

The Old Guard could not depend on La Follette. Nor could it depend upon Senator Borah, a brilliant orator and supreme debater. He was a vigorous black-haired man with strong features and a pleasant deep voice, and no one looking down from the gallery could fail to notice him. He was powerful and persuasive in debate, and there was something Websterian in his looks and manner in action. The first impression he gave was one of audacity and courage; but too often it was observed that he lacked the courage or the inclination to carry through. He would march gallantly up to the enemy's guns and seem about to take them by storm, and then, mystifyingly, he would wheel around and march back again. Thus he met with the little group of Republican rebels that opposed the Payne-Aldrich bill, participated in their discussions and seemed in accord with them, but on the final roll call, when the others voted as they had talked in the conferences, Borah voted for the measure. Was it timidity, expediency or just party regularity? No one can say positively, but he incurred the displeasure of the Old Guard without winning the confidence of the dissenters. A New York publisher once asked me to write a book on this phase of his character, but I personally liked Borah, and he had written a friendly review of my *Jefferson and Hamilton* for the *New Republic,* and my heart would not have been in the job.

The actual leader of the Old Guard was Boise Penrose of Pennsylvania, a political boss of an unsavory type who had absolute faith in the power and virtue of money. In debate he had the offensive manner of a bully. He was ruthless, unscrupulous, arrogant and lacking in finesse. His utter contempt for the rights of the masses was so transparent in his speeches that they did his cause more harm than good. The occasional combats between the enormous, domineering Penrose and the slight, almost frail John Sharp Williams were among the most enjoyable spectacles the Senate offered. It was a battle between an awkward mastiff and a small thoroughbred. There was no bad blood between these men. Penrose appreciated the brilliant qualities of his opponent, and if Williams abhorred the principles of the Pennsylvanian, he respected the brutal frankness with which they were avowed. But in a contest of wit Penrose was at a disadvantage. His blows were crude, like those of a bludgeon, and Williams came back with brilliantly poised rapier thrusts; the awkwardly swung bludgeon did not often make contact, while the rapier cut the big man to pieces.

Almost as reactionary as Penrose, though on an infinitely higher plane, was Elihu Root, who had rendered distinguished service in the Cabinet but whose Senatorial career did not add an inch to his stature in history. He wandered in and out of the chamber, contributing little, if anything, to constructive statesmanship, and he seldom spoke. His few speeches were those of a lawyer addressing a court, without the slightest pretense to eloquence, but closely reasoned and highly sophisticated. While he was speaking his features did not relax their customary lines of severity and his brow was corrugated with thought. He was precise in his diction, and I was fascinated with his occasional hesitations when he was clearly searching his vocabulary for the exact word. His voice was not pleasant, but his reputation assured him a most respectful attention.

Whatever may have been Root's manner in the cloakroom, his manner on the floor implied unbearable boredom and distaste for his colleagues—for most of them. He sat near Henry Cabot Lodge, and by their manner the two gave the impression of holding themselves aloof from their inferiors. They symbolized the old aristocracy of the defunct Federalist Party which, for all its brilliance, never spoke the language of the common man.

Root offered little, but he protested vigorously against all progressive legislation. In his farewell speech, which I heard, he seemed pessimistic because the income tax imposed a hardship on the great corporations; because railroad legislation for the protection of the shippers imposed a hardship on the railroads; because the Federal Reserve System would undermine the financial foundations of the American system. He had a great legal mind, but he clearly belonged to an age that was passing, and I have no doubt he retired to private life with satisfaction.

These were halcyon days for the Democrats in the process of rejuvenating their party, while the Republicans were pessimistic and depressed. The Democrats could contemplate any verbal battle without uneasiness, and investigating committees were prying into questionable proceedings and finding political gold. I would have but a faint recollection of the investigation into the Lawrence, Massachusetts, textile strike but for the memory of one man who fascinated me. The lawyer representing the strikers was unimpressive in size but had a most arresting face, very serious and with brows lined with concentration. Because of the deeply seamed brow he bore some resemblance to the portraits of Rufus Choate, another superb lawyer of Boston. He was modest in his manner, but this rather little man dominated the scene. He was Louis Brandeis, soon thereafter to begin a brilliant career as Associate Justice of the Supreme Court. The delay of the Senate in confirming Wilson's appointment of Brandeis was ascribed to religious prejudice, but the real reason was his liberal point of view. Years later I found him to have a rich sense of humor and a love for a laugh.

Out of the hearings on the money trust one scene alone is graphically recalled. J. Pierpont Morgan the elder was on the stand. He was an old man and he seemed strangely shy and nervous. I had observed him with astonishment because of his enormous nose with its reddish glow and its hills and valleys. The lawyer for the committee was the famous Louis Untermyer, tall, slender, elegant, with an almost sinister suavity in his manner of questioning. Just as Morgan took the stand, I had noticed an old man with white hair enter and find a seat close by and directly facing Morgan. It was Joseph H. Choate, leader of the American bar, former ambassador to England and long the legal adviser of the banker. He looked like a saintly bishop grown old in grace. I wondered if he was there to guide his client with sign language. I watched him closely throughout, but I did not see the movement of an eyebrow or a finger.

Many years later, I sat with Untermyer in his stateroom on an

75

Atlantic liner and recalled the incident to him. He gave me his version of that day. "It was clear that Morgan was frightened," he said, "and I questioned him in the most kindly manner possible, but when he could not recall the name of his most famous partner I knew there was something wrong, and I suggested a recess. I called in Morgan's lawyers, a small army of them, and told them that they might reassure him, since I knew he had not been the active director of the company for some time; that the only reason I had summoned him was that were he not called the public would get a wrong impression. They admitted that he was nervous and not well, and they seemed very grateful. It was a mistake. When Morgan died in Italy soon afterward, I was roundly abused for having driven him to his death by my brutal examination."

When I saw this brilliant man for the last time, his condition was similar to that of Morgan. I was home on leave from Spain and at his request I had driven to his castlelike house on the Hudson to see him. I found him in a lofty room, stretched out on a sofa talking with his granddaughter, who rose and left. Having been summoned, I was a bit puzzled by his nonchalant, almost unfriendly reception. At length when I mentioned Spain he amazed me by asking if I had ever been there. I told him I had been there some time as ambassador. "No, no," he said sharply. "I know the ambassador to Spain well. Claude Bowers is the ambassador to Spain." When I told him I was Claude Bowers he was embarrassed and found excuses for his failure to recognize me. Two or three months later he was dead.

The Senatorial investigation that impressed me most was that into conditions in the West Virginia coal fields, where the miners lived under feudalistic conditions, miserably underpaid in non-union mines, brutally treated, shamelessly exploited, and denied the right to collective bargaining. The Paint Creek settlement had been invaded by gunmen and gangsters thoroughly equipped as a private army, under the hired leadership of the notorious Ernest Gaujot. These men swaggered with drunken irresponsibility into the cabins of the miners, often committing crimes.

Just before the Republicans lost the Senate the United Mine Workers had asked Senator Borah to present a resolution calling for an investigation, and he had passed it on to Senator Kern when the Democrats took over. Kern presented it perfunctorily, having no idea of its importance, but he was startled by the flood of telegrams from men high in industrial and financial circles, urging him not to press the resolution. One day a personal friend high in the organization of a great banking firm in New York called him long distance to appeal to him "as a friend." I noticed Kern's indignant expression as he rang off with the words, "I'll see you in hell first." Clearly the resolution had some importance. At this time I called Kern's attention to a small newspaper item about Mother Jones, beloved of the miners, who had been arrested in the region and was awaiting trial by a court-martial, though the civil courts were open. I suggested that it was incredible that an old woman of her celebrity was to be tried without attracting more notice in the press.

"Yes," Kern said, "there's something here that stinks."

That day he called up the resolution, with pointed observations on the arrest of Mother Jones. Governor Haywood of West Virginia thereupon issued a statement to the effect that the old woman was "detained but in no sense confined," and that she was enjoying life "in a pleasant boardinghouse" with a private family.

The next day a copy of the Cincinnati *Post* was secretly tossed through an open window of the miserable miner's hut where the old woman was "detained." Thus she learned of the battle in the Senate. The friendly miner who was forced to be her jailer communicated with her from the cellar, by means of notes in a tin can attached to a string from a hole in the floor of the prisoner's room. She wrote a telegram to Kern with instructions for the miner to file it some miles away, since if filed in town it would be suppressed. Kern read it to the Senate:

"From out of the military prison walls where I have been forced to pass my eighty-first milestone of life, I plead with you for the honor of the nation. I send you groans and tears of men, women and children as I have heard them in this state, and I beg you to force an investigation. Children yet unborn will rise and bless you."

This telegram finally attracted attention to events behind the iron curtain of the mining region. The Governor hastily ordered Mother Jones's release, but she refused his condition that she should not leave the state, and a few days later she appeared in Washington.

I knew something of this woman's tumultuous life: she had lived

77

for months in the desolate mountain and mining region of West Virginia organizing the half-starved miners, living in their wretched cabins and on their meager fare. I knew that in the great anthracite strike she had marched at the head of the miners to meet the soldiers; that she had been swept emotionally into her militant career by the Pullman strike; that despite her age she had gone into the mining region of Colorado and harangued miners on mountainsides in zero weather, had been driven hither and yon by private armies and had been pricked by bayonets into an icy stream and compelled to hold her skirts up to her waist as she waded.

The day she walked into Kern's office I could scarcely believe that she could be the firebrand of whom I had heard, so grandmotherly did she look. Her eyes, however, were keen, penetrating and sparkling, and her voice was rough and heavy from speaking outdoors in winter weather. For some days this woman of more than eighty tramped the marble corridors of the Senate Office Building, personally giving Senators the benefit of her knowledge of conditions. Occasionally she came to my office for a brief rest.

She astonished me by the moderation, the fairness, even the toleration, of her estimate of men. Learning that she had seen Senator Penrose, I asked her opinion of him, expecting an explosion. He was not really as bad as he thought himself, she said, speaking as one would of an erring child. "One must always allow for a man's background, his environment, his contacts and his sources of information. I have no doubt he honestly believes in the ideas he represents. He has never known the seamy and tragic side of life. So with many of the reactionaries. I do not hate them—I understand and I pity them."

Footsore but undaunted, she made the rounds of all the Senators, and the resolution was adopted after a bitter debate. This, I think, was the first clear-cut victory ever won in the Senate by labor.

Five years later she called on me in Fort Wayne. Though she was now more than eighty-six, the intervening years had not visibly weakened her physically and her spirit flamed as always. At lunch she seemed to find something missing. I asked if she would like something to drink, and her face brightened. "May I have a stein of beer?" she asked, adding, "I find that when I'm very tired beer is a restorative." She went on to speak of her bad reputation. No, she was not a drunkard. She had never been drunk in her life.

Beer when she was tired, a bit of whiskey when she had spoken in the sleet on a frozen mountainside. And profane? Yes, at times she was profane, but always in public, and when necessary to lift the miners from their apathy. "One must adjust one's language to one's audience," she said. "Men working on starvation wages, living in miserable huts, facing death daily in poorly equipped mines, are apt to be profane, and when necessary I speak their language." When I asked her why she did not write her autobiography the superstition of the Irish peasant came out. No, no, she wouldn't think of such a thing. Didn't I know that people died soon after writing their autobiographies? "I'm only eighty-six and I'm not ready to die."

The part that Senator Kern had played in William Jennings Bryan's strategy at the 1912 Baltimore convention—which ultimately resulted in the nomination of Woodrow Wilson—makes an interesting footnote to history.

The National Committee had designated Alton B. Parker as the temporary chairman and keynote speaker, and Bryan was convinced that this foreshadowed a reactionary platform and nominee. He immediately announced his opposition and his intention to nominate one of three men instead, and one of these was Kern. Though he was devoted to Bryan, nothing could have been more embarrassing to Kern, for he was personally fond of Parker and had toured Europe with him the year before. It would also put him in conflict with the greater part of the Indiana delegation.

The night before the convention opened I sat with him in the hotel while friends made separate visits to Bryan in an effort to dissuade him from nominating Kern as temporary chairman. Each returned to report a stern and chilly reception and no success. At length Kern went himself.

"You agree, John, that the designation of Parker indicates a reactionary setup in the convention?" Bryan asked. And Kern agreed.

"And that the convention has been packed to some extent with delegates eager to meet the demands of the bosses?" Kern agreed.

"And that the rank and file of the party throughout the country is not in sympathy with these plans?" Again Kern agreed.

"Then," continued Bryan, "the rank and file must be put on notice of what is planned, and it must be done the moment the gavel falls, and the issue must be made on a comparatively unimportant matter to give time for the reaction of the rank and file to reach the convention before irreparable harm is done."

Agreeing to this, Kern urged that Bryan's own name be submitted as the substitute for Parker.

"No," said Bryan. "I must make the speech and make the issue. I cannot nominate myself. I must speak, and I shall be insulted and booed, and that will be news with color that will attract national attention, and the rank and file will reach the inevitable conclusion. No, John, I shall put you in nomination, and you'll have to do what you think proper."

When Kern left Bryan that night he was much depressed, and ill as well. He did not sleep, and sitting on the edge of his bed, he made his plans, which he kept to himself.

The next day Bryan made his speech and was booed as he had hoped. He closed by nominating Kern.

Kern took the platform. As he passed Bryan he did not even glance at him. He began with a plea for harmony and party solidarity. Then, referring to Parker in terms of respect and affection, he said that he and Parker could sit down at a table and in ten minutes agree upon a chairman satisfactory to all. He appealed to Parker, sitting with the New York delegation, to agree. Parker said nothing. Then Kern appealed to Murphy, the Tammany chief, "who holds the New York delegation in the hollow of his hand," to permit Parker to respond. Murphy, grimly chewing gum, did not bat an eyelash.

After a moment of dramatic silence, Kern continued, "If there is to be no response, if this is to be a contest between the people and the powers, the cause to which I subscribe is so great a cause that I am not fit to be its leader. If my proposition for harmony is to be ignored, and this deplorable battle is to go on, there is only one man fit to lead the hosts of progress, and that is the man who has been in the forefront for sixteen years, the great American tribune, William Jennings Bryan. If you will have nothing else, if that must be the issue, then the leader must be worthy of the cause, and that leader must be William Jennings Bryan."

Sick and ashen-hued, Kern was led from the platform, and again he passed Bryan without a glance. The latter, according to his admission to me in a letter, had had no intimation of what Kern would do. It was not a prearranged plan, but had it been it could not have been more effective. That night when Kern entered Bryan's room the Commoner rushed to him beaming and, throwing his arms about him, said, "How did you ever think of it? That was the smartest thing you ever did."

Of course Bryan was defeated, but the rank and file had been given dramatic notice and delegates were deluged with indignant telegrams from home. As a result, Ollie James was made permanent chairman and Kern chairman of the platform committee. The victory of the progressives was complete and Bryan had achieved it with the aid of Kern. Other things were to happen later to determine the Presidential nomination, but the speeches of Bryan and the act of Kern in the beginning, with the response of the rank and file, had put the fear of the Lord into the delegates, and the plan for a reactionary platform and a reactionary candidate was made impossible.

It was at the Baltimore convention that I first saw Cardinal Gibbons: a slight, frail creature, looking almost ethereal as he walked down the center aisle to open the convention with prayer; and soon thereafter I met him personally under unusual circumstances.

My fascination with the genius of John Philpot Curran and the other great Irish orators had led me to make many speeches on them and had culminated in my writing my first book. Senator O'Gorman was interested and suggested that it might be advantageous to submit the manuscript to Cardinal Gibbons. Seeing no reason why I should bother the seventy-nine-year-old prelate, I tried to avoid the meeting, but when O'Gorman saw Monsignor Russell of the Washington Cathedral and arranged the meeting, there was no escape. I went to Baltimore with fear and trembling, much concerned over what a meeting with a cardinal entailed. Thus early I began to stumble over protocol.

At the Cardinal's house the door was opened by a small boy, who ushered me into the reception room and said he would inform the Cardinal. As I sat down to wait, my back to the door into the hall, I heard the boy running up the stairs. I was struggling with the problem of how to begin the conversation when I heard rapid steps coming down again, and, with a frown of annoyance on my face, I turned to see what the boy had to say. To my horror, I saw Cardinal Gibbons already before me. He saw at a glance that he had caught me unaware, and, noting my confusion, he began fluttering about arranging chairs to give me time to recover. This almost feminine tact endeared him to me from the start. Then he sat down facing me and, in familiar fashion, began to talk about his boyhood in Ireland. I was impressed by the expression of his keen Irish eyes. Seen in the convention, he had seemed a saint; now, with his pleasant voice, his manner sweet and charming, he seemed no less so, but those eyes denoted also a wise man, a dominant leader and a statesman. While he appeared a man who loved his fellow men and knew tenderness, it was quite as clear that in any battle for his faith he could be a warrior.

At length he said, "When do you want this introduction?" It had not occurred to me as possible that he would write an introduction to my book, but, hiding my astonishment, I set a date.

"Very well," he said. "Send me the manuscript and you shall have it."

Thus it came to pass that Cardinal Gibbons wrote the introduction to my first book, *The Irish Orators*. I left him with the feeling that all the labor of research and writing had been richly rewarded by the privilege of meeting this truly great man, whose memory will always be cherished in America regardless of differences in creed.

And now a footnote to Irish history—on the Easter Rebellion in Dublin during the First World War, and its repercussions here.

When the Englishman Sir Roger Casement was arrested in Ireland by the British for complicity in the Irish Easter Week rising in 1916, it was a foregone conclusion that his trial, which followed immediately, would result in his condemnation for treason. American sympathy for him was high—this was before we entered the war—and Senator Martine of New Jersey, whose heart was as big as his judgment was bad, offered a resolution in the Senate asking clemency, but couched in scarcely diplomatic language. It was sent to the Foreign Relations Committee for revision. In view of the certainty that there would be other arrests, the resolution was reframed to ask clemency for "political prisoners" without a direct reference to Casement. It passed the Senate late on Saturday evening, I think. As I recall, the execution was set for Tuesday, in London. On Wednesday the press reported that the resolution had been delivered that day—a day after the execution. This seeming delay, which appeared on the surface to have been calculated, created consternation among the Administration Senators and indignation among the Irish. Senator Kern instructed me to ascertain just what had caused the delay.

I found that the resolution had been sent to the White House on Saturday night. Then I went to the State Department to see Frank Polk, Under Secretary of State. When he heard the object of my visit, he closed and locked the door and said, "This is dynamite. When the resolution passed the Senate I knew its engrossment would make it reach us late, and I also knew the importance of having it reach London promptly. So on Sunday morning I put the code room to work, and on Sunday afternoon it was sent. That very night it was delivered in London to the proper officials. So you see we took extraordinary precautions to see that it was delivered in ample time before the day set for the execution. On Monday morning Sir Cecil Spring-Rice, the British ambassador, came in with London's answer, to the effect that Casement was not considered a political prisoner. Of course this was a quibble, but if we were to announce to the press that the resolution had been delivered in time and that that answer had been given, the Irish would say that the Martine resolution had been changed to make it easy to deny the plea for clemency. So we're damned either way, and the best policy is to say nothing."

Sir Cecil had left with Polk photostatic copies of alleged extracts from Casement's diary indicating that the prisoner was a homosexual. He had been condemned for treason and the only purpose in distributing these photostatic copies of alleged extracts from the diary was to create prejudice against the prisoner, on behalf of whom such distinguished Englishmen as William Archer, Arnold Bennett, Gilbert K. Chesterton, John Galsworthy and Israel Zangwill had pleaded for clemency. Casement has been dead for forty years, but the authenticity of the diary extracts is still being bitterly challenged. An Irish poet put his protest in verse:

Afraid they might be beaten
Before the bench of time,

They turned a trick by forgery
And blackened his good name.

At the time of the trial, however, a young Irish sculptor, knowing of my interest in the Irish question, had warned me that word
had gone down the line to be cautious about Casement; and soon
I was to learn from one of the leaders of the Irish movement in
the United States that they had been distrustful of Casement for a
very definite reason.

My book on the Irish orators had brought me into contact with
John Devoy, editor of the *Gaelic American,* a great Fenian and the
head of the Irish militants here. During my conversation with Polk
he said that our government knew Devoy had been involved in the
Easter Week rising, but that, while he would be permitted to fret
awhile—knowing that his involvement was known—nothing could
be done to him. Some time after this I was invited to a dinner in
New York at the home of the daughter of O'Donovan Rossa, the
Irish patriot whose funeral in Dublin a little while before had been
the occasion of a great demonstration there. At this dinner I found
John Devoy. After dinner we were placed in a room alone, and we
had a talk that I shall always remember for its drama.

Devoy, then a very old man, was still of herculean frame, broad
of shoulders, with a thick chest partly concealed by a beard. His
entire life had been given to the fight for Irish independence. That
night he told me a story I believe has never been printed before.

"Roger Casement came to New York after the war began," he
said, "and asked to be sent to Berlin as an agent of the Irish here.
We knew him as a poet, a highly cultivated man and a great British
consul. Soon we had reason to doubt his judgment. At length we
got him off our hands by sending him to Germany, hoping to forget him. But the man was unbalanced. One day I was shocked to
receive a letter half an inch thick, written in huge script on page
after page, setting forth the most fantastic ideas imaginable. Of
course it had been read by the British agents. I wrote him pointing
out the absurdity of his action, but, undiscouraged, he continued
to send me letter after letter in the open mail.

"Meanwhile, one day a young Irish girl, just arrived by steerage,
came to see me with a letter from Padhraic Pearse, Plunkett and the
other brilliant young leaders of the rising of Easter Week. It said

that, while unprepared for action, they had learned that the government was about to disarm the Irish Volunteers, and since this was intolerable they had decided on Easter Week as the time for the rising. They asked me to send money and arms. This amazed me. These men had brilliant minds. I could send money, but how could men of their intelligence conceive it possible for me to send them arms? Then, not wanting them to go up against the guns unarmed, I worried about it, until it occurred to me as possible that Germany could get some arms to them. I took it up with the German embassy in New York. They agreed at length to furnish some arms and ammunition, and I informed Pearse.

"Then another Irish girl came with a letter asking that the delivery be made at a specified spot, and between three consecutive dates. I could understand the significance of the place of delivery, but the dates meant nothing special to me. I sent this note to the embassy.

"A few days later another girl came with another letter instructing that under no circumstances should the delivery be made before the last of the three days given. But by this time the boat with the arms was at sea, and it had no wireless facilities. Nothing could be done.

"It was at this point that Casement came into the picture. He was in a hospital in Germany and he had heard that the Germans were sending arms to Ireland. Assuming that the young men in Ireland thought that he had made adequate arrangements, and greatly concerned, he begged that he be sent to Ireland in a submarine to head off a premature rising. Some distance from shore he was put in a collapsible boat, which actually collapsed, and Casement, who was not strong, walked in water to his shoulders. Found by one of the Irish patriots, he was put in an old ruined house, and the Irishman went off in search of a conveyance to take him to Dublin. Casement's groans attracted the attention of an officer who happened to be passing, and he was arrested. He asked to see a priest, to whom he explained his mission, and the priest agreed to get a letter to the revolutionary leaders in the capital. When it arrived it caused confusion. Because of it the rising was called off everywhere but in Dublin, where the leaders thought the arrangements had gone too far to be canceled. That was why the rising was confined to Dublin. Casement had committed a grave blunder and would suffer in reputation but for the fact that, blunder though he did, he gave his life to the cause."

This story, all the more dramatic because simply told, by a very old man who had seen another dream shattered, was of the very essence of drama. Devoy's involvement, as indicated by Polk, had become known through a raid on the German embassy in New York, where letters were found bearing the notation "Submitted by John Devoy." This, of course, was before we entered the war, and treason was not involved.

Another footnote to history, concerning Bryan's resignation as Wilson's Secretary of State:

Washington was a diplomatic battleground to determine the position of the United States in the First World War. The city was swarming with secret agents and propagandists of Germany and Britain. The prevailing sentiment in Congress was one of sympathy with the Allies but of opposition to our participation in the war. The climax came dramatically in the opposing views of Wilson and Bryan, resulting in the latter's resignation from the Cabinet.

The record of Bryan's state of mind on the eve of his resignation has never, so far as I know, been fully put in print. Some years after the events, William Gibbs McAdoo, then Secretary of the Treasury, told me a story which throws a strong light on the character of Bryan. One day when McAdoo was entertaining guests at luncheon, Bryan stopped in on his way home. He was pale and clearly distressed and nervous. He had confidence in the friendship of McAdoo, none whatever in that of most of his other colleagues in the Cabinet. He had stopped to tell McAdoo that he could no longer continue in his post, holding the views he did, and that he intended to resign. McAdoo begged him to do nothing until they could talk it over, and he made an engagement at Bryan's home after lunch.

There he found the Commoner in mental anguish. McAdoo pleaded with him to reconsider his decision, assuring him of Wilson's affection and warning him that his resignation would be misunderstood and resented by the public. But Bryan was adamant. He respected the position of Wilson, but he could not share it with a clear conscience, since he thought it would lead to war.

McAdoo then asked if he could talk with Mrs. Bryan alone. The

Commoner retired to another room, and McAdoo begged Mrs. Bryan to exert her influence to dissuade her husband. "I'm afraid it will destroy him politically," he said.

Mrs. Bryan replied that she thought it probable, and that Bryan had a full realization of the probable political repercussions. "But you know William," she said.

When Bryan re-entered the room, McAdoo made a final appeal and then said, "You're distressed, nervous and depressed. I want you to promise to take the weekend to think it over and get some rest. Spend the weekend with Blair Lee at Silver Springs, and give the matter your prayerful consideration."

Bryan agreed. He went to Silver Springs and spent most of the time walking alone, but he returned convinced that he owed it to his conscience to stand firmly on his decision.

This is an incident in history necessary to an understanding of the character of a very great human being. Bryan's resignation had the political repercussions he had expected. This is not remarkable in view of the passions of the time, but it is remarkable that we have waited for a quarter of a century for a just and intelligent interpretation of Bryan by the historians.

The nation was now marching with long strides toward war. My first definite indication that Wilson was preparing for war came with the return of Senator Kern from the White House, whither he had been summoned along with Senator William J. Stone, chairman of the Senate Foreign Relations Committee, and Representative Henry Flood, who held the corresponding position in the House. Kern returned pale, tired and worried. "It's terrible," he said.

Feeling was now running high and tempers were on edge. One day I heard Senator Stone, who opposed war, speaking with such indiscreet bitterness that the Senate lost its dignity. Insults and threats were hurled about, and for a moment it seemed that Stone might be physically attacked on the floor. When his fellow Senator from Missouri, James A. Reed, rose to speak in a conciliatory tone to calm the storm, it was clear that sentiment against Germany was at high tide, since Reed usually counterattacked and seldom appeased.

John W. Kern's term in the Senate ended in 1917, following his defeat for re-election. The debt the Wilson Administration owed Kern has never been properly acknowledged, and probably never will be now. He was the Administration's floor leader in the Senate during the four years of its greatest constructive achievement. Among the Democrats in the Senate were several so intensely individualistic or ultraconservative that almost invariably some were off the reservation at some stage of the legislative proceedings, and it was Kern's delicate function to conciliate them and compromise their differences. His personal popularity with his fellow Senators contributed mightily to the passage of several highly controversial measures. This, I am sure, would be acknowledged by his colleagues. So pressing, continuous and arduous were his duties, so constantly, day and night, was he engaged in conferences and caucuses, that during these four fruitful years for the Administration he often did not appear at the office for days at a time, and the responsibility of making day-to-day decisions fell to me.

During the enervating days of Washington summers Kern was tied to his post, constantly on guard, with a notebook in his hand telling him where the absentee Administration Senators could be found in case of an unheralded roll call or some other emergency. Not a few of these gentlemen were ornamental Senators who deserted the stuffy chamber for the ball park and for the horse races in Maryland, while Kern, then on the shady side of his sixties, had no diversion or relaxation; but the vital importance of his work was not appreciated by the press.

A desired measure would be pending which could pass or fail by a narrow margin, with some Democrats holding out against it, and with Kern pleading and arguing day and night, until, out of deference to him in numerous instances, the rebellious ones would succumb to his pleading. ("Oh, well," I once heard Senator Reed of Missouri say, "if you feel so strongly about it I'll vote for the damn bill.") When at length enough votes had been pledged to assure the bill's passage, often through Kern's tact, diplomacy, popularity and patience, and the day was set for the full-dress debate before the roll call—then, when the galleries were packed and the drama was at its height, the absentee Senators flocked in from the race track and the ball field to deliver showy speeches that tickled the visitors and impressed the news correspondents. Kern never spoke on these occasions, and he knew them to be dangerous, for

88

the orators might say something to create resentment and upset the apple cart. The spectacular debate determined nothing in such a case; through Kern's diplomacy the issue had already been settled in the conferences while the Senators now in the limelight were enjoying their freedom.

The bill would pass, the people in the galleries would assume the victory to be due to the orators, and the press, finding copy and color in the discourses of these speakers fresh from the race track, would feature them. Because Kern was not an exhibitionist, but, on the contrary, was averse to self-advertising, was even secretive, he got no credit from the public. I doubt that Woodrow Wilson had a proper appreciation of his deep indebtedness to the self-sacrificing statesman and clever politician who had not figured in the drama of the full-fledged debate. But I have no doubt that Kern literally killed himself during these four years, for he died a few months after he left the Senate.

Kern's defeat for re-election in 1916 meant I was to leave Washington, and it was high time. Two years would have been valuable, but the status then of a private secretary of a Senator, even though the latter was his party's floor leader, was not impressive and certainly not profitable in any sense. It was largely because of the feeling that I was wasting time that I decided to write *The Irish Orators*. I wrote it at night in our office. When I left Washington I felt I had nothing to show for this period but this book. I was a bit worried over my audacity in writing the book at all, and I was not certain it would not be frowned upon by Senator Kern, who knew nothing about the writing or even the publication until Champ Clark, Speaker of the House, told him about it. I learned this from a letter to me from the Speaker. It surprised and delighted me, and I still cherish the letter, the first I ever received about a book of mine. He wrote:

Two or three days ago I went down to the dining room for breakfast, sleepy headed and sleepy eyed. I had sat up all night reading your book on the Irish Orators. I told Senator Kern to tell you that in my judgment it is one of the most interesting books that has been written in this country in a quarter of a century. As evidence of my belief I state that I sat up nearly two whole nights reading it. Your book will have an honored place in my library.

A few days later he had me as his guest of honor at a Speaker's luncheon, where he repeated to the guests what he had written to me.

A day or two after that, when I was on the floor of the Senate, Vice-President Marshall sent me a note from the rostrum:

Not until a few days ago did I have the opportunity to begin reading your book and let me say at the outset that I did not stop reading until I had finished it. You have certainly demonstrated that to teach history in connection with the actions and utterances of great men is more attractive and also more instructive than in the usual way. I have learned more of Irish history of the last two hundred years by the perusal of your book than I had from all the literature on the subject that I had read before.

These encouraging letters more than anything else turned my ambition toward the writing of history.

Before the expiration of Kern's term I was offered the editorship of the Fort Wayne *Journal-Gazette*, at that time the foremost Democratic paper in Indiana, and so, without regret, I left Washington and turned back to my native state.

CHAPTER VII

War, Politics and the League
of Nations

FORT WAYNE was then a thriving industrial city with no little
charm. We found an old brick house on West Berry Street, around
which cluster all the memories of this Hoosier interlude. I retain
a sentimental attachment to this house with its French windows
looking out upon the lawn and the tree-lined street. I had scarcely
any social life, my entire time being divided between the office and
my home. My position on the *Journal-Gazette* was that of editorial
writer, but since I selected my own subjects and treated them in
my own way without consultation, it was more nearly that of an
editor in chief. The complete independence accorded me made the
work interesting and agreeable. On the first Sunday after my arrival I voluntarily wrote two columns of reminiscences and observations on the Washington scene and its actors, under the caption "Cabbages and Kings," and the popularity of the experiment
was such that I was unable to discontinue the feature during my
six years with the paper. This, together with the editorials on
Sundays, took up the entire page of seven columns. I suspect that
this feature on the personalities and activities of the actors in Washington from 1911 to the end of 1917 is more complete than any
that will appear hereafter, but it did not occur to me to publish the
collection in book form.

Our war with Germany began a few days after I assumed my
duties. Thereafter almost all my editorial leaders dealt with phases
of the war and, later, with the League of Nations, which we vigorously supported against the unscrupulous propaganda and mis-
representations of its partisan enemies.

To my surprise, I was plunged into politics almost immediately on my return to Indiana. In the state convention of 1918 I was chairman of the platform committee, which would not be worth mentioning had not President Wilson played a part. It was one of the earliest of the state conventions of that year, and Colonel Hollister of the Democratic National Committee placed in my hands certain resolutions dealing mostly with postwar policies which Wilson wished incorporated in the platform as a model for other conventions that would follow. Particular pains were to be taken, he explained, that no intimation should be given as to the source of these resolutions, and this would be difficult. I took into my confidence only one member of the committee, who was to move the unanimous adoption of each of these resolutions without discussion when they were read. Once when the committee showed a disposition to question the resolution, I was forced to say that it came from a "very high source" and that I hoped it would not be questioned. Clearly the members understood, and all the resolutions brought from Washington were included.

This was the year of the deadly flu epidemic, when people were dying like flies in autumn, and the beginning of the speaking campaign was postponed from week to week. When it did open the week before the election, it was grotesque. I spoke but once, in Angola, and the scene was both amusing and ghastly. I faced an audience that wore masks, presenting a most ludicrous appearance. That year Wilson lost the House through what some thought a blunder in urging the election of a Democratic Congress. Had he asked for the election of a Congress that would support the Administration on all war issues, the critics would have us believe, the result would have been different. The appeal for the election of Democrats certainly drew the party line, but it had been drawn before. His enemies were infuriated by Wilson's international prestige, and we were moving toward that bitter hysteria of blind partisanship that was to put the United States in opposition to the League of Nations. I doubt that the result of the election would have been different had Wilson not made his partisan appeal.

In the state convention that year the leaders offered me the nomination for secretary of state, which was the head of the ticket, but that position made no appeal to me, and I declined.

Unexpectedly, I had a more important role in the state convention of 1920. Vice-President Marshall was designated temporary chairman to make the keynote speech, and Governor Ralston was to be the permanent chairman and to discuss state issues. When the manuscript of Marshall's speech was read by the party leaders, they were disappointed by the rather bromidic praise of the Wilson Administration and the League of Nations. The Vice-President was a conservative, and also it was common knowledge that Marshall felt he had not been accorded proper recognition by the President. I am sure there was some justification for his resentment. While we were engaged in a great war he had not been invited to sit in the meetings of the Cabinet, and he felt he did not enjoy the intimacy with the President to which his position entitled him. Even so, it had been assumed that his keynote speech would warmly praise the President and the League of Nations Covenant.

From a conference of the party leaders in Indianapolis, Governor Ralston telephoned me to ask that I make the speech that fell to him as permanent chairman, and that instead of confining my speech to state issues, as was customary, I devote the greater part to national issues, the Wilson Administration and the League. Ralston would take over as permanent chairman at the conclusion of my speech. It was not a pleasant task that was assigned me. I had a real and abiding affection for Tom Marshall, who had left the Senate to sit beside me at my mother's funeral, and who had always been a friend. I was not at all sure he had been treated with proper consideration. But my feeling for Wilson and the League was paramount.

I had known Marshall well for twelve years. He had a likable personality and was rich in whimsy and wit. His familiar conversation, which sparkled and glowed, was always clever. He had something of the eternal boy in him which reminded me of Barrie's Sentimental Tommy and Peter Pan. Grass-roots common sense illuminated by wit and humor—that was Marshall. He was popular on the platform as a humorist before he was thought of as a statesman, but he uttered many serious thoughts in jest. His tone was conversational and familiar. He talked and did not rant, and though he was less eloquent than instructive and amusing, there was in his speeches much homey sentiment to reach the heart. During his eight years in Washington he and his charming wife won the hearts of Washington society by their simplicity, their freedom from pose and their interest in people. His drollery and wit made him an ideal table companion, and he was constantly quoted in the capital.

Unquestionably, the state convention heard Marshall's speech with uneasiness and disappointment. My speech, with its ardent praise of the Administration and the League, followed his and was warmly applauded—and by none more warmly than by Marshall. When I sat down beside him at the close he leaned over, placed his hand on my knee and said, "Claude, I've tried to help the President, but he wouldn't let me." To my embarrassment, I realized that he knew my speech was intended to put in what he had left out, but if he felt any resentment he never showed it, and our friendship continued until his death.

In that year's campaign I spoke with him in Fort Wayne, and two years later we were on the same platform in Richmond. While he spoke with his usual cleverness, his speeches lacked the fervor and conviction which had come to be expected of him. Had Wilson retired when incapacitated by illness, Marshall would have become President; I believe Wilson's failure to step down rankled in the breast of the Vice-President.

The 1920 national convention in San Francisco lacked the courage to make the League of Nations the issue, though this was done by Governor James M. Cox, the Presidential nominee, during a call on Wilson by Cox and Franklin D. Roosevelt, his running mate, as related in another chapter. Foes of Prohibition would have preferred to make Prohibition the issue. Years later in an editorial in the New York *Evening World* I was to say that Wilson actually sent a wet plank to San Francisco for incorporation in the platform. This assertion was based on a statement in Joe Tumulty's book on Wilson after Wilson's death. The editorial aroused the curiosity of Senator Carter Glass, who wrote me a sharp denial, setting forth the facts as he knew them. In his letter he said that "one man" did strongly urge on Wilson the sending of such a plank. Wilson, he added, certainly was opposed to Prohibition and had vetoed the Volstead Act, but it seemed improbable that he would have subordinated the League to Prohibition. Saying that he was withholding an article for the *Atlantic Monthly* pending a reply to his inquiry, Senator Glass went on:

I was well aware in 1920 that a certain person was urging Mr. Wilson to send such a declaration to the San Francisco Convention, but it is incredible to me that any such thing was done, and I am writing to ask you to give me your authority for the statement that it was done.

At the very earnest personal request of Mr. Wilson I was made chairman of the Committee of Resolutions of the San Francisco Convention. I went from the White House to the train for San Francisco after an hour's discussion of the proposed party platform, the great part of which I had already drafted.

I have reason to assume that Mr. Wilson would have given me any such draft of a proposed provision had he decided to ask its incorporation in the platform. So far from doing this, he distinctly agreed with me that such a thing would be extremely unwise.

As chairman of both the sub-committee and the full Committee on Platform I know perfectly well that nobody assuming to speak for Mr. Wilson presented any such proposition. Hence I am interested to have you tell me, before the publication of the article I have prepared, why and how you reached the conclusion so positively stated in your editorial.

I had no recollection of the editorial, but an investigation disclosed the source of the claim. It is worth noting that the date of Senator Glass's interest and his letter was September 4, 1928, when his party had made Prohibition an issue in the campaign. But in 1920 the ground swell against Prohibition had not developed, though opposition was developing. I had given him my reason for not injecting such a controversial subject in my keynote speech in 1928, and he agreed with my reasoning. He added, "Smith, if elected, as I frankly told him in Albany, could do no more about altering the Eighteenth Amendment than my barn cat."

It was during my Fort Wayne days that my intimate friendship with Senator Beveridge began. During my boyhood I had seen him occasionally in his home, but for almost twenty years I had seen him only on the platform or in the street. He went to Fort Wayne to speak at a memorial meeting for Theodore Roosevelt, and after the meeting he invited me to his room at the Anthony Hotel, where he talked for two hours. He was in high good humor, for he had just finished his brilliant biography of John Marshall. That night it was evident to me that he was eager to return to the Senate. This would mean a primary fight for the nomination against the Republican incumbent, but he had no doubt of victory in the primary. He was not so sure about the election. He knew that his old enemies would be gunning for him, but he was tempted to try.

A little later he telegraphed me that he was speaking on Marshall in Plymouth the next night and would like to see me there. I went, and, sitting on the edge of the bed in his room in the hotel, he told me he had reached a decision—he would fight for the Republican nomination and gamble on the election. Despite our radical differences in politics, this confidential relationship was to continue until his death.

During the primary fight he spoke in Fort Wayne and I found him in the midst of his milling supporters in the lobby of the Anthony. He drew me into the elevator, took me to his room and denied himself to visitors. He was in a hilarious mood. In our conversation, mention was made of the deadly feud between Wilson and Senator Lodge, and I suggested that the latter's hatred of Wilson stemmed from the parallel careers of the two men. Both had been professors; Lodge, as the editor of a magazine, had Wilson as a contributor, and the editor had a supercilious attitude toward the contributor; both were historians; and Wilson had passed Lodge in the race and had become President and a world figure directing a world war. I suggested that the hatred of Lodge smacked of academic jealousy. Beveridge was washing his face after shaving, and, with water running down his cheeks, he turned and said, "By George, I believe you have hit it."

His speech that night was the last political speech I was to hear him make. It was entirely different in phrasing and delivery from his method in his early period. The Beveridge of the "March of the Flag" speech was no more. He spoke conversationally, as though chatting with his audience, cleverly and brilliantly, but without the dramatization of which he was a master in his younger years. He was nominated in the primary.

That year I might have had the Democratic Senatorial nomination. I had spoken at the Democratic state banquet at the Claypool in Indianapolis, with Cordell Hull, then the national chairman, as the principal speaker. The party leaders expected from Hull a sound, statesmanlike speech packed with solid meat, but they could not count on him for a fighting speech that would send the party workers back home in militant mood, and I was asked to supply that need.

That night I had a dangerous cold. My voice was a croak, and when I talked there was a disconcerting crackle in my ears. By sucking a lemon while the others ate I managed to clear my voice. In his memoirs, Cordell Hull refers to my speech as "red hot and eloquent" and as having "attracted wide attention." In truth, the reception of the speech was such that immediately afterward there was some canvassing on the feasibility of nominating me for the Senate. However, I was very tired and almost ill, and, more decisive, the organization was bringing pressure on Governor Ralston to take the nomination. I had no hint then of his reluctance to take it, and my intimate friendship with him from boyhood would have made a contest with him repugnant, as well as absurd. During the two previous summers my wife and I had been guests of the Ralstons at their beautiful country house, Hoosier Home, near Indianapolis.

I mention this incident because of the aftermath. Soon after his nomination Ralston wrote me that he had just heard that had he not been a candidate I would have been, and that had he received the slightest intimation he would have refused the nomination and supported me, since it was against his judgment to abandon a lucrative law practice at his age.

During the campaign, which resulted in his election, I spent a night at Hoosier Home between speaking engagements and was awakened at dawn by voices in an adjoining room. It was Ralston going over his speech for the day with Mrs. Ralston, his best critic and adviser. That campaign was unique in my experience, since the opposing candidates, Beveridge and Ralston, were my close friends and both had honored me with their confidence.

Fortunately for Beveridge, I think, he was defeated by hostile factions in his own party. He turned at once to the writing of a biography of Lincoln in the grand manner of the Marshall book. When I saw him soon after the election his defeat had been put behind him and he was aglow with his usual enthusiasm over his delving into Lincoln source material. Though in his sixtieth year, he seemed like a man in his mid-forties, and his boyish exuberance had abated not a bit.

One day he wrote me that he had valuable Lincoln material under heavy insurance in his house, and that if I would run over to Indianapolis he would show me something that would "knock your eye out." I took the next interurban.

He showed me, first, a copy of the *Sangamon Journal,* the old Springfield, Illinois, Republican organ, announcing that on the Saturday night before the Senatorial election (in 1858) Lincoln would address his fellow citizens of Springfield in "the effort of his life" and answer the "lies" of the campaign. He then showed me the *Journal* of the Monday morning following the meeting. Numerous men had spoken and the entire front page was filled with the speeches, but Lincoln's was dismissed in a few lines at the bottom of the page. It appeared that "the Hon. A. Lincoln also spoke" but that owing to "lack of space" it was impossible to print his speech.

"And what do you think of that?" asked Beveridge.

"*Hamlet* with Hamlet left out," I replied.

He then showed me Lincoln's notes for the speech. The headings were numbered points on which he proposed to touch, and among these was the notation that he was "not opposed to the fugitive slave law."

It was Beveridge's theory that night that Douglas had forced Lincoln in the debates into a more extreme position on slavery than the Illinois leaders thought wise. This had not been bad in the abolition strongholds, but the Republicans around Springfield were old-line Whigs who had no sympathy with the abolitionists and only an academic interest in slavery. They were alarmed lest Lincoln's speech defeat the state ticket, and they had little confidence in Lincoln's election. The meeting at Springfield on the verge of the election the following Tuesday offered an opportunity to reassure the more conservative Republicans there; and since the speech could not be printed because of "lack of space," the abolitionists elsewhere would not know that Lincoln had qualified what he had implied earlier in the campaign.

That night Beveridge was swamped with manuscripts, papers

and books, and he was using a magnifying glass to spare his eyes. For five years he was to work unceasingly on the Lincoln biography. What he would have done with the Springfield speech is conjectural, for his hand was stayed by death just as he was finishing with the debates.

My interest in the Irish overtook me a little disconcertingly in Fort Wayne when the Irish leader Eamon De Valera, who had escaped the vigilance of the British police and reached the United States as a stoker on a steamer, visited the city to make a speech. On his arrival in New York, John Devoy and Judge Daniel F. Cohalen, the brilliant but autocratic Irish-American leader, took him in tow with a view to using him against Wilson and the League of Nations. At any rate, his speeches were critical of Wilson and not at all calculated to advance the cause of the League, then under attack by the Republicans. Cohalen had organized the Friends of Irish Freedom, which many Irish joined with no realization of its political significance. Because of my *Irish Orators* and my well-known partiality for the Irish, the branch of this organization in Fort Wayne was very friendly with me, and I was asked to make one of a committee to go to a neighboring town to meet De Valera and escort him to the city. Having learned of the tone of his speeches and not relishing the idea, I made an excuse. That evening, however, after his arrival, I was invited to a small dinner in his honor preceding the meeting he was to address, and this I accepted.

I was disappointed in De Valera. He impressed me as conspicuously non-Irish. Tall and gaunt, funereally somber, apparently without a bit of Irish humor, he sat at the table looking down at his plate without a smile and with scarcely a word to the man beside him. I missed the wit, the humor, the conversational brilliance and eloquence of the Currans, Grattans, O'Connells and Meaghers with whom I had associated Irish leadership. He was accompanied by Harry Boland, a clever, scintillating young Irish patriot who did embody my concept of the Irishman.

I was seated on the platform that night before De Valera spoke when Dan Callahan, a well-known lawyer, a leading Democrat and a supporter of the League, came to me with a flushed face. "What do you think that damn fellow wants?" he asked. "He gave a typed resolution to Pat Breen, the chairman, and asked him to

have it introduced. Without reading it, Pat gave it to me to introduce." It was against the Wilson policy and it paid tribute to the
two Republican Senators from Indiana who were against the
League. "I told Pat I would see them all in hell first," Callahan
concluded.

A little later, Callahan came back with Charles Niezer, a banker,
who had agreed to serve as the chairman of the reception committee with the understanding that American politics would not be
introduced. The two asked me to accompany them below the stage,
where the local Friends of Irish Freedom were in session. Niezer
reminded the president of the group about the conditions under
which he had accepted the chairmanship of the committee, and he
warned that if anyone introduced the resolution he would either
denounce it or ostentatiously leave the platform and the hall. There
was embarrassment and consternation, for I am sure the Irish were
no more prepared for such a resolution than Callahan or Niezer.
The result was that the resolution was not introduced.

After the meeting, Callahan and I went to his office to celebrate,
and then to the Anthony Hotel in search of Niezer. We were told
that he was with "the President in his room." We knocked on the
door and entered. Someone said, "Here they are now."

The local Irish were sitting in embarrassed silence around the
walls. De Valera was standing with his back to the footboard of
the bed, expostulating angrily with Niezer, who stood facing him.
The coldness of De Valera had disappeared and he was in a rage.
He was far from silent now. His face was flushed.

Niezer retained his poise and temper, confining his interruptions to De Valera's flow of infuriated eloquence to one phrase:
"That may be all right for you, Mr. President, but we are Americans."

The climax came when De Valera burst forth with a statement
that shook the Irish around the wall: "My one purpose in making
this tour is to have that resolution adopted, and had I known it
would not be adopted here I would not have come to Fort Wayne."

In all other meetings addressed by De Valera the resolution was
adopted. Years later, M. J. MacManus, in his biography of De
Valera, said that the purpose of the tour was to create sentiment
for the recognition of the Irish Republic, and that the Irish leader
favored the League of Nations and understood why it was impos-

sible for Wilson to recognize the republic at that time. Perhaps, but such was not the impression left in Fort Wayne.

Later I was to meet De Valera at some small dinners in New York where he talked more freely, though still without much wit or humor, and the bad impression I had formed of him at the first meeting was largely wiped out.

Another Fort Wayne incident in the days of the First World War: It was at this time that I saw and heard Eugene V. Debs for the last time. This was just two weeks before his arrest in Cleveland and his imprisonment in Atlanta. He was, of course, a pacifist. Unknown to him and unnoticed in the rear of the hall, I followed his speech curiously to see how he would manage. The audience was composed almost entirely of Socialists. Debs was speaking conversationally, and, while he denounced war as a means of settling international disputes, his denunciation was concentrated on the military clique of Germany as responsible for the war. This was precisely what all speakers at meetings to sell bonds and raise money for the war were doing. We also denounced war and insisted that this war was to end war.

After he closed, I went to the platform to greet him as an old friend. He seemed pleased, and the next morning he spent an hour in my office discussing the progress of the war and talking about mutual friends in Terre Haute. He did not utter a word to which the most supersensitive patriot could take exception. It seemed to me at the time that, with the realization that his every word would be microscopically examined by secret agents, he had prepared his speech with meticulous care. As he proceeded eastward, speaking in various towns in Ohio, I followed his speeches as reported in the papers of these towns; they followed precisely the line of the harmless speech I had heard. Consequently I was shocked by his arrest in Cleveland. I am afraid that he was arrested because he would not publicly renounce the tenets of his political faith, and that his arrest was a blot on the fine record of the Administration. He was not a traitor. He was not a revolutionist. He was, rather, an evolutionist. He had no faith in force. He was an idealist, a poet and an honest man.

In prison he was beloved by prisoners and keepers alike, and when, after the war, many people interceded for his release, President Harding sent instructions to the warden to send Debs unaccompanied to Washington on his agreement to return to prison afterward. No higher compliment was ever paid a man. Harding was enormously impressed by Debs's personality and conversation, his lack of bitterness and his transparent honesty, and shortly thereafter he was released. But the prison years had told heavily on him. He died five years later, in 1926.

It was the encouragement of Beveridge that led me seriously into the writing of political history. I had long been collecting material for a book in justification of Jackson's "Kitchen Cabinet." There was a tendency, by people ignorant of politics and unaware of the fact that political parties and politicians are an indispensable part of the democratic process, to belittle and malign Amos Kendall, Frank P. Blair and Isaac Hill and their relations with the colorful figure in the White House. The very conservative school of historians had been condescending toward Jackson himself and his overdue crusade against the embryo plutocracy that was then assuming threatening proportions. Jefferson's election in 1800 had definitely determined that ours should be a democratic republic, but with the passing of the years the people had lost sight of fundamental principles, and plutocracy had been slowly but surely making progress. When Senators and Congressmen snubbed the levees of the President of the United States to flock to the levees of the president of the national bank, only the blind could have been ignorant of its significance. Jefferson had triumphed for democracy in 1800; it was the historical mission of Jackson to reawaken the democratic fervor.

With the money power of his day arrogant and active, using money, credit control and intimidation as weapons, Jackson's crusade called for a close, systematic organization to direct, drill and munition the masses, and foremost among practical politicians qualified for the work were Kendall, Blair and Hill. Following the "Era of Good Feeling"—which was everything but that—the country was tending toward personal government and a personality cult, not based on well-defined principles, and it was the mission of Jackson to create a government by parties.

Beveridge agreed with my estimate of the Kitchen Cabinet, but he urged me to extend the scope and include the party struggles of the Jackson period, to make the book a political history of the regime. Absorbed with political history all my life, I had found most political histories lacking in something I thought important—background; there was too little of the personalities and motives of the leaders, too much of a disposition to accept an official document as conclusive without inquiring into its political antecedents. It seemed to me that it was not enough to know that the people had reacted to this or that measure in this or that way, but that it was vitally important to know on what information, correct or incorrect, the people had acted, and to know something more of the atmosphere in which they moved.

I had in mind William Cobbet's *Porcupine's Gazette*, which resorted to the methods of yellow journalism as early as 1798 and printed sensational falsehoods to influence public opinion in support of the Alien and Sedition Laws when the fervor of the fanatics was dwindling. Under scarecrow headlines it announced that a French army had landed in South Carolina and was marching on Philadelphia, burning houses, raping women and kidnaping children. Of course no French army had landed or had thought of landing, but this scandalous lie had its effect. Fear lashed many into a frenzy, and mobs fared forth to attack Jeffersonians and wreck Jeffersonian newspapers. Because it was a lie old-school historians thought the Porcupine story beneath the dignity of history, and, while they noted the action of the mob, they ignored the reason for the action. Lies have played a conspicuous part in determining the action of peoples, and these lies are an essential part of history. Nothing that has determined the action of peoples is beneath the dignity of history.

In a tiny, dusty room on the ground floor of the *Journal-Gazette*, writing to suit myself and without serious concern about a publisher, I wrote *The Party Battles of the Jackson Period* after the paper had been put to bed. When finished, the manuscript was a length that would require two volumes. Beveridge insisted that I submit it to his publishers, the Houghton Mifflin people, and I sent it on hopefully, but without much confidence in its acceptance. Very soon Beveridge wrote me that the manuscript had been sent to Dr. William E. Dodd, head of the department of American history at Chicago University, and that this was fortunate since Dodd was one of the liberals among the historians. Soon thereafter he wrote again, saying that Dodd's report was "positively enthusi-astic." Then came a letter from Ferris Greenslet, editor of the pub-lishing house, accepting the book but urging that it be condensed to one volume. Dodd was opposed to the reduction, but I accepted Greenslet's advice, much to my later regret.

I learned at this time the importance of a title to a book. In correspondence with the publisher I had referred to the manuscript descriptively as "party battles of the Jackson period" with no thought of using it as the title. It smacked too much of a cold, dull study of political technique. But the book had already been copy-righted as *The Party Battles of the Jackson Period* and the pub-lishers thought the title was "as good as any." An incident disil-lusioned them as to that. The Chautauqua corporation then dis-tributed annually to its members books of fiction, biography and history, and its agent, in search of a history, called on Houghton Mifflin at their New York office. The Jackson book was offered. Looking at the title, the agent shook his head. He was asked to take a copy and glance over it en route to Boston and throw it out the window if he found it dull. On his arrival in Boston he went to Houghton Mifflin and ordered five thousand copies. The title gave no inkling of the human side and the drama. No matter what the text, my advice to young historians is to give serious thought to the title.

I was not prepared for the flood of good reviews that poured in from Boston to San Francisco, but I was delighted by the special approval of the elements I had thought lacking in most political histories. Nicholas Roosevelt in the New York *Herald Tribune* thought it "history as it should be written." The New York *Times* cited the success of Lytton Strachey in "applying psychological methods and insight to the writing of biography" and concluded that I had "subjected a whole political period . . . to psychologi-cal treatment." Beveridge in the Indianapolis *Star* wrote that "al-though he deals with the established facts he does so in the manner of the dramatist and the result is as fascinating as a novel by Du-mas." The Boston *Herald* recognized my purpose in saying that "in the colorful background that most historians have ignored he gives a very humanizing illumination of an era unique in our politi-cal history."

One letter, from James M. Beck, then Solicitor General of the

United States, gave me special pleasure and resulted in a warm friendship. Although I admired Beck's ability, brilliance and eloquence, he had become my pet aversion because of his attacks on Woodrow Wilson, and when the press announced that he was under consideration for the embassy in London I wrote a thoroughly nasty editorial. Ten days later a letter came from the "Office of the Solicitor General," and, having no doubt it was an excoriation, I invited my colleagues on the paper to enjoy it. It was a letter in warm praise of my book. That was the beginning of a close friendship with Beck which continued until his death. I have often reflected on the number of men, once pet aversions of mine, who became cherished friends on closer acquaintance. It is an illustration of the ancient truth that one cannot hate a man one knows.

It is a matter of some pride to me that all my books on American history have changed opinions on men and measures. In a later letter, Beck wrote me that *Party Battles* had changed his opinion as to the propriety of Jackson's vigorous action toward the French on the spoliation claims. "I had always thought," he wrote me (November 24, 1923), "that in the embroglio with France, Jackson had acted rather boorishly; but your book convinces me that his attitude and manners were those of a dignified and courageous American President and that the attack upon him by the Great Triumvirate [Clay, Webster and Calhoun] in the Senate was petty and ignoble."

Later I was puzzled to find Beck, a distinguished Republican, leaning strongly in fundamentals toward the Jeffersonian concept of politics. In his review of my *Jefferson and Hamilton*, I was astonished to note, his sole criticism was that I had made Hamilton out to be a greater man than he was. When I expressed my surprise to John W. Davis he gave me an explanation of Beck's career, which he described as "a tragedy."

"He was a brilliant young Democrat in Pennsylvania with unusual power as an orator," Davis said, "and he was looked upon as the fair-haired boy of the Democracy of that state. Cleveland had appointed him district attorney, and when, in 1896, Cleveland left his party on the money issue, Beck in loyalty to his chief did likewise, but instead of going with the Gold Democrats he went all the way over to the Republicans. The Republicans were jubilant and generous in their praise, and Beck remained with them. But he was never accorded the recognition his ability deserved, since his dedication to Republican elemental principles was suspect. He was made Solicitor General under Coolidge and made a brilliant record, and toward the twilight of his days he was sent to the House of Representatives. The truth is that Beck was a convinced Jeffersonian. Had he remained where he belonged he would have had a more brilliant career, and I, who knew him, had the feeling that he was not happy over his shift."

The publication of *The Party Battles of the Jackson Period* was to change the course of my life again, because of the favorable impression it had made on Frank Cobb, the brilliant editor of the New York *World*. He had spoken of it in complimentary terms to Arthur Krock, then with the *World*, who knew me, and Krock told Cobb I was writing editorials for the Fort Wayne *Journal-Gazette*. At this time an editorial writer was needed on the *Evening World*. I learned later from Herbert Bayard Swope that for some weeks the editorial page of the *Journal-Gazette* was read by Ralph Pulitzer, Swope and Cobb. Soon I was asked to meet Krock in Indianapolis, and I was invited to join the *World*.

An acceptance meant a definitive separation from Indiana, where I was known, and a final abandonment of all political activities. It was not an easy decision to make. Sentiment argued on one side and common sense on the other, and in the end common sense prevailed. But it was with much sadness and many misgivings that I broke with old associations and went to New York. The final shove toward this decision was given by Beveridge, to whom I had appealed for advice. "I have thought your matter over as well as I can and my first judgment is confirmed that you ought to take the New York offer," he wrote. "Of course it means a radical and definitive change in your life and there are a good many reasons pro and con. But weighing these, it seems to me that the balance is decidedly for the New York venture. But whatever you do, good luck and God bless you."

CHAPTER VIII

Under the Gold Dome

THE NEW YORK *World* had already known national prestige, and also degradation, when Joseph Pulitzer, a journalistic genius of the first order, took possession and again raised it to the heights as a militant crusader for liberalism. The Pulitzer Building, where it was published, was a showplace of the town at the time of its erection, and tourists paid fees for admission to the tower, which rose to the then sensational height of fourteen stories. The tower's golden dome loomed impressively on the vision of passengers on incoming steamers, and Pulitzer was enormously proud of it. This pride in the tower, where the editorial writers worked, amused Henry Watterson, a friendly rival, who suggested that Pulitzer bore holes in the tower "to let the darkness out."

My room was on the top floor of the tower, looking down on the City Hall entrance and park, and from its balcony I witnessed some spectacular scenes—the hysterical welcome to Lindbergh, the less impressive reception of Queen Marie of Romania, the noisy greeting of a swimmer who had braved the English Channel, and the sadly silent reception of Madame Curie, who was not a flyer, a swimmer or a queen, but merely a genius who, with her husband, had served mankind. Later I moved to another room in the Pulitzer Building where there were two impressive desks, one ornate and of mahogany, the other of California rose wood; I wondered at the serenity of the room, since one desk had belonged to Joseph Pulitzer and the other to William Randolph Hearst, who had once occupied an elaborately furnished office in the Pulitzer Building.

The *World* staff at that time could not, I am sure, have been surpassed, if equaled. Frank Cobb, who alone among journalists had enjoyed the absolute confidence of Woodrow Wilson, and whose brilliance as an editorial writer was unequaled, was on his deathbed when I reached New York. Few of the staff that had served under the great Pulitzer remained. John Heaton, old and gray but with the pink complexion of a schoolgirl, carried on the old tradition, and for him I had a great affection. The others were recruited later, and most of these who were not then famous were about to become so.

The brilliant career of Walter Lippmann had begun when he was a star on the *New Republic*. He was then a handsome young man with luminous, intelligent eyes. On the *World* he wrote his editorials in microscopic script with a pen. They were lucid, logical, perfectly phrased in impeccable literary style. When on the *New Republic* he had been the idol of the militant young liberals. He had thought himself a Socialist during his Harvard days, but he had begun to take on the pale cast of relative conservatism, and many of his erstwhile admirers had become his most severe critics. He had written some notable books and he was becoming something of a political philosopher.

Darting hither and yon about the tower, an enlivening figure, bubbling with energy and enthusiasm, his bright eyes beaming from behind his glasses, was tall, slender Charley Merz. He was of Midwest origin, and he too had had his initiation on the *New Republic*. His editorials were based on meticulous research and were dependable. When the *World* folded up he went to the New York *Times*, where the qualities so manifest on the *World* led, after a short time, to his selection for the very important post of editor in chief.

Rushing tempestuously in and out of the various offices, usually minus a coat, and talking incessantly and brilliantly in a booming voice was the closest adviser of Ralph Pulitzer, Herbert Bayard Swope, whose reportorial brilliance had made him famous. He was the most scintillating conversationalist I have ever known.

Arthur Krock, an old friend from the days when I was Kern's secretary, was Pulitzer's assistant. He had been trained in his profession under the eye of Henry Watterson, and I had known him as the Washington correspondent of the Louisville *Courier-Journal*. Later he was to have a distinguished career as the head of the Washington Bureau of the New York *Times*.

Sometimes, though not often in the daytime, a gargantuan figure, a towering mountain of gross flesh, could be seen and heard in the tower, speaking in a thin, high-pitched voice that was shocking because of its contrast with the huge physical proportions of the speaker. This was Alexander Woollcott, the drama critic, a prime favorite with the players. His criticisms were always brilliant and sometimes caustic. His book *While Rome Burns* had infinite charm. His reputation as a wit and genius may have been a bit exaggerated, but he could be immensely amusing even when, as usual, he was studiedly rude. He appears full length in the play *The Man Who Came to Dinner*, which was patterned after him with a touch of malice that did not prevent him from acting in the title role.

Almost as huge in bulk was Heywood Broun, whose column, avidly read by liberals and intellectuals, had the journalistic merit of calling forth either rapturous applause or indignant hisses. He was the *enfant terrible* of the staff and often a source of annoyance to the shy Ralph Pulitzer and the cautious, more conservative Lippmann. When he went out on the warpath with paint and feathers against President Lowell of Harvard, who had advised against the commutation of the death sentence of Sacco and Vanzetti, and referred to Harvard as "Hangman's House," he narrowly escaped cancellation of his contract. Another columnist who was a prime favorite in those days was Franklin P. Adams (F.P.A.), who conducted "The Conning Tower," in which appeared clever paragraphs and poems of his own and of contributors.

Moving quietly, almost silently, certainly unostentatiously, about the tower was Maxwell Anderson, who interested me greatly. He had then written two successful plays, one of them *Saturday's Children*. I got the impression that his ambition was lofty but purely literary, and that he regarded his job as an economic necessity rather than as a pleasure. Serious and dedicated to his ambition as a dramatist, he was too busy to join the frolics of Broun, F.P.A., Woollcott and Laurence Stallings at the famous Algonquin dining table. (At that time stenographers strained their budgets to lunch at the Algonquin and see their favorite columnists in the flesh.) I noticed that Anderson spent much time with Stallings, who conducted the book page. This young man had left a leg in Argonne Forest and was articulately bitter over his experience with the Marines. Almost daily he appeared with Anderson at the editorial round table in the *World* restaurant, and the latter sat in silence with an amused expression, listening to Stallings' interminable talk. In those days Stallings was promising a book page that would be unique, but he never was to get around to it. The secret of the association of these wholly different men was out when we learned that they had written a war play, *What Price Glory?* On the opening night I thought it would fail because of the sulphurous profanity put into the mouths of the Marines, but the public was in the mood for it and the play had an enormous success. This had no noticeable effect on Anderson, who had written successful plays before and would go on to write others of great literary merit, and he went about with his usual modesty, but Stallings became a bit exalted and lost interest in the book page. When he came to me for information on the dress of men in the days of Jackson I learned that he and Maxwell were collaborating on a play about Old Hickory. It was a dismal failure, and this ended the collaboration of the two.

Stallings was soon displaced by Harry Hansen as literary editor. Hansen was tall and slender, with a scholarly expression, and was as quiet as his predecessor was boisterous. He had distinguished himself as a critic on the Chicago *News* and as the author of *Midwest Portraits*. As a reviewer he was more concerned with setting forth the merits or demerits of a book than with exhibiting his own cleverness.

On my floor of the tower was the studio of Rollin Kirby, one of the most brilliant political cartoonists America has produced, more subtle and a finer artist than Nasby of generations before. Intimately familiar with the political scene and with literature, he had a rare capacity for satirical interpretation, and time and again he received the Pulitzer Prize. It was a treat to watch him, seated before a big wooden easel, creating cartoons more powerful than a thousand arguments. He alone conceived, as well as drew, his masterpieces, and one of the saddest results of the scrapping of the *World* was that it deprived him of the proper medium for his genius.

Not long after my appearance in the tower we were joined by James M. Cain, who wrote editorials in the lighter vein, for he had a sense of humor not easy to associate with *The Postman Always*

Rings Twice and other novels of his with their unsavory characters and tough dialogue.

It was under the gold dome that my friendship with Allan Nevins began. At intervals he joined the staff. Serious, intensely earnest and a hard worker, he gave the impression that at that time he seldom played. He told me that he aspired to a chair in American history at some university, an ambition realized when he became a professor at Columbia, where he was later head of the history department. It was after his *World* days that he wrote numerous biographies and histories that have made him one of the most distinguished historians of our time.

I shared a suite in the tower with Harold Pollard, who supervised the editorial policy of the *Evening World*. Slim and always immaculately dressed, he had been the favorite secretary of Joseph Pulitzer and had been with him on his yacht one day when his employer startled him by saying, "How suddenly it got dark!"—though it was still daylight. Pulitzer had become blind. Pollard remained with Pulitzer on the yacht, where the publisher lived during the years of his affliction until his death. Having previously been dramatic critic on the New York *Times*, it was his duty in the assignment of jobs among the several secretaries to keep the blind genius informed as to new plays and books. These reports never aroused Pulitzer's ire, as did those of the secretaries reporting politics and finance, and Pollard became the favorite. One night at dinner, Ireland, another secretary, remarked that he was writing a play. Pulitzer, much interested, asked what he was calling it. "I thought," said Ireland, "of calling it 'The Importance of Being Pollard.'" I found Pollard's reminiscences of Pulitzer always fascinating.

Such were the men of the *World*—certainly a goodly company beneath the gold dome.

I soon found that the *World*, an independent-Democratic paper, put most stress on independence, and that its association with the Democratic Party was due entirely to its militant liberalism, which almost always arrayed it with the party of Jefferson—whom Pulitzer revered. Some remark of mine at the round table in the restaurant drew from Heaton, staring at me with sincere wonder, the question, "Do you really take your politics seriously?" I am afraid I did, and do. I am sure that democracy will ultimately and inevitably fail if the people cease to take their politics seriously.

I was to learn much about the rocks and shoals of American politics in the Democratic national convention in Madison Square Garden in 1924. All the portents of reason pointed to a Democratic year. It was notorious that the Harding Administration had contributed nothing to public confidence in those in power, and though Harding had died, the personnel of the Administration had not greatly changed. The corruption of the time was appalling.

In 1923 the Presidential aspirations of William Gibbs McAdoo had seemed certain of fulfillment. He had distinguished himself brilliantly in the performance of multitudinous and vitally important duties under Wilson during the war. In the early summer of that year I was asked by McAdoo to meet him in Chicago. I had not met him before. I thought his personality pleasing and impressive. Tall, thin, graceful in bearing, he was youthful in spirit and manner, though he was then almost sixty. His deep-set eyes, sometimes quizzical, thoughtful and humorous, sometimes sad, suggested those of Lincoln. These eyes, and the arch of his brows, gave him a striking appearance.

"I see the Ku Klux Klan is out for you in Texas," I said.

"Yes," he replied, "and against me in Indiana."

He then explained the hostility of the Hoosier Klansmen as being caused by a story that he had had a picture of the Pope stamped on some silver certificates when Secretary of the Treasury. I told him I had heard the story but had not seen the certificates. Taking one from his pocket, he pointed to the tiny head of a man in the corner wearing a cap presumably popular in the days of Columbus which the overly credulous might be persuaded was the cap of the Pope.

"The funny thing about it," he said, "is that this is a reissue of a certificate issued first in 1862—which proves that Lincoln was a tool of the Pope, too."

I did not know him well enough to inquire into the charge that he was the candidate of the Klan. A little later, Dixon Williams of Chicago called on me at Fort Wayne to ask me to look after McAdoo's interests in Indiana. Nothing could have been more stupid, since my services to the party had been through voice and pen, and I was utterly ignorant of the rudiments of organization.

Then, too, something else made acceptance impossible. There was a disposition in Indiana to urge the claims of Senator Ralston to the nomination, and he had been my friend from my childhood. With Ralston as a candidate, McAdoo could expect nothing from Indiana. I suggested that McAdoo should talk with Taggart, the powerful, popular leader of the organization, and this advice was taken. Their conference at French Lick resulted in an agreement that McAdoo would not contest in Indiana, but that he would be urged on the Indiana delegates to the national convention as second choice. I was then asked to undertake the task of seeing that the agreement was carried out, but that autumn I moved to New York and my personal association with the McAdoo movement ended many months before the convention.

In New York that winter and spring there appeared to be no probability that Governor Al Smith would be a candidate, but I found an undercurrent of bitter hostility to McAdoo. His independent distribution of patronage in New York under Wilson had aroused the animosity of Tammany Hall. No spot in America could have been more dangerous to McAdoo's candidacy than New York City, but when the solemn assurance was given that the New York press would accord fair treatment, McAdoo, who could have vetoed the selection of New York as the convention city, agreed. It was a grave blunder.

In the months intervening between my arrival and the opening of the convention McAdoo was in New York several times, and each time I lunched with him in his room at the Vanderbilt Hotel. In May he showed the tremendous strain of the campaign. He was noticeably thinner, his face almost peaked, albeit there was fire in his eyes and nothing in his manner to denote weariness. He said nothing about Al Smith other than that he could not be nominated. He thought if Ralston ran the effort would kill him. He was bitter only against Senator Oscar W. Underwood of Alabama, whom he charged with putting the Klan tag on his candidacy.

"Do you think I ought to say any more about the Klan?" he asked while mixing his salad. He was willing to join all the candidates in a common statement on the Klan, he said, but he objected to being singled out. "Why isn't Smith asked to state where he stands?"

Dumfounded by the question, I concluded that he was mentally more tired than I had thought.

Later, on the eve of the convention, I called at his headquarters in the Vanderbilt to see Colonel Hollister, and as I was leaving McAdoo appeared in the hall and called me back. He led the way to a room where one light was burning. There were dark rings under his eyes, and during the hour I was with him he yawned repeatedly from sleeplessness. Stretching himself out comfortably in his chair, he talked about the Klan tag attached to him, and he offered an interesting explanation. In 1912 Wilson's candidacy in Texas had been managed by Cato Sells and Tom Love, who had been remarkably astute in organizing the state, and McAdoo had enlisted their support for himself. It was not until they had organized Texas thoroughly for him, he said, that he learned of Sells's connection with the Klan, which was then powerful. He said that to have dismissed him at that juncture would have been to concentrate the Klansmen against him everywhere.

Confident that night of winning, he was interesting himself in a running mate. At one time, he said, he had thought of Smith, but the suggestion had brought in alarming verification of the deadly danger of a religious feud when some fanatics warned him that, if elected, he would be assassinated to make way for a Catholic President! "There's no point in attempting to reason with a fanatic," he said.

It was five days later, during the convention, that I saw him again, and again without design. With Sybil, my wife, I was making the rounds of the headquarters of the candidates. By accident I met him in the hall, and he asked me into a private room dimly and depressingly lighted by a single lamp on a table. He still looked tired, but there was fight and anger in his eyes because of the treatment he was receiving from the New York press. He was bitter, too, against the city's reception committees, which he denounced, quite accurately, as anti-McAdoo propagandists. In angry tones he said that attempts were being made to seduce his delegates with gin and whiskey, and he named three or four of his men who had been stupidly drunk since reaching the city. It was the last time I was to see him before his defeat.

Unknown to the general public to this hour, the most dramatic figure in that convention was Senator Ralston. I was close to his Waldorf-Astoria headquarters, where Tom Taggart was in charge. Delegates were constantly going in and out, and the moment a visitor arrived a colored servant of Taggart's appeared as if by magic with a cool, sparkling Scotch and soda on a silver tray. These were the days of Prohibition and Taggart was a most perfect host. I have never known a man of such charm and magnetism as this genial Irish leader. Handsome, always smiling, in perpetual motion, gracious and graceful in his bearing, ever seeking opportunities to bestow a favor, never bitter even to his political foes, greatly admired by them, his pleasing personality as well as his rare organizing ability had maintained him in the unquestioned leadership of his party in Indiana for more than thirty years. His supreme ambition was to cap his career as leader with the nomination of a Hoosier for President. In the Madison Square Garden convention he felt the hour had struck.

My own heart naturally was with Ralston, who had carefully concealed his concern over his health from the public. When I was still in Fort Wayne he had telephoned to ask me to substitute for him as a speaker in Ohio because his physician had forbidden him to go. Later, one night at Hoosier Home, I learned that his kidneys were affected and that he had been put on a diet. Nothing could have been more annoying to this robust trencherman, who amazed me when I was a guest at his country home by the enormity of his breakfasts—hot biscuits with much butter, ham and eggs, cereal drowned in thick cream, and three large cups of coffee. He was heavy (he bore a striking resemblance to Grover Cleveland) and the reducing process was to be hurried; and this had a bad effect on his heart.

Ralston ranked high among trial and corporation lawyers of the state. His political speeches were always pitched on a high plane, without vituperation or trickery, and if not eloquent they were powerful in the marshaling of facts. No one ever questioned his sincerity and certainly not his honesty or ability. His modesty added to his popularity. A staunch organization man, he was in line for the highest honors and he was nominated and elected governor. I treasure his inscribed photograph with the grossly exaggerated words, "With gratitude for what you did to make me Governor of Indiana." His tenure disclosed great administrative ability. It was not marred by petty partisanship and he concentrated on public service. No governor has ever been more popular or more admired, appreciated and loved. It was much against his judgment that he was later nominated for Senator against Beveridge and elected. Among his colleagues in the Senate he was greatly admired, and leaders like Carter Glass thought him an ideal Presidential choice for 1924. But when plans were made to have him endorsed by the Indiana state convention he was as much distressed as jubilant.

The latter part of March 1924, Sybil and I were weekend guests of the Ralstons in Washington. He looked better than in November, but with the loss of forty pounds he had been so weakened that he was in doubt whether he should permit the state convention to launch his candidacy. We sat up until one-thirty in the morning discussing what he should do. He realized the possibility of his nomination in the event of a deadlock and was keenly conscious of his condition. Most of his physicians opposed his candidacy, but one of them thought he might, with discretion, go through the campaign. I could only suggest that in the event of his nomination he could avoid the customary continental tour and could receive delegations at Hoosier Home, as Harrison had done in 1888 and Harding in 1920. He thought he might make major speeches in New York and Chicago.

It was the last time I was to see him, for he clung to the old-fashioned sense of dignity which precluded the personal appearance of candidates in the convention. Later I learned that his moods were variable. One day he would think it "foolish to be thinking of the Presidency when I have to take medicine to keep alive," and the next he would be discussing a possible running mate. Such was the tragic situation of Ralston when the convention met. Meanwhile Taggart, with his usual finesse and resourcefulness, was working cunningly undercover, in secret conferences with national leaders, and he frequently called on me to prepare statements for the press.

We now come to unwritten history, certainly a footnote to history: the story of a man who refused the Presidential nomination when it was his for the asking. The bitter feud of Smith and McAdoo had made the nomination of either impossible, and the prolonged balloting had found not a few delegates short of money.

On July 7, Taggart called me to the Waldorf. He was preparing to make a drive for Ralston and asked me to prepare a statement for the purpose. I wrote it in accordance with some suggestions. Among these was a description of Ralston as a "conservative progressive." When Senator Pat Harrison of Mississippi read it he urged the striking out of the word "conservative."

I did not know at the time that Taggart had a promise from McAdoo. The next day the drive began, and when the convention adjourned in the afternoon Ralston's vote had been increased by two hundred, with every indication—considering the agreements made with numerous leaders—that at the night session he would be nominated. McAdoo had agreed to release to Ralston all his delegates, except those of California, and this, with the pledges of other leaders, would account for about six hundred votes. With the convention worn out, and with many delegates forced to borrow money to pay hotel bills, that much of a spurt would have ended the contest.

Now for the real drama of the convention behind the curtain. That night I went to the Prince George Hotel, headquarters of the Hoosiers, to accompany them to the Garden. As I entered the lobby I was accosted by an Indiana delegate with the startling news that late in the afternoon Ralston had telephoned Taggart, thanked him for what he had done and said that he could not take the nomination. Taggart, boyishly happy a moment before, was stunned.

"Do you mean it?" he asked.

"Yes, I mean it."

"Then I wish you would send me a telegram to that effect," said Taggart.

The telegram had been received, and, to protect himself from the charge of bad faith, Taggart had summoned all the leaders who had agreed to go to Ralston, read it to them and released them from their pledge. At the Prince George, Taggart asked me to sit in on the state caucus he had called. When it was called to order, Taggart walked over to a piano in a corner of the room, backed up against it, related simply what had happened, and read the telegram. He was bitterly disappointed, and in reading the telegram his voice broke. It was to be Taggart's last convention.

That Ralston sorrowed more over Taggart's disappointment

than over his own was manifest in a very long letter he wrote me on August 4, in which he said:

I would not be human . . . if I did not admit to you that the course I took was not easily determined upon. While I do not assume to be stronger or better balanced than the average man, yet I feel that there are few men who would have taken the course I did on what seemed to be almost conclusive evidence of my approaching nomination. I shall therefore, in a way, always regret that I could not see my way clear to court the nomination, and the sting of this regret will increase in severity as the years come and go. Really the thing I most profoundly regret is the disappointment my final decision brought to my friends . . . my uncompromising friend of a quarter of a century, Senator Taggart, who was, and is, of course incapable of having a disloyal thought toward me. Taggart has long been distinguished for his brilliant leadership of men, but he never displayed it to greater advantage than in this instance and he never made a finer impression upon the country than he did in the exercise of his generalship in the New York Convention.

The reasons for his decision were noble:

For reasons I will some day explain, I felt that I owed it to myself, to my family, to my party and to my country not to allow the nomination to come to me. Feeling this, and being both a party man and a patriot, I could take no other course than I did.

This unwritten history may not be "history in the grand manner," but it reveals the human side of political history, without which it would be deadly dull. Many years ago William H. Crawford, a most distinguished statesman, while stricken and in his bed, passionately persisted in his ambition for the Presidency. Ralston perhaps was the more unselfish patriot. In less than a year he was dead.

We must now return to the convention, where the Democratic Party was committing suicide. Underwood's charge against McAdoo had injected a religious issue into politics, and Smith's candidacy accentuated it. At a time when the Democrats were in a position to challenge Republican special-interest policies and to crucify the opposition on the live issue of corruption, the delegates met with the religious issue uppermost in their minds, with the enemy press vigorously fanning the flames of religious hates, with leaders subordinating both party and country to their personal ambitions. Under the wise and patriotic leadership of Cordell Hull, the national chairman, everything humanly possible had been done to assure a campaign for progressive principles and for purging the public service of corruption. The choice as chairman of Senator Thomas J. Walsh, whose inquisitorial genius had exposed the Teapot Dome oil scandal, had this in view. But throughout the convention the streets were flooded with newspapers diverting attention to a religious quarrel. It was in an atmosphere of insensate hate that the convention met.

My first view of the sad spectacle was during a mob scene. Franklin D. Roosevelt had finished his speech nominating Smith when I arrived. The scene beggars description. A mob composed mostly of young men and boys had taken possession of the floor and was endlessly parading up and down in the aisles with a band, shouting hoarsely, and to this horrid confusion mechanical devices contributed not a little. Sirens from the fire department had been put to work in the hall. A few boys with voices of limited range could have continued the noise for days. Finally, when the galleries resembled those of the French Convention in the period of the Revolution, Senator Walsh, finding it impossible to restore something of the dignity of a deliberative body, expressed his willingness to entertain a motion to adjourn the convention to another city. Roosevelt, standing on the platform, holding on to the railing, was appealing to the crowd to stop the disgraceful scene, and he succeeded for a moment, but a little later hell broke loose again. A demonstration of voices and marching delegates would have been a deserved tribute to Al Smith, but this actual occupation of the floor by a reckless mob determined to rule or ruin put the demonstration beyond the pale. The experiment was based on a false psychology. It was thought it would sweep the delegates off their feet; instead it outraged them, for the convention itself had been degraded. This mob spirit was to dominate the galleries throughout the many days necessary to destroy the possibility of a Democratic victory.

The next mob scene came, as was expected, in the fight over the platform plank on the Klan. Those who thought it a sufficient repudiation of the Klan to reiterate the Jeffersonian position on religious liberty and toleration were denounced as Klansmen. The Republicans, whose platform had not mentioned the Klan at all, were free to play both ends against the middle.

One day after a prolonged struggle in the committee on resolutions, Homer S. Cummings was recognized to explain to the convention the committee's delay in making a report. He was a tall, fine-looking man, but he sagged from exhaustion as he made his frank and honest statement. There was sheer drama in his description of the scene in the early morning when the committee, unable to agree, had adjourned for a few hours. Someone had recited the Lord's Prayer, and others had joined. Bryan had asked for divine guidance. Referring to the controversy, Cummings said, "We began to wonder what would happen if the issue were thrown into the convention, we began to think of the future of the Democratic Party." But all too few were thinking about that.

At length the fight was forced to the floor in the debate on the platform, which did not mention the Klan by name but left no doubt of the party's attitude toward religious intolerance. The Garden was packed. The very air was electric and ominous.

Bainbridge Colby was the chief spokesman for the minority insisting on a specific denunciation of the Klan by name. A man of striking appearance, he was a fine orator, careful in his diction, perfect in his enunciation, a bit satiric and brilliant, and he pleased the galleries.

Bryan closed for the majority report in one of his greatest speeches. It was to be his farewell bow to Democratic conventions after eighteen years. He was ridiculed and abused for this speech. I heard it. It was magnificent. It was the one speech free from hate. No man ever won a better right to a respectful hearing. There was not one drop of religious bigotry in his blood. Time and again he had demonstrated his complete freedom from religious prejudice. As Secretary of State he had regularly attended the famous breakfasts after the Pan-American Mass. He was a friend of Cardinal Gibbons. But none of this counted in his favor with the mob, which was there to hoot and jeer, determined that he should not be heard.

For some time Bryan's health had been failing. He had lost weight, and his great frame seemed to droop. Age had stamped its lines upon his face. But time and again he awed the mob into silence by the wisdom and nobility of his utterance. His tribute to the Catholic Church as an institution that had withstood the assaults of centuries and did not depend for life on a resolution of a political convention brought a momentary hush. Bryan did more to inflame the Klan against him than any other speaker, but this made no impression on the intolerants. Toward the close there was a touch of pathos in his observation, which was to prove prophetic, that this might be his last convention, and the mob brutally broke into applause. Turning blazing eyes toward the galleries, he retorted, "Don't be too certain—I may change my mind." The mob had the grace to laugh.

The roll call was dramatic. The majority resolution won by a margin of one vote, and that was the death warrant of the party in 1924.

The next day, in talking with Josephus Daniels, who loved Bryan, I realized how deeply the religious issue had cut. In the committee he had voted for a specific naming of the Klan. "The truth is," said Daniels, "I felt so strongly I should have taken the floor and spoken in favor of the minority report, but I found it painful even to vote against Bryan."

The damage, deadly and certain, had been done, but, as though the convention were determined to destroy the party's prospects completely, there was to be prolonged balloting ahead on the nomination. The contest had become disreputable. "My God," Theodore Dreiser wrote me, "is this the meaning of Democracy?" The Republicans were laughing. The press was pouring oil on the flames. Thus hate grew. Something might have been saved from the wreck had both McAdoo and Smith withdrawn with a plea of harmony, but neither would budge an inch.

That night I had my last close-up contact with Bryan. How changed he was from the handsome, virile, dynamic figure that had stepped out of the window of the State House in Indianapolis in 1896! That night he came up the aisle fanning himself with a palm leaf fan, looking worn and sick and much thinner than I had ever seen him. He made a tragic picture. He who in the darkest days had rehabilitated and galvanized a great party bordering on collapse and had made possible the nomination of Wilson; who for more than a generation had been surrounded by idolaters in every national convention, walked alone, almost ignored. It seemed an unpardonable affront to a great crusader whose work was done. As he approached our delegation, I rose to shake his hand and congratulate him on his fight to keep religion out of politics. He smiled and seemed startled by the novelty, and as he passed on down the aisle he looked back, still smiling.

Up until now even historians have failed to do remote justice to Bryan. When writing an editorial about him on his death I was astonished to find Ralph Pulitzer concerned lest I make a complimentary comment on this man who had made history for a quarter of a century. For the first and only time during my work on the *World* he summoned me to his office. I suggested that a man who for more than twenty years had been a famous national figure, who had three times led the party of Jefferson and Jackson, had been openly credited by Woodrow Wilson with having kept the cause of the people alive and active in dark days, and had pioneered for constitutional reforms that at first had been denounced and then accepted, could not lightly be dismissed with an editorial shrug. It was clear that Ralph was a bit jumpy about it, but the editorial appeared as written.

Now back to the convention. When, too late, McAdoo and Smith released their delegates, the contest—in which no one was greatly interested now—had simmered down to John W. Davis and Oscar W. Underwood, both conservatives. With Smith no longer a contender, the galleries were all but deserted. The convention hall was like a sepulcher. Everyone was dispirited, disgusted, for no one now thought the party had a chance. I was with the Indiana delegation at this stage, when Taggart said to a lieutenant, "Let's end it—who shall it be?" "Toss a coin," was the cynical reply, and on the tossing of a coin the Indiana delegation went to Davis. Taggart moved the nomination by acclamation and this was done with a few ghastly cheers.

It is a pity that so splendid and able a man as Davis should have been put forward as a sacrifice into an impossible situation. His brilliant intellect, his rare charm of manner, his polished, thoughtful oratory deserved a better opportunity. In his mental processes he bore a resemblance to Woodrow Wilson.

On the opening of the national headquarters at the Murray Hill Hotel in New York, before a real organization could be perfected,

Davis, who had liked my book on Jackson, asked Ralph Pulitzer to release me to headquarters to stop the absurd stories being sent out from there. This old hotel with large rooms and lofty ceilings made a mildly sentimental appeal to Democrats, for it was here that Grover Cleveland's campaigns had been planned and directed. It now seemed more like a mausoleum, since the soul had fled. It was in these depressing rooms that I first met John W. Davis personally and fell under the spell of his delightful personality. Tall, graceful in manner, he was dressed in a gray suit. His fine open countenance and his smiling mild blue eyes combined to make him handsome. He began by saying, his eyes laughing, that he wished me to destroy the "Coolidge myth" and to create a "Davis myth."

That same day, in the room of the vice-chairman, I was to note his abhorrence of theatrics. A dozen city Irish of third-rate importance had been called in to enlist them in combating the prejudice that had already been created against the nominee among Irish Catholics. These had told the vice-chairman that some of their people were cold toward Davis because he had been ambassador to England, and others because they resented the defeat of Smith. Unexpectedly the door opened and Davis appeared. Everyone rose, the Irishmen lined up, and Davis went down the line shaking hands cordially but with the dignity with which he would have passed down the line at a diplomatic reception. It was a fine cordiality, but not the kind these men understood. He should have punched them playfully in the chest or slapped them vigorously on the shoulder. Then he turned and looked at the visitors, apparently a little shy and uncertain what was expected of him.

Finally the vice-chairman spoke. "These men are here to help elect you," he said, almost accusingly.

Davis smiled and said, "Strength to their arms. We want every man in the boat and every man with an oar."

There was another embarrassing pause, and the vice-chairman surprised me with an impatient outburst. "Tell them you are an organization man!" he roared.

Davis admitted he was an organization man, looking a bit annoyed by the way he was being put through his paces, and then turned quickly to Mike Hennessy of the Boston *Globe* and engaged him in conversation. Clearly Davis did not qualify as a back-slapping, baby-kissing politician. His speeches, pitched on a high plane, delivered with dignity, without ranting, were addressed almost entirely to the thoughtful minds—and, alas, all voters do not have such minds. His irony, pleasing to some, was beyond the appreciation of many. Though a man of very strong convictions, he gave no outer exhibition of his capacity for wrath. There was not the fierce fire of the killer in his eyes and he never pounded the table or tore a passion to tatters. He had just made his speech of acceptance, a beautiful and brilliant performance, and I jokingly suggested that when he got out on the stump he might want to "slug" a bit. He smiled good-naturedly. "Yes," he said, "some others have told me that I must bend over the table."

The atmosphere at the Murray Hill became depressing. There was much running about, but apparently with no fixed destination. Groups gathered about James Hamilton Lewis, but he was not discussing campaign plans. A member of the finance committee, hard pressed for funds, asked Joe Tumulty how to raise money. "Take over the Mint," he said, and everyone laughed.

The effect of the Madison Square Garden convention was to deepen my depression as to the future of the more liberal party. There was every reason why it should have won in 1924, but its chances had been wrecked by the clash of personal ambitions, the vanity of a few politicians and the injection of the religious issue. It was humiliating to a Jeffersonian to feel as I did, that this deadly issue had been tossed among the Democrats to divide them, in the spirit of the sadist who throws pennies into a crowd of street gamins to see them claw one another.

It was therefore a relief to turn from the contemporary scene to write *Jefferson and Hamilton*, the history of a day when the Jeffersonians presented a solid front and knew what it was all about.

CHAPTER IX

My Jefferson Year

In OCTOBER 1924, McAdoo, just returned from his European tour and still sensitive over his defeat, asked me to join him at the Vanderbilt Hotel for a walk ordered by his doctor. We tramped to Fifth Avenue and trudged along to Central Park.

In front of the University Club he stopped and, pointing to the building, said with a grin, "That place is historic. It was there that Woodrow Wilson offered me the portfolio of the Treasury."

Just then Bernard Baruch joined us, and after a moment he pointed his finger at McAdoo and puzzled me by saying, "Mac, Bowers is the man to write that book."

McAdoo seemed embarrassed, and the subject was dropped. What the subject was I did not know until just before Thanksgiving, when Baruch telephoned me at the *World* asking for a copy of *The Party Battles of the Jackson Period* that very day. He then explained that political friends of Woodrow Wilson had canvassed the field and decided that I should be chosen to write the authorized biography of the President. Baruch was going that day to Washington to have Thanksgiving dinner with Mrs. Wilson, and he was going to urge my selection upon her. He learned, however, that Mrs. Wilson had found among the papers of her husband what appeared to be a commitment to Ray Stannard Baker. Had I been designated, my work would have been cut out for me for some years ahead.

Since the idea had not once occurred to me, the disappointment was not keen. Then, too, I was already zealously at work writing *Jefferson and Hamilton*. That idea had been germinating in my mind ever since I read myself into the Jeffersonian fold in preparing my boyish oration on Hamilton in my Shortridge days. One day Governor James M. Cox, the Democrats' Presidential nominee four years before, telephoned me in Fort Wayne urging me to write a book on Jefferson. Beveridge's biography of Marshall had followed the line adopted by most historians for forty years, of belittling the philosopher of American democracy or at least damning him with faint praise. Two generations had been brought up on adverse propaganda, and Cox thought it necessary directly to challenge this trend. In his memoirs, Cox ascribes the writing of *Jefferson and Hamilton* to this telephone conversation, but in fact I had already begun collecting material for the book.

For at least two generations youth had been fed on the theory that Jefferson was primarily responsible for the Civil War because of the Virginia and Kentucky Resolutions framed by Jefferson and Madison, that he was a liar and a hypocrite, that he was a mere dreamer and an atheist without any sound claim to statesmanship; and the climax of this campaign of misrepresentation had appeared in the scurrilous biography by Curtis. To me he is the greatest of all Americans, the architect of American ideals. The story I had in mind would describe the conflict with Hamilton over fundamental principles, and I felt I could do full justice to Hamilton, for whose honesty and genius I retained the warm admiration of my boyhood.

My office under the gold dome of the *World* looked down upon scenes of the years of their Homeric struggle. The narrow streets of this part of old New York had changed but little. By walking the thoroughfares known to these supreme antagonists of our history I hoped I would be able to capture the very feeling of their times. I found the narrow street near old Kings College where Hamilton the student walked at twilight, meditating on his future; saw Hamilton's home, the Grange, trying to visualize it in the days of his greatness. Through visits to Philadelphia I tried to re-create in my mind the town in which these two men fought their battles, its taverns where in toasts they damned their enemies. Though it was not so important, I visited the home of Freneau, who dedicated his clever pen to the support of Jefferson, and found his grave, with his beloved dog buried beside him.

Firmly convinced that there is no more effective source for historians in the capturing of the atmosphere of other days than the contemporary press, I laboriously turned the yellowing pages of newspapers of the period from 1789 to 1801 in the Astor Library, and through them I absorbed the spirit of the past. The men with whom I was dealing were then as real to me as my own contemporaries.

The book was very well reviewed, not only by historians but also by leading statesmen not given to the writing of reviews; and not only by Democrats but by Republicans as well. Senator Beveridge devoted a full page in the Boston *Transcript* to a remarkable review which was released simultaneously to the Indianapolis *Star*. Senator Borah contributed a fine review to the *New Republic*. James M. Beck, Solicitor General in the Coolidge Administration, reviewed it for the Philadelphia *Public Ledger*. Franklin D. Roosevelt did the review for the *Evening World*, the only book review he ever wrote. John W. Davis wrote the review for the morning *World* and William Gibbs McAdoo for the *International Book Review*. Dr. William E. Dodd of the University of Chicago reviewed it for the New York *Herald Tribune*.

The London edition, put out by Constable, was elaborately reviewed not only in England but in the press of India, Australia and South Africa, and these reviews were as favorable as those in the United States, though papers in Bombay and Calcutta were moved to vigorous polemics as to the relative merits of Jefferson and Hamilton. The book has had a continuous sale now for thirty-three years. In 1948, twenty-three years after its publication in English, a German edition was published in Berlin, and some years later Capelli published an attractive illustrated Italian edition in Bologna.

In the spring following the publication, John Heaton, the grand old man of the *World*'s staff, representing the donor on the Pulitzer Committee, told me confidentially that *Jefferson and Hamilton* would receive the prize. I knew nothing about the Pulitzer Prizes, and I certainly was incapable of writing history to conform to the political views or prejudices of any committee. Heaton explained that the three historians who advised the committee on history and biography had unanimously recommended the book and had added significantly, "No second choice." Consequently Heaton was shocked when the committee rejected their unanimous choice. When four years later the historians recommended my book *The Tragic Era* and were again ignored, it seemed clear that I was on the blacklist of the committee. Heaton emotionally told me what had been done the second time, but it did not matter. When the historians were rejected the second time, Lewis Gannett reported in the New York *Herald Tribune* that the 1930 award showed a sharp division in judgment between the historians and the committee of editors of metropolitan newspapers who were all of one school of political thought. The two books were in complete harmony with the views for which Joseph Pulitzer had vigorously fought, but Pulitzer was dead.

Nothing pleased me more than the fairness and generosity of Beveridge in his review of *Jefferson and Hamilton*, since the book was a challenge to the interpretation of Jefferson in his book on Marshall. Newton D. Baker told me later that Beveridge had told him that had he read *Jefferson and Hamilton* before writing his Marshall he would have greatly moderated his tone on Jefferson.

We had become the warmest of friends. I saw him invariably on his visits to New York at tea, luncheon or dinner, and he never failed to fascinate me. At this time Beveridge was at work on his biography of Lincoln, and I found him an ardent admirer of Stephen A. Douglas. One day, in discussing the effect of a dramatic death on fame, he said, "If Caesar had died peacefully in his bed he would be less interesting to posterity than Cicero; if Lincoln had not been murdered he would have run afoul of the same fanaticism and demagogy that persecuted Andrew Johnson and would probably be an object of controversy to this day; and if Woodrow Wilson had dropped dead on the platform while pleading for the League of Nations, the emotional reaction might have changed the course of history."

On one of his visits to New York he found nothing in the theaters worth seeing, and he amused me with the suggestion that I undertake a play. He thought some chapters of my book disclosed a sense of drama. The idea of attempting a play seemed absurd to me, but I was to have the same idea urged upon me by Jesse L. Lasky and Warner Brothers, apropos of my book on Jefferson. At a meeting of the directors of the Jefferson Foundation, Lasky told me that he had long thought a picture on Jefferson was needed and that he would speak to me about it before leaving the room. When I said I was utterly ignorant of the art of a dramatist, he replied that my part would be confined to working out the plot and that experts in the art would dress it up. He invited me to discuss it in his office, but I did not respond.

Later Warner Brothers telephoned me that they were deluged with protests from Jeffersonians because of the snide treatment of Jefferson in the picture on Hamilton in which George Arliss distinguished himself. The picture was making money, its production had been expensive, and they could not afford to remove it from the screen. They thought the only way to satisfy the Jeffersonians would be to produce a play on Jefferson, and they wanted to discuss it with me. I felt that any fictionalization might reflect on my reliability as a historian, so I declined and threw away an opportunity to make money.

But for *Jefferson and Hamilton* I might never had met Colonel House, Wilson's friend and adviser, who was a most interesting man. I was invited to lunch in January 1926, with the explanation that he had received a dozen copies of my book for Christmas and felt he ought to know me.

He was living simply in an apartment house. A dour Irish maid admitted me to the drawing room and left. Silence. The ticking of the clock sounded like the beating of an anvil. After a while the maid returned, tiptoeing or wearing rubber soles, and started a wood fire in the grate. The drawing room was comfortable, with large sofas, rugs and pictures and a fine portrait of Mrs. House. I went into the library, a small room with books to the ceiling, and there the famous Colonel found me. He too came in noiselessly, like a kitten—a man of short stature, with narrow shoulders and mild features. His manner implied timidity—and he was far from timid—as he sat on the edge of his chair and explained about the books.

Thereafter I saw him occasionally for some years until I went to Spain, and invariably on New Year's Day, when it was his custom to invite ten or twelve friends to lunch. One was almost certain to see there Nicholas Murray Butler, John W. Davis and Norman Davis, and sometimes there was a guest of honor. One year it was Paderewski. When the great Pole entered the room, wearing a flowing tie, and in the manner of a politician gave each guest a hearty handshake, he seemed less formidable than I had feared, and when he directed the conversation into political channels I felt at ease. That day he discussed informally the problem of the Polish Corridor, admitting that the division of German territory was naturally resented, and suggesting a solution that seemed fantastic. He proposed a tunnel under the Corridor, with several railroad tracks, through which Polish goods for export could be conveyed to a port that would be placed exclusively in possession of the Poles. Thus the ground above would remain German territory.

I always enjoyed the conversation of Colonel House. He was most partial to Clemenceau, whom he had visited in his cottage on the Brittany coast. He had found the Tiger stiff and stubborn at the peace conference, but more dependable than Lloyd George. "One might have to struggle with Clemenceau for hours to get an agreement," he said, "but once made it could be dismissed as settled. But Lloyd George! I have known him to agree unreservedly to some line of action and then go immediately into the session and take the opposite line."

Apropos of the visit during the war of Marshal Joffre and Viviani, the brilliant and eloquent French Premier, he told an amusing story illustrative of the character of the two men. Viviani, who with all his brilliance was a peacock in vanity, had been shocked when he rode up Broadway in New York with Joffre to find himself, the head of the French group, ignored, while the multitude shouted lustily for the Marshal. When the visit was over a dispute arose between them as to the time of departure. Joffre was for taking the first boat out, which would sail by the light of the moon, but Viviani, not so hardened to shot and shell and more fearful of submarines, insisted that they should not sail until the dark of the moon, and he was the head of the mission.

Later, when I told this story to McAdoo, he matched it with another, illustrative of the orator. Just before the arrival of the French mission, Arthur Balfour of England had visited Washington, and Woodrow Wilson had attended the joint session of Congress to hear him. When the President failed to appear in Congress for the Viviani speech, a friend of the latter, going to the Frenchman's room, found him pacing the floor in a state of hysterical indignation, insisting he had been snubbed and insulted. When Wilson was informed, he explained that his knowledge of French was not perfect and that Viviani spoke with such lightning rapidity it would have been impossible to understand him. Of course he had read Viviani's speech. It was scarcely an adequate excuse, but undoubtedly the real one. To smooth the ruffled feathers of the peacock, the President gave an elaborate dinner in his honor.

Colonel House was most interesting in discussing Wilson. The world then knew of the break in their intimate relations which had begun in Paris. The Colonel insisted that he did not have the remotest idea how it had come about. He thought Wilson had been dangerously overworked in Paris, where he had insisted on giving personal attention to his voluminous correspondence and had declined the Colonel's offer to act as supersecretary to separate the wheat from the chaff. He thought Wilson's nervous tension might have been responsible for the misunderstanding. However that may be, there can be no doubt that House at one stage rendered services of great value to the President.

At this time I was given another version of the break between them. One evening I was the speaker at a dinner of the Women's National Democratic Club in Washington, when Senator Carter Glass sat beside me. I had admired him from afar but until that night had never seen him. As I was speaking I glanced at him, and a sourer, more disapproving expression I had never seen on mortal face. It was so disconcerting that after several glances had revealed the same expression I resolutely refused to look. When at the conclusion of my speech Glass paid some warm compliments I was the more astonished. I mentioned my experience to Admiral Grayson, Wilson's friend and physician, who laughed heartily, explaining that the expression that had worried me was habitual with the Virginia statesman. Thereafter we became the best of friends.

It was the next day, when I was lunching at the Metropolitan Club with Grayson, Dan Roper and John Barton Payne, that Grayson gave me his version of the breach in the relations between Wilson and House. He said that in Paris House had urged upon the President a certain line of action or policy to which Wilson was averse. Immediately after this, Wickham Steed had an article in the London *Times* strongly favorable to the British line which House had urged. The morning it appeared the Colonel, going to the Crillon as usual, found the President engaged for the moment, and Mrs. Wilson, in greeting him, observed that the President had read with interest "his" article in the London *Times*—since the Steed article was precisely along the line that House had urged. The Colonel said nothing, and a little later he left without seeing Wilson.

These stories of the breach, while coming from men close to the situation and differing in character, may have no historic value, but they can give the future the tone and temper of the time. Incidentally, it should be noted that House and Grayson, both close to the President, disliked each other.

All through 1926 my life seemed to revolve around Jefferson. Years before, my wife and I had made a sentimental journey to Monticello, climbing the road in a broiling sun up the hill that leads directly by the family cemetery to the house. It seemed deserted. With some difficulty we attracted the attention of the custodian, and through his kindness we were permitted to see the entrance hall, but no more, since Monticello was then the private property of Congressman Jefferson M. Levy of New York. The last years of the great philosopher had found him in financial difficulties. Too many decades of self-neglect in the service of his country, too many reverential pilgrimages of strangers to be housed and fed, had reduced him to the necessity of selling his library, which was to become the nucleus of the Congressional Library of today. Soon after his death, the property on which he had lavished his tenderest care and the beautiful house he had designed and loved beyond any other spot on earth were sold to a stranger, and in the stranger's family it had remained until the hour I first saw it. To many it seemed discreditable and disgraceful that the property was not acquired by the nation as a patriotic shrine.

This thought obsessed the beautiful and charming wife of Martin Littleton, the distinguished trial lawyer and orator, then a member of Congress. (I have an unforgettable memory of her from the day of the unveiling of the monument to L'Enfant in Arlington: President Taft attended and Elihu Root and Ambassador Jusserand spoke, but most memorable to me is the picture of a beautiful woman in a bonnet leaning against a pillar of the Arlington mansion. This was Mrs. Littleton. Years later I astonished her by telling her I could describe her dress that day and astonished her more by doing so.) She threw herself impetuously into the task of arousing

Americans to a realization of their disgraceful neglect of Monticello, addressing small societies, importuning men and women,
buttonholing statesmen. She was to fail, but not completely, since
her crusade made an impression. A short time later the Thomas
Jefferson Memorial Foundation was formed, with Stuart G. Gib-
boney as president, and Levy agreed to a sale, fixing a handsome
price. The work of this organization, of which I was governor and
director, was to raise the money. The country was organized.
Solicitors scoured the cities for contributions. The children of the
schools contributed their pennies and dimes. No one deserves more
credit in this work than Theodore Fred Kuper, a young New York
lawyer, who was literally a dynamo in action. At length enough
money was raised to make the purchase possible.

Finally plans were made for the presentation of Monticello to
the nation on July 4, 1926, the one-hundredth anniversary of Jefferson's death and the one-hundred-fiftieth anniversary of the Declaration of Independence. Our party left New York in a special car
on the evening of July 2. The next day we had an experience with
an amusing confusion of values. We drove to Montpelier, the home
of Madison, in an adjoining county, to receive an ungracious welcome from the housekeeper of the mansion, which then belonged
to one of the Du Ponts. The lady stood militantly at the door with
a cold and condescending expression that never could have
launched a thousand ships nor burned the topless towers of Ilium.
A bit timidly, as an approach, one of the party inquired if this
was the home of James Madison. The lady sniffed audibly. Clearly
she felt we did not appreciate the importance of the establishment.
"This is the house of Mr. Du Pont," she replied loftily, and we
were given short shrift.

On the way back, we ran into a rainstorm and were forced to
break our journey in a little village noted for years for the luscious
fried chicken sold by an old Negro woman. We sat in the car and
ate chicken, and, since I was to speak at Monticello at four o'clock
and hoped something would happen to prevent it, the rain was welcome. But, unhappily, we drove into the grounds of Monticello at
four sharp. Just then the rain began again and those assembled had
to crowd into the entrance hall, on which the gallery looked down.

Tremendously impressive to me was the ceremony Sunday afternoon dedicated to Jefferson's Statute for Religious Freedom. The

speakers included Rabbi Goldenson of Pittsburgh, representing the Jewish faith, Father Lyons of Georgetown University, representing the Catholics, and Bishop Manning of New York, representing the Protestants. All faiths were to join in placing wreaths on the grave of the common benefactor of them all. The grounds near the mansion were covered with wreaths. At the appointed time the procession was formed, headed by a band, and with the clerics in the fore, followed by the others, we marched down the hill to the unpretentious grave of the greatest of Americans. I was amused to note the dash with which the rabbi swung along to the music of "Onward, Christian Soldiers." After the placing of the wreaths, we marched back to the mansion for the speeches, just as the rain came down in force to drive us all into the house again.

The speakers spoke from the gallery, and the scene was colorful. The house was almost dark, and since the clerics read their speeches, light for their manuscript was furnished by a candle held by an old white-haired Negro who might have been one of Jefferson's loved household servants revived for the occasion. I can see him now, standing close to Father Lyons, holding the candle, with the other clerics on either side, the flickering flame throwing both lights and shadows on their faces. Bishop Manning could not forget that Hamilton is buried in Trinity Church graveyard, and he surprised us by praising Hamilton's theories rather than Jefferson's. I learned later that the bishop was so concerned over being called on to pay tribute to the author of the Declaration of Independence that he consulted Dr. John Finley of the New York *Times* as to the propriety of appearing!

The formal presentation to the nation was on Monday afternoon in the library of the University of Virginia. Secretary of State Kellogg read from manuscript at some length, and he was noticeably reserved in his tribute to the philosopher of democracy. Senator Walsh spoke brilliantly and without notes. It was then that President Alderman of the university spoke, in presenting me with the Jefferson medal for the writing of *Jefferson and Hamilton*.

Nicholas Murray Butler had told me that Woodrow Wilson thought Alderman the greatest living American orator, and that day Felix Warburg told me that in his youth in New Orleans, when Alderman was the head of Tulane University, he had often heard him, and that he was the most brilliant orator he had ever heard. It would have pleased Wilson to know that Alderman was selected to deliver the nation's tribute to him in the official funeral oration at the joint session of Congress, a very choice masterpiece. In 1926 Alderman had been suffering for some time with tuberculosis of the throat, which affected his voice, and his public appearances were then rare. That day at the university he spoke from a manuscript, which he inscribed and gave me on the conclusion of his speech.

I quote briefly from his speech, partly because it could be taken as an answer to the partisan reticence of Bishop Manning and Secretary Kellogg, but mostly because it contained the most treasured compliment ever paid me, and touched precisely on the reason I had written the book:

Jefferson and Hamilton is a book that will live. There is in it extraordinary vitality and color. It is free from passion and prejudice. A judicial fairness informs its pages. Its sources are varied and dependable. Under the touch of your imaginative genius, Mr. Bowers, the epic story of the formative period marches like a living procession of furiously contending men, dominated justly by the figure of Thomas Jefferson, so portrayed that the gross caricature of him built up by malice and misunderstanding fades from sight, and there emerges a calm, courteous, versatile, patient, steadfast, courageous statesman, alike a master of philosophical theory and statement and a master in managing men, a robust hater of ignorance, tyranny and intolerance, an apostle of peace and a lover of nature and mankind. . . . All honor to Claude Bowers, who has destroyed the monstrous Jefferson of passion and prejudice, of myth and fable, and restored to the vision of his countrymen the myriad-minded statesman and philosopher who forgot the titular honors of the world in the proud reflection that he was the author of the Declaration of Independence, the Statute of Virginia for Religious Freedom, and the father of the University of Virginia.

It was this book that brought me into personal contact with President Coolidge. That year, 1926, Congress created the Jefferson Centennial Commission for the observance of the hundredth anniversary of Jefferson's death. I was made a member of the commission by the President, along with Henry Ford, Felix Warburg, Thomas Fortune Ryan and President Alderman. Vice-President Dawes and Nick Longworth, Speaker of the House, with the leaders of the two parties in House and Senate, were the representatives of Congress.

It was at the initial meeting of the commission in the East Room of the White House that I had my first view of the Yankee President. We were seated facing a small table against the wall when the President was announced. Then he appeared—a slight, slender man, looking down his nose, not even glancing to his right or left or making any sign of recognition to the Congressional leaders who were his friends. He sat down at the table and, without once looking up, began reading a telegram from Warburg. Thus far it was clearly the silent Coolidge of the gossips. Then, having read the telegram, in which Warburg offered to contribute $100,000 to the Monticello fund if a like amount would be subscribed by a Catholic and a Protestant, Coolidge soberly said, "I will authorize Senator Robinson to notify Vice-President Dawes that it is the sense of this meeting that he donate a like amount."

Then he smiled, and I was fascinated by his smile, for he smiled without opening his lips, and the effect was to spread his face and to narrow his eyes almost to a squint. Nevertheless, it registered undeniable mirth. After that he joked at intervals, though the jokes were not side-splittingly funny. I noticed that his ruddy face was without a line, with nothing to indicate the cares of his high office.

Having been made secretary of the commission, I went to the table and was introduced. I had often heard that his handshake was feeble and flabby, but the warm and hearty handshake I received convinced me that the gossip came from ignorance or malice. But not a word did he say. When, a moment later, we went into the grounds for a group picture and I stood beside him, his uncanny silence was unbroken. Not a word was exchanged, and yet the impression of cordiality was there.

It was my last view of Coolidge until, some time later, on the invitation of the state of Tennessee, I made the speech on Andrew Jackson at the unveiling of his statue in the Capitol. Governor Horton was there to make the presentation speech for Tennessee, and President Coolidge to make the speech of acceptance on behalf of the nation. We were to meet in the room of the Minority Leader, just off Statuary Hall, and on entering the room late and finding Longworth and Everett Sanders, the President's secretary, both known to me, just inside the room, I joined them for a chat. When

I observed someone circling around us, I assumed that I had committed some error in protocol. Looking around, I found President Coolidge standing alone against the wall, while the others stood in groups aside. As I approached to greet him I was wondering what to say, in view of my previous experience with his silence, but just as I shook hands I was drawn away to meet some others.

Finally we filed into Statuary Hall and to the platform improvised for the ceremony. There was a delay in starting, and, feeling impelled to say something to the President beside me, I remarked that his last predecessor from Massachusetts had made the greatest speech of his life in that hall when it was the House of Representatives, in defense of the foreign policy of Andrew Jackson. There was a moment's silence. Then he cleared his throat and with a Yankee drawl said, "I well think he might." Since it was difficult to hang any further conversation on that comment, the conversation closed. But I had talked to Coolidge and he had answered.

Apropos of this experience and the tradition about the Coolidge silence, I asked a Senator who had spent a weekend at the White House if he had found the President a difficult conversationalist. He said that at meals when there was other company present Coolidge seldom said a word, but that in the evening when alone with his guest he talked incessantly and pleasantly. "But," the Senator added, "if I touched on politics or policies he became as close as a clam."

After his retirement from public life, when an organization with which I was associated planned a distribution of books to places throughout the country that had no access to public libraries and I wrote to Coolidge asking his approval and co-operation, I received a reply from Northampton, dated October 23, 1930, that sheds some light on his opinion of books and reading.

Your very interesting letter has been received and I feel certain that everyone will approve your proposal. It is probable, however, that the motion picture and the radio are sources of education quite as great as that formerly afforded by books. I assume also that proper attention will be given to the kind of books. There are a great many published now that do not appear to me to be particularly helpful.

I think I ought to add that my experience of being brought up in the country where I came into contact with a great many people who never read books leads me to the conclusion that the harm from lack of books can be overemphasized. Society as a whole could not exist as we know it without a great many readers of books but very many individuals can get along very well without reading books, especially if they have access to newspapers.

It would be a mistake to assume from all this that Calvin Coolidge was a dull man lacking in ideas. He himself read many books, and no doubt he found not a few that he could have done without. And as to his silences, he was rich in Vermont wisdom, and his observations may have taught him that very often silence is golden.

I am afraid he was a bit suspicious about the reliability of Democrats in relation to history. I was asked by the Centennial Commission to prepare the Presidential proclamation to be signed by President Coolidge, and it did appear above his signature as I wrote it. I knew he had read it, since he evidently had not heard that in Jefferson's draft of the Ordinance of 1784 on the Northwest Territory he had included a prohibition of slavery which was finally stricken out because of sectional pressure, though Jefferson was unyielding. One day I had a telephone call from the White House. Was I sure that this prohibition was included in Jefferson's draft? I was, and it remained in the President's proclamation.

It was as a member of the commission that I first met Vice-President Dawes, whose picturesque mannerisms and reputed profanity under provocation had created a general interest in his personality. A meeting had been called in the office of Senator Royal S. Copeland, one of the members, primarily in the hope of devising ways and means of persuading Henry Ford and Thomas Fortune Ryan to match Warburg's offer of $100,000 for the purchase of Monticello. Dawes arrived late; the Senate was preparing to adjourn and there was the usual jam.

He was impatient to get the picture-taking ordeal over. "Damn it, hurry," he said. "Must get back to the Senate. Might be another tie vote. I got hell not long ago when I was not on hand to break the tie for my crowd. They never mention the many times I *am* there."

He sauntered into the room with his familiar underslung pipe and the usual bad-boy grin on his face. When I was introduced he said, "I have never met you, but I have spent a number of evenings with you"—referring to *Jefferson and Hamilton*. Sitting down, he grinned, looked meditatively at his pipe and added, "I will say that you didn't do a damn thing to my old hero, Hamilton. I would read some assertion of yours and say out loud, 'That's a damn lie,' and then I would look down at the citation and find it was from an actual letter of Hamilton's published in his works edited by Henry Cabot Lodge." He gave his head a shake. "You can't get away from that sort of thing," he added. He agreed, however, that Hamilton had been fairly and honestly treated, not misrepresented, and that he appeared in the book as a great genius.

CHAPTER X

The Dance on the Rumbling Volcano

EVERYONE, especially the future victims, seemed extraordinarily happy during the years 1926 and 1927. The stock market was reaching new heights, and therefore the country was considered "prosperous." Every semblance of control over the misuse of wealth and corporate power had been withdrawn, and robust individualism was paying enormous dividends to a few. The atmosphere and psychology of New York in these years bore a striking resemblance to those described in accounts of London just before the bursting of the Mississippi Bubble. Half of the people I knew, living in a fool's paradise, were joyously anticipating riches through the magic of the stock market, which had become literally a gambling den. The speculators were not confined to those with means who could afford to gamble and lose. They included a good portion of the entire population. Riding in the subway to Park Row each morning, I observed that the girl stenographers crowding the cars, who had previously preferred the highly spiced tabloids with their lurid tales of scandals and crimes, had suddenly become sober and intellectual in their taste: the tabloid had given way to the New York *Times*. I was puzzled by the transformation, but the mystery was solved when I noticed that the girls turned at once to the market page. These stenographers were playing the market on their meager earnings. My own friends urged me to "move with the times" and "make a fortune on the market"; and when I was not impressed, they looked their disgust and threatened to let me walk in my rags when they rolled by in their Rolls-Royce cars. Not a few of these friends soon lost all they had and went deeply into debt. But such was the spirit of the times that those who could not see that the country was prosperous beyond precedent were frowned upon as chronic pessimists, if not unpatriotic. Yet even that early the employment agencies were jammed with jobless men and women vainly seeking work.

My most intimate friend for many years was Frank Oliver, then a member of Congress from the Bronx. One evening during these abnormal years I stopped with him for a call on Charles A. Buckley, his district leader, and I was amazed to find a long line of unfortunate men and women stringing from the leader's door into the hall. A sorrier company I had seldom seen—old men crippled, old women with careworn and frightened faces, younger women with babies in their arms. We were admitted at once to the private room of the leader, who heaved a sigh of relief since he needed a few minutes' relaxation before seeing more of the crowd and struggling with their problems. Thus I learned that not everyone was prosperous and happy and getting rich in New York.

Incidentally I learned at that time why Tammany had such a grip on the poor of the tenements. The scene I had witnessed was repeated constantly throughout the year, not just in election periods. A woman with a sick and helpless husband had an eviction order because of nonpayment of rent, and money was furnished to save the family from the street; a child was doomed to lifelong invalidism unless an operation were performed, and it was sent to a surgeon and the cost of the operation guaranteed; a man with a family of hungry children was out of work, and contacts were made with some business and the man got a job. It was this humanitarian service between campaigns that made Tammany strong with the poor. When, on the eve of an election, some righteous reformer appeared before these unfortunates with a denunciation of Tammany it was easy to imagine the reaction. "Where were you when my child was sick?" "Where were you when they were about to turn me out into the street?" "Where were you when I needed a job to feed my children?"

At any rate I saw quite enough in those days to realize that the prosperity of the country was artificial, one-sided and grossly exaggerated.

Even so, I was personally content, since I was deep in research for *The Tragic Era*, a book on the Reconstruction Period. This took me to Lancaster, Pennsylvania, the home of that picturesque old fanatic Thad Stevens, to visit the brick house where he had lived alone, waited upon by a Negro woman described by neighbors as his mistress. Whether she was or not is immaterial, though it was not denied by him. I talked with some who had seen her, and all agreed that she was a kindly, accommodating woman worthy of respect. I was told that when a painter passed through the town, Stevens had him paint her portrait on wood, and I was promised a view of the picture, a promise which was not redeemed.

But I was to hear other things about Stevens I had not heard before. Joseph F. Guffey, who would become Senator from Pennsylvania a few years later, had written a friend about my planned visit, requesting him to act as my cicerone. One day this friend took me to a very old man who had been superintendent of schools in the days of Stevens, and on the way to his house my guide told me that some time before, when chatting with the old man, he had been told that Stevens, who never married, had a daughter. The guide could not broach the subject on our visit, but he hoped the old man would tell me what he knew. Unhappily, while the latter talked freely of many things, the daughter was not mentioned. Directly from his house we went to call on Judge Brown, also oldish, and, to our amazement and delight, we were scarcely seated when the jurist said, "Of course you know that Stevens had a daughter." We hardly moved a muscle, and the judge continued, "When I was a very young law student I was assigned by the court to make a catalogue of Stevens' library. In rummaging about, I opened a drawer, and there, to my astonishment, I found letters wrapped about with a pink ribbon. I read them. They were from this daughter, acknowledging remittances. I know people who knew the woman, and these say she was the image of her bachelor father and a very talented woman. She married and went West. I have no idea who her mother was, but I imagine it was a woman Thad knew in Gettysburg before he moved to Lancaster."

Discoveries such as this diverted my interest from the state of the country. One day a large box was delivered at my apartment, and inside I found enough manuscript to have filled some volumes. I had said to Dr. Andrews, the Baltimore historian, that to get the feel of the atmosphere of Reconstruction days in the South I would like to see family letters and diaries kept at the time by people of no political importance, but that I knew of no possible way to find them. He offered to write to his friend the head of the Daughters of the Confederacy, who could ask women of the hundreds of chapters all over the South to go into old garrets and trunks in search of manuscript. I was to follow his letter to her with one of my own a few days later. She told me my letter arrived the morning after she had read a paper at her literary club on my *Jefferson and Hamilton*, and perhaps this helped. The result was the box, with its scores of intimate family letters reflecting the fears and feelings of the time, and diaries, some written by young girls, all throwing a white light on the actual living and thinking of the people. Reading these, I really lived as a contemporary through those tragic days.

Such was my primary interest through these two years. With greed gone mad in the market place, the populace of New York had their Roman shows to divert them from their worries. Conditions certainly were abnormal, and the atmosphere was just right for the hysterical acclaim of Lindbergh after his flight to Paris. Admirable though this achievement was, the popular reaction amounted to sheer hysteria, whipped up by the press. Perhaps the times were so sordid and money-mad, so crassly materialistic, that the public was starved for something romantic and spectacular. The New York *Times* devoted pages to the flight, and Lindbergh became the darling of the multitude that was verging on disaster. The hero worship was so extreme that when Clarence D. Chamberlin made his flight soon afterward and almost reached Berlin, the insolence of the man in trying to match our popular hero was greeted with growls from the crowd.

From the *World* tower I witnessed the Lindbergh reception at City Hall. The streets near the park were congested hours before his arrival; the *World* was forced to close and lock its doors to prevent an invasion, and I had to sneak into the building by the back way. The windows of surrounding buildings were packed, and not a few spectators found perches on the roofs. A military band entertained the patiently waiting throng.

And then the hero came. Mounted police surrounded his car, and the crowd roared its enthusiasm when the bareheaded youth, serious and clearly astonished, alighted and ascended the steps to the stand. Fourteen stories up came the voice and the words of Mayor Walker, but the words of Lindbergh did not climb so high. Then, with the flyer seated beside Mayor Walker in a car, the procession moved up Fifth Avenue to Central Park while women fainted and men screamed their adulation.

"The poor dear boy," said Pollard's wife, Crystal Herne, who was with us in the tower. "They should let him go to bed."

He had received a greater ovation than Dewey on his return from Manila Bay, greater than Theodore Roosevelt on his return from Africa, greater than Woodrow Wilson on his return from Paris with the Covenant of the League of Nations. Clearly there was some confusion as to values, but this was typical of these two mad years of excitement and false hopes.

Soon we had another Roman holiday, when Queen Marie of Romania was making her tour of the country, and from my window in the tower I looked down upon her reception. The rain had fallen in sheets that morning and there was but a fringe of the curious awaiting her arrival. Despite the rain, the show had to go on. First came the smart-looking soldiers, headed by the cavalry, with the band playing the national anthems of the two countries. Drawn up before City Hall, they stood immobile as statues. At length, the Queen. To my surprise she was received in silence, a curious silence. It had been quite different when Gertrude Ederle came back from her swimming of the English Channel to be received with the shouts of thousands. But Queen Marie had done her part. Her military entourage was brilliant with color, and on the balcony of City Hall she stood with her hand on the wet railing and smiled and waved, though there was no response. Mayor Walker being with her, the party seemed merry, though the silence of the crowd must have been embarrassing. Marie was really regal in appearance and bearing, but the charm of which we had heard so much was not apparent from the balcony, and really her nose was much too large.

And then one day came Madame Curie to have her greeting, but not fifty onlookers were waiting for her. She did not rate a reception comparable to that of those who flew the sea or swam the Channel, and again I marveled. We wanted action comparable to the hectic hurry on the market. Thus we moved on like children laughing too much to hear the rumbling of the volcano.

Franklin D. Roosevelt, standing in the rain in 1944 to urge the fourth election of Robert F. Wagner to the Senate, paid him the perfect tribute when he said that "he deserves well of humanity." It is with some pride that I can claim to have had a part in his first election in 1926.

I became involved, if behind the scenes, under peculiar circumstances. In 1924, though the Republican Presidential nominee carried New York State, Governor Al Smith was elected for the third time and his nomination for President in 1928 seemed assured. But he had one more hurdle ahead. He was up for his fourth term in 1926 and in the event of his defeat he would be eliminated. His friends and followers in New York were gravely apprehensive. Not a few urged a trade with the Republicans, who could have thrown enough Republican votes to Smith in exchange for enough Democratic support to re-elect Senator James W. Wadsworth. Whether such a trade was ever seriously considered by the leaders I do not know, but such trades were not without precedent. Since party principles were not involved in the governorship and were in the Senatorship, this seemed intolerable to me. I therefore wrote an editorial in the *Evening World* calling attention to the spread of this gossip throughout the country and the natural reaction of loyal party men, which could reflect unjustly on Governor Smith, who had no part in it. When nothing happened, I wrote another, stronger than the first, which called forth a statement from Judge Olvany, the Tammany chief, announcing that of course the organization intended to nominate a Senatorial candidate to elect him. In a third editorial I credited Olvany with sincerity, but said that the dissemination of the trade story had made such an impression that it would be necessary for the Democrats to nominate a man everyone knew they did not wish to sacrifice. Soon thereafter it was announced that Wagner, then happy on the State Supreme Court bench, one of the ablest and most respected men in the party, would be nominated. Nothing could have been more satisfactory. He was able, absolutely honorable, liberal, and popular.

Soon after this announcement, Vincent Leibel, law partner of Wagner and later on the federal bench, telephoned an invitation to a dinner with Wagner at the Manhattan Club, with but two others present. That night I saw one of the most constructive humanitarians I have ever known. Wagner entered the private dining room briskly, putting aside his coat and cane while apologizing for his tardiness. He was short in stature, and his strength and character were in his then thin brown face lighted by intelligent gray-blue eyes. He mingled dignity with an air of familiarity. The secret of his popularity was manifest at a glance. His voice was warm and honest, and he talked with fluency and force. No one could doubt his courage and decision. Born in Germany, he had come to New York with his father as a child, and through hard work and family sacrifices he had secured an education and been admitted to the bar. The story of his early struggles was told me by Wagner in the *World* tower the morning after the election. He had served constructively in the Legislature and had made a favorable impression on citizens of good will.

After coffee, I listened in silence to the early part of the conversation. Wagner said the leaders had wished the nomination upon him without notice, and that in the state convention a week later he would have to make a speech. Had he been a gubernatorial nominee he would have felt free of embarrassment, since he had served in both branches of the Legislature and was intimately familiar with state issues and problems. But he had not given very intensive study to national issues and he was being precipitated into a Senatorial contest against a man who had served twelve years in the Senate, dealing with them. He felt, therefore, the need of advice and assistance at the beginning. He was in doubt about the World Court, since the League and all its accessories were still subjects of acrimonious controversy, and into the Mexican problem a religious question had been injected.

We had a talk about these issues, and I also suggested that in the beginning he concentrate on Wadsworth's record on Prohibition, which was obnoxious to the greater part of New York. That year Wadsworth, who had voted to pass the Volstead Act over Wilson's veto, and had approved the successive platforms of his party that had avoided the issue, was posing as a foe of Prohibition. There was a wide space between his pretensions and his record, and the success of Wagner would depend on the attitude of the liberal element. Wagner had been aggressively against Prohibition from the beginning, and I thought the issue with Wadsworth was made to Wagner's order. In the end I was asked to draft the convention speech. I also wrote a second speech, and in this connection I had it impressed upon me that I was in New York, not in Indiana. Leibel, reading my draft and finding the classic quotation "Beware of the Greeks bearing gifts," suggested that perhaps it might be stricken out. This was perfectly satisfactory to me, but I expressed curiosity as to the reason. Leibel replied that there were a great number of Greeks in New York and they might misunderstand. No doubt he was right.

At these dinners my admiration for Wagner grew. He had a fine mind, a good heart and high ideals of public service. He had an innate sympathy with the working masses, then all too rare. He was absolutely clean and honorable. When he was in the State Senate, it was understood by his law partners that a retainer fee of more than five thousand dollars should not be accepted without consultation with him. One day a great corporation appeared with a ten-thousand-dollar retainer fee and was told that Wagner, then in Albany, would have to be consulted. On his return for the weekend, he said that this corporation had very able lawyers regularly employed and needed no legal advice from him, and that the manifest reason for the sudden desire for his services was the fact that the corporation was interested in certain legislation pending before a committee of which he was chairman. "Send the money back," he concluded. And that attitude was all too rare.

After the first two speeches, Wagner began his speaking tour in upstate New York and within a week he had found his stride and needed no more assistance.

Whatever may have been the attitude of party leaders of consequence, many of the underlings continued to talk about Wadsworth's hostility to Prohibition and to urge a bipartisan bargain. While no newspaper attacked Wagner, he received editorial support from none except the *Evening World*. Three weeks before the election, I began running a daily Wagner editorial, aimed directly at those who pretended to see little difference in the records of the candidates on Prohibition. Day by day these were reminded of Wadsworth's vote to pass the Volstead Act over the President's veto, and of his uniform support of his party's platforms. Emphasis was placed on Wagner's liberalism and constructive interest in social and labor legislation. No one on the *World* interfered, but no one commented—no one but Arthur Krock, who said to me one day that I was making a "great fight" for Wagner and that he hoped he would win.

On election night I went to the office to write the postelection editorials, my mind wholly on Wagner, and with many misgivings. Quite early his election was assured. About two in the morning the telephone rang. It was Wagner, who called to thank me for the little I had done in his campaign—and that too is much too rare.

The next morning he came to my office. He was happy, but he seemed embarrassed that his precipitation into the campaign had caught him unprepared. He said he intended to spend the time intervening before taking his seat in making an intensive study of all the national problems "so I will never again be taken unaware." How well he did it the record shows. And that morning I got a glimpse into the mind and heart of Wagner. "I was born out of this country," he said, "and this is the highest honor that can ever come to me. I intend to be worthy of the opportunities America has given me." And then he added wistfully, "My only regret is that my mother did not live to see my election."

This is behind-the-scenes history that would mean nothing if Wagner had meant nothing in the Senate. Serving longer than any other previous Senator from New York, except Rufus King in the first days of the Republic, he rendered more distinguished and constructive service than any other Senator of the commonwealth. No member of the Senate in our history has done so much or fought so hard for social justice, and no New York Senator before him had such a record of constructive statesmanship. He sacrificed his life to his sense of civic duty. I recall a day I spent with Senators Barkley, Guffey and Wagner in Paris. The Congressional session had been a grueling one of constant battle, like most of those of the Franklin Roosevelt regime, and these Senators were on vacation. Wagner had just arrived. He looked terribly tired and worn, in desperate need of rest. That very day of his arrival a cable from Roosevelt begged him to return at once to undertake a task no one else could perform, and the next day he abandoned his vacation and returned to work. Thus he continued until the end, when he collapsed.

I have dwelt on my connection with Wagner's first fight for the Senate because there is nothing in my life of which I am prouder.

Our intimate relations, political and personal, continued through the years, and at his request I put him in nomination for his second term at the state convention in 1932. The last time I saw him was after his election for the fourth time. He greeted me by throwing up his hands and saying I was "the greatest prophet since Biblical times." He had been worried over the election in 1944 and I had written him the prediction that he would run ahead of Roosevelt— and he did.

Thus despite my supposition that my removal to New York would divorce me completely from politics, I soon found myself involved, though my activities were in the wings or behind the scenes. During these two years, 1926 and 1927, the political pot was simmering in preparation for the Presidential campaign of 1928. With the re-election of Al Smith as governor in 1926 there could be no reasonable doubt of his nomination, but he had enemies and rivals who were not prone to concede it.

When I dined and spent the evening with McAdoo in his hotel room, I learned that the former Secretary of the Treasury had by no means abandoned his Presidential aspirations. I had often lunched and dined with him in New York and I had no idea that this particular dinner had any political significance, especially since Mark Sullivan, the able Washington correspondent of the New York *Herald Tribune* and an ardent personal friend of Herbert Hoover, was one of the party of three. McAdoo was to speak before the Ohio State Bar Association the following week and I had seen a copy of the speech he had prepared. It was a stout Prohibition speech, clearly designed to draw the line between the drys of the West and the South and the wets of the East. It seemed certain to me that it would definitively put him out of the Presidential race, since the anti-Prohibition wave was mounting.

That night McAdoo was looking fit, with a springing step, a good color and high spirits, but when I advised against a Prohibition alignment there was a very noticeable cooling of the atmosphere. During the conversation, in developing the theme that the liquor interests were corrupting, he told of an attempt by a representative of the so-called liquor interests to buy his influence just after he had retired from the Cabinet. He had been offered a $100,000 retainer to represent them before the United States Circuit Court and the Supreme Court in an attempt to have the war-time Prohibition law declared unconstitutional. "I was completely flabbergasted," he said. "I had never seen a hundred thousand dollars [*sic*]. At length I told him that while I appreciated the offer, I could not take the retainer. He asked why. I said, 'You don't want to retain my legal services, since I've been out of the practice for years. You want me because you feel that I've built up some kind of reputation resting on the confidence of the people.' 'Certainly,' said the man. 'Reputation is always considered in a retainer.' 'Precisely,' I said, 'and I don't feel it would be giving the people a square deal for me to betray their confidence.' " McAdoo mentioned the man's name.

It was evident that he wished to be a candidate, but he assumed the attitude of one soliciting the opinion of others. He said that Smith's candidacy meant wet and reactionary domination which he himself would not tolerate, but, he asked, why should he himself run? Thereupon he called the roll of other possible candidates, and the two other guests bowled them over, one by one.

Then, too, continued McAdoo, where would the necessary campaign fund come from? Sullivan thought the Prohibitionists ought to raise it. I said but little, shocked at the prospect of another bitter contest like that of 1924. I did suggest that his strength was in his progressive and not his Prohibition views, and at this point the atmosphere was frigid. Knowing Mark Sullivan's intimacy with Herbert Hoover, destined for the Republican nomination, I had the feeling that Mark was less interested in McAdoo's career than in creating another schism within the Democratic Party. I did not blame Sullivan at all, since he was a Republican, but it seemed astonishing that McAdoo did not suspect the journalist's interest in his candidacy on a Prohibition platform.

Toward the close of the evening McAdoo looked tired. Then sixty-four, he was extraordinarily well preserved, but it seemed doubtful that he could stand the bitter fighting in another convention.

Two days later I saw him again at the Hotel Plaza. He was beaming with satisfaction over the reception of his speech before the Ohio Bar Association, which the New York *Times* had printed in full, more than a page. He described his reception as unusually cordial, but he was clearly disturbed by the tone of the *Times* editorial, which said that the speech had eliminated him from the Presidential race.

When I next saw him, two months later, he seemed disillusioned as to his Presidential prospects. He said he would not lift a finger and was not at all sure that he would run. He had a good law practice and he thought it stupid to dissipate his energies in politics. He had opened a law office in Washington, while retaining that in Los Angeles. "This," he said, "will give me an excuse for spending half my time in Washington, where I have friends and the kind of social life I like."

Five months later he sent me a copy of the letter he had written positively announcing that he would not be a candidate. The same day he telephoned to ask my opinion of the letter. I told him I thought it was wise. He talked quite happily about it and as though he meant it. He was to remain in politics and later to enter the Senate from California, but never again was he to figure as a candidate in a national convention.

But the track had not been entirely cleared for Smith. In November 1927 Senator James A. Reed of Missouri asked me to call upon him at the Waldorf. I was rather shocked by his appearance. I recalled him as I had seen him first in Washington fourteen years before: a magnificent physical specimen, with a fighter's face, and a genius in debate unequaled by any of his colleagues. Now he was slightly stooped and his hair was perfectly white. His face, while ruddy, seemed a little shriveled and was much wrinkled, and he appeared much older than his years.

Long before this he had compromised his position in his party because of his feud with Woodrow Wilson, but a few days before I saw him he had delivered a brilliant philippic against the Coolidge Administration at Sedalia, Missouri, and he had been endorsed by the State Committee for the Presidential nomination.

That day I found a woman sculptor at work at a bench on a bas-relief of the Senator. He had been posing all afternoon, reading the while. His fine profile lent itself beautifully to the work. "I don't know what she intends to do with it," he said, "but I guess she hopes to sell it." When I suggested that it might serve as a campaign piece the next year he laughed, but said nothing. But he did say that he had not made his Sedalia speech for the purpose of launching a Presidential campaign. "If that had been my intention I would have left out the personalities," he said, and this seemed sincere. Referring to his endorsement by the State Committee, he said he could have stopped it, and would have but for the fact that the committee on two previous occasions had read him out of the party. "I always hoped," he said, "that one day they would wipe that out, so I let them go ahead the other day."

It seemed incredible that a politician as wise as Reed could have conceived it possible that the party would so completely repudiate Woodrow Wilson as to nominate one of his most virulent enemies. Even that day he talked with unrestrained bitterness against the war President. "If we had elected Champ Clark," he said, "there would have been no war and the other countries would have let us alone."

But he was clearly a candidate.

Meanwhile, in New York few doubted the nomination and election of Al Smith. There was nothing to indicate that a religious war of fanaticism would be waged against him, but here and there one could sense an opposition to his nomination. I was not involved at that time, personally or emotionally. *The Tragic Era*, on which I was at work, kept me occupied. I think I was more interested in Theodore Dreiser in those years than in any of the aspiring politicians. It was in his apartment that I had contact with men and women of the literary world. I hardly knew Carl Van Doren when he stopped at the table where I was lunching at the Players club to ask me what I was writing; and when I told him I was working on *The Tragic Era* he startled me by saying that he would take it for the Literary Guild without seeing the manuscript. He had discussed *The Party Battles of the Jackson Period* in complimentary terms in a lecture at Columbia University before I went to New York, and I was to be deeply indebted to his friendship in my literary work, but among the writers it was Dreiser with whom I was on most intimate terms. Putting aside the premonitions of economic disaster and the maneuvering of politicians, we shall now spend a little time with him.

CHAPTER XI

Memories of Theodore Dreiser

To ME the most interesting and significant literary figure in the New York of the first and second decades of the century was Theodore Dreiser. In Terre Haute, where he was born, I had heard many stories about his family. That community took great pride in his brother, Paul, whose "On the Banks of the Wabash," written in part by Theodore, had been accepted as the regional song. The family had lived in sordid poverty, and he himself has recorded the pathetic story of his boyhood in an autobiography. His father, a German immigrant, was so obsessed with his religion that most of the little money that he made was given to the church, and to prevent her children from going barefoot in winter the mother worked as a scrubwoman in a hotel. For this Theodore was never to forgive his father. The family lived in a small house, which is now being preserved as a memorial, across the street from the county jail. To my amazement, the Terre Hauteans appeared to have little appreciation of the infinitely greater work of Theodore, preferring the song of Paul. Dreiser's *Sister Carrie*, which shocked the Philistines with a realistic treatment of human problems in fiction, had probably persuaded them to join in the silly crusade against him.

On the appearance of his novel *The Genius* and his autobiography, I had written a review and an editorial in the Fort Wayne *Journal-Gazette*, and a mutual friend sent him a copy of the editorial. He wrote me a note of appreciation that impressed me as sincere. "Thank you very much for your editorial," he wrote. "You write an editorial as colorfully as you write a book. One mistake, however. Paul and I were born in different houses in Terre Haute. Our family had to move, evidently to keep ahead of the rent collector." When, later, I sent him my review, he wrote: "The same morning that brought your review of 'The Genius' brought the enclosed from The Times here. Yes, I guess from several straws that the wind is slightly veering in Indiana. This review of yours should do as much as anything—a fine piece of writing, really. I like it ever so much and I am obliged to you. . . . If you come this way drop me a line and have dinner with me. I hope you do."

I concluded that despite his affectation of indifference he was hurt by the attitude of his native state, and that a friendly review from that quarter pleased him. He asked me to get in touch with him if I was ever in New York and gave me his address and telephone number. It happened that within a month I went to the New York *Evening World,* and, being alone in the hotel one night, I called him on the telephone. He said he would be up immediately.

I was in the lobby when he appeared. Tall, stout, with a large, roughhewn face, he was almost elephantine in his movements, and he impressed me instantly as coming from peasant stock. I noticed especially his queer blue eyes. His manner was simplicity itself. There was nothing of affectation, no pose. With him was Helen Richardson, a beautiful young woman with laughing eyes and a perfect complexion, who later was to become his wife. We sat for a while on the balcony overlooking the lobby of the McAlpin Hotel and then went to the Prince George for sandwiches and beer. As he talked I noticed his now famous eccentricity—a never-ending rolling and unrolling of his handkerchief. He talked frankly of the poverty of his childhood and the supercilious attacks upon his work by the more precious critics. Though it was clear that these had hurt him deeply, for he was extraordinarily sensitive, they appeared that evening to amuse him, for he chuckled as he talked.

"I don't read criticisms or reviews," he said. "Even when they're intended to be friendly they often take a slant that is not flattering, so I pass them up." He paused, then smiled and chuckled again. "Do you know Dr. Smyth, long literary editor of the *Times?*" he asked. I knew him as the editor of the *International Book Review,* for which I had written some reviews. "I met him at a sort of book-men's dinner," Dreiser continued. "I had never met him before, and he came around to my chair to tell me how glad he was to meet me, and that he had been one of my most persistent boosters. As a matter of fact, his paper had been one of my most severe critics, and I told him so. He remonstrated. We had been drinking some, and I was in the mood to be offensive, so I filled a water glass half full with liquor and said to him, 'If you're a friend of mine, you'll drink this with me.' I had no notion that he would do it, for it was a deadly potion and he seemed delicate and not young. But he did. Under my direction we got him upstairs to a room and got a doctor. It was some days before he was out. I called up to see how he was, and he answered in a feeble voice that he was all right. 'No hard feelings?' I asked. 'Oh, not at all,' he said. After that we were friends."

That evening, in reminiscent mood, he recalled his experience as a callow reporter on the New York *World*. It was in the days of the elder Pulitzer. Everyone was kept on his toes by that colossus, and Dreiser recalled that the city room was always throbbing with nervous tension. Every day cables poured in from Pulitzer's yacht in the Mediterranean, slashing viciously at some story he did not like and giving orders. "I often went home sick at my stomach from nervousness and worry," said Dreiser, "though no one ever said anything to worry me." Finally he was discharged from the paper.

Soon afterward I visited Dreiser in his apartment on West Eleventh Street, in Greenwich Village. The block was old-fashioned and attractive, and he lived in one of the Rhinelander Gardens houses, a long row of three-story brick houses with wrought-iron balconies and deep front yards, the property of the old aristocratic Rhinelander family. Dreiser lived on the ground floor in two rear rooms—large rooms with the lofty ceilings of spacious times. I entered through his bedroom, where a huge and very high three-quarter bed first caught my eye. By the door was an antique walnut cupboard with glass doors which could be used for either books or china—the property of the Rhinelander family, left there in storage. Dreiser called attention to it, moving his hand over it almost reverently, for its beauty appealed to him.

From the bedroom one entered the study, a much larger room with wide, high windows that looked out over a back yard where someone's washing was flapping on the line. A bright May sunshine was pouring in. In the center of the room was a long table on which he wrote. Beside it, on a small table, stood a typewriter of ancient make. On one side wall hung the picture of a woman, and opposite, against the wall, was a bookshelf made of boxes. Most of the books were in fresh jackets, gift copies from the authors or publishers. On top of the bookshelf stood a coffee percolator. On the broad window seat was a stack of manuscript, much marked, and Dreiser explained that he was writing *An American Tragedy*. "I call it that," he said, "because it could not happen in any other country in the world."

That day Dreiser was in the best of moods, smiling and laughing heartily, and seeming in excellent health, his face ruddy. As always, he played incessantly with his handkerchief as he talked. I soon learned that he preferred almost any other subject for conversation to his own books, but I managed to draw him out a little bit on his work.

"I have heard that you like *Twelve Men* better than any other of your books," I ventured.

He shook his head.

"No, I like it because of my portrait of Paul, but I wouldn't say that I like it better than any other," he said.

"*Jennie Gerhardt?*" I hinted, merely to get his estimate.

"No, I don't like Jennie so much. I formed a dislike for it almost as soon as I had finished it. I wrote it in an emotional mood and liked it immensely in the process of composition, but almost immediately afterward I concluded that I had overdrawn Jennie. I think so still."

"I have known some women after whom she might have been drawn," I ventured to say.

"Well—" and he laughed—"I can't say that I ever have." Then, after a pause: "Some people think *Sister Carrie* the best. I like *The Genius* best of all. There's more of myself in it. I don't know. I get all sorts of preferences from other people." With a chuckle, he added, "Liveright [his publisher] likes *The Titan* best, maybe because he too is a bandit."

He then shifted the conversation to politics—a subject that interested him strongly, though I was to find that his views were mostly fantastic.

"Do you think that democracy has worked out in this country?" he asked in a manner that indicated clearly that he did not. "Do you think this form of government is the best?"

I admitted that at times plutocracy had been in the ascendancy. But, I said, this was not because of but in spite of our democratic system, and I reminded him that when the people were aroused, as when Jefferson overthrew the Federalists and when Jackson unhorsed the national-bank plutocracy, the rule of the people had been real under our institutions.

"I don't know of any better form, do you?" I asked.

But he did not reply.

That his skepticism was real is evident in the inscription he wrote later in a gift copy of *An American Tragedy*: "To Claude Bowers, whose duty and business is to crystallize and visualize for America that democracy which as yet is a vague and nebulous dream."

Suddenly he said passionately, "You enjoy life, don't you? Do you never get morbid, depressed and disgusted?"

And with that question I knew he had lifted a curtain on himself.

I soon saw that Dreiser looked out with some distaste on the world about him, and that much pondering on man's inhumanity to man had made him a little bitter. All this appears in his novels, his pity for the frailties of man, his compassion for the underdog. This gave the tone to all he wrote. About this time he wrote me: "I greatly acknowledge your evaluation of my writing principles. I think it springs from a fairly close observation of the working principles of life. There is the old saw, to know all is to forgive all, although in some cases in my experience, it seems hard to believe."

One day when he was walking with me on the street in a happy, hilarious mood, we passed a wretched old woman in rags and with misery etched on her face. "God, look at that!" he exclaimed. "Is there any excuse for that?" His mood changed at once and we finished our walk in gloomy silence. It was not an affectation of sympathy for human suffering with Dreiser, it was real.

At dinner one night in my apartment he expressed an unfavorable opinion of the movie industry of the time—an opinion to be strengthened soon when he went to court in a vain attempt to prevent the mutilation of a novel of his. That night he looked upon the movies as a failure, primarily because of what he termed "the ignorance and spiritual and dramatic limitations of producers and artists." He thought the movie stars "shallow-pated, pretty creatures who have no knowledge of psychology or of life." Of the directors he had a view scarcely more favorable. Apropos of the recent murder of a director soon after he had entertained Mabel Normand, the actress, described by the press as a star of the first magnitude in her time, he illustrated the mentality of the stars by citing Miss Normand's tribute to the dead director as a great intellectual because, she said, "you can ask him the meaning of any word and he can tell you."

This poor opinion of the directors, along with the players, was to have an unfortunate sequel for me. One night as I was leaving a party at Dreiser's and, in a downpour of rain, had just caught a taxi, a woman of my acquaintance who had also been a guest appeared with another woman on the sidewalk, and I proposed to drive them to their homes. The strange lady was strikingly beautiful. During the drive, my friend observed that Dreiser cared little for the movie stars. "Yes," I replied, "he says they are morons and that the directors are very little better." There was silence in the taxi. We reached the apartment of the strange lady first, and after she had left I inquired her identity of my friend. "Her husband is quite a famous movie director," was the crushing reply.

Soon after moving to New York, my wife and I were guests of Dreiser at dinner. He had proposed some place in the Village and had written a reminder: "Friday at six or seven, suit yourself, it's OK with me. Do you mind ringing my door bell? There are dozens of these evil dens within a few blocks, and, Satan aiding, it will not be too much trouble to walk. Besides, crime is so rampant here that it is interesting to observe it as it proceeds."

It turned out to be the Russian Bear, on Second Avenue near Twelfth Street, frequented by Bohemians and radicals who thought themselves enamored of the Soviet. Bearded, spectacled, vociferous, gesticulatory, they roared applause when a dark-skinned fellow sang Russian songs none understood.

That night Dreiser again amazed me by his interest in politics and his abysmal ignorance of it. He was a radical thinker, that was clear. He resented Wilson because of the war. The Democratic national convention at Madison Square Garden was but a few days off, and he seemed keenly interested in McAdoo's candidacy. Later I was to conclude that his partiality for McAdoo was due less to McAdoo's political character than to the Tammany affiliations of Governor Smith, his competitor. "Of course," said Dreiser, "if La

Follette is nominated I shall vote for him." It was a safe wager that he would not vote at all.

A few days later I sent him two tickets to the convention. The day after he attended I received a letter from him: "Thanks for the Convention tickets. (See Index World Morgue, Convention Series, 1924.) Also how are you? That horrible Convention all but did for me. I gave up on the 18th Ballot and did not return. (Texas votes 60 for McAdoo.) As to dinner next week—sure—only I'll have to call you up on Monday or Tuesday. I am still hard worked. Just got back from a side job in Detroit—that wretched burg. All that I have in view is apple pie." (We had a Virginia cook who made good apple pie that Dreiser liked.)

When I saw him next I asked his impression of that rowdy convention. An expression of pain or loathing contorted his features. "My God," he said, "one session was enough for me. And is that the way we're governed in a democracy?"

The night at the Russian Bear he had tried to smoke a cigarette, and he did it gingerly, awkwardly and in evident distress, spluttering and coughing. I was astonished to learn that he was not a smoker. Laughing, he said that when, years before, he was the editor of a women's magazine, he occasionally was invited to little parties at the houses of some of his women associates, and invariably the air was blue with the curling smoke of the cigarettes of the women. Once, in sheer desperation, he determined to join them, only to struggle and sicken. "There I was," he said, "a six-footer of ample poundage, growing giddy in doing what every woman was doing with evident relish, and I was ashamed."

At this time he was working steadily on *An American Tragedy*, the manuscript of which I had seen in the window seat of the apartment on Eleventh Street, and the publisher was announcing it for publication in the fall. In September I asked him about it.

"It will not be ready until spring," he said.

"But the publisher—" I began.

"I can't help that," he barked angrily. "You can't write any faster than you can."

A little while before, a woman who was managing a small theater in a basement in the Village had surprised me by her bitter comments on Dreiser. I asked him if he knew her. Again the expression of physical loathing and mental torture, and he groaned aloud. "Oh, what's the use of talking about her?" he gasped. And then he talked about her. "A vampire without passion, but with a keen appetite for money," he said. "She gets her actors and actresses for nothing, holding out the futile promise that some manager from Broadway will drop in and pick them up. She lives in the cellar and has little expense. She plays her sex against men who are in position to help her—especially newspapermen. If you're expecting to get anything out of it, forget it. She smiled all over me when she thought she could use me. The first thing I knew she was producing one of my plays without leave. I tried to stop her and make her pay, but she only smiled and went ahead." And then, with a heavy sigh: "Why, I had to get a lawyer before I could make her stop."

It had been a mistake to mention the woman, for Dreiser remained gloomy throughout the remainder of the evening. Perhaps that gave acidity to his remarks about Frank Harris' erotic autobiography, which had been forbidden in New York. Harris had written Dreiser from France offering him a set for fifteen dollars. "No art," snorted Dreiser. "Nothing but the nastiest stories, without any art in the telling even, and illustrated with obscene pictures having no connection with the text—pictures of the kind you pick up on the streets of Paris when no one is looking."

He twisted his handkerchief a while in silence.

"I think that Harris is about three-fourths genius," he added, "but the one fourth that is not kills the other three fourths."

The first time Dreiser came to dinner in my apartment I had enticed him with the promise of apple pie, Hoosier variety. "How about Wednesday, May 21 next?" he wrote. "And if the apple pie is what it should be—fair Indiana pie—I will partake of it. But where do I travel to?" He evidently liked the pie, since I find another later note from him: "And I never ate better apple pie. Only my manners cheated me of a second piece." And much later, apropos of another dinner invitation: "All I have in mind is apple pie."

One of the most enjoyable evenings I ever spent with him was in the winter of 1925, after he had left his apartment on Eleventh Street and taken one in Brooklyn. My wife and I were invited to a duck dinner he had promised to supervise in the cooking. He had sent me a note giving the street number and the number of his telephone, with directions on how to reach his place. We found the street, but there was no such number on it. I rushed to a drugstore telephone and told him of our trouble.

"Then you're just a block away," he said.

We renewed the search, but it was no use and again I had recourse to the telephone. It turned out that absent-mindedly he had given the telephone number as the street number of the house as well. I had his blunder in his own handwriting, but I found him thoroughly annoyed and resentful, though he did greet us with rather sour laughter.

It was a fantastic Dreiser that loomed in the doorway. He wore a blue smock such as a painter uses, to protect his clothing against grease and gravy, since he had personally seen to the cooking of the duck. Never had I seen him in a happier, more boyish mood. The apartment was simple but comfortable, with a piano, many books, easy chairs. After the cocktails he brought in the duck, wheeling it in on a serving table. The cooking of that duck had been a rite. He explained very earnestly that it was of prime importance that duck should be cooked just right. Never in a restaurant had he had duck cooked properly. This one had to be. Helen Richardson had been impressed with the importance of the rite, and though she had been afraid to leave the kitchen in the afternoon, all she was permitted to do was to stand and wait while he pottered about the stove.

At length the serving table was wheeled up to the very small table where we ate, and the big burly man in the blue smock presided and served the duck with the glowing pride of an artist contemplating his masterpiece.

We discussed Booth Tarkington over the rapidly disappearing duck, and Dreiser, the realist, gave his version of the mission of the novelist as an interpreter of his time. He was disappointed in Tarkington as an interpreter of life. "He does not know reality, does not know life, work, the average human being, or sex," he said. "The best and most ambitious thing he has done is *The Turmoil*, and I thought he was going to do something with it. The subject was big—a modern captain of industry and his reaction to society, and society's reaction to him. But he had this industrialist a dreamer, getting things in a mess until a poet with no business training stepped in, waved a magic wand and brought order out of chaos.

It's not real life. If he had dealt only with the raw realities, what a marvel he would be with his exquisite style."

When *An American Tragedy* was published no one was more astonished than the author by its enthusiastic reception. Sherman of the New York *Herald Tribune*, who had been such an uncompromising purist earlier that he had severely condemned *Sister Carrie*, was almost fulsome now in his praise. That surprised Dreiser most of all. "I wonder," he said thoughtfully, "if the book is any good." With all his erstwhile enemies praising his latest work, Henry Mencken, who had been his valiant champion against the field of hostile critics, was tardy in coming forward. I reminded Dreiser that Mencken had made his reputation by being against the field and perhaps his inclination had not changed. He laughed —but the adverse criticism came.

Abnormally sensitive to criticism, Dreiser had left New York just before the publication date to escape the reviews, and on his return from Florida he invited Sybil and me to dinner. He and Helen were living in a hotel at the corner of Broadway and Sixtieth Street, and we went out to a little Italian restaurant nearby for dinner. The novel had been a sensational success and it was announced that the movies had bought the screen rights for an extravagant amount. All his life Dreiser had been true to his ideas and ideals, seeing his best novels suppressed or belittled, reaping scant monetary rewards from any of them; and now, at length, he was acclaimed, and the money was rolling in. With the shame-faced expression of a man confessing to having taken advantage of a blind man in a horse trade, Dreiser said, as though unable to believe it himself, "What do you think? They gave me ninety-eight thousand cash!"

I had heard that he had had some difficulty with Liveright, his publisher, at a dinner at a hotel to discuss business arrangements with Lasky, the producer. That evening Dreiser described the actual event. There had been a dispute about some phase of the arrangements and Liveright had called Dreiser a liar. The novelist rose to his full six feet one inch and invited Liveright to stand up. Taking discretion to be the better part of valor, the publisher did not budge from his chair. Thereupon Dreiser took up a cup of coffee, dashed it into Liveright's face and stalked unmolested from the room. Chuckling over the incident, he added that Liveright had been writing him "love letters ever since."

I saw Dreiser after his return from Europe, when he was bubbling with enthusiasm for the Scandinavian countries and over "the wholesome beauty of their women and their indifference to the capitalization of their charm." Vienna had impressed and depressed him as a dead city, poverty-stricken and pitiful, but he was enthusiastic about Czechoslovakia. President Masaryk, who had recently written a book about America and devoted an entire chapter to Dreiser, invited him to the palace as his guest and the novelist finally found a politician he could admire. The picturesque old statesman had told him of his plans for the development of the country and had insisted on its capacity to sustain forty million people. "But why change?" Dreiser had asked, thus illuminating his own taste. The old man had smiled knowingly. "Because we must progress," he replied, laughing.

In England Dreiser had been surprised by the mania for things American. "Dramas from America that we consider third-class here are playing to crowded houses," he said.

The next time I saw Dreiser he had entered upon a new but, happily, temporary phase. It was a long cry from the old-fashioned rooms on Eleventh Street with the neighbor's washing flapping on the line outside his windows to the imposing studio apartment at 200 West Fifty-seventh Street. There was one very large room, the ceiling two stories high, with a balcony on the second floor off which the bedrooms opened. Off the large drawing room was a tiny dining room, which was seldom used, and off that a kitchen. In the drawing room a fire was blazing, and a long sofa was drawn up in front of it. A few paintings were on the wall, one a large canvas of a woman in the nude. A Russian wolfhound lay on a rug in front of the fire. It was a corner apartment, and high stained-glass windows looked out on two streets. A piano stood in one corner, an ornate writing desk in another. Dreiser was dripping with prosperity.

This apartment was vastly different from his former habitations, and it seemed to me less the atmosphere and environment for Dreiser and his work. I knew he had grimly struggled against adversity, producing some great novels, and I wondered if the luxurious surroundings would not dull his pencil. I was rude enough to ask him point-blank, but he misinterpreted what was in my mind.

"No," he said, frowning. "I see no one during the day, and it's quiet up here"—for his apartment was high up.

It seemed to me that for a moment Dreiser had made himself a subject for a Dreiser novel—the poor boy whose life had been one of intense labor in very simple surroundings, darkened by abuse and injustice, who had had his dreams of more luxurious living and who now was in a position to realize his dreams. What would prosperity do to the writer? I wondered.

He had written me a note saying that he was having "Thursday Evenings" and that since "all the seven arts" would be represented he expected there would be "good talk." Years before, he added, he had had a small salon on Tenth Street until too many came and they became argumentative and quarrelsome, and since it gave him headaches he had given it up.

That first "Evening," Dr. Abraham Brill, who had introduced Freud to America, was there when we arrived. Soon the other guests poured in, and cocktails were served generously. A large man with rather scant sandy hair and a blond mustache appeared, and Dreiser introduced me to Ford Maddox Ford, the English novelist, who was in New York as a visiting critic on the *Herald Tribune*. He lived in Paris. He explained that he had been gassed in the war and could not live in London because of the climate, though I believe there were other reasons as well. Dreiser thought his salon the most interesting in Paris. He seemed that night a gross monument of indolence—too indolent even to enunciate clearly, and it was difficult to understand him. Learning that I was on the *World*, he complained that we had misquoted him and had refused to make a correction. His real grievance was that we had said that he had "a little wisp of hair."

"Now look at me," he said. "Does my hair seem as thin as all that?" I really thought it did. He did not talk shop, but drifted lazily along with quaint small talk. We left that night as Ford was leaving with a beautiful, rather voluptuous woman we assumed to be his wife. In the taxi the lady became eloquent on children, and Sybil asked about hers. Rather mournfully, she replied that she had none of her own, but that she did much work among the poor children. Ford looked amused. The explanation of his amusement came the next day when I was telling a young woman on the *World* about Ford and his wife. "I understand that he does not marry them," she said.

That first night Dreiser, in his blue smock, seemed boyishly, radiantly happy, but disappointment was just around the corner. That night a comely and neat colored maid passed the cocktails; the second of the Evenings found a butler in charge. Dreiser again appeared in his smock, which could have stood a washing. The company was larger. The butler constantly passed around with cocktails and whiskey, and few passed the cup by, since this was in the days of Prohibition. Dreiser took me over to a large meaty-faced man, with not much in his appearance to suggest the leader of a religious flock, and introduced Dr. Percy Grant, the Episcopalian minister at St. Mark's-in-the-Bouwerie, who had been shocking the hierarchy by staging dances in the church. But he was interesting, and he won me by his praise of Bryan.

But the most interesting person there was Elinor Wylie, the poetess and novelist, who had just published her novel on Shelley. Hers had been a colorful career. After her matrimonial complications she had begun to write poetry and fiction, and she wrote exquisitely. She was then married to William Rose Benét, also a poet. I had met her first at the home of William E. Woodward, whose provocative biography of Washington had just been published. She appeared a little late that night. Beautiful, very girlish, a little wild in her exuberance, she stood in the middle of the room displaying a new gown with the delight of a child, fairly glowing in response to the compliments her dress and manner invited. A woman of great talent, if not of genius, a literary craftsman of finesse, she always seemed to me a peacock spreading its tail to invite admiration. It was not possible to doubt her vanity, but her friends loved her none the less for this weakness, while freely commenting upon it. That night at Dreiser's when she approached him with an offer to read at the next party some of the poems of her "boy friend," meaning her husband, an ill-natured woman exclaimed, "See, she's determined to be the center next time."

Meanwhile I listened for the sparkling conversation promised by Dreiser and heard none. The next time two male servants passed the cocktails, and Dreiser abandoned his smock for a dinner coat.

The personnel of the party had also changed. The two Van Dorens, Carl the critic and Mark the poet, were there, and Joseph Wood Krutch, the brilliant drama critic of the *Nation*, Ernest Boyd the Irish critic, Liveright, and many lesser lights who appeared with pretty young girls, drawn more by the free liquor, I suspect, than by the promised "talk." Some sat in circles on the floor, flirting, exchanging witticisms, and it was worth a journey to see Ernest Boyd's whiskers bob when he laughed.

Dreiser viewed the scene with darkening brows. "I'm afraid these parties are going to get wild," he said plaintively. He walked about trying to engage some of the guests in "talk," but they would have none of it.

But the next week there was an improvement. I had received a note from Dreiser: "Wassermann the German novelist, Max Reinhardt the Berlin producer, Frank Walsh the lawyer and Otto Kahn are all due here Thursday night. Thought you might want to know." The guests that night were notably different. There was no flirting on the floor, and the company was more impressive and better dressed. It was the night of the initial performance of the opera *The King's Henchman*, by Deems Taylor and Edna St. Vincent Millay, and quite a number came in afterward in evening dress. I was taken over to a short stout man with a glistening face and introduced to Max Reinhardt. His appearance was disappointing, since he looked more like a stockbroker than the great artist that he was. Otto Kahn, fresh from the Metropolitan, handsome, distinguished in bearing, ingratiating in manner, mingled with the company. In the dining room sat a man who reminded me of a gypsy—slender, not tall, with narrow shoulders and the suggestion of a slouch. I had seen many like him conducting gypsy orchestras. His face was dark, his black eyes darted here and there. He was surrounded by a group of admiring women. This was Jakob Wassermann, author of *The World's Illusion*. He mingled but little with the guests.

This was the most distinguished company that was to attend these "Thursday Evenings."

It was after this that Dreiser went to Russia. On his return he seemed in the best of health and spirits, and he appeared pleased with his Russian journey. From Helen Richardson, however, I heard a different story. Accompanied by a Soviet guide in his me-anderings, and suspecting that he was being managed, Dreiser barked too many questions, and the guide wondered if he were entertaining a capitalist spy unaware. His departure was accordingly delayed. Helen, hearing nothing from him, went to Istanbul, expecting a message there. Nothing. Unable to speak the language, ignorant of the customs of the country, she was distressed until she found a Turkish taxi driver who had lived in New York, and she clung to him as to the rock of salvation. At length she heard that Dreiser was having trouble getting his exit permit. He finally emerged, greatly depressed and nervous, and Helen hurried him to Paris to revive his spirits. But from Dreiser I heard nothing to indicate that his Russian sojourn had not been a veritable delight. His sole complaint was that the Russians had a rule forbidding an unhappy ending of books or plays.

The "Thursday Evenings" were renewed after his return, and they reached their climax on an evening crowded with entertainment. An attractive young Hungarian woman, who had scored a triumph on the Berlin stage the winter before, sang. She had a beautiful voice, her manner was charming, and she sang songs then in fashion with a verve that brought resounding applause and many encores. But her triumph almost deprived us of the privilege of hearing Nina Koshetz, formerly a famous soprano in St. Petersburg in the time of the Czar. This artist was huge in girth, but with a pretty face. She had been warmly acclaimed by the critics after her recital in Carnegie Hall. But she was ruffled by the triumph of the other singer, and when asked to sing she complained that she could not do so until all smoking had been stopped for half an hour. The smokers extinguished their cigarettes. But at the end of the stated period the buxom artist still was petulant and refused. Dreiser coaxed; she was adamant. He then tried to put his arm around her, but there was not arm enough. However, the coaxing finally succeeded. She sang marvelously well, with a dash and spirit that were truly moving.

After she had finished I congratulated Dreiser, who seemed boyishly happy, on the brilliance of his entertainment. Looking mysterious, he said, "The best is yet to come." Finally a dozen Congo Negroes, all but naked in costumes representing various animals and birds, filed into the room with their tom-toms and swept into a Congo dance. It was a warm evening, the room was close, the air was anything but pleasant. Dreiser watched the performance with sparkling eyes. To him this was the best. Here was something primitive. Another side of Dreiser was revealed.

One day in March 1930 I found Dreiser alone in his huge living room working at an enormous writing desk made out of an old piano. He wore neither coat nor vest. For the first time I noticed a large portrait of him by Wayman Adams, another Hoosier. That day he was on a rampage because, with the money already subscribed, the people of Terre Haute had done nothing about the memorial for his brother Paul. "What they ought to do," he said, "is buy the old house, which can be had for a song. I promised to give them Paul's organ and some other things of his that could make an interesting museum, but they have big plans and nothing is done." A few years later the old home was bought and a beautiful boulevard bearing Paul Dreiser's name was built along the banks of the Wabash.

That day he told me an interesting story about Will Bobbs of the Bobbs-Merrill Company of Indianapolis. Dreiser had been having a hard time some years before, and Bobbs had tried to persuade him to return to Indiana, offering him ten thousand a year whether he gave his books to the Bobbs firm or not. "I didn't want to leave New York if I could help it," he said, "but I was glad of the offer. It gave me some encouragement to find that someone thought I was worth that much money."

Meanwhile, in October 1929, the stock market had crashed. Billions in paper fortunes were wiped out. Stocks fell, and with them dividends. Dreiser had invested his small fortune on the advice of Otto Kahn, and there were whisperings that it was gone. Actually, though his income from dividends had been drastically cut, his stocks were good. However, through either necessity or choice, he soon abandoned the elegant studio apartment, and the parties were over. And then I had an unpleasant slant on human nature. Not a few of those hanging on to the outer fringe of "literature" who had fawned upon Dreiser and enjoyed his hospitality seemed sadistically delighted with the rumors that he had been ruined in the crash. Those who had once sneered at his style resumed their sneering.

Happily, just before the crash a speculator on the market, in immediate need of money to cover his losses, sold Dreiser forty acres of hill and dale in Westchester County, near Mt. Kisco, and one June day we were invited out. "I am in and out like a shuttle," he wrote. "Took a place near Katonah (also Mt. Kisco) and am doing over an old cabin. Wish sincerely some Saturday or Sunday you and yours would motor over. There is verandah enough to accommodate a small convention. I will give you a drink."

Near the center of the grounds was a single house, a cottage with a terrace formed by a huge rock, on which we found Helen sleeping in the sun. After a while, Dreiser, who had been out walking, appeared with Max Eastman, both in blue shirts, which went well with their white hair and ruddy complexions. Dreiser wore hiking boots, and the man of the studio had become a country gentleman. Bubbling with enthusiasm, he took us to where he had formed a swimming pool in low ground that was fed by springs; and to a hill, shoulder deep in grass, which commanded a splendid view of the country about; and to a little thatched cottage near the house, built by the contractor who had undertaken to reproduce the cottages of Washington's army at Valley Forge. It had one room, with a bed for an overflow guest, and a table on which Dreiser wrote.

There we sat and talked politics, of which Dreiser still knew exceedingly little. He was bitter against Al Smith, and he gloated over the denunciation of my keynote speech at Houston by the "capitalist press." That day he insisted that we were headed toward an undisguised plutocracy which would pave the way to a totalitarian state. He was working industriously at the time on *The Stoic*, the third of a trilogy, the other two being *The Titan* and *The Financier*.

It was a long time before I saw Dreiser again. He had gone to the mining region of Kentucky to investigate personally and write about the treatment of the miners, and his presence had been bitterly resented by the operators and the newspapers they controlled. He took with him a young woman secretary, and the local Sherlocks conceived the happy thought of setting a trap for him. Soon the charge rang over the country that the young woman had entered Dreiser's room one evening and remained all night. This was demonstrated to the satisfaction of the sleuths, because they had set a match against the door and by morning it had not been knocked over. The foes of the miners were beside themselves with simulated indignation over an immorality no Kentuckian could understand. The rest of the country laughed. Instead of treating the story with silent contempt, Dreiser, overwrought, startled everyone with the public announcement that the charge was fantastic because he was "impotent."

It was immediately after his return to New York that I saw him, in his room at the Ansonia Hotel. Soon after leaving Kentucky he had been indicted for adultery. The sole purpose was to keep him out of the coal fields and his pen out of the service of the miners. The press, which had found no space for the outrages committed against the poor devils in the mines, reeked with the shocking charge that Dreiser had committed an offense that no Kentuckian could tolerate. The telephone was ringing constantly, and he answered with barks. Not once did he sit down, and he paced the room like a caged lion, bitterly describing the treatment of the miners, and indulging in profanity that amazed me, since ordinarily he never swore. On the table was a pitcher of wine, and time and again he stopped to fill a glass and drain it with a swallow. Pausing in his restless pacing, he gave a contemptuous description of the activities of the local sleuths.

"I told them I was impotent," he said, twisting his handkerchief. "They can't prove I'm not."

To get his mind off his obsession, I called attention to a picture of an old man and woman, his parents, on the mantel, with the observation that he resembled his mother rather than his father.

"My God, I hope so!" he shouted.

In the summer of 1932 I accompanied a hopeful author to Mt. Kisco. Having forgotten the way, I asked directions to Dreiser's house. Finally a storekeeper told me that it was on the Bedford Road, but that it would be well to inquire for Dreiser's next-door neighbor "since more know his place than Dreiser's." I recognized Dreiser's place, however, when we came to a blue fence with red trimmings. The old farm cottage had been burned the year before, and Dreiser was occupying the house he had designed and had built. It was a Swiss house with decidedly futuristic decoration, the interior lurid, with many colors. The Russian wolfhound came lazily to the car to greet us. We found Dreiser in the large basement room he had converted into a study. A huge table, a few chairs with enormous high backs, a sofa covered with red plush, a bust of a novelist friend of his, a photograph of himself when he emerged from Russia—such were the furnishings. Dreiser was seated at the head of the table, his white shirt unbuttoned at the neck, shoes without socks, gray trousers. He seemed in perfect health, though his bitterness had merely moderated. On the table before him were many typewritten sheets he was correcting. This was *The Stoic*.

A little later, when Frank Oliver and I were driving in Westchester, we found ourselves at Mt. Kisco, and since Oliver had not met Dreiser I suggested a call, not without a warning that we might expect a gruff reception. The rain was coming down in torrents. Again Dreiser was in his study, with Helen and two friends from France. As I expected, our first reception was scarcely cordial. "Sit down, sit down, sit down," he barked. But Oliver's incomparable gift as a mimic and story teller soon won him over. Never from Dreiser had I heard such boisterous laughter, as he stood rubbing his hands together and asking for more.

When Oliver began a story on a Communist, I wondered what his reaction would be. He perked up to listen.

It was the story of a soapbox orator in Union Square who was telling how "ven th' Revolution come" everyone would eat "strawberries mit powdered sugar and cream," when an auditor interrupted: "But, mister—" "Vat for you interrupt?" "But, please, I don't like strawberries with powdered sugar and cream." "Aha!" roared the orator. "Vell, ven th' Revolution come, you vill HAVE to eat strawberries mit powdered sugar and cream."

Dreiser roared with laughter.

We spent a memorable afternoon, looking out on the rain-drenched fields, listening to the crackling of the logs in the wide cheery fireplace, and with the wolfhound, superlatively dignified, adding an ornamental touch. I had never seen Dreiser in such a delightful humor. I knew he was pleased when he asked Oliver why he wasted time in Congress when he could make a fortune on the stage. He insisted on accompanying us through the rain to the car.

For years the mystery of *The Stoic* remained. When I saw him working on the manuscript at Mt. Kisco I was told it was the last draft. In the early spring of 1933, at a dinner at Alma Clayburgh's, he said he was withholding it from publication until the book trade improved, since it would be a large and expensive book. Years passed. The book trade revived, but the book did not appear. Inquiries by letter failed to elicit a reply about the lost book. And I was not to see Dreiser again, for that spring I began my twenty years as an ambassador, first to Spain and then to Chile.

When years went by, twenty years, without the publication of *The Stoic* and with nothing appearing from his pen, I wondered if I had been justified in my fear that his financial success would chill his creative power. He was now living in California, and years before he had told me that it was impossible for him to write there because it was "too beautiful." Meanwhile the American Academy of Arts and Letters had given him the Gold Medal for Literature, and literary reviews were placing definitive estimates on his work and his place in American literature. He had come into his own after he was seventy. His death brought the announcement that he had left two novels ready for publication. *The Stoic* had dwindled to a small book, with the ending left to the imagination of the reader; it had turned into something vastly different from what he had at first intended. The other novel published after his death, *The Bulwark*, more than most of his other books reveals the man, his tenderness, his sympathy with the weaknesses of human nature, his deep undercurrent of religious feeling. It is a psychological study of Dreiser.

I have attempted this portrait because to me he is one of the most heroic and significant figures in our literary history.

CHAPTER XII

Behind the Scenes in 1928

AFTER THE ELECTION in 1926 there could be no doubt of the nomination of Governor Smith for the Presidency in 1928. His triumphant re-election as governor in 1924, when New York State went overwhelmingly for the Republican national ticket, and his re-election in 1926 for the third time sufficiently attested his phenomenal popularity. His picturesque personality made him the subject of constant gossip from coast to coast. His rough and ready manner of dealing with opposition was suggestive of another Andrew Jackson. His record in the gubernatorial office had never been equaled in New York. In social legislation of a humanitarian nature he had been both a crusader and a creator. His sympathies had always been with the underprivileged. No living New Yorker had his comprehensive grasp of the problems of the commonwealth; in the state constitutional convention some time before he had been called "the most useful member" by Elihu Root. It was utterly absurd to brush aside the legitimate claims to the nomination of a man four times a successful governor in the important Empire State. No one but knew that had he been a Protestant the idea of challenging his claim to the nomination would have been thought ridiculous.

I had an intense curiosity about this remarkable man before going to New York, and when I noticed that he was to speak at a political rally in Brooklyn in the municipal election of 1925 I found my way to the meeting. He was received, as usual, with an ovation, but during the first five minutes of his speech I was shocked by his rough, harsh voice. There assuredly was nothing in it to suggest polish, but in a few minutes the charm of his personality, the warmth of his smile, put the voice out of mind.

Unhappily, his personality, his charm and smile, could not be transmitted over the radio, and I am sure that his radio speeches in the campaign of 1928 did him some harm, since the radio accentuated the roughness of his voice. "Listen to that voice," one Prohibitionist would say to another. "Clearly a whiskey voice." And actually it was nothing of the sort.

The story of his political rise from the sidewalks of New York is typically American. Elected to the Legislature, he and James A. Hoey, also a new member, alighted from the train in Albany and, carrying their satchels, went in search of simple lodgings. Sitting silent in the Legislature, Smith observed that bill after bill was called up and hurried to a vote without analysis, explanation or discussion. It was offensive to his nature to vote blindly on anything, and he found, to his disgust, that his colleagues voted blindly on most measures. He arranged that all bills introduced be sent to him, and they were taken to his lodgings for a minute scrutiny. Soon thereafter the green young legislator from the neighborhood of the Bowery astonished his colleagues by his intimate familiarity with almost everything. This was embarrassing, since time and again he rose to point out the trickery, the absurdity or the viciousness of the phrasing and intent. Thus he attracted notice and commanded respect.

About this time a group of women of the highest social circles in New York City, who were interested in social service, were trying to get certain measures through the Legislature. They found it impossible to enlist the interest of members of their own strata of society in the Legislature, who brushed them off with promises not very seriously given and quickly forgotten. They appealed to the rough but serious-minded young man from the region of the Fulton Fish Market and were amazed by his instant grasp of the significance of their measures and delighted by his enthusiastic sympathy with them. Thus he soon became the one man in Albany to whom they turned, and never afterward were they to lose faith in him. I am sure that this was the beginning of Smith's ascent to fame and popularity.

He was a realist, very practical, and he was honest. From the beginning he mastered his subject. He formed his opinions on the hard, cold facts. In many speeches I heard him make, one sentence stood out vividly, for it was never absent. Setting forth the position

174

of the opposition fairly, he would turn to the papers on the table before him, seeking the right one, and say in his rough tones, "Well, let's look at the record." And he never falsified or doctored that record.

Throughout his gubernatorial terms he had to deal with hostile Legislatures, and there were constant battles. It was his method to summon the opposition leaders to his office, remove his coat, lock the door, put the key in his pocket and, giving them a profane tongue-lashing such as they would have taken from no one else, announce that the business of the state took precedence over everything else and that they would not leave the room until an agreement had been reached. Thus in numerous notable instances he literally lashed his opponents into acquiescence.

Even so, in 1928 many Democrats without a drop of bigotry in their blood feared that it would be unwise to nominate him for the Presidency, because he was a Catholic. Most of these were not unmindful of the fact that a surrender to this fear would be interpreted as an acceptance of the narrow prejudices of the day, but they felt that to challenge those prejudices would mean defeat in the election, which the party could not afford. Others, however, felt that the party could not afford to yield to prejudice. After all, if the Democratic Party stood for anything, it should stand foursquare for religious freedom and toleration, which had been one of the pillars of the temple Jefferson had raised. For more than a hundred years his party had not shirked a clash with the enemies of toleration, and it dared not mar that record now. The issue was squarely before it. Better defeat in one campaign than the marring of the record and the surrender of the principles of more than a century.

The first conclusive evidence of party dissensions appeared in arranging for the Jackson Day banquet in Washington. For years this banquet had been the occasion of the meeting of the National Committee and leaders from all over the country. The candidates for the Presidential nomination had always been invited, had always attended and spoken. In 1928 all the candidates were invited as usual, but it was arranged that something in the way of a keynote speech should be made by a principal speaker who was not among the contenders. It was in the choice of this speaker that a feud was threatened. The Republican press enjoyed the situation and reported on the progress of the quarrel, until finally I read with amazement and disgust that it might be necessary to abandon the banquet entirely. It was easy for a Democrat to be a pessimist in those days.

Then one morning I read in the New York *Herald Tribune*, under a Washington dateline, that the leaders had been able to agree on my designation as the principal speaker. It seemed so improbable that I gave it no thought until the report was verified by Clem Shaver, the national chairman, in a telephone conversation with me. I was in the midst of work on my book *The Tragic Era* and impatient with interruptions. That was made clear to Shaver with the suggestion that, until the convention had chosen a new party leader, John W. Davis was the official head of the party and should be designated regardless of possible critics. Shaver promised to test the suggestion. The next day he reported back that the committee could make but one unanimous choice. There was no escape.

The incident indicated too plainly the continuance of the dissensions, the persistence of the feud of personalities, the immolation of party interests a second time within four years. Never had there been a more impressive need for party solidarity. Corruption, flagrant and now a part of history, reflected the condition of the public service. The exploitation of the great mass of the people by a privileged few with the knowledge and even the co-operation of the government had never been more open. It seemed appalling that confronted by these conditions the opposition party should be dividing into hostile groups readier to fight one another than to make common cause against the common foe. What kind of speech could one make from the heart under the circumstances?

Manifestly, one kind only—a thoroughly Jeffersonian, Jacksonian speech on the fundamentals, shaming the party for dividing on the nonessentials. It would be rash to mention these dissensions and thus add fuel to the flame. Clearly it would be bad taste to criticize the leaders who were clawing at one another. But there was a way it could be done, to say bitter things without offense—by putting it all on Jackson. What did Jackson stand for? What enemies did he encounter? What sort of party discipline did he enforce? How did he win his victories? In answering these questions it would be possible to say the things that should be said. If they could not be said bluntly, they could be insinuated and the audience could take them or leave them.

A few days after the announcement of my selection I was asked by Franklin D. Roosevelt to call on him at his Liberty Street office with the Fidelity and Deposit Company of Maryland, and, since he was the principal adviser of Smith in his campaign for the Presidential nomination, I assumed it was to make suggestions regarding the speech. I found him seated at a huge desk. At that time he looked his age, but no more. His face was smooth but for some lines, not deep, across his brow. His finely chiseled face was patrician. His gray-blue eyes were expressive. His manner was charming, genial, sometimes boyish, and he laughed a great deal. I had seen him before, but only casually. He had written a long review of my *Jefferson and Hamilton* for the *Evening World* before I knew him well. I was sure I had been invited that day to get better acquainted. His secretary had called me earlier to ask what I would like for lunch, which was served in the office at Roosevelt's desk. We lunched on fish, potatoes, cheese and tea and talked politics.

He spoke intimately about conditions generally and about Smith's campaign. It was evident that the Tammany politicians distressed him at times because of their inability to comprehend conditions nationally. He told me of a recent conference where the decision had been made to name managers for Smith's campaign in New England, New York, Pennsylvania and New Jersey. Roosevelt had asked if they intended to ignore the rest of the country. The New York politicians doubted if any managers were needed elsewhere, but under Roosevelt's insistence they finally agreed to name one Western man "for window dressing," as they put it. Roosevelt was also annoyed because it was apparent that they expected to win in the cities and to ignore the country and the small towns. This, thought Roosevelt, was because Smith had won his victories in the cities; the Tammany men did not realize that while the cities dominated New York State, they did not then dominate the nation.

Throwing back his head and laughing, he told a story illustrating the typical ignorance of the New York City politicians at that time about the country west of the New Jersey coast resorts. In the preconvention fight of 1924 some Kansas delegates called to see Smith, who was out attending the christening of the daughter of an Irish friend. At length he appeared, entering like a breeze, in a swallowtail coat, a silk hat at a rakish angle, and with the usual cigar in his mouth. "Hello, hello, my boy, and how's things?" he said, addressing Roosevelt. The latter introduced his callers as delegates from Kansas. "Hello, boys," said Smith, shaking hands. "Glad to see you. Y'know, the other day some boys were in from Wisconsin and I learned somethin'. I always thought Wisconsin was on this side of the lake. It's on the other side. Glad to know it. Glad to know more about the place where the good beer comes from." And this to the delegates from a strong Prohibition state.

Roosevelt told other amusing stories about Smith that day, and it was evident that he had a warm affection for him. He told a story on himself as well. When he was just starting out in politics in Dutchess County the local boss gave him some don'ts: "Don't be seen smoking cigarettes in public," "Don't wear white clothes," "Don't wear yellow shoes." About this time he was asked to speak at a Columbus Day affair at Peekskill. He conferred with no one about his speech. The diners at the banquet were all Italians and very devout Catholics. In the course of his talk he thought he would strike a popular chord by saying that he had his associations with Italy through a close relative. "A young and adventurous fellow," he described him, "with a flare for liberty, and being in Italy in 1848 he had joined the glorious legion of Garibaldi." He had forgotten Garibaldi's battles with the Catholic Church, but his hearers had not. He was surprised by the silence.

My assumption that I had been summoned to discuss what I was to say in Washington turned out to be wrong. Roosevelt did not ask me what I proposed to say, and not even by indirection did he make a suggestion. It was a delightful luncheon.

My speech, then, was prepared in a spirit of indifference, or at least of resignation, as to its reception. Naturally mention should be made of the immediate issues raised during the preceding eight years, but the heart of the speech would be an analysis of Jackson's methods. In defining the kind of leader he had been it would be possible to hit directly at those who were betraying the party to its enemies:

He was too wise to enter a conflict with enemies, spies and traitors in the rear.

He had no patience with the timid or the time server, and he ordered the Miss Nancys and the Sister Sues back with the scullions and the cooks to make way for two-fisted fighting men upon the firing line.

His strategy of battle was to center on a single issue, brush all extraneous matters out of the line of march, and, the strategy determined, close debate and concentrate on victory.

Imagine, if you can, an Iago insinuating himself into Jackson's camp to propose the division of the party on evolution or the theory of relativity and living to report progress to the enemy that sent him.

He never fought with ping-pong sticks—he gave his men battle axes and artillery.

He never soft pedaled his approach to conflict—he rode to battle waving a warrior's sword and shouting commands, and he rode at the head of the column.

He never inquired whether a policy would be good for the North, South, East or West, for he knew if it were really good it would be good for the masses of the people everywhere.

He fought the common enemy; he waged no civil wars.

Under his courageous leadership, the jingle of the golden coin could not intimidate the army that he led, and the enemy barricades could not stop it, and the machinations of the enemy could not divide it, and thus he moved to inevitable and immortal victories for popular government and the economic rights of man.

And how did he do it? By giving the people a fundamental issue that had a meaning at every fireside in every home in the country. He pointed to the entrenchments of monopoly and he said, "We will take that." He called attention to the increasing arrogance of class rule, and he asked the masses to follow him to battle for the restoration of a government of equal rights for all and special privileges for none.

So much for the spirit of dissension on nonessentials.

But there was something more that was revolting to a Jeffersonian and Jacksonian in the talk of the times among certain Democrats. These were the defeatists with but a hazy conception of the fundamental differences in the governmental concepts of political parties, and these could find no issue at all on which to fight. They also said there was no real difference between the two schools of political thought. And with these in view I said:

But someone asks what Jefferson and Jackson have to do with present-day problems and conditions; and the answer is that there is scarcely a domestic issue that Jefferson thought for and Jackson fought for and Wilson wrought for that is not a vital living issue at this hour.

If the party that these men stood for stands today where these men stood, for equal rights for all and special privileges for none—there is an issue.

If it stands where these men stood, against monopoly and autocracy in government and industry—there is an issue.

If it stands where these men placed it, for the rule of the majority and the greatest good to the greatest number—there is an issue.

If it believes, as these men did, that the debaucher of the ballot box and the hucksters in high places who sell the nation's birthright to line their pockets belong to the penitentiary and nowhere else—there is an issue.

And to put it all in one sentence: If it stands where these men stood, for democracy and against the oligarchy of a privileged class—there, there is an issue that can mobilize the people and make them march with waving banners and the will to victory in their hearts.

To my astonishment, the speech was more than an ordinary success. The dining room of the Mayflower Hotel was packed with members of Congress and party leaders from all over the country. The press correspondents were all in readiness with sharpened pencils for a Kilkenny cat fight, for there had been everything but harmonious talk in the lobbies. John W. Davis, presiding, made one of his excellent speeches, and I followed. I had expected my speech to be heard in a reproving silence. Instead, there were constant interruptions, a series of demonstrations—one especially, around the table of Senator Walsh of Montana, to whom I had paid a brief tribute, and once all the diners were on their feet. At the close there was an ovation, and John W. Davis said it was the best political speech he had ever heard. To a speaker prepared, as I was, to be coldly heard, this reception was amazing. Carter Glass wrote (January 18, 1928) that the speech was "powerful in conception and presentation—a classic performance"; Meredith Nicholson, the novelist, wrote that it was "no dead stuff—all alive and with some bully sentences—long fellows that cracked like a whip when the end came and greatly tickled my stylistic sense"; and Senator (later Justice) Hugo Black wrote that it was "the greatest exposition of Democracy since Jefferson's day" because based on fundamentals.

Certain it is that some of the speeches prepared for the occasion were instantly put aside. Senator Reed of Missouri made an entirely different speech from the one he had prepared. My speech had accomplished one purpose—it made it at least embarrassing to inject a controversial note.

That night and during the next day I heard frequent suggestions that I be made the keynote speaker of the national convention five months later, and the next night Senator Hawes, a great friend, gave a dinner for me at his house with Senators Reed, Robinson, Harrison, Swanson, Pittman, Tydings, Broussard and George, all of whom agreed to the plan. Even so it seemed impossible, since the honor traditionally fell to a Senator or a governor, and, not much concerned, I returned to my less disturbing work on *The Tragic Era*. Then, too, I had heard nothing from any of the leaders in New York, and up until that time I had not met Governor Smith. Nor, aside from Senator Wagner and Franklin Roosevelt, was I personally known in the circle of his advisers.

Soon thereafter I was asked to dinner by Elisabeth Marbury, the national committeewoman for New York. When I was speaking at the banquet I had noticed her seated directly in front of the speakers' table, and after I sat down she had nodded approvingly several times. I supposed the dinner engagement was connected with the banquet speech.

She was living in a charming old New York house, done over by her friend Elsie De Wolfe, in Sutton Place on the East River. A short flight of steps brought me to the cozy little library where she received her friends. The walls lined with books, the comfortable fireplace where live coals glowed, the huge easy chair in which she sat, her cordial greetings from the chair, for she was too heavy to rise with ease—all are familiar to the many who have crossed her threshold.

She did not rise, but leaned forward with extended hand. "You must be a courageous man," she said, "to call alone on a woman whom you do not know and who is neither young nor beautiful."

We talked for an hour about people, politics and books, and then went to the Embassy Club for dinner. There she broached the keynote speech, saying she was urging it on Smith. A few days later she telephoned me that the Smith people had lined up for my selection.

Since she was a remarkable woman, a picture of her may not be out of place.

Elisabeth Marbury was one of the most clever and fascinating women of her time. Hers had been a unique career. Her father had been a lawyer, and socially her family was of the best in the days of her youth, when the best was meticulously tabulated in society. In her prime she had been remarkably successful as an international agent for authors, playwrights and artists, with offices in New York, London and Paris. In one of the most crowded autobiographies of achievement, *My Crystal Ball,* she had told with rare charm and humor of her innumerable adventures with men of genius. Sardou, Barrie, Clyde Fitch, Oscar Wilde, the foremost writers of plays and novels, were her intimate friends at the time she was introducing to the American stage the best offerings of the French and English theaters. She knew them as friends, and her long association with them had enriched her conversation with anecdotes. Possessing as she did a mind masculine in its appreciation of the realities, her attention had been drawn to politics when Theodore Roosevelt, with whom she had romped as a child at Oyster Bay, was breaking with his party and with a fervor almost touched with religious fanaticism was launching a new party that would make the brave new world a better place. When Teddy grew tired of crusading and returned to his old party, Elisabeth became disillusioned as to reform and reformers, and, finding the Democratic Party closer in principles to the Bull Moose than the Republican Party, she became a Democrat and a member of Tammany Hall. At the time I knew her she had one of the best minds with the best judgment among the leaders of that venerable organization. She was consulted and respected by the leaders. It was she who insisted that the Tammany delegation to the Houston convention should not decorate its special train with Tammany banners, and that the band should not play "Tammany" in Houston. She understood perfectly the popular conception of that organization over the country. Why stir prejudice?

She was indeed of huge dimensions; her face was overheavy with pink flesh and her eyes were a bit weary from the weight, though darting satirical glances all the while. I think she found amusement and satisfaction in satirizing life and the people with whom she dealt. Her tongue was salty with sarcasm and her conversation sparkled with witticisms, not always kindly, but always to the point. She had strong convictions and she expressed them strongly. Naturally she made enemies, for people with strong convictions are always resented by people with bromidic minds.

She was a bit sensitive because of her size. On my first call, as we were leaving for dinner at the Embassy Club, it took her some minutes to go down the short flight of steps with the aid of a crutch cane. I had to follow very slowly, and she may have been embarrassed, judging by the aftermath. Apropos of nothing previously said, and with this in mind no doubt, she said she had suggested to Al Smith that she should resign as national committeewoman and make way for a younger person. She was then almost seventy.

"What's the idea, sister?" growled Smith.

"I'm no longer young, my legs are bad, and I can't get around easily," she replied.

"Sister, we don't want you for your legs, we want you for your head," he rumbled in his hoarse voice.

And so she continued through two more Presidential campaigns and until her death.

She admired Dreiser for his work, but found him more than ordinarily trying at times. Young Phil Kearney had just dramatized Dreiser's *An American Tragedy*, which had been a financial success. He was young, handsome, erratic, and interesting enough. It was Marbury who invited him to the task. "I sent for Phil Kearney, a bright young fellow," she said, "and gave him the two volumes, which everyone said could not be dramatized, and told him to read it over and let me know if he saw a play in it. He came back in a few days with a sketch. 'Now,' I said, 'you've sold yourself to me. You must now sell yourself to Dreiser and Liveright.' Dreiser was fascinated with him, and the work was done."

Kearney had momentarily dropped from sight and I asked her what he was doing. "Nothing," she said. "Just running around. He won't do anything more." Not long afterward he committed suicide.

The house in Sutton Place presented a cross section of political, social, literary and artistic New York. It was as nearly like a Paris salon of other days as could be found in the city. The hostess, seated in her chair, was at ease conversationally, whether the talk turned on books, plays, music or politics. One day the talk over cocktails turned on the number of seemingly intelligent men in high financial circles who occasionally consulted oracles or fortunetellers. Marbury chuckled and her chair shook. It reminded her of the woman pretending to hold converse with the dead, who had asked to see her "at once" because she had an important message from "a dear friend." She was given an appointment.

"And who is this person who is distressed about me, and why?" Marbury had asked.

"Let me think," said the woman, tapping her head. "It begins with *R*—a person of political distinction. Do you know who it could be?"

"The only person of that description I knew was Teddy Roosevelt, whom I played with as a child and followed some time later in politics."

The messenger of the dead concentrated, and her face brightened. "Yes, it is Roosevelt."

"And why is he distressed about me?" demanded Marbury.

"Because of your present politics," said the messenger. "He says you were with him and now you are with the Democrats. It hurts him. He is much distressed."

"Well, that's funny," snorted Elisabeth. "Teddy, of all people! Ask him if *he* ever changed from one party to another. Changed his principles at the same time, too."

The messenger was shocked. "We can't talk with him or question him," she said with a shudder.

"Again that's funny," stormed the irreverent Elisabeth. "He comes down here to tell me about myself and I have a right to ask him a few questions."

The messenger became solemn. She raised her hand impressively. "He's going . . . he's fading . . . he's fading away."

"Hold him!" shouted Marbury, thoroughly incensed. "Hold him! He can't pull a one-sided debate on me. There are a lot of things I want to say to him."

But Teddy had faded away.

That day some politicians were present, and we lunched in the little brick-floored dining room downstairs, the small-paned windows of which looked out on a little garden with irregular stone steps leading down to the river. She impressed me as the wisest politician in the group.

It was in that charming room later, before the Houston convention, that I had my first warning that my idea of a proper keynote speech might not conform with that of others high in the councils of the party. Norman Mack, the national committeeman, and former Ambassador James W. Gerard were with me alone and, while no direct suggestions were made, there was a very evident intention to enlighten me as to what, if anything, should or should not be said. After they were through I was a bit puzzled. Gerard was sure that we should make it clear that as to the tariff we could and should make it as high as the Republicans. Mack thought this a little strong, but suggested that we might at least soft-pedal the subject. Neither could see any point in referring to the desperate plight of the farmers, or to the treatment accorded labor at that time. My idea that something should be said that would be pleasing to progressive Republicans, liberals and independents made no hit at all. They feared it might drive from Smith some great industrialists and monopolists, who I knew would not support a Democratic nominee under any circumstances. I went away with the uneasy thought that a militant Jeffersonian speech would greatly displease some party leaders. I decided, however, to say precisely what I thought should be said.

A few days later I got a more agreeable impression from conversations in Washington with two leaders for whom I had a profound admiration, Senator Thomas J. Walsh of Montana and Cordell Hull. The latter was fundamentally sound on Jeffersonian principles, and no one in the preceding five years had even approached the service of the former to the party and to clean government. He was the symbol of protest against the corruption of the time. Through him, I wished to verify and fortify what I planned to say on the subject. He went about answering questions meticulously and methodically. On every question he summoned his secretary and had the evidence in the oil scandal brought. Then he would read this slowly and carefully. When, after the convention, it was intimated that the delectable creatures involved in the corruption had been lied about, I had the satisfaction of knowing that every single charge and reference had been checked from the official records by Walsh himself. Hull was in accord with the general tenor of the speech throughout.

Once only I discussed the proposed speech with the New York party leaders, whom I met at the Manhattan Club with Franklin D. Roosevelt: Surrogate Foley, Judge Joseph H. Proskauer, Senator Wagner and Judge Olvany. New York could not have assembled a finer lot of men, and no fault was found with the outline of the speech. "That suits me one hundred per cent," said Proskauer. When I outlined what I proposed to say about dollar diplomacy and military intervention in South and Central America, Roosevelt smiled wryly. "But don't forget Nicaragua," he said. This intervention was under a Democratic Administration. I replied that it was because I had not forgotten it that I proposed to protest against such interventions.

At this meeting there was some discussion of the Vice-Presidential nomination. It was agreed that Cordell Hull would be an ideal nominee but for his traditionally Democratic position on the tariff, which was distasteful to some of the New York contingent. Roosevelt suggested Senator Alben W. Barkley, whom Bernard Baruch had mentioned to me some time before as a good Presidential candidate. There was a friendly suggestion of Senator Harry B. Hawes, but he was dismissed on the ground that it would not be well to have two "dripping wets" on the ticket.

That day Roosevelt looked in perfect health, seated, but he used two canes, and it was with difficulty that he made his way to the car in which he drove me to the *World*.

More interesting, as sidelights on history, were a few small dinners to discuss the platform. The first was held in the apartment of Senator Wagner and was attended by Wagner, Gerard, Foley and Senators Peter Goelet Gerry of Rhode Island and Key Pittman of Nevada. Senator Pittman had been selected by the Smith followers for the chairmanship of the committee on resolutions, and this was the first opportunity some had to feel him out. He made a fine impression, for he had keen intelligence, excellent judgment, consummate tact and a saving sense of humor. It was at this meeting that it was decided that Tammany's delegation was not to appear in Houston in special trains three and four days before the opening. Pittman, no enemy of Tammany, warned that the press correspondents would feature the Tammany appearance and create the impression that the Smith movement was primarily that of Tammany Hall. Foley was not hard to convince, and he agreed to urge upon the organization the abandonment of the original plan to appear in force early. It was also agreed that Tammany would remain in the background as much as possible and permit the Smith supporters from other states to take the lead, and that in the event of an attack on Tammany the organization would remain silent and indifferent. Soon I was to find that this in no way corresponded with Smith's own idea.

The discussion passed to Prohibition. Some of Smith's friends, including the Governor himself, were bitterly resentful of the attempt of the *World* to force the Governor into a declaration before the convention. I learned that at a private meeting Smith had asked Ralph Pulitzer of the *World* if he thought he should be forced into a declaration before the Republican convention met, and Pulitzer agreed that he should not. The outcome was an agreement that the *World* would say no more until after the Republican convention. Proskauer announced at the Wagner dinner that Smith would make no further statement until after the nomination and then would make his position clear in his acceptance speech, when he would express the opinion that national Prohibition was wrong, that such matters should be left to the states, but that so long as the law remained on the statutes he would try to enforce it.

Again the tariff came up, and Gerard reiterated the view he had expressed to me at Elisabeth Marbury's. This shocked Senator Wagner, who stoutly insisted on a traditional Democratic stand. Pittman smiled his inscrutable smile and said nothing.

A few days later Governor Smith telephoned, asking me to meet him at the Biltmore Hotel and saying that he had "some ideas about taxation." This was disturbing, since my speech had already been distributed to the press, but I hurried to the Biltmore. It was a very unconventionally clad figure that met me at the door of his room. He had arrived a few minutes before from Buffalo and was about to leave again. He evidently had just taken a bath and finished shaving, since the suds were caked at his temples. He wore a bathrobe, which was thrown back, and old-fashioned underwear that reached to his ankles and fit like tights, giving a grotesque appearance to his thin legs. When, frequently, he had to go to the door to turn someone away, he went at a dogtrot, his skinny legs in tights most conspicuous as he ran. But his thin face, actor's profile and penetrating blue eyes, his fluency and clarity in explaining what he had in mind, his magnetism and dynamic force, stamped him as an outstanding individual, a real person.

It was not taxation he had in mind. Sitting down at a table in front of one of the tall wall mirrors and motioning me to a chair beside him, he said in his husky voice, "I'm afraid that at Houston an attack will be made on Tammany. If it is it should be answered on the spot. When Bryan made his attack in the Baltimore convention I told Charlie Murphy it should be answered right away, but he thought differently. The next day, when it was too late, he changed his mind and put up Stanchfield, who made a botch of it. Now, if an attack is made at Houston it should be answered on the spot, and *you're the man to make the answer*. You're not a member of Tammany—I don't suppose you've ever been in a Tammany club in your life. The Democrats over the country respect you, and you're the man to make the answer."

He then proceeded to set forth what he thought should be said. Talking earnestly, gesticulating with clenched fist, looking in the mirror as he talked, the way an actor would, he set forth the argument. It was a good one. But it was startling to be asked to assume this responsibility in addition to that resting on the keynote speaker. It was in direct contradiction to the agreement I had heard made by the inner circle of his advisers not to reply to any attack. I wrote Judge Proskauer, reminding him of the agreement, and I heard no more about it. However, no attack was made.

It has often been said that a great actor was lost when Smith went into politics, and on this occasion he gave an exhibition of his histrionic talent. He had Governor James M. Cox and myself as an audience as he acted out a story about former Governor Sulzer of New York, an amusing and amazing figure. This politician, tall and slender, had once been told that he resembled Henry Clay, and thereafter he tried to accentuate the resemblance. He wore a lock of hair on his forehead in imitation of the great Kentuckian. He had made himself invincible in his Congressional district even against the frowns of Tammany when he was in the House of Representatives, claiming credit for everything that pleased his constituents, many of whom were Russian Jews. He opened his campaign for governor in his district just after the Senate, under the leadership of Senator Raynor of Maryland, had forced the abrogation of a Russian treaty because of the mistreatment of Jews, and he shamelessly claimed the credit.

Smith, giving an imitation of Sulzer on that occasion, stood up in his tights, pulled an imaginary lock of hair over his forehead, assumed an impressive frown and an air of great solemnity, glared around a moment at his imaginary audience and said in stentorian tones, "All over Russia tonight the Jewish people are on their knees praying for Bill Sulzer."

Then he acted out the dialogue between Sulzer and Martin Glynn, the nominee for lieutenant governor (who had a sense of humor), as they drove away:

"Bill, you made a fool of yourself tonight."

"And what's the matter now, Martin? What did I do? You're always worrying about little things. It's a wonder you aren't in a sanatorium. What did I do?"

"You said that all over Russia tonight the Jewish people are on their knees praying for Bill Sulzer."

"And so they are, Martin, so they are. What's wrong with that?"

"Merely this: Most of the audience was made up of Russian Jews, and they know that when the Jews of Russia pray they don't get on their knees."

"Ah, but, Martin, that may be usually true, but when the Jews of Russia pray for Bill Sulzer *they always get on their knees.*"

It was a few days after this that I attended a meeting of the platform group and had an opportunity to observe Smith in action. We dined at the Lotus Club, and Senators Pittman and Wagner, Surrogate Foley and Judge Proskauer were present. An entire platform had been prepared for discussion, plank by plank. Al Smith literally exploded when Pittman read the proposed plank on international affairs. It was sound enough, a bit overcautious, but couched in the ponderous language of diplomacy. The Governor first read it over in mocking tones, while Pittman, who was then all but a stranger, looked on keenly, clearly surprised, but plainly interested in studying the man.

"Now, what does that mean?" stormed Smith. "No one knows what it means. I know a little, but it gives me a pain in the back of the neck to get it. Our people are not the professors and the fancy boys down at the Union League Club. We want a platform the man in the factory and the corn row can understand. Now let me try my hand."

Everyone was interested. Few thought that Smith had ever given a moment's thought to foreign relations and international affairs. He clenched his fists for gesticulation, the cords in his neck stood out, his face flushed, he looked at the floor, and he delivered a speech instead of a plank, but one that astonished me by its keen comprehension of world problems and our relations to them. His lack of familiarity with federal procedure was occasionally shown by his frequent questions as to the relative roles of the President and the Senate, but there was everything disarming in his honesty in asking, and admirable in his instant comprehension.

There was a moment of silence when he finished, and then Proskauer said, "Al, that comes very near to the League of Nations."

Smith did not reply.

Occasionally during the evening he would make a suggestion that Proskauer or Pittman would combat, and with admirable open-mindedness Smith would say, "I'm licked," and settle back in his chair.

On the Prohibition plank he objected to the proposed pledge to enforce the Eighteenth Amendment. It could not be enforced, he said, and he would not stultify himself by promising the impossible to the people. He was willing to say that he would do his best to enforce it, leaving him an opportunity to amplify in his speech of acceptance. Finally he wrote on a slip of paper: "The Eighteenth Amendment is part of the fundamental law of the United States. We hold it to be an economic and not a political question. We promise a solution of its enforcement or its amendment as experience may teach."

Proskauer and Senator Wagner interposed to say that he meant "social," not "economic," and it developed that he had in mind the amount of money the people would be willing to spend on enforcement. In the end he tore the slip of paper in two and threw it on the floor.

His husky voice and his manner, when in earnest debate, of talking a second or so out of the corner of his mouth were unpleasant, but his personality filled the room. It was a strange room for such a conference, with portraits of Whitelaw Reid, the Republican aristocrat, and William Winter, the drama critic, neither of whom would have felt comfortable there, looking down from the wall.

Fastidious gentlemen might be distressed by the mannerisms of Smith, who was a sort of Andrew Jackson of the sidewalks of New York, but no one could or did question his intellect. At a dinner at Nicholas Murray Butler's soon after Columbia University had made Smith a Doctor of Laws, I heard Sarah Butler tell an illuminating story illustrative of the man's vast fund of information and his great ability. It was the custom for Butler to give a dinner in honor of those receiving honorary degrees, with representative citizens among the guests. Each recipient of a degree was invariably called upon for a speech. Butler, who was fond of Smith and appreciated his true worth, was distressed over the necessity of calling on him without notice in the presence of gentlemen of the academy. He was fearful that the cynical might get a wrong impression. But there was no escape from the custom. In presenting him, Butler referred to the fact that, with the exception of De Witt Clinton, Smith was the only man who had been governor of New York four times. This gave Smith his cue. To the amazement of all present, he began a comparative analysis of government in New York in the days of Clinton and in his own time which, Butler thought, if reduced to writing and polished here and there, would have been as fine a thesis for a doctor's degree as any he had seen. It was a remarkable performance, but then Al Smith was a remarkable man.

CHAPTER XIII

Politics Turns Putrid

In April I was selected as the temporary chairman and keynote speaker of the national convention in Houston in June. Meanwhile I was again interrupted in my work on *The Tragic Era* by speaking engagements. In March when I spoke at a Democratic banquet in Kansas City and met Harry S Truman for the first time, I was surprised to find that Senator Reed's candidacy was not taken seriously, but that Missouri would pay him the tribute of its support. In April I delivered the Founders' Day address at the University of Virginia. It was a militant reassertion of Jeffersonian principles. President Alderman, who was ill, wrote me a congratulatory letter, and the Charlottesville paper said it was a speech overdue, since previously the address had sometimes been made by men having no sympathy with Jeffersonian ideas and ideals.

From Virginia I went to Washington, on the invitation of the state of Tennessee, to make the formal speech on Jackson at the unveiling of his statue in the Capitol. At the conclusion, when surrounded by people saying the usual pleasant things, I was startled by a finger shaking under my nose and a lady speaking with much emphasis; more surprised to find that it was Alice Roosevelt Longworth, the wife of the Republican Speaker of the House and the daughter of Theodore Roosevelt; and still more astonished by what she was saying: "This country has never been more corrupt than it is today. What it needs is another Andrew Jackson to clean it up. If the Democrats had the sense that God gave a goose, they would make corruption the issue and they could sweep the country." But I was to find that they did not have that much sense.

En route to Houston, we stopped for a day in New Orleans, sweltered in the heat, rode about in search of a breeze and finally retired to a room in the St. Charles, where a huge electric fan gave some relief. When we entered the station that evening the special train bearing the delegates of Georgia, the Carolinas and Florida, comprising the anti-Smith bloc, was pulling out, the rear platform packed with cheering men. We had entered our train when the special with the Massachusetts delegation drew up on a parallel track, and from the observation car we enjoyed the antics, since Holman Hamilton, a student at Williams College, later the biographer of President Taylor and a professor at the University of Kentucky, had drilled the Negro porters in "The Sidewalks of New York," and these, with the delegates, were lustily singing.

We reached Houston to find it baking in the most deadening heat we had ever felt, but soon Jesse Jones called and took us to his breezy apartment on top of the Lamar Hotel, where we found Mrs. Woodrow Wilson. I had not met her before. She was natural and charming, with a delightful schoolgirl giggle.

A reference to a current story that President Harding had Negro blood elicited from her an interesting sidelight on the character of Woodrow Wilson. He and Mrs. Wilson had been sitting on the portico of the White House when Tumulty appeared in a high state of excitement, exclaiming, "We have them now." He then told the story. Wilson was shocked and instantly forbade its use politically.

Still more interesting and human was her story of her first impressions of Wilson. She had a woman cousin who was an idolator of the President. "I heard so much about him from her that I became prejudiced against him," she said. Later, on learning that Wilson would attend the theater one night, the cousin insisted on going. At that late hour tickets were difficult to get, but the future Mrs. Wilson told the ticket seller that she had "a lunatic along" and that if he wanted to avoid a scene he had better produce the tickets, which he did. Their seats were close to the Wilson box. "Mr. Wilson was never less inspiring," she said. "He was tired and he yawned constantly." But the cousin never took her eyes from the box and saw nothing of the play. When, some time later, the cousin appeared with shining eyes to announce that she had wangled an invitation to the White House to "just shake hands," Mrs. Wilson rebelled. "I certainly am not going," she said. "I've lived in Washington many years and have never been inside the

White House. However, I'll drive you down and wait for you." This she did, driving around and around the grounds until the cousin appeared.

The hour with Mrs. Wilson is my most pleasant memory of those dreadfully hot days in Houston.

The opening session of the convention was set for night in order to reach the radio audience, which was then something new. The heat that day was intense and in the afternoon there was a fierce storm, with startling electrical effects that I feared would put the radio out of commission. When the time came for me to go to the convention the rain was coming down in torrents. I found the lobby of my hotel deserted, since everyone had gone to the convention hall. No taxi could be found and I did not have, nor could I borrow, beg or steal, an umbrella. In my predicament I appealed to a casual acquaintance, the sole man in the lobby. He hurried to the door and a moment later motioned me to follow. He had stopped a large car in the street and was standing beside it. Clearly the occupants had agreed to drive me to the hall. To my embarrassment, I found the car occupied by three priests. Fearing as I did a campaign of fanaticism because Smith, a Catholic, was a candidate, it seemed highly inept that I should be driven to the hall by three priests, but the night was stormy, rain was falling, press photographers would hardly be waiting at the entrance, and I took a chance. Had it been a clear night, photographers would have taken pictures of my arrival and the intolerants would have made the most of it. The most respectable papers would have published the pictures without comment, but with full knowledge of the effect on the bigots. No pictures were taken, and it remained my secret and that of the priests. When I told the *World* staff of the incident that night they laughed. "It's a great story," they said, "but not for the *World*."

The hall, which could seat eighteen thousand, was packed, and the roof, in spots, was leaking. My keynote speech that night broke precedents, since, contrary to custom, it received perfect attention and there was a long demonstration in the middle of it, with a parade of the standards of all states and territories.

Having attended several national conventions and been a delegate to some, I had definite ideas of what a keynote speech should

194

be. The usual thing was to outline the record of the party when it was in power, and, if it was out of power, to set forth principles and policies to be used if it was called to power. Invariably the speeches were read and little attention was paid, while the delegates engaged in low-toned conversation. My conception of a keynote speech was something other than a review, especially at a time when the average man had concluded that there were no elemental governmental principles involved in elections, which were nothing but a struggle for the loaves and fishes of patronage. That spring I had heard Walter Lippmann tell an audience of Democratic women that criticisms of Republican politics should be much restrained, because the majority of the people were Republicans and their sensibilities should not be hurt. I was convinced of the contrary: that the great majority of the people were Jeffersonians and that the line should be sharply drawn between the two schools of political thought to permit the electorate to know what fundamental principles were involved. My purpose, then, was to draw that line. Later, when the speech aroused such fury among the ultra-conservatives, I knew it was due not to what was said about the transient issues of the hour, but to the sharp line I tried to draw on fundamental principles. Those who feared plain speaking even in political polemics were shocked. Those who had persuaded the average man that the two parties or any two parties were merely teams contesting for patronage were even more offended by my attempt to draw this definitive line between the fundamentals of the two schools of political thought:

The issues are as fundamental as they were when Jefferson and Hamilton crossed swords more than a century ago. To understand their conflicting views on the functions of government is to grasp the deep significance of this campaign.

Now, Hamilton believed in the rule of the aristocracy of money, and Jefferson in the democracy of men.

Hamilton believed that governments are created for the domination of the masses, and Jefferson that they are created for the service of the people.

Hamilton wrote Morris that governments are strong in proportion as they are made profitable to the powerful, and Jefferson knew that no government is fit to live that does not conserve the interest of the common man.

Hamilton proposed a scheme for binding the wealthy to the government by making government a source of revenue to the wealthy, and Jefferson unfurled the banner of equal rights.

Hamilton would have concentrated authority remote from the people, and Jefferson would have diffused it among them.

Just put a pin in this: There is not a major evil of which the American people are complaining now that is not due to the triumph of the Hamiltonian conception of the state. And the tribute to Hamilton in Kansas City [at the Republican national convention] was an expression of fealty to him who thought that the government is strong in proportion as it is made profitable to the powerful, who proposed the plan for binding the wealthy to the government by making government a source of revenue for them, who devised the scheme to tax the farmer to pay the factory, and whose avowed purpose was to make democracy a mockery and a sham.

Then, turning to the fallacy, cleverly imposed on many, that Lincoln and Hamilton belonged to the same school of political thought:

What a comment on the confusion of the public mind on the elementals of American politics when a great party is able to claim joint parenthood in Abraham Lincoln and Alexander Hamilton.

Why, you cannot believe with Lincoln in democracy and with Hamilton against it.

You cannot believe with Lincoln that "God loved the common people or he would not have made so many of them" and with Hamilton that the people are "a great beast."

You cannot believe with Lincoln that "the principles of Jefferson are the axioms and the definitions of a free society" and with Hamilton that they are the definitions of anarchy.

You cannot believe with Lincoln in a government "of the people, by the people and for the people" and with Hamilton in a government of the wealthy, by the powerful and for the privileged.

There are Lincoln Republicans and Hamilton Republicans, and never the twain shall meet until you find some way to ride two horses going in opposite directions at the same time.

Except for applause, there was absolute silence during the delivery, which I planned to consume no more than forty minutes. It was intended as a fighting speech. During the tribute to Woodrow Wilson the convention rose. The sensational feature of the reception was wholly unexpected by me. In touching upon the legitimate grievances of the farmers, in disclaiming any thought of paternalistic treatment of them, I said, "We do demand that privilege take its hands out of the farmer's pockets and off the farmer's throat." I had not expected even a handclap here, but instantly the delegates from agricultural states sprang up cheering, and, taking their state banners from their sockets, they started a march around the hall. State after state joined in the procession, to the amusement of Mencken of the Baltimore *Sun* when the "horny-handed sons of toil" of the New York delegation joined in the parade. This demonstration continued for twenty minutes. In the midst of it, Ralph Pulitzer, publisher of the New York *World*, sent me a note: "Never before has there been a demonstration like this during a keynote speech."

The Democratic press was warm in praise, with the exception of the *World*, which was able to restrain itself. The attacks of the Republican press were violent at the time and continued throughout the campaign in some papers. At any rate, unlike most keynote speeches, it was not forgotten overnight or treated with the contempt of silence. And when weak-kneed Democrats cringed before the vigor of the attack I recalled the comment of Jackson's fighting lieutenant Isaac Hill, who under similar circumstances clapped his hands and said, "I have hit them, for they flutter."

I soon sensed some distress among certain of the local advisers of Governor Smith. The Governor had listened to the speech on the radio with a group of newspapermen, and he had seemed pleased; but when the New York papers, all Republican or mugwump, began their attacks, I have no doubt he was worried. My first intimation that the speech had frightened some of his advisers came with the discovery that, contrary to custom, it was not printed and distributed by the National Committee. I learned later that national headquarters was astonished by requests from party organizations all over the country for copies of the speech, and it was finally published with the Jackson Day speech in the campaign book, under the caption "Authoritative Pronouncements of Democratic Principles." Criticism of the speech was confined largely to New York City.

Among the flood of letters I received, the one that pleased me most of all was from Alfred Harcourt, the publisher, with whom I was not acquainted:

I have seen enough disparaging remarks on your keynote speech that I cannot refrain from writing you that I thought it was a grand job. Carl Sandburg was staying with me at the time and we both listened to it with the greatest enjoyment. It was a great relief from the usual political oration, and yet it was beautifully phrased, and, to us at least, came off perfectly. It was fine and refreshing and I must make you my compliments on it.

More than ever I was persuaded that the sooner the two parties discontinued their disposition to run in parallel lines and got down to first principles and the fundamental differences dividing the two schools of political thought, the better the prospect of preserving· our free democratic institutions. Senator Hugo Black, later to rank among the greatest members of the Supreme Court, wrote me in agreement with this thought.

That Al Smith did not share the opinion of bipartisan New York Democrats about the speech is manifest in a letter of August 7, inviting me to a luncheon at the Executive Mansion in Albany for a discussion of his speech of acceptance. Unhappily, my reservations were made for a trip to Europe and I was unable to attend.

By a coincidence, I had repercussions of my keynote speech years later in Chile from two distinguished American visitors. When I was driving Henry Wallace to the country home of President Ríos he told me that the speech had given him the final shove into the Democratic Party in 1928. Two years later, on the same road and on the same mission, President Hoover surprised me by saying that he had heard the speech on the radio. I held my breath, expecting an explosion which did not come. He said he had had some "fun with the boys" because of the Biblical quotation, "To your tents, O Israel," with which I closed. "I said," he continued, "that maybe the Democrats had to live in tents, but that we Republicans were substantial enough to live in houses." It was not scintillating, but we both laughed heartily, and it was the only mention of politics during Mr. Hoover's visit to Chile, which I greatly enjoyed.

What convinced me that I had served my purpose was the publication of the speech in full in an English magazine two months after the convention, with the explanation that it had persuaded the editor that there were fundamental differences in principles and philosophy between the two political parties in the United States after all.

In late August I went to Hot Springs, Arkansas, to "notify" Senator Joseph T. Robinson of his nomination for Vice-President —a silly custom. At St. Louis I joined the small party of John J. Raskob, who, though a Republican, had been made national chairman by Smith. Hot Springs was gaily decorated with banners bearing the inscription "Our Joe." The ceremony at night was just outside the Arlington Hotel, the spectacle impressive, with spectators on roofs and leaning out windows.

Returning to the Raskob car after the ceremony, we found the table spread for a feast, and I found my prejudice against Raskob melting in the warmth of his personality. It was my first contact with him. He was a little man with serious brown eyes. One could almost see his mind work, and it was a good mind. Occasionally he smiled, but most of the time he was serious. During the journey back I was surprised to see him take from his bag a copy of *Ariel*, the André Maurois biography of Shelley. An executive of General Motors reading about the poet would have seemed incongruous even if he had not then been engaged in a political campaign. He seemed a symbol of efficiency. Though he appeared modest, there was a decisive note in his conversation. At various points local politicians joined the train to ride to the next station and urge their political necessities. They wanted assurances about campaign funds and speakers. They would enter the car jovially to see a fellow politician and would find themselves in the presence of a quiet, undemonstrative man of business. This momentarily drove the joviality from their faces. Then, as Raskob gave them his ideas about organization, patterned after that of General Motors, they became silent and clearly disappointed. They had never known a party manager like Raskob. I sat aside and studied their faces with amusement.

I am going into this campaign with some detail because of its numerous unique features and its lessons that must be learned if American institutions are to survive. The campaign of 1928 was the most disgraceful and threatening in our history up until that time. At some periods, happily wide apart, waves of religious and racial intolerance had swept over the country, but never had there been anything so widespread and sinister in its implications. It came so suddenly and was so incredible. It was not the candidacy of Smith that inspired it, since it was in full blast some time before. The nomination of Smith, a Catholic, only added fuel to the flame. Soon the favorite outdoor sport in some states was parading in bed-sheets and pillowcases and burning crosses on the hilltops at night.

Although it is naturally denied, there is not a scintilla of doubt that the Republican managers expected to profit from the bigotry and gave discreet encouragement to its growth. Millions no doubt were innocent of complicity. Years later Herbert Hoover told me in Santiago that he had publicly repudiated that phase of the campaign against Smith, and though I do not recall this public repudiation I have no doubt he did.

It was difficult to meet the issue without giving primary importance to intolerance. The general feeling among Democrats was, the less said the better. Besides, in most places it was a subterranean force that refused to fight in the open. It was a campaign of poisoned whispers.

While many of his advisers thought it unwise to meet this anti-American issue forced upon them, it was impossible to convince Smith that he should remain silent, and he insisted on one of the most gallant and magnificent acts of his career. He was not running away from his faith; he was not defending it; but he was defending one of the most sacred tenets of Jeffersonian democracy. He determined to make one speech on this phase of the campaign, and with his usual courage he went to the capital of a state where one of the Senators of his party had deserted because of Smith's church affiliations. In my opinion, that speech in Oklahoma City was easily the greatest of the campaign. The effect, however, was as feared by those who sought to dissuade him. Among intolerants it made religion the paramount issue. Herbert Hoover told me later that in his opinion it was a tactical mistake. But in the final appraisal of the character of Al Smith, this speech is of lasting importance to history.

From the *World* tower, where, with my pen, I played a meager part against this anti-American propaganda, I followed the campaign with increasing amazement not unmixed with amusement, despite the tragedy it implied. Volumes could be printed about the mad things said and done. I editorially urged that a systematic collection of the "literature" of intolerance be made and preserved for historians in the future, and this was done. But there were a few ridiculous incidents brought to me by personal friends that may serve to lighten the sadness of this story.

My most intimate friend at the time, Frank Oliver, spoke during the campaign in a small town in Delaware. Himself a Catholic, he was chagrined on entering the hall to find the Democrats' nominee for Congress discussing the religious issue.

"They say," the orator was saying, "that if Smith is elected the Pope will come over here and run the country. Now, let's see about that. As you know, I'm a Presbyterian. Last year my pastor went to Rome and called on the Pope. A lovely old man came in. He was the Pope, and he said he was always glad to see Americans because he can't come to America to see us. Now, to understand that you must know how the Catholic Church is run. When a Pope dies, they go out and pick his successor and they shut him in the Vat-i-can, and he never can leave there any more. And if he sticks his head ten inches outside the Vat-i-can he automatically ceases to be pope." Turning triumphantly to Oliver, who had been educated by the Jesuits, he said, "Ain't that correct?"

Oliver, being a good party man, had to nod his head in assent—with his fingers crossed.

"So you see," continued the orator, "the Pope can't come over here and run the country."

That day the local leaders pointed out to Oliver an old man who seemed a caricature of the Civil War veteran, standing on a street corner. He was told that this man was on the payroll of the opposition party and that his work was to stand on the street and pass out a certain line of talk. "We're going to have you introduced to him as a young man who is thinking of voting for Smith, so that you can get his line," Oliver was told.

When he was presented, the old man looked up with a cunning eye and said, "Young feller, you seem to have had good up-bringin'."

Oliver admitted that he had had a good home environment.

"Well," continued the old man, "this is all there is to it: If this man Smith is elected, the Pope is goin' to come over here with all his wives and concubines and live in the White House and run the country. Y'may not have noticed that Catholics in droves are goin' into the Army, for if Smith is elected they're goin' to take over the country and make the Pope President."

"Well," said the amazed Oliver, playing his part, "I won't stand for that."

"I didn't think y'would," said the old man.

After the election I had lunch with Mrs. Champ Clark and her daughter Genevieve Thompson, and the latter told me of an experience of hers at some point in Oklahoma where a Democratic community had gone wild on the religious question. Since the women were the worst offenders, it was thought that perhaps a woman speaker might have a good effect, and Genevieve was asked to go from her home in New Orleans. When the train drew up at the station in the little town, the station was black and there seemed to be no lights in the village. The conductor advised her to get back on the train, go to the next town and spend the night there, but Genevieve replied that a committee was to meet her and she would take a chance. She went into the station. At length a big man wearing a huge hat flashed a powerful searchlight in her face and demanded her business there. She explained.

"Wal," he drawled, "they ain't goin' to be no meetin' and they ain't goin' to be no committee. I reckon the best thing y'can do is to stay all night with me an' my old woman an' take the train out tomorry mornin'."

Since there was nothing else she could do, she went, and on the way to the house she found that her host believed that there is no real baptism except by immersion, sprinkling being insufficient, a mere halfway measure.

The next morning the "old woman" appeared at the breakfast table. She was scrawny, yellow, with black hair parted in the middle and plastered down, feverish dark eyes and sunken cheeks.

"Wal, I understand yer for Smith," she said accusingly.

"Yes, I'm for Governor Smith."

"Wal, I ain't," said the hostess with vehemence.

"Well, perhaps you're a Republican."

"No sir, I'm a Demmycrat, my dad was a Demmycrat, my granddad was a Demmycrat."

"Then why are you against Governor Smith?" asked Genevieve.
"He's a Catholic."

"I don't want to be impertinent," said Mrs. Thompson, "but I'm a Protestant and yet I'm for Governor Smith. Why are you so bitter against the Catholics?"

The eyes of the woman blazed, the muscles in her sunken cheeks twitched, and she brought her clenched fist down upon the table with a resounding whack.

"They brung in *sprinklin'!*" she cried.

Such incidents were not at all unusual. All over the nation, in village, town and country, during four months of the campaign they were being repeated in fantastic forms; printed propaganda of the most libelous sort was being mailed and distributed even at the doors of the churches. Never in our history had so many Americans turned venomously against American traditions, principles and ideals.

I have gone into this campaign because this anti-American movement should be a warning against future movements of this sort. It resembled a fascist movement in that it was based on hates, prejudices and demagogy. It was a revolt against the Bill of Rights, and yet millions were mobilized under its banner. The Hitler movement in Germany had its origin in a similar appeal to racial and religious hate. If it did not eventuate in fascism in America it tended dangerously in that direction. Marching men in uniforms of bedsheets and pillowcases, the fanning of the flames of hate, the burning of crosses, intimidation—all quite similar to events in Germany in the 1930s. The movement had its storm troopers too. The time came when in Indiana in a Republican state convention the head of the Klan in that commonwealth stalked down the aisles with a gun in his holster in plain view, giving orders. Happily, this man ended his career in the penitentiary.

The theory of the fanatics was that Al Smith was "the Catholic candidate" and that all Catholics supported him. He lost New York State partly because of the Klan strength there, but he probably could have carried the state had all the Catholics there supported him, and they did not. Catholics in big business, for instance, did not permit their religion to alienate them from the Republican Party.

No Democrat in public life was a more devout Catholic than

Senator Tom Walsh of Montana. Soon after Smith's nomination I received a three-page, single-spaced letter from him, expressing his fear that he might not be able to support him unconditionally, because of Smith's opposition to the Great Lakes–St. Lawrence waterway. He believed the project was of the greatest importance to the farm states in the marketing of their products. "Hoover, as you know, is committed to the project, is enthusiastically for it," he wrote. "Twenty-two states have officially endorsed it. New York alone among the forty-eight has gone on record against it, insisting on the utilization of its so-called 'barge canal.'" He ascribed the opposition to "the railroads leading from the West to New York City" and to "the power trust." The strong opposition of Smith to the Great Lakes–St. Lawrence waterway he ascribed to the selfish or "provincial" views of New York, and he thought that possibly it had been imposed upon him as governor of New York. But "what can I say to the people of Montana about what President Smith will or will not do?" he asked. He had told the people, both from the platform and in the Senate, that their dearest interests were involved, and how could he warmly support a candidate openly opposed? He hoped that though as the spokesman for New York Smith had to go along with New York sentiment, as President he would respond to the demands of the rest of the country of which he would become the spokesman—but how could he, Walsh, be certain? In a statement he had "said what I could for the nominee . . . but how wholeheartedly I can enter into the campaign for him is still uncertain," for the reasons set forth in his letter to me.

Here was one of the two most conspicuous Catholics in public life refusing blindly to follow a candidate because of his religion. Just what understanding he may have reached with Smith is not revealed. His position, however, based on political and economic grounds regardless of the nominee's religion, stands out like a red light against the Klan's propaganda that Smith was primarily the candidate of a religion rather than of a political party.

Soon after the election, Smith went south on a prolonged vacation. I saw him for the first time after his return at a dinner at the home of Ed Flynn, the party leader in the Bronx.

He arrived looking fit after his rest, his color ruddy, his eyes bright, his step springy. Mrs. Smith was with him, and nothing could have been more charming than his devotion to her. During the cocktail interval he held forth with boyish enthusiasm on the Bronx of their courtship days, when she had lived there and when, he said, "it was a wilderness." He had had a job in the New York County (Manhattan) sheriff's office which called for the delivery of summonses, and no one relished an assignment to the Bronx, since the houses were widely scattered. On a Thursday young Smith offered to deliver all the Bronx summonses on condition that he would not be called upon to report until the task was finished, and the sheriff agreed. That night the young lover appeared at the home of Katie's family, and when it grew late a gentle hint was given. "But I'm staying all night," he said, and he explained the bargain with the sheriff.

"The next morning," he continued, "I got Katie's brother's bicycle, and by Friday noon the job was finished and I had two and a half days to wander with Katie on the commons and along the riverbank." He recalled the strategy with all the gusto of a mischievous boy, while Katie smiled.

During the dinner he was amusing and little was said about the campaign and the election, but it was evident that he resented the poor showing in Manhattan. The suggestion was made that New Rochelle and another place might be annexed to the Bronx. Someone broke in with the reminder that the majority in these towns were Republicans.

"Take them in and make them Democratic," said Mrs. Smith.

"And you might annex Manhattan and do the same," Smith said sourly. "You can have my full share of Manhattan."

That night he told a story that throws light on his very human, kindly traits. An Italian policeman had been about to sail on a vacation to Italy, and Smith, then governor and in the heyday of his popularity, had decided to see him off. "I thought it might mean good treatment for Tony on his trip," he explained. All the officers of the Italian liner were standing at salute when he and his party arrived. Asked what he would have to drink, he said, "No drink— I want some Italian spaghetti." The party was shown into the dining room, and the stewards brought two huge portions of the spaghetti the guest craved. He had asked for another helping when he noticed it was ten minutes of six; the boat was scheduled to sail at six, so he canceled the order. A stiff-necked officer retired, and a moment later the captain, in gold braid, very formal and military, appeared, walking like a soldier on review, bowed, saluted and said, "Governor, the boat will sail when you have had the spaghetti." The boat was an hour late in sailing, but on the trip Tony was treated like a prince.

The most touching thing Smith said that evening was apropos of the election. In Georgia, just before, he had heard of a convent school where the girls had prayed for his election and had been bitterly disillusioned and disappointed by his defeat. "I decided to go to the school and talk to the girls," he said. "I said to them, 'I understand you were kind enough to pray for my election, and I thank you for it. I hear you're disappointed because nothing came of it. Well, girls, remember this—it's in the Bible: "Thy will be done on earth . . ."' "

There was a dead silence at the table.

That same evening the Ringling Brothers circus was having its formal opening for the season in the Bronx, and Smith, a friend of John Ringling's, was to be master of ceremonies. On the way there from Flynn's, he was constantly exclaiming about the growth of the Bronx since the days of his wooing. Thirty years before he had been permitted to exercise the horses of a firehouse, and he was peering out the window in an effort to find the site. "Yes, there it is!" he cried excitedly. At the circus the band played "The Sidewalks of New York" and Smith waved his derby and beamed, and inside he vied with the smallest boy in his enthusiasm.

At this time he had been made the manager of the projected Empire State Building which was to rise on the site of the old Waldorf-Astoria Hotel, internationally famous for its cuisine and for the celebrities who had sojourned there. The day he presented inscribed copies of his autobiography to a few friends, he had been watching the men at work demolishing the old structure and he seemed rather sad. The historic hotel was a part of the old Manhattan that he loved, and I gathered that he thought that something of the old life was passing out.

"In the banquet room where I've spoken so many times and attended so many dinners," he said, "it was pathetic. Those great gold and brass moldings and decorations in the corners that I supposed were really costly—nothing but gilded plaster. And the chandeliers! They looked magnificent hanging, but on the floor—

just junk. I went down thinking I might pick up something for my apartment, but there was nothing there worth having. It was pathetic."

His was a unique personality, colorful, unforgettable, and he will never be forgotten in New York.

CHAPTER XIV

The Year of the Bursting Bubble

THE YEAR 1929 was to become memorable for the bursting of the bubble of stock market prosperity toward its close. While a few men of penetration could see the approach of disaster, these, like angels, were few and far between; and despite the increasing unemployment and the agricultural depression, the vast majority were convinced that nothing could happen to disturb the complacency of the fool's paradise. During the first half of this year that was to end so dismally, I found my friends devoting most of their conversation to the stock market, to the fortunes being made on paper and to the ease with which such fortunes could be made.

Happily for me, I was not a speculator and had other things to occupy me that year. I had finished my research for *The Tragic Era*, and during the first six months I wrote and rewrote the manuscript. I had found this research on the Reconstruction years more fascinating than I had expected. It was a liberal education in that period of American history. I had not set out to prove any preconceived theory of my own, but to set down the facts, whatever they were found to be, and I was making discoveries that sharply challenged interpretations of fifty years.

I had always assumed that the popular impression of Andrew Johnson, passed on through historians either writing in a partisan spirit or lacking the courage to attack a prejudice, was the correct one. I was to emerge from the research convinced that not more than four or five other Presidents have approached his defense of American institutions and ideals, and that none has fought such a gallant battle for constitutional government.

I had accepted the old slander that he was a drunkard and that he was drunk when he spoke in Cleveland in 1866 and replied to insults from the audience. This incident occurred during his "swing around the circle," when day after day he had spoken in numerous cities. I knew he had made the swing to arouse the civic conscience of the people in defense of the peace plans of Lincoln. So through many newspapers I followed him on this tour, reading all the speeches published in the contemporary press, and I found them constitutionally sound, dignified, pitched on a high ethical plane. It was because of the favorable impression he was making that the radical Republicans who had taken over the party of Lincoln—whom they hated along with his postwar plan of conciliation —found it necessary to meet his patriotic crusade with a fusillade of falsehoods, the favorite weapon of the demagogue. These made their stand in Cleveland. En route to Cleveland from his last stop he had engaged in conversation on serious matters, and he was perfectly sober. But his enemies knew he had been trained in the rough-and-tumble methods of the Tennessee hustings of prewar days when the speaker who failed to reply vigorously to interruptions from the audience was considered weak or timid, and they knew, too, that Johnson had a temper. Thus the insults hurled at him in Cleveland by his enemies, and by men who were enemies of the Lincoln plan of reconstruction, were answered angrily, and the damage was done. "How disgraceful," they cried, "that a President should bandy words with a crowd!" "Of course he was drunk," many insisted. But my research showed that his speeches on his "swing around the circle" had been statesmanlike, patriotic, and unanswerable except with abuse.

I learned that an old friend, Grace Julian Clark, daughter of George W. Julian, one of the most conspicuous of the abolitionists and a leading member of Congress during the Civil War, possessed a diary of her father's. It had not been intended for publication, but, on my request, the daughter placed two volumes covering the period of *The Tragic Era* at my disposal, and there I found something of the spirit of those mad days, something of the hatred and contempt aimed at Lincoln by the leaders of his own party. One notation, written on the day of Lincoln's death, startled me. It recorded the proceedings and the tone of a party caucus in which the prevailing sentiment was one of hostility to Lincoln's plan, and it concluded with the observation that the general feeling among the leaders was that Lincoln's death "was a God-send to our cause."

And that cause was the cause espoused and led by Thad Stevens and the radicals! Thence onward, the growing hatred of Johnson reflected the hatred of the radicals for Lincoln's plan of conciliation.

But Johnson had been unfortunate in that he had incurred the resentment of both political parties. The Democrats could not forgive the man who had left his party to go on the Union ticket in 1864, though finally his chief support came reluctantly from the Democrats in Congress; and the Republicans, taken over bag and baggage by the extremists, hated him for interfering with their plans for the punishment of the South. There was no one, at first, to champion his cause or to defend him personally.

I think I rendered a real service to history in bringing about a revaluation of Andrew Johnson which has now been accepted. The nearest relative of the maligned President wrote me on the publication of the book to thank me for the justice I had done him. When I began I had no thought of defending Johnson, whom I supposed undefendable. I followed the trail of truth, however, and the real Johnson emerged. And later Nicholas Murray Butler told me that when he was a child in Elizabeth, New Jersey, his father had taken him to see Johnson on his "swing around the circle," and that my portrayal of him was borne out by his own recollection of Johnson's impressive and dignified appearance.

The Tragic Era had a good reception both in the North and in the South and was a Literary Guild selection. The historian Dr. David S. Muzzey of Columbia University, in his review in *Current History*, began with the admission that while a sad story had been told it was a true one and that perhaps "the time has come to tell it." I was deluged with letters, especially from the South, and eight months after publication Franklin D. Roosevelt wrote me from Warm Springs:

It may interest you to know that since I have been down here for the last two weeks at least a dozen good people have spoken to me about "The Tragic Era," and they have not been confined to Georgians or southerners. The book, more than any other book in recent years, had a very definite influence on public thought.

This book kept me home after office hours at the *World* and the year for me was serene and happy. There were a few diversions.

I spoke at the unveiling of Jo Davidson's statue of Robert M. La Follette, Sr., in Statuary Hall in the Capitol in Washington. It is the most living of the statues there, showing La Follette seated in the Senate, his hands grasping the arms of his chair as though he were on the verge of springing to his feet, with an expression of whimsical incredulity on his face, as I saw him in the flesh many times. That day Statuary Hall was packed with his friends, followers and political associates, though among them were not a few who, like Senator James Watson of Indiana, had no use for his political views while having a secret admiration for his genius and courage. I was to speak toward the close, and there were too many speeches, most of them too long; even so, Fola La Follette twice sent a note to her brother on the platform asking me not to cut my speech "one inch." It was well received. At least one man in the audience, aside from the family, was pleased, for Senator Norris of Nebraska sat beaming and smiling broadly when I said that La Follette "did not have to await the conclusion of a party caucus to determine the dictates of his conscience."

That summer Sybil, our daughter Patricia and I sailed for Europe on the *Berengaria*, visiting England and France, spending most of the time in London and Paris and their environs, but for me the greater part of the year was passed prosily enough in New York between our apartment and my office in the tower.

One day we lunched with Colonel and Mrs. House in their apartment, and the conversation revolved largely around Clemenceau. Mrs. House drew a charming picture of the old man at his place on the coast of Brittany in a village of fishermen, where he spent some summers. She described the house as really that of a fisherman, surrounded by sand. "He sticks things in the sand and wonders why they don't grow," she said. His workroom faced the sea and was all windows; he had built a kind of shed where he could be out of the sun and enjoy the ocean breeze.

I was interested by the Colonel's observation that a mistake had been made by Wilson in not placing Root and Taft on the peace commission. "That would have assured favorable action in the Senate," House said. "He should have said to Taft, 'You've been interested for years in a League of Nations. I want you to concern yourself with that.' He could have put me on with Taft and I could

have headed off anything in Taft's mind that might have run
counter to Wilson's plan. Taft would have been easy to work with.
And to Root he should have said, 'You're recognized as one of the
world's greatest international lawyers. You protect us there.' "

He then told me a story not generally known, of the resignations
resulting from the appointment of the peace commission. Ambassador William G. Sharp, accredited to Paris, wanted to be on it, and
when he heard that Wilson preferred to have Newton D. Baker
on the commission he took it as a personal affront, since both were
from Ohio. "I tried to reason with him," said House, "calling his
attention to the fact that none of the other nations included their
ambassadors in Paris, but he was miffed and so he resigned.

"Then, too," said House, "while McAdoo was not keen to go, I
thought he should be on to handle the financial matters, but Wilson
wouldn't appoint him, and when McAdoo heard that Baker might
go on, he, who had been eager to return to private life, also resigned
from the Cabinet. And then Baker, who had been reasonable
throughout, decided not to go."

It was on another occasion at the Colonel's that he talked of the
pretensions of General Smuts of South Africa to the parentage of
the Covenant of the League. He said that all that Wilson owed to
Smuts was the mandate system. The President, he continued, had
wanted a tentative covenant ready so the discussions could revolve
around it. He had discussed it many times with House, and the
Colonel was asked to make a first draft. "I spent two days at Mag-
nolia writing it," he said. "It had twenty-three points and Wilson
worked over it trying to boil it down to thirteen—his lucky number."

And then the Colonel said a startling thing: "It's strange that the
only thing he struck out was the provision for a world court."

That autumn in a dinner-table conversation with McAdoo I
learned something about Jules Jusserand, for years the French ambassador in Washington. I had not seen McAdoo for two years. He
was thinner, with less color, and was much older and more mellow.
However, at his age he had taken to the air, possessing a plane of
his own in which he was traveling between Los Angeles, Washington and New York. I had never known him to be so animated, so
charming in manner or so interesting in conversation. Despite his

years, he was as straight as an Indian. At times he walked around the room, but most of the time he sat in a chair, one leg thrown over the arm, and talked. The conversation turned on his visit to France after the war, and he had little to say about it that was pleasant.

"After the convention in 1924," he said, "I was worn out and so was Mrs. McAdoo, who had not been quite well since, after sitting through all those days in an atmosphere of hate. So we went to Europe for a rest. When we landed at Cherbourg some French reporters met us and I told them we were there for a rest and implied that we didn't care for much attention. But when we got to Paris I found this was taken literally, for we were utterly ignored. One day, however, I was told that the French government was sending an invitation. They had heard that I wished to visit the battlefields, and they offered to arrange the trip and to send along an officer who spoke English. I preferred to go my own way, but it was urged that a refusal would seem ungracious, so I accepted. Just as I feared, it was a military program—an hour here, half an hour there. We were put in an old automobile I would not have hired. The officer, who spoke English poorly, wore me out. In two days we were back and weary. Then came the climax. The government submitted a bill for everything—for the automobile, for the services of the officer, even for the meals we had in a French fort."

I expressed amazement.

"It was no worse than was done to Wilson," he added. "When he went to France a special train was at Cherbourg to take him to Paris, and Wilson thought it a gracious act. But the French government submitted a bill for the train, and, much embarrassed, Wilson paid for it out of his own pocket."

Thus the conversation veered to Jusserand. McAdoo described him as pro-Republican, certainly unfriendly to the Wilson Administration. This did not surprise me in a diplomat accredited to Washington in those days. I had read numerous memoirs and letters of British diplomats who had been in Washington from the 1890s until 1913, and scarcely any of them had found anything to admire or even respect outside Republican circles. This was due in part, no doubt, to the fact that their position and taste confined their personal contacts to the rich social circles of Washington, New

York and Newport, which were almost entirely Republican. Thus foreigners formed their opinion of the personnel of American politics from these. Then came McAdoo's almost incredible story about Jusserand:

"When the war began for us and we entered, the Allies financially were on their last legs. Morgan and Company had about reached the end of their rope. I suggested to Wilson that loans be made to help while we were getting our army ready for the field. This was the time we got Congress to vote nine billion dollars. Five billion of this was for us, two for the loans, and two more for emergencies. We then loaned England two hundred million dollars. When I told the representative of the Bank of England what I proposed, his eyes filled up. When I made out the check my secretary suggested that I sign with two pens and give one to Sir Cecil Spring-Rice, which I did, and it seemed to please him. Then I made a loan of a hundred million dollars to France. Before that, Frank Cobb had been suggesting in the *World* that we 'give it to France and not loan it,' and one day Jusserand came in to ask about it— ostensibly on the instructions of his government. I told him it was impossible and unwise; that if we gave it, the people would think we had done enough, but that a loan could be repeated. Jusserand couldn't see it and was displeased—not only for that reason, but also because he thought France should have got as large a loan as England. I pointed out that England had made many loans to the Allies, and that we would make other loans from time to time to do the most toward ending the war. When I signed the check, I did it with two pens as before, and afterward I offered him one. 'I do not want it,' he said. I thought it the most ungracious thing I had ever heard."

Jusserand was a brilliant man, a distinguished social historian and an elegant speaker, and he was much loved and admired by the Americans, but he had no such comprehension of American institutions as John Bryce. In my early days with Kern I used to see Jusserand almost every evening on his habitual walk, which led past my apartment, accompanied by his American wife, who loomed impressively above him in stature. He was a short, bearded man, and he always seemed solemn on these walks. I had heard him in Arlington at the unveiling of the L'Enfant memorial, when Elihu Root also spoke, and I could not but notice that the Frenchman spoke a more elegant English than the American. He had been an intimate of Theodore Roosevelt, who probably molded his opinions on the personnel of public life; this could hardly have given him a favorable impression of Woodrow Wilson. He was an ardent French patriot, and while there were ample reasons for giving a bigger loan to England than to France it is not remarkable that he resented it. Even so, I cannot disassociate my impressions of Jusserand from the incident of the pen.

One night I dined at Nicholas Murray Butler's on Morningside Heights. Dr. Butler had grown mellower politically, and he found little to commend in the Hoover administration and something to praise in the Democrats' program. Wise as he was politically, apparently he was not a perfect judge of political acumen, for that evening he said that Franklin D. Roosevelt was a political dud. This was surprising, since at this time Roosevelt was enormously popular with the prosperous old families in New York because he too was of the aristocracy and could, they thought, be counted upon to stand by his "class." No one then could have foreseen that fifteen years later, when he was at the peak of his greatness and world renown, rendering service to mankind, he would be the object of the most violent abuse in these same circles. Later, Butler was to admire and support Roosevelt's foreign policy.

And then one gloomy day in October there was a sensational slump on the stock market, and tremors of fear ran through the city. The speculators, in over their heads, tried to console themselves with the thought that it was a freak manifestation arranged for some sinister purpose by some mysterious personage, and that the morrow would see the market booming as before. But on the morrow it was worse. Desperate men were crowding into the banks seeking money to cover themselves, and finding the bankers cold. Many were trying desperately to unload their suddenly worthless stocks. Those who could not sell—and no one was buying—and could not borrow, were facing ruin. And the third day it was still worse.

It was on the night of the third day that I attended a dinner for Winston Churchill in the home of Bernard Baruch, a close friend of the British statesman (who was spending his parliamentary recess in the land of his mother). There were not many guests, but these represented hundreds of millions of dollars. It was such a rich group in its representation that John W. Davis, head of the American bar and scarcely in want himself, came to me to say he was glad I was there, since it gave him less of an inferiority complex in the midst of so many "plutocrats." For there was Charlie Schwab, big, bluff, burly, associated with the steel business and many times a millionaire. The short, slight man with the keen eyes, sharp features and iron-gray hair was Gerard Swope of the General Electric Company, a vest-pocket edition of his brother, Herbert Bayard Swope. The large man with the strong, chiseled features one finds on old Roman coins, a bit cynical and sardonic, was Charles Mitchell of the National City Bank. The rather prim little old man with a white beard was Cyrus Curtis, owner of the *Saturday Evening Post* and the New York *Evening Post*, who had his finger in numerous financial pies. His white hair, bright eyes and pink schoolgirl complexion made him handsome. Former Colorado Senator Simon Guggenheim, a short, jolly man with a democratic manner, was in the company. And mingling with the financiers was George Wickersham, former Attorney General, a short gray man with a smiling face and a genial manner.

Had Churchill still been Chancellor of the Exchequer, anyone seeing him in such company would have suspected his mission to be that of negotiating a loan.

Knowing of the turmoil on Wall Street, with the economic and financial structure trembling to its base, I would have thought most of the guests of the evening would be in a huddle on the Street seeking means to save or restore financial order; I did not realize that these wizards of finance were as helpless as the ragpicker in the alley. I was puzzled by the general simulation of carefree levity, but later I could understand. They were entering a graveyard and they were whistling like the scared boy to keep up courage. For during the dinner the financiers on a powder keg gave the impression of abnormal gaiety. I was seated between Baker of the City Trust and Curtis, and I asked the former how things looked on the Street.

"It looks as if tomorrow will be worse than ever, from present indications," he said. So that was it.

I had read all that Churchill had written and I thought him the most brilliant and entertaining writer of political history since Macaulay. I had followed his career eagerly from the hour I heard him, fresh from his escape from a military prison in South Africa, lecturing in the English Theater in Indianapolis. He then was young. This night his appearance at first was disappointing. The dashing, audacious, brilliant fighting political orator I had envisioned was short, pudgy, thick-chested, with slightly rounded shoulders. He was a little bald, but he had the fresh English complexion, bright, twinkling pale-blue eyes and a small cherubic mouth. When I told him that although I was the youngest man present I had probably heard him before any of the rest, and described his appearance in Indianapolis years before, he was amused. He had read *The Tragic Era*, which Gilbert Chesterton had elaborately reviewed in an English magazine. In conversation his voice was peculiar, a little nasal, as though he had a head cold, and he talked choppily.

With the champagne, Churchill was introduced and he spoke conversationally for fifteen minutes, with numerous little whimsical touches and no attempt at purple patches. The pending economic tragedy was not mentioned, and he talked entirely on Anglo-American relations. He said that, while anxious for actual naval parity between the two nations, England was dependent on the sea for existence and this necessitated a navy strong enough to keep the breadline open. It was a pleasant, familiar talk.

After dinner I had an opportunity to talk with him for some time when he was in a reminiscent mood. Someone had suggested that the settlement of the Irish question had removed a bone of contention between the English-speaking peoples and that he was largely responsible. "No," he said, "Lloyd George was responsible. Of course, when the plan was proposed I had something to do with helping iron out the difficulties."

The party broke up at midnight, and the next day the market struck bottom. The panic and the long lean years loomed ahead.

The long depression, with millions dependent on charity for life, had the result of disillusioning the average American about the superhuman wisdom of the great financiers. Most Americans until then had kept a childlike faith in the capacity of bankers and great industrialists to do anything they wished. For some months it was pathetic to see how many clung to the illusion. One heard on every side that the market crash was due to some clever maneuver of some financial wizard for some selfish end, and that when the purpose had been served, these strong men of the Street would wave a magic wand and lo, everything would be as it was before.

It was wishful thinking. No one knew this so well as the idols of these optimistic people. They were as helpless as anyone, and some of them were more pessimistic than most. They who were of the magic circle knew it that night at Baruch's, and this explained the simulated levity of the evening. Since that period, the superman of Wall Street has passed into mythology.

That autumn Houghton Mifflin, my publisher, who had published the books of Senator Beveridge, asked me to undertake a biography of the Senator, who, after writing his monumental work on John Marshall, had died when an equally imposing work on Lincoln was half finished. I would have demurred had I not learned that Mrs. Beveridge hoped I would consent. Then, to my relief, I was told that Beveridge had kept all his correspondence of thirty years, comprising thousands of letters from national leaders. Eager to satisfy myself of the existence of this rich mine of information, I went one weekend to Beveridge's summer home at Beverly Farms, Massachusetts, where he had written his Marshall and Lincoln biographies.

The house was large and attractive, but he had built a platform in a tree where he had worked in warm weather. The letter files were on the top floor of the house, and there were the letters alphabetically filed for each year. And there on many weekends in the attic I was to examine the manuscript and select such as I required in New York. I came to look forward to these excursions to Beverly Farms, since they took me into a beautiful countryside where I could get the odor of trees and the smell of the sea. I had feared that restrictions would be put on the use of the manuscript, but I soon found that Mrs. Beveridge and the publisher wanted history and not an inspired panegyric. The letters were there to use, and some of them were of the sort that families often keep from biographer or historian; none was withheld or even discussed. My appreciation of Mrs. Beveridge grew through the months. She had worked with Beveridge in the writing of his great biographies, reading the manuscript and offering criticisms, and she had the instinct of a real historian. She never once interfered, never once asked what line I was taking. When the manuscript was finished I asked her to read it for the correction of possible mistakes as to facts. When it was returned with the sole suggestion that I give more space to the first Mrs. Beveridge, whom I had known when I was a boy, my admiration grew.

Though the enormous amount of manuscript material, including the exchange of letters between the political leaders of the period, convinced me that the book had some permanent value, I was surprised when Carl Van Doren asked for it for the Literary Guild. The reviews were uniformly favorable, that of Dr. John H. Finley in the New York *Times* especially so. Personal letters reinforced the judgment of the reviewers. When Ferris Greenslet of Houghton Mifflin, whose literary judgment was acknowledged, wrote me that "it seems to me the very best biography of any American public man that I have ever read," and Willis Abbot, then editor of the *Christian Science Monitor*, wrote me that he thought I had "done an amazing piece of work when judged by its literary, historical and political character," I was satisfied with the book. After twenty-five years I still sometimes receive letters about it.

Meanwhile the depression deepened and darkened and nothing was done in Washington beyond the giving out of assurances with monotonous regularity that prosperity was "just around the corner." We were to hear this constantly for four years of increasing misery, and the search for the "corner" was like looking for the end of the rainbow.

CHAPTER XV

The Deepening Gloom

THROUGHOUT THE YEAR 1930 the country was accustoming itself to the depression, which was deepening month by month. There was scarcely anyone who did not have personal friends who were in dire distress. The demands on private charity increased alarmingly, and no matter how generous the response it did not remotely meet the needs. Millions of workmen were in the streets pounding the pavement in hopeless search for a bread-and-butter job.

Throughout the year I was making regular journeys to Beverly Farms to work on my biography of Beveridge, and, aside from this, and my editorial work on the *Evening World*, I was responding to more invitations for speeches than ever before. Because of *The Tragic Era* I was overwhelmed with requests for commencement speeches in Southern universities, from many of which I received the honorary degree of Doctor of Laws.

The political pot was boiling over that year, and I had political speeches to make as well. The Administration was conspicuously unpopular. It seemed paralyzed as to action in the face of the greatest economic crisis in our history. It insisted that it was not proper to extend national aid to the unemployed and that this was the responsibility of private charity or of the cities and the states, whose resources were almost exhausted. The one measure on which, strangely, it pinned its faith was an absurdly high tariff measure, the Smoot-Hawley bill. With people starving, with trade languishing, it appeared to think that to increase the cost of living would somehow ameliorate the condition of the hungry, and that to wreck our foreign market would revive the dwindling commercial exchange. The measure was so utterly illogical that for one day the Administration forces lost control of the House to the Democrats and the insurgent Republicans.

I was in Washington that day, and I witnessed this first serious break in the Administration lines. The lumber schedule was up for discussion and action in the House, and Congressman Hawley, hailing from a lumber state, Oregon, was keen about it. The press of the nation, including scores of Republican papers, was in open revolt, putting the fear of the Lord into the hearts of the most robust partisans. Taking advantage of the situation, Crisp of Georgia, one of the cleverest of parliamentarians, who was leading that day for the Democrats, moved to put lumber on the free list. Speaker Longworth called for a voice vote, and, to his amazement and Hawley's consternation, the ayes won. Hawley stood in the aisle with his mouth open, mentally paralyzed, speechless. To give him a chance to recover sufficiently to move for a roll call, Longworth drawled slowly, "The . . . ayes . . . seem to . . . have it." He repeated it more slowly, but there stood Hawley, rooted to the spot and still speechless.

At length, his face flushed and very angry, Longworth did a most unusual thing. "Does the gentleman from Oregon wish to address the chair?" he asked, expecting a motion for a roll call. Still Hawley stood, his mouth open, paralyzed. Someone else finally made the motion, but the roll call did not help, since twenty Republicans, who had stood up for the high duty but feared a record vote, went with the Democrats.

Then came the sugar schedule, and the Democrats forced a reduction in the duty. The remainder of the afternoon the Democratic minority was in absolute control of the Republican House, and Crisp, in the absence of Jack Garner, sick with a cold, assumed the actual leadership of that body.

It was a comedy of errors all around, throwing a white light for consumers on the tricks of tariff making. For the confession was made that the cement bloc and the lumber bloc had agreed to vote for each other's graft. The cement vote came first and the lumbermen carried out their part of the bargain, but when the vote on lumber came, so great was the protest that the cement men ran out on theirs. Infuriated by the betrayal, the lumbermen rushed to Crisp, appealing to his expert parliamentary knowledge for some way to force a reconsideration of the vote on cement. The incident was a revelation to many Americans on how tariff bills are put through. That night everyone was laughing in the hotel lobbies over the bizarre events of the day. The old regime had just about reached the end of its string.

Early that year I attended a stag dinner for General Smuts in the home of Bernard Baruch. The last two Democratic nominees for President, John W. Davis and Al Smith, were there. That night Admiral Grayson, who had been the friend and doctor of Woodrow Wilson, told me of his plan to publish his White House diary when Ray Stannard Baker had finished his biography of Wilson. Senator Carter Glass was there with his crooked smile, very chatty and interesting, along with Senators Wagner and Pittman. There, too, was Governor Ritchie of Maryland, Adolph Ochs of the *Times*, Henry Morgenthau and Norman H. Davis. The latter joked on the possibility of the marriage of his son to a descendant of Ben Butler of Civil War fame, and Carter Glass of Virginia sourly observed that "the Butler spoons" would probably find their way to the Davis family. With Tom Chadbourne and Mitchell of the National City Bank talking business at the table, Judge Bingham, later ambassador to England, turned to me with the observation, "It's funny that when these New Yorkers get together they talk of nothing but money."

In a joking mood Mitchell turned to Eugene Meyer, who, with Baruch, was interested in legislation for the alleviation of the tragic state of the farmers. "And how are your farmers, Gene?" he asked with a smile.

"My farmers may save you financiers if there's to be any saving," Meyer said. "They're the people who may get you out of the panic, and if they won't we'll never get out. They continue to produce while your factories close."

Mitchell sobered. "I think you're right," he said.

One day I lunched with Edgar Lee Masters at the Players club. He appeared late with the explanation that he was working on a poem to supplement his "Jack Kelso." It was to be called "Gettysburg."

I have never known anyone quite like the author of *Spoon River Anthology*—so simple, direct, natural, so pessimistic over politics and so prone to ignore it because it distressed him. He was very like Dreiser in this regard. At this time Allan Nevins was planning to edit a series of American biographies, and I persuaded him to ask Masters to write the biography of Altgeld, for whom I knew the poet had an immense admiration. The idea appealed to Masters momentarily, but in the end he declined. "I found I would get my thoughts on things I want to keep away from for the peace of my mind," he said.

Tagore, the Indian poet, was then in the United States receiving the adulation of literary circles. I was shocked by the bitterness of Masters' denunciation of the man. Finally I was able to pin him down to his grievance. He said that the widow of William Vaughn Moody, the poet, had a tearoom near the University of Chicago, and that all literary celebrities visiting the city were expected to have tea with her. When Tagore went there he told Mrs. Moody that he had a few friends who would love to have tea with her as her guests. He was told that he might bring them. The next day he appeared with half a hundred husky compatriots, and Mrs. Moody had to scour the neighborhood for bread and cake. "Yes," snorted Masters scornfully. "Tagore is a grafter."

In the old days I had often wished to have Dreiser and Edgar Lee Masters to dinner, but I had found both chilly to the suggestion and had learned a possible reason for the estrangement. It seems that some years before the publication of his *Spoon River Anthology* Masters, then one of Dreiser's friends, was morbidly depressed over his inability to realize his literary aspirations. He had abandoned a lucrative law practice with Clarence Darrow to concentrate on writing and nothing had come of it. He was even hinting at suicide. Dreiser, who knew he was full of the Spoon River poems, had urged that he put them in form. "You're such a killjoy," he told him, "that I'm not concerned with what you do about yourself, but I am interested in seeing those poems written. Write them, and then, if you insist, go off and shoot yourself." Masters wrote the poems, and Dreiser peddled them about to all the publishing houses in New York without success. At length William Marion Reedy published some of them in his St. Louis magazine, and after these created a furor all the publishers wanted them. "I've seen very little of Masters for a number of years," Dreiser added. "It got so every time I saw him he was cross with me, and so I stayed away. I have no idea what it was about."

The subject was too delicate to mention to Masters, so I never heard his version of the cooling of their relations. Happily, years later, when Dreiser was given the Gold Medal for Literature by the Academy of Arts and Letters, he insisted that Masters, then ill, accompany him to the ceremony, and Masters did.

That year the political outlook was interesting. After the election of 1928 Mr. Raskob, the national chairman, delegated the active duties of the chairmanship to Jouett Shouse, than whom no better man could have been found. I knew him intimately and admired him. He did much to form the Democratic members of Congress into a compact organized group. He put experts to work collecting the material that formed the basis of Congressional speeches that were given a nationwide circulation. In Charles Michelson he found one of the ablest publicity men who ever served a political cause. Despite the overwhelming defeat in 1928 the party entered the Congressional campaign of 1930 perfectly organized for action and richly munitioned through Shouse. He had a hundred thousand copies of an article of mine in the *World* printed and circulated. And so with many others. That year I made a number of political speeches. My own interest in them now comes from incidents connected with them.

In February I spoke at a banquet of the Democratic Editorial Association in Indianapolis, and the next day I went to Terre Haute, where, at one of several functions for me, I had a peculiar experience that has puzzled me ever since. I have often thought that a clever essayist could write a charming essay on the adventures of a book, and this will illustrate: At a luncheon presided over by the mayor, a local labor leader was introduced to tell a story. He said he had long patronized a little junk shop and secondhand bookstore near where he worked, and that recently, while rummaging among his possessions bought there, he had found a copy of Byron's poems the inscription of which showed that it had been bought by a boy with money made on tickets for a Joaquin Miller lecture. He remarked that the book had marginal notations and that he was distressed to say that most of the marked passages were from *Don Juan*. He had been tempted to keep the book, but had concluded it should go back to the boy who had bought it—myself.

I remembered the book well. How it found its way into a secondhand store in Terre Haute, seventy miles from Indianapolis,

I cannot imagine, since I had never sold a book from my library. It probably had been loaned to a friend who, as is often the custom, failed to return it and later needed a little money. Thus after a third of a century Byron came back to me.

A somewhat similar experience later: When I was in Chile I noticed in a circular announcement of the Argosy bookstore in New York that among the old books offered was a first edition of my *Party Battles of the Jackson Period,* and since I had no first edition I ordered it. I had it some years before I noticed that it was an inscribed copy—from William Gibbs McAdoo to Tom Chadbourne as a Christmas gift in 1922. It evidently had reached the Argosy through the sale of Chadbourne's library after his death. I am sure that the bookstore too had overlooked the inscription, or the price would have been higher.

In April 1930 I was the speaker at a dinner of the Women's National Democratic Club in Washington in their new clubhouse on Connecticut Avenue. Among the numerous men who attended were Cordell Hull, Perry Belmont, some Senators and Dr. Jamieson of the Congressional Library. At the small round table where I sat, and at which Mrs. Daisy Harriman presided, were Mrs. Woodrow Wilson, Madame Grouitch, a Virginia woman married to the Foreign Minister of Yugoslavia, and, strangely enough, a Republican guest who arrived just as I began speaking—Alice Roosevelt Longworth. When the wife of the Republican Speaker threaded her way among the tables there was a gasp of astonishment from most of the women which sounded like a sudden breeze in the trees. I certainly had not planned to say anything about her father or her husband, but I did moderate a few expressions out of deference to her. She was not enamored of the Hoover Administration and, being a Roosevelt, had no inhibitions on the subject, and she cheered portions of the speech and laughed heartily at all the jibes at the Administration.

A week later I spoke at a state Democratic banquet in Cleveland, in the ballroom of the Statler Hotel. I looked forward with pleasure to this dinner, since Newton D. Baker had agreed to introduce me, and, though ill and running a temperature, he appeared. He was a small man, but no one could look into his face, with its penetrating dark eyes, without realizing that there was an extraordinary intelligence to explain his brilliant career at the bar and as Secretary of War. At this time he was being urged in many quarters for the Democratic Presidential nomination. He brushed the suggestion aside with seeming levity. When I told him of a talk with Mrs. Woodrow Wilson, who had expressed a preference for his nomination, he said he had been too close to the Presidency ever to crave the job, but this I could not quite believe. That night he was downcast over the fate of the World Court and puzzled over Hoover's failure to popularize himself, ascribing it in part to his incapacity for political leadership.

As we were leaving, an incident convinced me that Baker would have liked nothing better than the Presidential nomination in 1932. He had left the hall and was in the lobby, when he returned to the dining room to say to me in an undertone, "It's too early to decide on the matter you mentioned at the table."

During the last week of the campaign in 1930 I was asked by Shouse to make a political speech over a nationwide radio hookup, and I chose as my subject "The Collapse of an Administration." I had always found a microphone disturbing; still, it had been possible to ignore its presence when I was facing an audience. But to make a speech with the right tone and expression into a piece of mechanism in an empty room was not so simple, and I looked forward to the ordeal with trepidation. However, on entering the room I found a thirty-piece band that was to furnish music, and during the delivery of the speech I talked to the musicians and got the same inspiration as from any other audience. Even so, it seemed a waste of time and energy, for this was in the early days of the radio and I still found it hard to believe that people were really listening. But the reception was good and telegrams and letters poured in from every section of the country. Bainbridge Colby described the speech as "a terrific arraignment of the Hoover Administration without exaggeration," and Shouse thought it "the strongest speech of the campaign." Requests for copies of the speech came from Congressional candidates over the country. I was pressed to speak in Boston, and Peter Goelet Gerry asked me to speak in Providence, but it was impossible, and my one campaign speech was made over the radio. It was easy to make an opposition speech in those days.

The Democrats swept the country in 1930 and carried the House of Representatives. In New York Franklin D. Roosevelt was re-elected governor by a majority much greater than the one that had first elected him in 1928, and there no longer could be any doubt of his candidacy for the 1932 Presidential nomination.

In July I had spent a day with Roosevelt at his family home at Hyde Park—my first visit there, although I had been to his house in the city. The drive from Poughkeepsie to Hyde Park is through a beautiful countryside. The house looked mellow and attractive—a very large yellow brick, with a columned porch, softened by time. It reminded me of an English country house.

Mrs. Roosevelt appeared in the drawing room to say that the Governor wanted to initiate me into the mysteries of a farmer's life. When I reached the hall I found Roosevelt in a wheel chair, jovial but not looking so well, I thought, for his color was grayish and there were circles under his eyes. He was wheeled outside and two husky men engaged on the farm lifted him into a small car, in which he drove us to a grove of poplars whose trimming he wanted to supervise. He was without coat or vest, and his shirt was un-buttoned at the top. His mother had suggested a light coat, but he had impatiently brushed it aside.

Hardly had we reached the grove when the contractor for a bridge that was soon to be formally opened came to talk over the plans for the ceremony. "Foolish," said Roosevelt after the man had gone. "It could have been attended to better through correspond-ence."

It was soon evident that he knew all about trees, for, as he sat in the car, he directed which branches should be cut off, and how close they were to be cut. When one of the farm hands appeared with a scythe to mow the tall weeds, Roosevelt gave a shout of ap-proval, expressing surprise that the man knew how to use it. The youngest Roosevelt boy also had a scythe, and his father took some pride in that, warning him not to cut his shins.

In between times when he was directing the trimming of the trees, he talked politics. It was clear that the Prohibition issue an-noyed him not a little. He had his own idea of a plank for the state platform, to be headed not "Prohibition," but "Temperance." It differed little from the ordinary declaration for the repeal of the Eighteenth Amendment. It proposed a restoration to the states of the right to determine for themselves, with a pledge of federal support in the enforcement of Prohibition in states that preferred it, through a control of interstate commerce.

I told him I thought Smith had made a mistake in the convention of 1928 in sending his "wet" telegram after he had been nominated, and he agreed. "The telegram was sent on the insistence of Belle Moscowitz," he said. "It came when the convention was on its last legs, and, in the absence of Robinson, Pat Harrison was presiding. I showed him the telegram. 'My God,' he said, 'this will cause a riot!' And so we agreed that when all the business was over the telegram would be read, since we had to read it, and then I would immediately move an adjournment and Pat would put the question and declare its adoption."

At length Mrs. Roosevelt appeared, laughing, to say that we really must go to lunch, since others were waiting and hungry. It was then almost two o'clock. She stood on the running board and the Governor drove us back.

Roosevelt was in fine humor that day. He entertained the company at lunch by telling about his Harvard days, and about the place in Georgia where water ran uphill—an optical illusion that he then explained.

After lunch when the ladies went to the drawing room for coffee, Roosevelt had a conference with some politicians from Connecticut, while I sat on the porch and smoked. At length we were summoned to the drawing room with the announcement that Roosevelt was "in his corner" by the fireplace. Here we talked politics and personalities for a while. Then his secretary came to say that some foreigner was there to ask him about some "poles in the road." Visibly annoyed, he told her to find out about it and to take notes. Soon Mrs. Roosevelt entered, amused and apologetic, saying that the man simply had to see him about some "poles in the road." Simulating the manner of a petulant child, he said, "But I don't know anything about poles in the road." And then he added, "This is the way it is. I'm troubled more here with matters of this sort than in Albany."

I had been much impressed by Roosevelt's naturalness, by the delightful informality of the family and by his evident love of Hyde Park, and I was glad that I had seen him trimming the trees minus coat or vest and with his shirt open at the top.

But Presidential politics was now to the fore. That August I had lunch with Jouett Shouse at the Park Lane Hotel in New York and found him optimistic over the party's prospects for 1932. He had attended a conference of Raskob and Smith with Roosevelt. This was before the convention that was to renominate Roosevelt for governor. I learned later that the purpose of the conference was to persuade Smith to place Roosevelt in nomination, and to determine Smith's role in the campaign. Still later, I learned that Smith had issued an ultimatum that if he was to take part in the campaign for Roosevelt the latter would have to make clear publicly that he was a "dripping wet." Thus, for the first time, I foresaw the inevitable friction between the old friends. In New York it was an unnecessary declaration, since everyone knew perfectly well that Roosevelt was opposed to Prohibition. The only effect of a dripping-wet declaration would have been to put him on the defensive in the South, which was politically dry. It was not intended to be helpful to Roosevelt's candidacy for the Presidential nomination.

Political luncheons and dinners were multiplying. One day Bainbridge Colby asked me to lunch with him at a restaurant on Ann Street. I knew him for what he was, a very brilliant man, a polished orator. In appearance he resembled the pictures of the courtiers of the days of Louis XIV. He had that mingling of strength, cunning and romanticism. His handsome head covered with iron-gray hair, his strong, lean bronzed face, his brown eyes indicating his intellect, his full lips, gave me that impression. His voice was full-toned. His manner was not merely courteous, it was courtly. That day I found him a fascinating conversationalist. As in his speeches, his vocabulary was rich and colorful.

He told me how he had entered the Democratic Party in 1916 by way of the Bull Moose. He had made the speech placing Theodore Roosevelt in nomination at the Chicago convention, but scarcely had he finished his peroration when his candidate walked bag and baggage back into the Republican camp. Utterly crushed and disgusted, he could not bring himself to join the others on the homeward journey, and instead he went to a Chicago hotel and shut himself in his room with a bottle of rye and a box of cigars. When the New York *World* telegraphed him for his views on the situation he brushed it aside. "But finally," he said, "the rye and the cigars soothed me and I decided to send something to the *World*. I said that the Progressive Party was dead and that it would be wise to wait and see what the Democrats did. That went all over the country and caused some comment. Later I attended a dinner in New York addressed by Woodrow Wilson. It was the time he said he was playing for the verdict of mankind. Unexpectedly I was called upon, but I didn't commit myself. It didn't seem to be the time. But I did pay a tribute to Wilson and sat down. I was a little flustered, as one will be when called upon without warning, wondering if I had said the right thing. Suddenly someone took hold of my arm. It was Wilson. He had come all the way from his place at the table to thank me and to say he appreciated what I had said. That was the sweetest moment of my life." Soon after that he had gone over to the Democrats, to become in time Wilson's last Secretary of State.

That day he told another story of the Progressive, or Bull Moose, Party. Two calls were written for the first Progressive convention in 1912, one by Frank Munsey, the other by Colby. Theodore Roosevelt preferred the Colby call, but Munsey threatened to leave the party if his were not used, and it was. After Munsey left, Roosevelt said, "I have a profound respect for Mr. Munsey's checkbook."

I got the impression that day that Colby had aspirations for the Presidential nomination. He told me something I had not heard before, that at one time during the 1920 San Francisco convention there was a possibility that he might be put in nomination. Murphy of Tammany had told him that there was some sentiment for his nomination, and that it had been decided to "give him a run." But Murphy thought it would be unwise for Tammany or New York to lead off. His idea was for some state near the top of the roll call to lead off and for New York to follow. Just why this plan was not carried out he did not say.

I had no little admiration for the intellectual caliber of Bainbridge Colby, who unquestionably enjoyed the confidence and friendship of Woodrow Wilson. But with a Democratic victory almost inevitable because of the wretched economic condition of the country, it was too much to expect that the party would turn for a leader to one who had been associated with it only a few years.

Clearly it would make its choice between Roosevelt, Garner, Baker, Ritchie and others who had fought the battles of the lean years and felt that in the year of the harvest one of them should be the beneficiary of the sowing.

In the interval, in early 1931, came what Adolph Ochs of the New York *Times* described as a great tragedy to American journalism—the needless scrapping of the New York *World*, the greatest champion of liberal principles in the country.

I had just returned from Georgia, where I had spoken at the University of Georgia and at Oglethorpe University, and was unlocking the door to my office when Rollin Kirby, in passing, asked if I thought it worth while. He then startled me with the news that the *World* was being sold to the Scripps-Howard chain and would be scrapped. It was my first intimation that negotiations for a sale had been in progress, and I was no more ignorant of the proceedings behind the screen than others on the staff who had been on the paper for thirty years. Later I learned that Herbert Pulitzer, Joseph Pulitzer's youngest son, to whom the father had left a controlling interest, had approached Adolph Ochs with an offer to sell the *Morning, Evening* and *Sunday World* to the *Times*. The offer was refused. Ochs, who looked upon great newspapers as public institutions and not merchandise, was shocked, and he promised a counterproposition. This contemplated the turning over of the paper to members of the staff, with some financial assistance to cover the period of transition. No reply was made to that generous proposal. The sale proceedings were delayed because the sale could not be consummated without court action from Surrogate Foley, and during the interval a funereal pall descended on the staff. Lovely old John Heaton, who had been with the paper for years during the lifetime of Joseph Pulitzer, and to whom the *World* was as a child, was prostrated by the news.

Surrogate Foley was still considering his action when I attended a dinner of Roosevelt's at the Executive Mansion in Albany and stayed the night. All at the table were talking almost exclusively about the fate of the great newspaper. Roosevelt announced that he had arranged for any news touching on the sale to be promptly transmitted to him. The atmosphere was like that of people in a room adjoining that of a friend whose life was ebbing. The news that Foley had authorized the sale came while we were still at the table, and it was received with the solemnity with which the announcement of a death would be received.

Some time later, at a political dinner, Surrogate Foley told me of his grief in authorizing the sale, but said that all information in his possession indicated there was no possible way to save the paper. Later still I learned that there was a way. Adolph Ochs, who was abroad at the time, told a staff conference on his return that perhaps it was just as well that he had been out of the country, because if he had been in New York he would voluntarily have gone before Foley and shown how, with some changes, the *Morning World* could make money, thus eliminating the one reason on which Foley acted.

The sale was against the judgment or desire of Ralph Pulitzer. On February 24, 1931, I received a sad letter from Ralph:

In the face of this tragedy to our newspaper and of the personal catastrophe that it means to so many devoted World men, words seem worse than empty.

I must ask you to believe that the abrupt nature of the sale as well as the sale itself was unavoidable.

The depth of my own distress for the fate of the editors and the future of so many of the men with whom I have spent my working life I must leave to your friendship to realize.

With heartfelt thanks for your past loyal services to the paper and to me, I am,

Faithfully yours,
RALPH PULITZER

The grief of many thousands is reflected in a letter that Senator Wagner wrote me on March 2:

I never regarded myself as a sentimentalist, yet I had that "lump in the throat" feeling when I realized that the sun had set upon the Evening World. In a rapidly changing age I suppose we must learn to accept such events and hope that the ideas and ideals embraced in your editorial page will somehow find expression. In fact, knowing you, I am sure they will.

There can be no doubt that the scrapping of the *World* was not only the greatest tragedy in the history of American journalism but an equal tragedy to liberalism in the United States.

I was still at the dinner table in Albany when Hearst telephoned from California to Will Curley of the *Journal* to get me for a signed editorial column. Six years before I had declined an offer of a Hearst editorial position vacated by Norman Hapgood. When Curley invited me to his apartment in the Warwick Hotel I told him that many of my views were not in accord with those of Mr. Hearst, and that I could not write against my own convictions. He replied that I would select my own subjects and treat them in my own way, and that since my column would be signed it would be mine without interference. I accepted with some misgivings. I wrote signed articles for all the Hearst papers from coast to coast for two years and not one word was ever stricken out. Never once was I instructed to write anything. No one ever inquired what I was going to write or say. As an editorial writer I have never had such freedom of expression anywhere else.

In one editorial I injected a paragraph in commendation of something Al Smith had said. Because I had been treated so fairly, I took the editorial to Curley and told him that it contained a paragraph he might not want and that it could be stricken out without destroying the whole. He read the editorial carefully.

"What paragraph do you mean?" he asked. I told him.

"What's wrong with it?" he asked.

I replied that I found nothing wrong with it, but that I knew of the feud between Hearst and Smith.

"All the more reason we should publish it," he said. "It proves to the public that you're free."

Another incident, even more impressive to me: I had devoted two columns of satirical observations on a political interview with a great industrialist, and the next day, speaking in the home city of this man, I had repeated the substance of the editorial in a speech. Two months later, after the election of 1932, the city editor told me that at the time the editorial appeared the industrialist was on the point of signing an advertising contract of huge proportions, and that Hearst almost lost the contract.

I went to Curley. "You didn't tell me about the trouble over the advertising contract with ——," I said.

Curley's face flushed. "Who told you?" he asked.

I told him.

"He had no right to tell you," he said with indignation. "We had specific instructions from the chief never to mention the matter to you. Hearst stood firm and got the contract anyway. If he hadn't it would have been all the same as far as you're concerned."

I enjoyed my two years with Hearst. I wrote my editorials in my home and took or sent them to the office. Because my name was signed to them I had a new experience as an editorial writer: a great daily flood of letters addressed to me. Most of these were laudatory, some were abusive; from them I learned more about the public.

During his long life many derogatory things were said about Hearst, too few in commendation of many public services he rendered. Differing from him on many things, I thought him a great journalistic genius and a man of great ability. His occasional two-column front-page editorials were most powerful. He fought many a battle for social justice for which he was viciously assailed.

I saw him personally only once, when I was ambassador in Madrid and he was touring Spain. He came to the embassy residence, the palace of the Duke of Montellano, to see the famous Goya panels and the beautiful garden, and it was hard to associate the hard-hitting journalist with the modest-mannered, soft-spoken and kindly gentleman I met that day.

CHAPTER XVI

Gloomy Years—and Light Shafts in the Darkness

WHETHER Colonel House played an important part in the Democratic national convention of 1932 I have never known. At an interesting luncheon at the home of Elisabeth Marbury in January of that year I met him again. We had eggnog before luncheon, and there was some speculation as to whether Mrs. Roosevelt would object to the serving of cocktails. This was incredibly silly, since they were served in the Roosevelt home and Roosevelt always insisted on making them himself. I had seen him shaking them in his corner in the drawing room and had partaken of a number of his brew. That day I found that both House and Miss Marbury were for Roosevelt, and I was puzzled when she pointed to House with the comment, "He's our rock."

The traditional Democratic banquet on Jackson's birthday in Washington was held as usual, but there was significance in the dropping of the custom of inviting all the avowed candidates for the Presidential nomination to speak. Instead it had been decided that speeches should be made only by previous Presidential nominees, which meant John W. Davis, James M. Cox and Al Smith—two of whom at the time were undercover candidates. I was asked to preside as toastmaster. The significant thing was the exclusion of Roosevelt, who was the most conspicuous candidate.

Smith received an ovation when he entered the dining room. His speech, though not quite up to his standard, was more constructive than the others'. By urging federal action to meet the crisis of unemployment, he made a timely talk and a wise one.

That evening Jack Garner, now Speaker of the House, also received an ovation on entering and his ruddy face beamed. He too was then a prospective candidate. It seemed clear to me that it was the field against Roosevelt.

Three weeks later I lunched at the Waldorf with Jouett Shouse, and we discussed the statement by Newton D. Baker that the League of Nations would not be an issue in the campaign—a statement that had been accepted as an announcement of his candidacy. Many who hoped for Baker's nomination were criticizing him for his coy approach and his indisposition to wage a militant campaign. Shouse, who admired Baker, remarked, "In these days no one can hope for the nomination without an active fight."

The next day the opposition of Al Smith to Roosevelt came out into the open. With unnecessary emphasis he repudiated the story that he would soon be a guest of Roosevelt in Albany, and this was taken as a declaration of war against his former friend and champion. I know that on that very day a conference was in progress to persuade Smith to announce his own candidacy. I got the impression from men sponsoring that conference that, while they did not think Smith could be nominated, they hoped, through his candidacy, to make it impossible for Roosevelt to marshal the necessary two-thirds vote. Also, that with two candidates from New York neither could be nominated. The tragedy here was in the fact that Smith himself was confident of the nomination.

Meanwhile, Governor Harry Byrd of Virginia was about to enter the arena. In February 1932 I sat beside him at a luncheon at the Lawyers Club and he asked me to linger after the others had left, when he told me that in conversation with Smith he had found him wrought up with fear that religion might again be dragged in, and complaining that Roosevelt had not mentioned his own Presidential aspirations to him personally. This, I know, was true, but Roosevelt knew from the beginning that he could not count on the support of his old leader. The sole justification for the reference to religion was in the fact that many who would have liked to see Smith President did not want to go through another campaign like that of 1928.

Soon after this I had an hour alone with Jack Garner in the office of the Speaker in Washington. He was being urged to enter the race. Few men have had a more magnetic and pleasing personality. He was picturesque, with white hair and heavy long white eyebrows, always a bit disheveled. There was a golden warmth in his all-embracing smile, and in the blue-gray eyes could be seen a capacity for fire and fury. He was a fighter and looked it. When I told him that in business circles I was hearing many complimentary things about him, he instantly sobered. "Yes, I hear that, and that's what worries me. I'm wondering if my conservatism has been exaggerated." Later, after his nomination for Vice-President, an attempt would be made to convince conservative elements that he was a radical extremist. It was clear that day that, while eager for the Presidential nomination, he had no illusions.

He then told me an interesting story about the Hoover moratorium on intergovernmental debts. Hoover had telephoned him in Texas to ask for a sweeping approval of the plan. This he refused to give. Later, at a meeting of the Congressional leaders at the White House, it was he who had broken up the plan for a longer moratorium with cancellation as the evident intent. He told Hoover that it seemed that the leaders had been called in to write his message. "I had had a drink or two and got restless and I walked out into the hall," he said. "Senator Borah followed me and said, 'I'm glad you said what you did. I was waiting to see if someone else would say it, and would have said it myself if no one had.' The next day Borah told a press correspondent that he had always been a Prohibitionist but that two drinks of liquor had rendered a great service to the country the night before."

On the first of May I lunched with James A. Farley in his room at the Biltmore in New York. He was a man of attractive personality and political tact, combined with rare organizing ability, but until then his experience in national politics had been limited. He was to become perhaps the greatest campaign manager in our history. He formed personal contacts and friendships with party workers from the highest to the lowest, and precinct workers in forty-eight states spoke familiarly of him as "Jim." In Terre Haute early in that year's campaign I joined the party workers for refreshments after speaking and noticed that constant references were being made to "Jim." Assuming the reference was to some local politician, I asked, "What Jim?" Evidently astonished by my ignorance, they replied in a chorus, "Jim Farley." He had spent a few hours in the Hoosier city and was already established as a sort of next-door neighbor.

I had met him casually before the day of our lunch at the Biltmore, but had never really talked with him. Big, hearty, manifestly sincere, he made a deep impression upon me. Just what he wanted to see me about I could not guess, and when at length I left him I still did not know. It was evident that he was then utterly devoted to Roosevelt. He had been equally devoted to Al Smith, whom he still loved. When he was asked to manage Roosevelt's preconvention campaign, he had gone to Smith to ascertain whether he would be a candidate and had been given the distinct impression that he would not. No objection was offered by Smith to his managing Roosevelt's campaign. Farley had been shocked by Smith's belated announcement, since he could not honestly change his allegiance at that stage.

I was amazed that a campaign manager could be so frank and open, but it was this quality that was to make him so popular and so successful. He said that, "while some people think me crazy," he could not figure the possibility of a combination that could prevent Roosevelt's nomination. Taking a pencil and paper, he wrote down for the opposition Massachusetts, Connecticut, New Jersey, part of Pennsylvania, Ohio, Illinois, California, Maryland, Virginia, Texas and Missouri—much more than necessary to prevent Roosevelt's nomination. But he did not think these opposition votes could be held, and he was sure that if Roosevelt went into the convention with six hundred votes he would be nominated.

I asked him who would be nominated for Vice-President, and without a hesitation he said Cordell Hull. I am sure that at that stage this was in accordance with Roosevelt's plan.

In March and April there was a release from preconvention politics, and at this time I had an amusing encounter with Gertrude Atherton at a party at Alma Clayburgh's. She had just published her autobiography. I was surprised to find that the thin little woman in a very low-necked dress, with sandy-colored hair and old-fashioned bangs, was the author of *The Conqueror* and other, better novels. Having in mind her idealized portrait of Hamilton, I sat beside her on the sofa with the idea of talking with her about her hero. I am sure she had never heard of me or of *Jefferson and Hamilton,* and when I broached the subject of Hamilton she snapped, "When I'm through writing on a subject, I put it behind me." It was as though she had said, "I am Sir Oracle and when I ope my mouth let no dog bark." Soon she was put in a high-back chair by the fireplace, and there she sat in state. Part of the time someone was talking with her, but most of the time she sat alone, apparently preferring it, watching the other guests with expressionless eyes.

I had expected to see Dreiser. "I called him up," said the hostess, "and he began to grumble, 'Oh, a crowd—I don't care for such damn things.'" "Don't come," she had said. "Come some other time when no one else is here."

In April I went to Charlottesville, Virginia, to make the speech at the unveiling of Pericelli's statue of James Monroe, a ceremony that twenty-four governors from the governors' conference in Richmond attended. But visits to Charlottesville, though delightful, were never restful, because of the too generous hospitality of the Virginians, and the next morning we were glad to drive through the charming countryside to Lexington, where I was to speak at Washington and Lee University. I shall always remember that visit, the beauty of the country and of the little town, the luncheon with Mrs. Gaines, the wife of the president of the university, the visit to the chapel to see Valentine's exquisitely beautiful recumbent figure of Lee—but most of all, perhaps, the privilege of spending some time with Henry St. George Tucker, statesman, jurist, writer, in his delightful home. He was a handsome old gentleman with Old World graciousness. Summoning a venerable white-haired Negro, a bit feeble in his walk, who had a charm and courtesy that matched that of his employer, Tucker asked him if he thought he could make a real mint julep. The old Negro smiled expansively. He could, he would and he did. Then we walked in the garden and talked politics.

One evening in late June Senator Wheeler telephoned me that he had attended a "war conference" with Roosevelt in Albany, along with Cordell Hull, Senator Tom Walsh, Dan Roper and Major Cohen of the Atlanta *Journal*, and that it had been the unanimous decision that I should be asked to render a certain service, which all hoped I would give. I was to be called by Roosevelt the next day. On the morrow I was summoned to the national headquarters in New York by Louis Howe to receive "an important message" from the Governor. I assumed that I was to be asked to make the speech placing Roosevelt in nomination at the convention.

Nothing could have been more embarrassing, because of several complications. I was writing a political column for all the Hearst papers and it would appear daily during the convention in Chicago. At that time, Hearst was supporting the candidacy of Speaker Jack Garner. While my contract left me free in such matters, I could see that the delivery of the speech might be embarrassing to the paper in Chicago. Then, too, the New York leaders, in making out the list of the delegates at large from their state, had overlooked the keynote speaker of the last national convention, but the leader in Manhattan had telephoned me to say he thought I should be a delegate and to ask if I would go as a delegate from Manhattan, and I had agreed. I had no idea what the position of the organization would be in the convention.

The next morning Roosevelt telephoned, asking me to see him in Albany that night. I was met at the door of the Executive Mansion by the venerable butler with the cold announcement that Roosevelt was "not at home." I was protesting with no little irritation when I was interrupted by a boisterous laugh from a room off the entrance hall, and Roosevelt's voice: "Come on in, Claude."

I found Roosevelt seated on a sofa before a table, with Miss Le Hand, his efficient secretary, taking dictation. He was in a jovial mood. It had been announced that the findings of Judge Seabury in the investigation of the charges against Mayor Walker would be delivered to Roosevelt that night. "There will be a flock of reporters along insisting on some expression from me," he said, "and I want to skip them. Thus the butler's refusal to admit you, since I had forgotten to make an exception in your case." He added, "After all, this is my home."

A little later there was a rumble of cars in the driveway and the sound of many voices. The bell rang. The butler went to the door. We maintained silence, and Roosevelt had the expression of a mischievous boy awaiting the reaction to a trick. We could hear the butler saying that the Governor had retired and that the papers would be given to him in the morning. The door closed. The butler cleverly deposited the great sack in the hall, and there they remained for a long while, lest a curious reporter peer through the glass in the door. They were then brought in and placed beside the sofa.

When the accompanying letter from Seabury was placed in Roosevelt's hand and he read it, I was interested in his expression of distinct distaste. Reading it aloud, he commented on its failure to make direct charges or to ask anything. His observations on the letter were not complimentary. "No governor in a hundred and fifty years has ejected an elected officer on charges as vague as these," he said. "But Jimmy [Walker] has been guilty of so many indiscretions that in the accumulation it looks bad." I certainly got the impression that night that he was not keen on the removal of Walker, and that he suspected that Seabury had maliciously put him in an embarrassing position in the Presidential contest. Later he was spared the necessity of taking action by the voluntary resignation of the mayor.

This over, he asked if I would have a glass of beer. The servant brought in two bottles and when these were finished Roosevelt asked for a second round. Then he came to the point, the request that I make the nominating speech. I explained my difficulties, particularly as they related to the support of Garner by the papers running my editorials. I felt I could not agree without getting the consent of Hearst.

"Is there anything I can do?" he asked. "Can I get Hearst on the telephone?" And he reached for the phone. I suggested that this would be the surest way to get a negative answer, and that it would be better for me to submit the matter to him through the office. To this he finally agreed.

Then he outlined the tone of the speech he had in mind—very significant of what was to come later during his Presidency. He wanted a "fighting speech," and he enumerated the various points he thought should be emphasized. He mentioned Andrew Jackson and said he wanted a "fighting Jackson speech." I concluded that Jackson, more than Jefferson, was his idol. I had no doubt of his complete adherence to the Jeffersonian principles of democracy, but he clearly had a preference for Jackson's methods.

The next day a telegram from Hearst was received by Curley of the *Journal*. It said, "While I would not think of interfering in any way with Mr. Bowers' personal or political views and preferences, I think it would be less embarrassing to the papers if he did not too intimately identify himself with any one candidacy."

Bitter though my disappointment was, this seemed reasonable to me. I enclosed the telegram with a note to Roosevelt that I mailed that night. Thus was I deprived of the high honor of placing Roosevelt in nomination in 1932.

Any fear of his possible resentment was immediately removed by his reply of June 18:

DEAR CLAUDE:

Please do not take it too much to heart that things did not work out as we hoped. You must of course do what seems wise and for the best interest of all concerned. Certainly I would be the last to ask you to go against your own better judgment. You know and I know where your heart is and that you will do all in your power for me when the time comes. . . .

Had I had the slightest doubt of the inevitability of a Democratic victory that fall it would have been dispelled by what I saw and felt at the Republican convention in Chicago, which I attended in the press section to write daily editorials on the proceedings. The day I arrived the lobbies of the hotels were positively lonesome, almost deserted. I found Nicholas Murray Butler alone at the Blackstone, looking tired and discouraged, but prepared to make a fight for the inclusion in the platform of a straight-out plank for the repeal of the Eighteenth Amendment. The next day the town was still dull, with no enthusiasm. In the hotel lobbies the delegates were discussing everything but politics. On visiting the Indiana headquarters I failed to find one man with the slightest expectation of victory.

During the convention I went daily to the hall in Governor Horner's official car at a terrifying speed, the sirens screaming. The keynote speech made no reference to the dread realities in the country. No enthusiasm. The mention of Hoover's name was scarcely cheered and then, as if on second thought, a brave effort was made which amounted to nothing. It was clear that the sole interest was in the fight for the repeal of the Eighteenth Amendment.

The next night featured that fight. James R. Garfield, old, austere in appearance, read the platform, which ignored the des-

perate economic state of the nation, and the delegates drowsed
until the Prohibition plank was reached, when they perked up.
Garfield led off in the debate against repeal. When he said, "The
youth of today knows nothing of the taste of liquor," the galleries
naturally roared with mirth, and many booed. Garfield stood stern,
with a Calvinistic countenance. "I repeat—" he began, but his voice
was drowned by shouts from the gallery. When Senator Bingham
spoke for repeal he was well received. Nicholas Murray Butler,
who followed, was a disappointment. Clearly he was dead on his
feet, and I noticed that his hands trembled. What he said was by
odds the best thing said, but there was no fire. Then Ogden Mills,
arrogant, with his small, cold, supercilious eyes, spoke with great
vigor and made the best speech of the evening. It was after one
o'clock when the roll was called, and repeal lost by six hundred
odd to four hundred odd.

The next day when the nominating speeches were made I
watched the demonstration for Hoover with some amusement.
Most delegates looked as though scourged to the task. Heavy faces,
sour faces, without expression, certainly without enthusiasm or
conviction. Balloons were released to the ceiling, but they helped
very little. Most amusing was the insistence of the band on playing
"California, here I come, *right back where I started from . . .*"

The artificiality of the demonstration was shown when the
chairman held up his hand for silence and it came with the sudden-
ness of a shock. No one could have attended that convention without being convinced that the next President would be nominated in
the Democratic convention.

In the double role of delegate and commentator I attended the
Democratic convention, taking Sybil and Patricia with me. Knowing all the candidates but one, I made the rounds of their headquarters. My first call was on Al Smith. The outer rooms were packed
and I was immediately shown into his private room. He was seated
at a table by the window, cordial, jovial and without the slightest
indication of nervous strain. One of his men entered to propose
that Smith make a demand on the entire New York delegation for
its support, accompanied with a threat. Smith seemed startled.

"Oh, no," he said. "I wouldn't do that. I never would do that.
Every man is entitled to his opinion."

Thence to the headquarters of Governor Byrd, whom I found with his brother the Admiral and some other Virginians. Major Reed of Richmond, his manager, was complaining that no working arrangements had been agreed upon by the candidates competing with Roosevelt. He could not understand why there had been no meeting, and he was unhappy because Smith had taken the center of the stage, creating the impression that the nomination had to go to Smith or Roosevelt.

That night I attended a caucus of the New York delegation on the permanent organization of the convention. The National Committee had selected Senator Walsh of Montana for permanent chairman, and the opposition favored Jouett Shouse. The atmosphere was tense. Dan Cohalen spoke for Shouse, George R. Lunn of Schenectady for Walsh. Then John W. Davis, very handsome with his white hair and pink complexion, made an earnest plea for Shouse. Lieutenant Governor Lehman spoke with deep emotion and under a nervous strain, announcing that he had not yet decided but that he would make up his own mind. He was greeted with boos. When Smith entered later he was given an ovation, but not equal to that accorded Mayor Walker. The caucus voted to support Shouse.

Resuming my visits, I found Governor Murray of Oklahoma, "Alfalfa Bill," another candidate, standing in the door of his deserted headquarters in his shirt sleeves, without a collar, and with one suspender off his shoulder. Drawing me inside the room, he astonished me with a penetrating analysis of my book *Jefferson and Hamilton* and then introduced me to his wife, a charming and motherly woman. Thence on to the headquarters of Governor Ritchie, handsome, smiling and entirely calm, but not exuding confidence.

After Senator Barkley's keynote speech the next day, I went to Garner's headquarters, where Sam Rayburn was in charge. There I found Ruth Bryan Owens, daughter of the Commoner, an attractive woman with something of the magnetism of her father. Someone suggested that she should carry a cane now that she was a "lame duck," having been defeated for renomination to Congress.

"Oh, I always carried a cane when I lived in England," she said, "but with more swagger than you." Whereupon, taking a cane, she rose and strutted about with a kangaroo swing.

Roosevelt did not appear in the convention city until after his nomination.

The debate on the repeal of the Eighteenth Amendment came at a night session. Cordell Hull, speaking against a straight declaration for repeal, was much too judicial and argumentative, but the boos from the gallery shocked me.

Then Al Smith dramatically appeared on the platform to speak for straight repeal. His face was red and he beamed with smiles, for his ovation was tremendous and long continued. The galleries roared. Walsh wisely did not attempt to abbreviate the demonstration. Even Smith seemed surprised by his reception, and there was moisture in his eyes. His friends hoped that the demonstration would sweep the delegates into his camp.

The plank favoring repeal was overwhelmingly adopted.

The nominating speeches the next day were followed by the usual organized demonstrations, and the balloting began. There were three ballots that evening. The windows began to glow with the dawn. On the platform I noticed John W. Davis sound asleep. All around, delegates were resting their heads on their arms. It was nine-thirty in the morning when we filed out of the hall.

That day it was whispered that the Garner forces would go over to Roosevelt, and William Gibbs McAdoo took the platform to make the announcement. It was a mistake, in view of the Smith-McAdoo feud, since it gave to the action the appearance of a pre-arranged revenge. The galleries booed unmercifully. McAdoo took it coolly, though he was angry. In Spain two years later he was my guest in San Sebastián, and, walking along the Concha, he told me that he had realized the danger of having him make the announcement and that he had urged the choice of someone else, but without effect. Other states now followed rapidly into the Roosevelt column, and he was nominated. At the moment of the nomination, John W. Davis, standing beside me, murmured as if to himself, "What a pity."

Thus the road was cleared for the historic regime of Franklin D. Roosevelt.

Garner's nomination for Vice-President followed the next day. On Sunday morning I met Farley, Cordell Hull and other Rooseveltians, all in a high state of elation. Roosevelt had made his sensational flight to address and thank the convention. In the hall that day I found many of his friends apprehensive, fearing an accident, a plane flight being still considered at that time an act of daring.

I found Roosevelt in his room at the hotel, along with Louis Howe, seated by the window. When he saw me, Roosevelt threw back his head and laughed. "We must razz you for voting for Smith," he said.

Almost immediately he had a problem in his lap when someone entered to say that McAdoo was in the reception room and wanted to pose with him for a picture. Roosevelt's face fell. He asked my opinion. I thought it would be a mistake, since it would mean rubbing salt into the wounds of the Smith followers. He decided to say so frankly to McAdoo, and when the latter entered I left. There was no picture.

The sad feature of the convention for me was the failure of Al Smith to avail himself of the opportunity to make himself the hero of the day. It was known that Roosevelt on his way to the convention would stop at the hotel where Smith was staying. The defeated candidate was surrounded by men and women passionately devoted to his fortunes but irreconcilable in their bitterness because of his defeat. These persuaded him to leave the hotel before Roosevelt's arrival. Had he been better advised, he would have remained to greet the victor, would have ridden with him to the convention, have gone onto the platform with him arm in arm, and have moved to make the nomination by acclamation. An emotional reaction would have swept over the convention and Smith would have gone forth better loved than ever before. But when Roosevelt arrived Smith had gone, and there would be no meeting or greeting for almost three months. Those three months of silence would deprive Smith of many friends throughout the nation.

To me the most astounding revelation of the convention came with the speech of Senator Huey Long, who was to speak in support of a contested delegation from Louisiana. There was a general fear that he would mutilate the English language, tear a passion to tatters, make a vulgar exhibition and humiliate the party. When he appeared on the platform, nattily dressed, he looked serious and not at all like the comedian whom the public knew best. He asked freedom from interruptions pro or con, since they would be taken out of his allotted time, and thereupon plunged into his argument. Speaking rapidly in excellent English and with closely knit logic, he made one of the strongest and most dignified speeches of the convention. It was a revelation to me that there was a Huey Long quite distinct from the frothing demagogue with whom the public was familiar.

I gave him full credit in a signed editorial in the Chicago paper the next morning. That day a page came to me on the floor to say that Senator Long, then on the platform, wished to see me. I had never met him and I doubted if he would know me by sight. Certain that he wanted to thank me for the editorial, I went to the platform, introduced myself and congratulated him on his speech before he had an opportunity to say anything. Throwing back his shoulders and looking more belligerent than pleased, he roared, "As a rule I don't care a damn what any crooked newspaperman says about me, because they're mostly goddam liars, but you gave me a square deal and I want to thank you for it."

I was not quite certain whether I had been patted on the head or kicked.

Just before leaving Washington for Spain the following year, I was lunching in the Senate restaurant with Vice-President Garner when Huey Long, passing our table, paused to shake hands with great cordiality and to express regret that I was leaving the country. I replied that one of my regrets would be that I could not follow his speeches in the *Congressional Record*. "I'll send you the *Record*," he said, jotting down a reminder on a piece of paper—and he did.

When he passed on, I said to Garner that Long had charm. "Charm!" exploded Garner. "Too damn much charm. He has more charm than any man in the Senate, and that's what makes him dangerous."

In truth, he had become a very dangerous man at the time of his death. He had a superabundance of natural ability, in which rare cunning played a part. A more persuasive demagogue has never appeared on the American scene. The conditions of the time, with millions jobless and millions hungry, discouraged and desperate, were made to his order. It was so easy then to indict a system based on democracy. I have no doubt that he thought to play the part so successfully played by Hitler in Germany, and he was making threatening progress when a bullet put a period to his activities. Anyone who thinks it absurd that there is a possibility of fascism in this country would do well to ponder on the careers of Huey Long and Joe McCarthy.

CHAPTER XVII

The Revolution of 1932

I HAD KNOWN Roosevelt personally and politically for several years. He had been pleased with my treatment of his hero, Andrew Jackson, in *The Party Battles of the Jackson Period* and he had reviewed my *Jefferson and Hamilton*, the only review I think he ever wrote. The first time I saw him was in the spring of 1913 when, with some other subordinate officers of the Wilson Administration, he spoke one evening at the National Press Club. He was then about thirty and in the pink of physical condition—tall, handsome, athletic. His pronounced Harvard accent was a bit disconcerting to a Hoosier, but his personality exuded charm. Tragic as was the attack of infantile paralysis a few years later, I have no doubt it served the nation well. The years that bound him to his chair gave abundant opportunity for extensive and leisurely study, and this, I think, was the period of his intellectual growth. Years later, Senator Wagner, who had suffered a nervous breakdown from overwork, told me that Roosevelt had told him that enforced rest has its compensations. "I could not have kept going under the pressure of the last few years," Roosevelt said, "had I not accumulated stores of energy during the time I was physically inactive."

I think our friendship was based largely on our common interest in political history and his interest in my books. In the spring of 1929 he wrote me a letter that is not without significance:

Many thanks for your mighty nice letter. I am thrilled at the prospect of another book from your pen [*The Tragic Era*, published five months later]. I think it is time for us Democrats to claim Lincoln as one of our own. The Republican Party has certainly repudiated, first and last, everything that he stood for.

That period from 1865 to 1876 should be known as America's Dark Ages. I am not sure that we are not headed for the same kind of era again.

I do hope that this summer after I get back from Warm Springs you can run up to Albany or Hyde Park and give me a chance to talk to you about many things.

Meanwhile please let me tell you how very grateful I am for all the splendid editorials in the Evening World. They are a bulwark of strength.

My close relations with Roosevelt date from about this time. Apropos of his interest in political history, I was not surprised to see that Upton Sinclair in his novel *A World to Win* ascribed to Roosevelt a longing to write history after his retirement. Some time before, he had surprised me by saying that he had long had an ambition to write an adequate biography of Martin Van Buren. The Red Fox, as he was called, was a favorite of Jackson's, but no two men could have differed more in their methods. Van Buren was supercautious, conservative in action, and more of a clever manipulator than a fighter. "Better walk miles to see a man than risk a letter," was his motto. I suppose that Roosevelt's interest grew out of Van Buren's political sagacity, his organizing ability and the fact that he, like Roosevelt, was a product of the politics of upstate New York. It is a pity Roosevelt did not find time for the realization of his ambition, for his biography of Van Buren might have thrown more light on the character of the author.

From my return from Europe in September 1932 until the election in November, I wrote a two-column political editorial every day but Sunday which was published in newspapers from Boston to San Francisco having an aggregate circulation of several millions. These editorials were militantly Democratic, attacking the Hoover Administration all along the line. (There was an embarrassing richness of material that year.) They made no personal attacks on Mr. Hoover, but his policies were assailed tooth and nail. These editorials were used as directives by party committees throughout the country. Urging their publication in pamphlet form, Senator James Hamilton Lewis wrote that I was "possibly the only outstanding writer who constantly puts the principles of the Democracy as the guide of politics rather than the prospect of office." After the election Mr. Ritche of Mr. Hoover's staff said they were "the most damaging articles of the campaign." Letters of approval poured in from many Republicans, some fearful that Roosevelt might make a blunder to the benefit of his opponent. William Allen White wrote me facetiously in July: "How do you suppose Roosevelt is going to manage to elect Hoover? You Democrats never had such a hard job before and I almost despair of your success. . . . Still it's a great Party."

Soon after my return, Roosevelt invited me to Albany to have dinner and stay the night. Patricia and I arrived just as he was returning from a day's campaigning in Vermont by motorcar. We found him in "Franklin's corner" in the drawing room, shaking cocktails. Never had he seemed so boyish as he did in his enthusiasm over the cordial reception he had received in that rock-ribbed Republican state. I recalled to him the story of Samuel J. Tilden, who was repeatedly importuned to "address the Democracy of Vermont," until, weary of excuses and the persistence of the invitations, he replied that he would "be glad at any time to address the Democracy of Vermont in his library in New York."

Roosevelt threw back his head and laughed, but quickly said, "Well, you couldn't get the crowds today into Tilden's library."

That night he was in an exhilarated mood at dinner, the drive through the crisp air and contacts with the people having done much for his spirits. While we were at table his mother telephoned that some friend had sent fifty quail to Hyde Park and she wanted to know what should be done with them. He laughed uproariously. "In heaven's name, how can we ever eat them?" he asked. When told that they were live quail he gave minute directions where on the farm they should be placed and just what they should be fed.

Later, talking about Britain, he recalled a blunder he had made in Scotland at a garden show when he was unexpectedly called upon to say something. He thought he was making an impression as no doubt he was, by telling the Scots the difference between the American and Scottish ways of cooking vegetables. "You cook them in water," he said, "we in milk." Mrs. Roosevelt had been much embarrassed.

After dinner we went into the library, where a log fire was blazing. He sat in an easy chair before the fire, a table beside him, and Miss Le Hand went over some correspondence with him. Occasionally a servant brought in the telephone. He talked with

Governor Dern in Utah about the speech he was to make in Salt Lake City. Were there steps at the tabernacle where he was to speak? He had been asked to attend an Episcopalian service there, and he inquired about the steps at the church. Surely never in history has any man ventured forth on a continental campaign tour under such a physical handicap, but all he required was preparation.

The night before, Al Smith had held a conference with his friends regarding the position he should take in the campaign. He had not yet broken his silence since the convention. Someone from New York telephoned that he had attended the conference. Herbert Bayard Swope was to have informed Roosevelt, but up to midnight that night he had not called.

Then the secretary entered to say that Mr. ——, a New Yorker, wished to speak to Roosevelt from Idaho.

"But I don't want to talk with —— in Idaho," he said with his trick of pretended petulance.

Raymond Moley did the talking and explained that Roosevelt had retired. Mr. —— said he had telephoned to warn that Roosevelt (that excellent politician) should not pass through any state on his Western tour without greeting the people.

"What?" exclaimed Roosevelt incredulously. When the warning was repeated he laughed.

The scene that night was memorable to me: Roosevelt boyishly happy and in laughing mood, Miss Le Hand curled up before the fire on the floor like a kitten; and there was good talk until after midnight, when we retired. I noticed in the big hall large photographs of Al Smith and his wife. The tragedy of a strained friendship.

When I saw Roosevelt the next morning to say goodbye I found him propped up in bed working on a speech.

It was not until almost a month after this, at the New York State convention, that Smith and Roosevelt met—more than three months of silence on the part of the defeated candidate. Senator Wagner had asked me to make the speech at the convention putting him in nomination for his second term, and thus I witnessed the meeting.

The real excitement in the convention centered on whether

John F. Curry, the chief of Tammany, would persist in his efforts to prevent the nomination of Herbert H. Lehman for governor. Every effort was being made to whip him into line, and a story was circulating that at a conference for this purpose Al Smith had turned on Curry a battery of vituperation not unmixed with picturesque profanity that would not look well in print. Wagner was gravely concerned, and when I talked with Roosevelt on the phone and told him I had heard that the opposition would be withdrawn he was skeptical. On the morning of the day of the nomination, which had to be made before midnight, Curry had sent instructions to his men to be in their seats by 7 P.M., and this seemed ominous.

We sat in the torrid heat of the hall filled with perspiring people from seven until eight-thirty, doing nothing, while behind locked doors the leaders fought it out until Curry fell into line.

When Smith appeared on the platform to nominate Lehman, he was given an ovation. This was to be his first meeting with Roosevelt since the convention in Chicago. Roosevelt was seated in the center of the front row on the stage. With a debonair smile and manner, Smith shook hands with everyone in the front row as he approached the center. Roosevelt, in the meanwhile, had risen. Finally reaching his successful rival, Smith thrust out his hand cordially, and he was reported to have greeted him familiarly with "Hello, old potato," though this was afterward denied. The scene was dramatic, and the convention roared approval. For the benefit of the photographers Smith, whatever his inner thoughts and feelings, held on to Roosevelt's hand, beaming.

It was in nominating Lehman that Smith for the first time announced his support of the national ticket. Roosevelt then spoke from manuscript, a good, sound speech, but it was not so rapturously received as was Smith's. The reconciliation was to prove skin deep and was not to live beyond the election in 1932.

Soon afterward I had an amusing experience. I had gone to the Biltmore Hotel in New York to address a meeting of the Democratic Forum, arranged by Mrs. Roosevelt, and in the corridor I met Farley, who invited me to stay after the meeting and dine with Garner and some others on the same floor. I supposed it would be a small dinner of five or six, and I was astonished, on entering the room, to find at least thirty or forty present. One glance at the personnel convinced me of the purpose, though Farley had given me no intimation. There were a few politicians, but more numerous were businessmen and industrialists of very conservative views. The silly idea had been propagated by the Republicans that Garner was a radical of almost Populistic tendencies, and a scare had been thrown into these men by the thought that Roosevelt might not live through his term and that Garner, a "dangerous extremist," would become President. It was amusing that the ultraconservatives had no fear of Roosevelt, because of his conservative background, but actually were doubtful of Garner, who was ultimately to be prominent in the conservative opposition to some Rooseveltian measures.

That night, Garner was introduced first. Talking in a conversational tone and smiling his infectious smile, his red cheeks glowing, he made one of the frankest, most human, transparently honest speeches I have ever heard. He stressed the fact that his first political appearance as a youth, in a county convention in Texas, had been to oppose Bryan's silver views in 1896. He clearly made a favorable impression on his audience. I was startled when Farley next called on me. Still uninformed as to the purpose of the dinner, but suspecting what it was, I said some pleasant things about Garner and added that the only criticism I had ever heard in Democratic circles was that he was too conservative. I felt that would help reassure most of the diners.

The Garner confession of faith had an immediate effect. An important moving-picture magnate rose. He told of his early poverty, of his migration to the United States, of having met Mrs. Roosevelt and then Roosevelt, and of his attachment to them. He had gone to the dinner with the intention of contributing a certain amount, he said, but after hearing Garner's speech he had decided to double it. Garner rose, beaming, and rushed over to shake his hand. So the movie magnate became the hero of the dinner.

But Garner was to remain the problem child of the campaign. Though he had been in Congress for thirty years, and was one of the ablest debaters in the House, he had made few stump speeches in years, and never, or very seldom, outside his district. He had been stubborn about taking the stump in 1932, and, in fact, he was to speak but little. He had been persuaded, however, to make a radio speech on a nationwide hookup in reply to Hoover, and there was some fear that he would pull his punches. I met Sam Rayburn, later Speaker of the House longer than any other man in our history, in the Biltmore lobby, and he told me they were having trouble with Garner and asked me to see him and do my bit in favor of a robust attack. When I asked why he did not go himself, he said with a grimace that his old friend was annoyed with him for persisting in the plea that he take the stump. I found Garner in good humor, glowing as usual, and asked him if his speech was to be an attack. He said, "Mostly." I expressed the hope that he would make the attack outstanding. Then he surprised me even more. "I wonder if the people may not feel sorry for Hoover," he said meditatively.

The next night I listened on the radio and thought the talk one of the most effective and devastating speeches of the campaign.

I had left Indiana in 1923 with no intention of ever again making a campaign speech, but there was no escape in 1932. Toward the close of the campaign I spoke before old friends in Terre Haute and then went on to Detroit to close the campaign in the armory there. I remember that meeting clearly because it was there I first met and formed a warm friendship with Frank Murphy, then mayor of Detroit and later governor general of the Philippines, governor of Michigan, Attorney General under Roosevelt and Associate Justice of the Supreme Court. I had heard from several quarters of pleasant things he had said about my books and editorials. In some way I had formed the fantastic idea that he was a rough diamond, unschooled but rich in character and with a high idealism. When I met him I was not prepared to find him looking like an intellectual priest, and when I heard him speak I was amazed by the brilliance of his talk, the richness of his phrasing. I have seldom known a man in politics with such an appreciation of spiritual values.

That night the armory was crowded. Incredible though it seemed, I was assured that Michigan would go Democratic for the first time since it went to Franklin Pierce in 1852, eighty years before.

The moment I reached home, Louis Howe telephoned that Roosevelt was to have spoken that night over a nationwide radio hookup for forty minutes but that something had intervened and he wanted me to substitute. I made the speech, and on returning home I found a stack of telegrams, with one from Farley calling it "one of the best speeches of the campaign—yours and that of Carter Glass."

The next morning I went to Buffalo to close the campaign there. This was the most pleasant excursion of the year. Norman Mack, national committeeman, then over seventy, drove me with a small party over the International Bridge to Canada for lunch at the Erie Downs Country Club. In the afternoon I went with a small party to the station to meet Mayor Thatcher of Albany, who did not arrive. When we were waiting at the gate as the passengers poured through, it was amusing that Ogden Mills, Secretary of the Treasury, who was to close the campaign there for the Republicans that night, should loom before us. Though I had never met him, I had been vigorously attacking him through the campaign simply because he was by odds the ablest advocate of Hoover's re-election. When I was introduced he seemed curious and not very cordial; but when later after a Gridiron Club dinner in Washington I found myself in an elevator with him, he was cordiality itself. He was one of the ablest Republicans of his time, but an inescapable arrogance of manner deprived him of popular support.

From Buffalo I went to Syracuse to close the campaign there. The meeting was crowded and enthusiastic. There for the first time in years I was told that some manufacturers were trying to intimidate their workmen. The stormiest applause of the evening followed my denunciation of this lawless attempt and my advice to the workers to keep their own council and go into the secrecy of the voting booth with their sovereignty under their hats and vote their own convictions in defiance of these men who seemed to look upon them as chattels.

That was the Saturday night before the election, and my work was over. I had thoroughly enjoyed the old thrill of facing a militant audience with a fighting speech.

Roosevelt carried forty-two of the forty-eight states, and, as predicted, Michigan was in the Roosevelt column.

Following the campaign—and a surfeit of politics—there was a literary interlude. That winter William Butler Yeats, the Irish poet, visited New York. A few days before I met him, at dinner in Yonkers, I knew there had been some discussion among members

256

of the Irish-American Historical Society on the propriety of inviting the poet to some function. There was a feeling that Yeats was a bit critical of the Catholic Church, and a year before during a debate in the Dail on a divorce bill he had made a rather nasty attack on Daniel O'Connell as having illegitimate children "scattered all over Ireland."

Contrary to the rule, Yeats looked like a poet—tall, slender, of graceful figure, with very slightly stooping shoulders and with a great shock of white hair. He seemed either shy or bored and looked at the floor most of the time. Years before I had seen Eleanor Robson in his charming play *The Land of Heart's Desire*, and I told him I had seen the actress a few nights before at a dinner at General Donovan's for A. E. (George William Russell). He then showed some interest, remembering her in the play, and inquired about her. He talked but little at the dinner table, but afterward he read some of his poems, giving their background in prefatory statements, and he was thoroughly delightful in the reading. A little later I saw him at Mrs. Casserly's in Sutton Place, where he lectured on the literary revival in Ireland, speaking with perfect modulation and enunciation, and, at times, with dramatic effect, though he got this effect by soft rather than flamboyant methods. He explained that the youth movement which broke away from the Irish Party grew out of the bitter resentment of the young because of the stupid repudiation of Parnell at the behest of Gladstone. To me the highlight of his lecture was his story of going down to the waterfront as a boy to see the unloading of the casket of the great leader who had died of a broken heart.

But his story of the origin of the Abbey Theatre was both fascinating and amusing, his yarns about the dramatists diverting, his description of the tumultuous scenes in the pit of the theater in protest against the "insults" to Ireland very funny. The purpose of the intellectuals, he said, had been to emphasize the bad qualities of the race to bring about their eradication, but the noble intent escaped the rank and file in the pit. I am glad I heard him that night recite with tremendous effect his moving poem "O'Leary in the Grave."

But New York was not in the mood for literary or theatrical entertainment. That winter Katharine Cornell was appearing in the tragic play *Lucrece* and there was tragedy enough all about.

No one but an actress of the first order could have played the part, and Cornell was superb. But the drama was too tragic for those gloomy days when tragedy sat by the fireside of millions of suffering Americans. None of the theaters was ever filled, though only a short time before reservations had to be made in advance or outrageous prices were exacted by the speculators.

The state of the country was deepening into darkness, with millions jobless, with children suffering and some starving, with the harbor of New York almost deserted because the tariff had discouraged foreign trade, with importers and exporters closing their offices, their business ruined.

Pedestrians were constantly importuned by beggars—beggars who had once held responsible and dignified positions. I knew some men who were sleeping on the benches in railroad stations and living on a few pennies a day. The usual refrain in the streets was "Brother, can you spare a dime?" I knew a man who had held an important position and who was driven to selling apples and shoestrings in the street.

Desperation was driving men to crime. One night on returning home I found the iron grille gates to my apartment house closed and locked; no one was admitted until identified. An old man who lived in the house, entering by the back way to avoid the bitter winds on Riverside Drive, had been set upon by robbers, gagged and robbed. Though he was not badly hurt, the attack brought on a stroke and the next day he died. Just before this incident, a gang had boldly entered International House next door and emptied the box of the cashier.

Crime had us in a state of siege.

In sober truth we were on the verge of revolution. With the hammer of the auctioneer knocking down farms to the highest bidder because of nonpayment of taxes, the traditionally conservative, law-abiding farmers were on the warpath. When these men pushed into a courtroom where eviction proceedings were in progress, put a rope around the neck of the judge, carried him to a grove and were on the point of hanging him, the blindest must have seen that we were rushing toward revolution. And when striking farmers armed with pitchforks patrolled the highways leading into Chicago to prevent the delivery of milk the most incurable optimist must have had moments of misgivings.

It was in these days of darkness that thousands of young men, despairing of a future under democratic institutions and driven to desperation, began to become interested in Communism, which they did not understand very well. They were young and all they understood was that they could not be happy under things as they were.

The atmosphere and the conditions were precisely those that precede revolutionary storms.

At Hyde Park Roosevelt in his corner was pondering problems such as no other President had ever faced.

In early January at a dinner at Henry Morgenthau's the conversation was on the gravity of the situation, and Frank Vanderlip dripped with gloom. He found the real-estate situation in New York threatening—"terrible," as he expressed it—with general conditions dreadful. He thought Roosevelt should name a committee of outstanding businessmen to go to Washington and stay there exchanging views with Congress. Since outstanding businessmen, given a free rein during the Coolidge administration, had done much to bring the ruin and had not submitted a constructive thought to meet the situation, the suggestion seemed ironical to me. Morgenthau poked fun at Vanderlip's pessimism.

In every sector of society one saw the wreckage of hopes, ambitions, fortunes. One day Pat Hurley, Secretary of War in the Hoover Cabinet, told me of the tragedy in the life of the brilliant Attorney General Mitchell, who had to forego his lifelong ambition when it was within his grasp. Hurley insisted that Hoover's Attorney General was really a Democrat. Not infrequently in Cabinet meetings he would say, "I belong to a school of political thought with which it is impossible to reconcile this plan of yours. You must leave me out." With the retirement of Justice Holmes, Hoover had planned to put Mitchell on the bench and to make Hurley Attorney General. A canvass of the Senate had shown that the appointments would be confirmed. But when the President made the offer to Mitchell the latter said, "Mr. President, my one ambition for years has been for a seat on the high bench, but this depression has wiped me out and I must buckle down for the next few years to make money for the protection of my family. So I cannot take it now that it's offered."

In early February I spoke at a dinner in honor of Mrs. Roosevelt at the Waldorf and sat beside the guest of honor. She described to me her visit to the White House under the ciceronage of Mrs. Hoover, and her almost irresistible impulse to laugh on being shown the Lincoln bed of teakwood, black and heavily carved, with the headboard looming toward the ceiling. The picture had flashed upon her of the plight of the occupant if the headboard should ever collapse.

She talked a little of her plans for the kitchen, but in the midst of the levity of the occasion what impressed me most was her reply to my question whether she looked forward with pleasure to moving into the White House.

"As the time draws near," she said, "and I think of the terrible condition of the country, and of the high expectations from the change, it frightens me."

In late February Roosevelt announced his Cabinet, and the same day I was called to the phone by Raymond Moley.

"I have a pleasant task," he said. "The other night Roosevelt and Farley had a long conference and I was present. Farley said that you had done great work for the party, and I said that you were doing the greatest kind of work for liberalism and democracy through your books. I've been asked by the President to say to you that you'll be appointed ambassador to Spain. He asked me to get in touch with Hull so that he can notify you as he sees fit. I had Hull on the phone this morning and he's delighted. It's an interesting post just now, and I envy you."

It was to prove more interesting than he thought, but I doubt if he envied me a few years later.

Three days before the inauguration, a dinner was given for me at the Astor in New York. It had nothing to do with my appointment, since this was still secret. Ruth Bryan served beautifully as toastmaster, and complimentary speeches were made by Josephus Daniels, Frank Murphy, Jim Farley, Senator Hawes and Mayor O'Brien of New York.

Meanwhile I had been selected to make the only speech at the banquet of the Electoral College in Washington the night before the inauguration. I have a vivid remembrance of the grimness, the feeling of depression bordering on hysteria, in Washington on the eve of an occasion usually given over to hilarity. In the afternoon

I had visited several Senators at the Capitol, and, without a single exception, I found them solemn and gravely disturbed. One Senator told me he thought that the banks still standing were sound, but that hysteria was abroad, and huge withdrawals were threatening all. Another Senator told me that $43,000,000 had been withdrawn from banks within ten days. I was told that the Federal Reserve Board had sat late the night before and proposed the suspension of gold payment, but that Roosevelt had vetoed the plan.

On the eve of the inauguration conditions were so somber that hotels were refusing payments in checks. Rich men high in the business world with large balances in the strongest banks found their checks worthless in the hotels. This in the capital of the United States!

At the Electoral College banquet I was introduced by Farley. Just before the dinner I met the notorious Father Coughlin, who had been asked to deliver the invocation. For sheer arrogance and offensive conceit, I have never seen another such face. At the conclusion of my speech, which was studiedly free from partisan jubilation because of the gravity of the hour, he sent a note to Farley offering to say something if desired. Farley made a grimace and declined the offer. It was a more unusual occasion than I had known.

After the dinner I had a letter from Michael Francis Doyle, chairman of the Electoral Commission:

The Committee, appreciating the fact that your address was the outstanding feature and did much to add to the brilliancy of the occasion, sends this expression of their appreciation and gratitude. We hope it may also be treasured in your mind as being the first meeting of Presidential electors of the United States in one body, and that your selection as the only speaker is a tribute of the regard in which you are held by the Democracy of the nation.

The great throng that faced Roosevelt at the inauguration was not the traditional laughing, jubilant crowd. It was serious, sober, intent on the inaugural address. This was on Saturday. On Monday morning it was announced that all banks would be closed until investigated; that all found sound would be immediately reopened, backed by the government. This was the kind of decisive action with which the country had not been familiar for four years.

Thereafter Roosevelt was to move rapidly and with daring. History will record that he saved the nation from ruin and revolution.

In a few days Roosevelt telephoned me from the White House. "That Spanish matter is all right," he said. "I'm a little embarrassed about so many people from New York. Can I send your name in as from Indiana?"

"I've voted in New York for eight years," I said, "but you may do as you wish, since you're the dictator"—referring to the all but dictatorial powers granted him in the crisis.

I heard a gasp, and then a hearty laugh. "Have you any property in Indiana?" he asked.

"I have not."

"Do you have any of your things there?" he persisted.

"None."

"Then I guess I can't do it. I think I'll send your name in as from Indiana and New York," he concluded. (I had been presented as temporary chairman of the Houston convention in this way—as from Indiana and New York.) "I'll send it in tomorrow."

The reaction in Spain to my appointment was friendly. It now seems significant that Ambassador Cárdenas in Washington seemed interested solely in ascertaining what, if anything, I had written about the forced departure of King Alfonso XIII in 1931, when the monarchy was replaced by the Spanish Republic. A career diplomat under the monarchy who had been retained by the Republic, he would later turn against the republican government and become Franco's agent in the United States.

The morning I reached Washington I called on Cordell Hull, the new Secretary of State, who was looking tired. No one could have thought that he would go through twelve grueling years of international crisis before retiring, at the age of seventy-three. I paid my respects also to William Phillips, the Under Secretary of State. I had been warned that his stiff, cold manner would be disconcerting, but I found this distinguished diplomat very human and cordial. Afterward I lunched at the Spanish embassy with Ambassador Cárdenas, and that same day I had my first official audience with Roosevelt.

The President was at his desk looking very thoughtful when I arrived. Then, as was his custom, he threw back his head and laughed. He said he was sorry I was going out of the country. When I congratulated him on the tidal wave of public approval of his dramatic measures to save the country from the danger of utter ruin, he again looked serious.

"But I'm always a pessimist," he said. "How long will it last?"

Though he looked well, there was a sobriety about him and a set look about the mouth that one month of tremendous responsibility had given him. Both the President and Hull had told me of their desire for the negotiation of a commercial treaty with Spain, and I was consequently puzzled when I failed to find a single subordinate official of the State Department who did not rather deride the idea. I confessed my bewilderment to Dan Roper, Secretary of Commerce, and urged the necessity of knowing whether a treaty would be seriously undertaken before I expressed myself in Madrid. He was sure the treaty was wanted, but he advised me to talk again with the President and Hull.

The next day I saw Hull again. He, an idealist, was becoming disillusioned early. Apropos of the various international conferences preliminary to the London Economic Conference, he said that "all these fellows come over with a big trunk expecting to carry away big concessions," and that he was afraid none had enlarged views and were "bent solely on some immediate advantage." He reiterated his desire for a trade treaty, but he admitted he had pressure upon him from all sides against lowering the tariff barriers.

On May 2, 1933, I had my farewell talk with Roosevelt before sailing. He seemed much less harassed than before. His office looked out on a beautiful green lawn, and while I was with him he gave instructions that no flower beds were to be planted to break the continuity of the greenery. Apropos of the proposed treaty, I told him that some, fearing for the American telephone company in Spain, property of the International Telephone and Telegraph Corporation, which had had some difficulty a little while before, had proposed holding off a commercial treaty to use it as a club for the protection of the corporation.

"Of course," he said, "the matter of the Tel and Tel is simple. The company entered into a contract in good faith and has put its money into building a great telephone system. We expect, of course, that the terms of the contract will be observed." But, with a vigorous shake of the head, he waved aside the idea of using the trade treaty as a club. "Oh, of course not," he said. "That's the old diplomatic method, outdated now."

(Incidentally, the Tel and Tel had no trouble of any consequence during my tenure, and during the Spanish Civil War it continued to function on both sides of the lines.)

And then Roosevelt said something indicative of how his mind was working: "One thing I want you to find out when you get over there is what would be the effect of my making an appeal over the heads of government leaders to the peoples of the world. I'm greatly disturbed over the trend of the world toward dictatorships. I'm a Jeffersonian democrat, despite some of the laws enacted recently in Congress. Italy is gone. Japan is gone. Germany with Hitler is becoming a menace. Now I can see that Spain has a potentiality of becoming again one of the foremost nations. She isn't one today. I don't know positively how she stands on democracy, but I'm anxious to have Spain on our side of the table."

On reaching Madrid I was assured by Fernando de los Ríos, Spanish Minister of Foreign Affairs, that the Spanish government would heartily welcome the President's suggested appeal to the peoples of the world against the totalitarian drift, and I so informed the President. I was to think of this many times between July 1936 and June 1939.

As I was leaving, Roosevelt gave me an inscribed photograph and said, "I wish that whenever you find anything you think I should know, even though you have sent it to the State Department, you would send me a copy with such observations as you may care to make to me personally."

I am sorry I did not avail myself more fully of this privilege during the Spanish war.

CHAPTER XVIII

The Embassy in Spain

WE SAILED for France on the initial voyage of the *George Washington* in mid-May, proceeding immediately to Madrid, where I presented my credentials as ambassador the first of June.

Madrid was a typical European capital with a million population. The leisurely tempo, the beautiful tree-lined streets, the circles and the monuments bore a resemblance to the Washington I knew before the First World War. The tone of the city was political, not commercial or industrial. The Prado, a treasure house of art, was equal or superior to the Louvre in Paris. Because of my interest in history I was especially fascinated by the older sections of the town through which the centuries have marched, such as the Puerta del Sol, where the soldiers of Napoleon were mowed down by infuriated patriots, where the Republic was proclaimed in 1931, and where at midnight on New Year's Eve boys and girls assembled to eat their twelve grapes, one with each stroke of the clock on the Ministry of the Interior a short distance away.

The Plaza Mayor, a few steps beyond and entered from several streets through stone archways, was steeped in history, and here I was to make many sentimental journeys. Here the medieval buildings, once residences of the nobility, had become tenements, and on the flat roof of one of them a frame house had been built and one could see the occupants sewing or hanging clothes on the line to dry. Here, with a little imagination, one could visualize the scenes of other days—the festive gatherings, the dancing in the street, the bullfights with nobles in the role of matadors, and the terrible drama of the Inquisition. The balcony of the Casa de la Real Panadería, the old bakers' guildhall, interested me, since from this point of vantage Charles I of England, then Prince of Wales, with his gay companion the Duke of Buckingham, had looked down on the bullfight arranged in his honor.

It is customary to write with distaste of the Castilian plains about Madrid, so dusty, with so little vegetation, with few trees and with their scorched yellow earth, but I came to love those plains. I was to make many journeys to the surrounding country—to the Escorial, the most impressive, inspiring and yet depressing structure in the world, with its royal apartments, its monastery, its beautiful cathedral, its library and art gallery, and its dark marble crypt in which rest the caskets of all the Spanish monarchs from the Emperor Charles V to King Alfonso XII; to El Pardo, my favorite among the royal palaces because here one felt that human beings had lived domestic lives. I never visited the palace without driving in the great hunting park of the kings just beyond, with its low rolling hills and stunted trees.

Our government did not own an embassy in Madrid at that time. We rented the palace of the Duke of Montellano, one of the grandees of Spain, and had both the residence and the office in the same building. The palace and grounds occupied a full city block and gave entrance on three streets—the Castellana, one of the broad avenues of Madrid, and two quiet shady streets, Cisne and Fortuny. The house, designed by a French architect forty years before, was beautiful and comfortable. When, many years later, Franco announced that the grandson of Alfonso XIII, who was being educated in Spain, would be living in an apartment in the Montellano Palace while taking his military training, because the dictator wished him to live in an atmosphere of "austerity," I marveled at his choice of the word.

To a reasonably simple Hoosier, the marble dining room, with its painted ceiling, and the long ballroom adorned with portraits by Boldini and Zuloaga of the beautiful Duchesses of Montellano and Arión had special charm, but the best of all was the little Goya room, designed exclusively for the famous Goya panels. The dining room, the ballroom and the hall opened on a broad marble terrace the width of the house, looking out over a very large formal garden with horse chestnut trees, flowers, statuary and a fountain. The garden was so shut in by shrubbery that one could dine at night on the lighted terrace with a feeling of perfect privacy. One walk in the garden was especially appreciated, since it was bordered by a row of trees whose branches overarched to form a delightful green aisle. By the tennis court was a little stone summerhouse for tea or bridge. Nothing could have been more beautiful and restful than this garden, especially at twilight or in moonlight, and Queen Victoria of Spain, who was a friend of the Duchess, had loved and frequently visited it.

I particularly recall one moonlight night when Franklin Roosevelt, Jr., just out of Groton and ready for Harvard in the fall, visited Spain with a classmate and we had them as our guests. The first night, seeking some form of entertainment and noting their keen interest in bullfights, I arranged for Sidney Franklin, the American matador, to come in after dinner. We were sitting on the terrace when the matador appeared, dramatizing his entrance. The eyes of the boys popped. He was an excellent matador, with a sense of drama, and the boys sat on the edge of their chairs, leaning forward so as not to miss a word. Now and then Sidney Franklin took a cigarette, and the son of the President literally sprang across the terrace with a lighter. The matador's dramatic dialogue went on and on while the moon traversed the sky, and the dawn was breaking when we went to bed.

I understand that young Roosevelt left Spain with a stuffed bull's head, the gift of a Spanish well-wisher, which delighted him but was something of a problem to his mother and the White House staff.

Another well-remembered moonlight night we had Ernest Hemingway and John Dos Passos and their wives as guests. Naturally it was after a bullfight that I first met Hemingway. He was then an enthusiastic friend of the Republic and spent much time in Spain following the corridas and the fiestas.

There in these pleasant surroundings we were to remain till the summer of 1936. In this house before the Spanish Civil War I wrote two books, *Jefferson in Power* and *The Spanish Adventures of Washington Irving*, finding much material for the latter in the archives of the embassy.

The monarchy had fallen without the firing of a shot two years before I reached Spain. The Republic had adopted a thoroughly democratic constitution and had chosen Alcalá Zamora as its first

President. The Cortes, popularly elected and consisting of 476 members, legislated in the old chamber mellow in history since the days of Castelar. The political party or coalition having a majority in the Cortes constituted the government.

Alcalá Zamora was a small, handsome man with lustrous brown eyes, graying hair and mustache, and a complexion hinting of Moorish blood. He was a leader of the Madrid bar and several times had served as a minister of the King. He was innately conservative and devoutly Catholic. In his character were many virtues and some weaknesses that were to prove his undoing.

The government was headed by Manuel Azaña as Premier, by all odds the greatest statesman of the Spanish Republic. Brilliant as a writer and biographer, all-powerful as an orator and debater, progressive as a thinker, profound as a political philosopher, he was to prove himself the most convinced and militant democrat at the head of any European government during the period of appeasement of the Axis in the early phases of its war on "decadent democracy." I knew him well and found him fascinating. Though a progressive, he had the conservatism of common sense. His great orations were closely knit conclusions of sound logic expressed in the purest language free from tasteless floridity and demagogy.

The titular leader of the opposition was Alejandro Lerroux, long the republican leader during the monarchy. When the rightists triumphed in a general election and Lerroux became Premier, my personal and official relations with this picturesque veteran of seventy were always pleasant. He had an intriguing personality, colorful because of the traditions that clung to his career. A short, stoutly built man, erect as a ramrod despite his years, he not only was meticulously correct in his dress but he was something of a dandy. His socks always matched his tie, and a blue-edged handkerchief always protruded from his upper pocket. It had not been so always; in the days when he posed as the champion of the proletariat in Barcelona he had worn flannel shirts, unbuttoned at the top to prove he had hair on his chest. His manner was gracious and ingratiating, and he had great charm. His old eyes had penetrated all the secrets of politics and he knew most of the answers. As an orator he had more words than ideas, but the words poured from him with the ease and melody of a mountain stream.

I have described Lerroux as the titular leader because the real leader of the rightist coalition was José María Gil Robles, the head of the CEDA, the Catholic party, which during the Lerroux regime was numerically the strongest in the Cortes. This remarkable man had organized the victory by persuading all rightist parties to unite in a common front, and by making promises to all and sundry that could not all be redeemed. To escape embarrassment, it was said, he stepped aside that Lerroux might become Premier. By the nodding of his head he could have toppled Lerroux from his throne any minute, and because the old veteran knew it he voluntarily bowed to the will of the ambitious young leader. I am convinced that Lerroux was a sincere republican and fundamentally a democrat and I do not think he realized that there were times when his government was whittling away the Republic. His supreme ambition had been to become Premier and he was willing to pay almost any price to retain his station.

Gil Robles was a clever man whose rise in politics had been spectacular. He was an orator who depended for effect on the emotional fervor of his declamation. He did not approach Azaña, but he was better than Lerroux. His position was difficult to define. He was believed to be a monarchist, and, while he never openly avowed himself such, he never convincingly declared himself republican.

He was a somewhat enigmatic figure even to his own followers. Many who joined the CEDA in the belief that it was a monarchist party, secretly pledged to bring back the King, later became disillusioned and restive. Others thought him a fascist and found themselves mistaken. Yet he helped prepare the way for the rebellion and was apparently in close co-operation for some time with its future leaders. Then when the rebellion broke out the CEDA disbanded, and for many years of the Franco regime Gil Robles lived in exile. Emotionally, I am sure, he would have liked to see the King return, but the cause to which he was truly devoted was the cause of the Catholic Church.

The CEDA was a large party and it included elements which had very little in common with each other—reactionary landowners and extreme conservatives on the one hand, and on the other a group which would have liked to make of the CEDA an instrument for social progress after the ideas of Pope Leo XIII. There was even talk of a land reform program, but the bulk of CEDA support and finances came from groups that would never permit interference of this sort and the reform program disappeared early. The political left was so convinced of Gil Robles' monarchism and his intention to betray the Republic that when Lerroux gave Cabinet posts to some members of his party there was a general strike and a brief revolt, which was put down at once everywhere except in the northern province of Asturias. The Spanish Foreign Legion was brought over from Morocco to deal with the Asturian miners and crushed the revolt with a severity and violence that aroused lasting bitterness among the working classes.

These three, Azaña, Lerroux and Gil Robles, were the outstanding leaders during my time in Spain before the Civil War.

Madrid then had its season for official entertaining. It began with the President's dinner to the diplomatic corps on the first of January and ended early in June. President Alcalá Zamora had offices on the ground floor of the imposing Royal Palace, but he lived in his town house near our embassy. The royal apartments were used only on special occasions, because of the cost of heating the enormous structure. Sometimes the stately salons were all but frigid, though on the occasion of state dinners great fires blazed in the fireplaces and took off the chill. The dinners were served in the state dining room at a very long table colorful with flowers and lighted by candles in splendid silver candelabra. The silver service still bore the insignia of the King. Following the dinner we filed into the throne room for the entertainment, and I have a vivid recollection of seeing La Argentina dance there to the music of her castanets.

In the diplomatic corps were a number of interesting and clever men. The nuncio, now Cardinal Tedeschini, tall, handsome, elegant, suave and velvety, seemed to have stepped out of the period of Talleyrand and Metternich, for he was a consummate and wise diplomat of the old school. He astonished me on my initial protocol call by his familiarity with my *Irish Orators*, then out of print a quarter of a century. I remember him most vividly as I saw him occasionally on my drives in the Casa del Campo, where, on the rustic road, I met him walking, his car following to pick him up when he was tired. I was to witness the ceremony at the palace when Alcalá Zamora placed the cardinal's red cap on his head. It was not surprising to me later that he was one of the three most favored cardinals in the election of a new pope in 1939. One of my colleagues told me that King Alfonso XIII had been somewhat bitter against several members of the diplomatic corps, among them the nuncio, for not having taken some steps to show support of the monarchy. Cardinal Tedeschini had told my friend that the King, then living in exile, had seen Pope Pius XI and endeavored to turn him against Tedeschini. "But," said Cardinal Tedeschini, "His Holiness is an old man, and when the King began his criticism of me he noticed that His Holiness was nodding. He changed the subject and His Holiness woke up. Then the King began again. But immediately he observed that His Holiness was nodding."

My most cherished friend among my colleagues was Sir George Grahame, the British ambassador, who, being a bachelor, seemed to me a lonely man. Though he had been born into a very conservative county family, I was to find him more liberal than my other colleagues. Tall, rangy, his shoulders slightly stooped because of his height, he would have attracted attention anywhere and I am sure he would have preferred it otherwise, for he was a shy and modest man. Once, admiring a painting on one of his walls, I asked the name of the artist. He blushingly replied that he was guilty. "I dabble a bit for my own amusement," he said. He wrote short stories that were shown only to his intimate friends. I thought them too clever to hide away, but the mere suggestion of publication threw him into a panic. His political judgment was of the best, and well before the fall of the monarchy he had warned London of the growing unpopularity of Alfonso XIII.

My relations with Count von Welczeck, the German ambassador, were most cordial. Preceding me in Madrid by seven years, he had been a favorite hunting companion of the King. He was a great landowner, a thorough aristocrat in the better sense. He had entered the foreign service somewhat against his will, on the insistence of his father. "I wanted to be a farmer," he told me. Tall, slender, courteous, he was socially popular. He admired pretty women and loved to dance. I know that he found the Nazi regime at that time offensive and not a little absurd. It was his fate to be transferred to Paris a few years before World War II; however, he resigned before the storm broke. On the afternoon of the day of the memorial service for Hindenburg in Madrid he spent the afternoon in our

THE EMBASSY IN SPAIN

garden, and through a long intimate conversation I came to know him.

Another interesting colleague was the Mexican ambassador, Genaro Estrada, famous as the author of the "Estrada doctrine." Short in stature, a little stout and very quiet, he gave the impression that he was more the poet than the politician. Some of the most pleasant memories of my Madrid days cluster about him and his beautiful and charming wife, then in her early twenties, who was no end bored by her enforced association with the other ambassadors and ambassadresses, most of them old enough to be her parents. Protocol made me her table companion at numerous dinners, and I found her as refreshing as a breeze on a sultry day.

Among the women of the corps the most stimulating and clever was Princess Elizabeth Bibesco, wife of Prince Antoine Bibesco, the Romanian minister, and daughter of British Prime Minister Asquith and the famous Margot Asquith. She was small, attractive, and sparkling in her manner and conversation. She had a rich sense of humor, but her brilliant wit was devastating and her sarcasm deadly. Her talk was epigrammatic, like her novels, and these epigrams were disconcerting since they came with the rapidity of machine gun fire, and at times with much the same effect. I am sure she cared little for the conventions and liked whenever possible to put aside diplomatic protocol. Our first dinner in Madrid, before I presented my credentials, was at her table. She admired Azaña and took liberties with him in conversation; at the other pole, she was a friend of young José Antonio Primo de Rivera, founder of the Falange party, and after his death in the Spanish Civil War she dedicated a novel to him. When I told her how much we appreciated her great helpfulness and kindness in our first days in Madrid, an expression almost of wonder spread over her face. "I don't have a reputation of that sort," she said.

In my many trips by car to all parts of the country, I found Spain lovely and fascinating. When the heat of summer became oppressive, one could roll along in a day to the refreshing greenery of the Basque country or to the sea at San Sebastián; when the gloom of winter settled sadly on the city, one could quickly reach Andalusia and the blue waters of the Mediterranean at Málaga. These motor trips were delightful, since the roads were perfect and at intervals, at the edge of small towns, were charming *para-dors,* inns for the traveler, where one could count on excellent meals and sleep in comfort in clean beds with fresh linen.

These journeys of thousands of miles took me through many villages, some as old as Spanish history, all dusty with time, and picturesque. The primitive threshing in the fields, the windmills such as Quixote saw and fought, the patient donkeys with loaded panniers plodding along bearing old women with wrinkled faces or young girls with sparkling eyes—such was the drama of the highway. On these journeys I came to understand the observation made long ago that "the real nobility of Spain is the peasantry." Courteous and always helpful, they had great self-respect, pride and dignity.

Time and again we made the short trip to Toledo, near Madrid. An impressionistic picture of the town would be cold and austere. The narrow winding streets and the plaza have little physical beauty to commend them to tourists, but visitors with a sense of history and some imagination will find them thrilling because several civilizations have passed and left their imprint. One can sit in the historic plaza and let fancy run riot, for it reeks with drama, romance and tragedy. A bit gruesome to me was the "Bloody Gate" on one side, with its balcony whence princes and ecclesiastics once looked down coldly on the scenes of the Inquisition. Passing through the gate and down uneven steps worn rough with the tread of generations, one found the medieval tavern where Cervantes once stayed and which before the Spanish Civil War was still ministering to the needs of man and beast. There in the cobblestone-paved court the chickens still scratched and clucked and the air was redolent of the old stable where peasants left their mules and donkeys on market days, as when Cervantes once looked down from the balcony. I am glad I saw the old tavern before it was wrecked in the struggle for Toledo. Here one could easily transport oneself in fancy to the days when the ladies of easy virtue in front made sport of poor Quixote.

We always visited the little church, to stand before El Greco's masterpiece "The Burial of Count Orgaz," and lingered in the cathedral so intimately identified with the political and spiritual history of the country. I never had enough of the treasure room, to which access could be had only in the company of three priests, each with a key. The treasures are priceless—gold and silver and precious stones, and the raiment of dead cardinals studded with emeralds and pearls. There in the cathedral are El Greco's paintings of the disciples. No spot in Spain impressed me more than Toledo. I especially remember walking through the narrow old streets at night during an official fiesta in the town and hearing the music of guitars from the latticed balconies.

In Seville I remember the old palaces steeped in history, the narrow streets with awnings stretched across them to protect pedestrians from the sun, and the marvelous drama of Holy Week, the most impressive I have ever seen, when the hotels are filled to overflowing and many find lodging in other towns not too far away. The purely religious motive was not so predominant as it had once been, but it was still there, and the gay folks with their drinking and laughing could not shut it out. In Granada we rambled through the rooms of the Alhambra and visited the great gardens of the Moors. I am sure the majority of Spanish roosters live in Granada, for invariably I was awakened in the morning there by the crowing of cocks. We made several journeys to the walled town of Ávila to visit the convent of Saint Teresa and the ancient church built into the town wall as part of its protection in old times, with the figures of warriors one on each side of the entrance to remind the visitor that the Church had been a fighting force; to Córdoba with its memories of the Jewish philosophers and the Moors, and its great cathedral that was once a mosque; and to Segovia and San Sebastián, the first impressive, the second amusing in summer.

And I always remember with particular affection the small town of Alcalá de Henares, the birthplace of Cervantes, near Madrid. Soon after our arrival in Madrid Elizabeth Bibesco recommended it to us as the most charming and interesting small town in Spain, and she was perfectly right. The buildings of the old University of Madrid there for the most part belonged to the Army and were not open to the public, but one room, once reserved as the dining room of star students in ruffs and with swords, is now a restaurant for tourists. We often lunched and dined there, and in the winter we were grateful for the slightly elevated stone fireplace whose dancing flames drew out the chill of the mountain air. While waiting to be served we would go out into the court to enjoy the architectural beauty of the old building with its pinkish glow imparted by time, its gargoyles worn smooth by the rain and sleet of centuries. Thence into the room where great savants lectured to students now for centuries turned to dust. Anyone who can stand unmoved in that room with its beauty and memories must be cold indeed.

During these years I formed an admiration and affection for the Spanish people. Even their chief fault comes from an overdevelopment of their chief virtue, their intense individualism, their extreme pride, the feeling that each man is a sovereign within himself. In the Spanish people is a strong vein of poetry, born of the mysticism of the race that is in their blood. I came to resent the superficial impression of foreigners that they are cruel. This impression springs from the bullfight, but one may question whether the killing of the bull, in which the matador imperils his life, is worse than the running down and killing of the fox. The foreigner answers that it is not sportsmanlike in that the magnificent bull never has a chance, and the Spaniard replies that it is not a sport at all, but a tragedy. I knew many Spaniards who did not care for the tragedy and never attended the fights, but I met no tourist whose chief interest was not in seeing the bullfight.

I know of no classless nation, and Spain like all the others has its social divisions. The old nobility of Spain and the newer aristocracy are a mixture of good and bad. Among them one finds culture of the highest order, intellectual distinction and taste, but also playboys who would not permit a vitally important election to divert them from a day's sport. Undoubtedly the nobility, as a class, had signally failed in its political obligations to the state and even to the monarch. Unlike the English aristocracy, which prepares a son for public life, the Spanish nobility looked upon politics as degrading. There were very few exceptions. When in the municipal elections of 1931 the monarchy was tottering, the greater part of the nobility, to whose support the King had a right to look, was standing aloof. Just as fatal to the nobility was the fact that for some decades the old landowning aristocrats had ceased to maintain real contact with the peasants on their broad acres or to recognize their responsibility to them. In former times they lived a large part of the year on their estates and the peasants thought the master could be counted upon as their friend and protector; but for years the masters had left the management of their domains to supervisors whose chief concern was to make the best possible showing in profit at the expense of the peasant.

The industrial workers and miners had a reputation for turbulence, but this fails to take into account that until the reforms attempted by the Republic no rights such as have long been acknowledged in England and the United States had been granted them. Thinking almost in terms of medieval serfdom, the dominant class had refused to yield the elemental rights to labor without a struggle. If they asked a mere living wage they were denounced as Communists, and their demand for safety devices in the mines and for an eight-hour day was called anarchistic and subversive. Americans who took these denunciations seriously and were shocked by Spanish strikes conveniently forgot that American labor has won its victories only by fighting and that we have had quite a bit of turbulence in the United States.

But of all the segments of Spanish society my greatest sympathy was for the peasantry. The peasants, though uneducated and living drearily in unfit habitations in dusty villages whence they trudge to the fields, have an innate nobility and a keen natural intelligence. I always found them courteous. On my first motor trip in Spain we were doubtful as to directions, and seeing a peasant by the road we asked him to direct us. He was an old man whose face had been lined by toil and weather. Coming to the car, he removed his hat, but with such great dignity that it was clear he did so not as an admission of inferiority but as one gentleman to another. He gave directions clearly and then added that if we wished he would ride on the running board to the next crossing and show us which way to go.

The middle class included merchants, professional people and intellectuals in general. I was fortunate in the friendship of poets, novelists, dramatists, painters and sculptors among whom were some of great distinction and international renown.

I profited much by the friendship of Salvador de Madariaga, famous as a scholar, historian, biographer and essayist. Representing Spain in the League of Nations, he made periodic visits to Madrid, when I saw him in my house and in his. He lived, when there, in an attractive house in a new development. He was a brilliant and fascinating conversationalist and his talk sparkled with wit and glowed with humor. Though on the verge of politics, he never really belonged to it, and I found him pessimistic over the totalitarian trend of the times. When I drove him home through the rain after the memorial services for George V of England, he expressed doubt about the future of democracy because its enemies were rapidly possessing themselves of the agencies of publicity through their wealth. He admired and respected Azaña, but it was Lerroux who withdrew him from his embassy in Paris to make him Minister of Education; and, while he accomplished much during his brief tenure, I am sure he was not happy in a rough-and-tumble political atmosphere and he was glad to return to more congenial duties in Geneva. He was almost unique in the League of Nations—he believed in it!

In Fernando de los Ríos, rector of the University of Madrid, I had one of my warmest and most cherished friends. Though he was deep in politics, as a deputy in the Cortes, Minister of Foreign Affairs and later ambassador to Washington, our conversations were mostly on books, writers and history. He lived quite simply in an apartment house, his rooms overflowing with books denoting his character. Big in body, mind and heart, he was worthy of his uncle, Francisco Giner de los Ríos, one of the most enlightened minds Spain has produced in a century. I saw Fernando de los Ríos many times in his apartment, occasionally in Paris, and he impressed me as a great humanist and philosopher. Being a democrat, he was to die in exile.

Ramón Pérez de Ayala, the novelist, I knew well and found socially and intellectually delightful. He was one of the best novelists of his time, but one of his books had concentrated upon him the resentment of reactionary elements. His republicanism, however, was more of the drawing room than of the arena. Azaña made him ambassador to the Court of St. James's. Slender, always well groomed, he had a courtly manner and a pleasing personality. He was fluent in conversation and could be immensely amusing. He could discuss the relative merits of bulls and matadors with real eloquence and judgment, and it was a liberal education in the art of the arena to sit beside him at a fight, as I have done. He was an intimate friend of Belmonte, the greatest of the matadors of the time.

Jacinto Benavente, the famous dramatist, winner of the Nobel Prize for Literature, was already a legend in Madrid when I arrived. Though perhaps his finest dramas were behind him, he was turning out sparkling comedies all the time. I do not know why he always reminded me of D'Annunzio, unless it was because he was small and wore a slight goatee. His bald head was impressive and he seemed something of a dandy, being always meticulously attired. His hands were tiny and I was fascinated by a great exotic ring on his finger which must have had a history. His was an almost extravagant courtesy. In the summer I found him often in front of his favorite café in San Sebastián and he invariably rose, lifted his hat and bowed.

Another friend was the distinguished poet and recipient of the Nobel Prize for Literature Juan Ramón Jiménez, a very shy genius who seldom left his ivory tower. He had a charming wife, and occasionally one or both were at the embassy. The bearded poet, whose health was frail, would sit in the warm room wrapped in a heavy coat, most of the time silently looking into the fire. He could not be counted upon to initiate a conversation, but once it had been begun by others he could talk pleasantly in the language of the Academy. I found him, a little to my surprise, an admirer of the poetry of Longfellow and Lowell, especially the latter.

Perhaps the most picturesque of the novelists was Valle Inclan, called the Anatole France of Spain, whose satiric novels depicting the free and easy court of Isabella II did much to undermine the hold of the monarchy. I never spoke to him, but I saw him occasionally sitting under a tree in front of the café he favored, always surrounded by his court of youthful admirers. Tall, very slender, with a thin El Greco face and a long, narrow beard, he seemed formidable. He was not easy to know, and the same was true of Unamuno, the great philosopher, who occasionally appeared in Madrid from Salamanca, where the Republic had given him a life professorship in the university. A truly great man, a profound thinker, he had been exiled by General Primo de Rivera and was supposed to be an uncompromising enemy of all dictatorships. I was therefore startled during the war in Spain to find in a fascist paper an interview in which he was purported to have said that the Spaniards were fit only for a dictator. I hoped that the explanation lay in the presence of a Franco officer during the interview, or that the paper had misquoted him intentionally. Soon he was saying, "These Germans swaggering possessively through the town I love will kill me." And he died during the war after a violent scene in the university.

Another friend of Madrid days was Count de Romanones, a former minister of the King and a liberal favoring a constitutional monarchy. He was a monarchist deputy in the Cortes, but he sat apart from the small monarchist party, which did not think a king should be hampered by a constitution. Though a politician, he was also an intellectual and the author of a number of important biographies and histories. He lived across the street from our embassy on the Castellana and I saw him in our house and in his beautiful and historic country place near Toledo. Our common interests were largely literary and historical. Crippled from childhood, he carried a cane. He had a roughhewn face and a brusque manner which was partly affected. His wit was biting, his sarcasm withering. He was by odds the ablest man politically of his class.

During the two and a half years of Azaña's leadership as Premier great and significant reforms tending to the destruction of a lingering feudalism were made. His program provided for the creation of a small peasant proprietorship in the land, through purchase, not confiscation, of parts of the enormous estates. Labor laws similar to those in the United States and England were enacted to raise the economic status of the workers. A program of building schools and training teachers was initiated, and this, perhaps, was the most important of all his reforms, inasmuch as when the monarchy fell there were more than nine thousand villages and towns without teachers and schools, and the illiteracy rate was naturally high. Unfortunately the schools of the religious orders were to be closed and many devout Catholics were unwilling to see the state school system replace the Catholic schools.

The agricultural and labor reforms, though much needed, aroused the hostility of powerful forces—the great landowners, the industrialists and the bankers. During the succeeding Lerroux–Gil Robles regime these reforms were reduced to a nullity. Anticipating the return of Azaña and the liberal parties to power at the polls, these forces prepared to take over the government by armed rebellion in conjunction with Army leaders and after receiving assurances of support from Hitler and Mussolini. Meanwhile the

Lerroux–Gil Robles government had been manipulating the Army and placing the future conspirators in strategic positions.

Such were the conditions when the general elections were forced in the late winter of 1935–36. The republican and democratic forces and the working masses were aroused to fever heat. When Azaña sought permission to speak in Madrid and was stupidly refused, a field outside the city just beyond the Toledo Bridge was taken for the meeting and a quarter of a million people poured in from every side by train and bus, on mules and on foot. The great orator of republicanism spoke for two hours to this enormous multitude without the slightest incident in the city.

And Azaña was swept back into power. In the first days of the Spanish Civil War Count de Romanones told me that the military rebellion had been planned before the election to have everything prepared in the event of a rightist defeat at the polls. He may not have known, though this seems improbable, that the bargain with Hitler and Mussolini had been made even before that. Since I have told in detail the story of these conspiracies in *My Mission to Spain*, I need not repeat it here.

The Spanish Civil War began in July. Most of the diplomatic corps had gone as usual to San Sebastián in the north of Spain for the summer. My wife was recovering from an illness, so instead of going to the hotel in San Sebastián for several weeks, as we had done before, we took a villa for the summer in Fuenterrabia, a quiet, picturesque village on the coast near San Sebastián. Ten days after the war began I was ordered by my government to leave Spain and join my colleagues of the diplomatic corps just across the French border in Hendaye. I then went on board the *Cayuga*, an American ship, to call at Spanish towns along the northern coast and evacuate Americans. When September came and the great hotel in Hendaye closed for the season we all moved on to St.-Jean-de-Luz just beyond, and here we were to continue during the remainder of the war. I established our chancellery in the Miramar Hotel and from this point it was possible to report fully on the activities of the rebels across the Spanish border. American war correspondents frequently called to tell me of conditions they could not publish because of the military censorship. Daily I read the Spanish papers of both sides and in the Franco press I found attacks on Roosevelt and on England and France, together with praise of Hitler, Mussolini and the "new order." It seemed that the struggle was to be between democracy and fascism.

With all the diplomatic corps accredited to the Spanish Republic stationed in St.-Jean-de-Luz, it was certainly the most unique "capital" in the world. It was a very old town, much older than Biarritz nearby, but such an influx of official foreigners had probably not been seen there since the remote days when the pompous courts of Philip IV of Spain and Louis XIV of France moved in for the marriage of the French King to the daughter of the King of Spain. Close to the waterfront stood the old palace in which the bride awaited the ceremony, and the palace facing the plaza where Louis XIV stayed was still there. Visitors were amused by the walled-up door of the church through which the great French monarch emerged with his new Queen, after which he gave instructions that the door should never give entrance or exit to anyone less exalted than this royal couple.

Most of the people who owned villas in St.-Jean-de-Luz were quiet and conservative, and the town had only one small night club, open in the summer for tourists, where I once saw the Prince of Wales, later Edward VIII, sitting in a corner alone with a sad expression. At the cocktail hour most people gathered at the Bar Basque, but anyone hungering for more hectic entertainment could find his way to Biarritz. St.-Jean-de-Luz was a dignified little town normally drowsing in an atmosphere of sweet serenity. Daily we went to a stationery store for the foreign papers and frequently to an old-fashioned and very popular English tearoom which had books to rent. We were fortunate to find a pleasant villa on the edge of the Chantaco golf course with big windows looking out in three directions over a lovely landscape. It rained much in the winter, but with the wind whipping the falling water into waves the scene was entrancing. In the green lush pastures cattle grazed in peace and sheep huddled together when the wind was strong. Here for two and a half years we were more than comfortably housed.

Ignacio Zuloaga, the foremost Spanish painter of the time, called upon me there one rain-drenched day. He was a man of large frame, scarcely gray despite his age, and he astounded me by his youthfulness, his vivacity and enthusiasm. He was living near San Sebastián in an old convent he had converted into a combined residence, studio and museum. Possessing a head of Saint Lawrence by El Greco which he considered among the artist's finest work, he had put it in a safe-deposit box in a bank in San Sebastián at the beginning of the Spanish war. When the fascists took the city the Loyalist government transferred the contents of the boxes to a bank in Bilbao, and Zuloaga was in terror lest the Basques, ignorant of the value of the canvas, misplace or mar it. He had been unable to sleep. I told him I would write Aguirre, head of the Basque government, if he wished and perhaps it might be possible to arrange for the painting to be deposited under the guardianship of some agency in France until the close of the war. He was boyishly grateful. But the next morning the lady with whom he was visiting came to tell me that Zuloaga had been unable to sleep, worrying that the acceptance of any favor from the Basques would arouse the resentment of the fascists; he would prefer for me to do nothing.

That day in my house he seemed more republican than rebel. As we sat before a blazing hearth he told me of his experience with the incomparable propaganda of the radio commentator of Lisbon. His friends, thinking to relieve the tedium of his isolation, had given him a radio, and he and his family gathered about it and turned it on. The first words he ever heard on his radio were these: "I am sorry to announce that the great Spanish painter Zuloaga has been brutally murdered by the reds." It was all news to him, but none the less thrilling. A little later he was "murdered" again in the newspapers, this time by his own people, the Basques.

I soon gathered that though his friends were all republicans, he had become a warm partisan of the fascists. When Mussolini arranged for an exhibit of his paintings in Rome he went all over to the fascists, and his last days were spent painting portraits of German Nazi officers and Italian Fascist generals. He was very good on uniforms.

During this time I personally wrote elaborate dispatches for Washington covering every phase of the situation, as Cordell Hull told his press conference at the time. Most of the ambassadors and ministers of those democratic nations which were soon to fall under the feet of Hitler showed marked partiality for the rebels who were backed by Hitler and Mussolini. It was lonesome for a demo-crat on that coast. Democracy had been shunted aside like a broken freight car on a siding, and the fascist and Nazi expresses had the right of way. The very word "democracy" was dropped from the vocabulary in fashionable quarters. Titled men and women from Spain who thought Franco was fighting for the restoration of the King made the fashion. The so-called international set was entirely pro-rebel.

I was there when Irún fell to the rebels because the "Non-Inter-vention" Committee prevented the delivery of ammunition waiting on the tracks at Hendaye for the Loyalist forces. I saw the pitiful parade of refugees, bewildered old men, trembling old women bearing burdens, children with frightened eyes, and young mothers carrying their babies, trudging along the road between Hendaye and St.-Jean-de-Luz. I was to witness the same scenes at Perpignan after the fall of Barcelona. But I do not have the heart for further discussion of the Spanish Civil War, which I have described in another book.

With the fall of Barcelona in January 1939 and the imminent triumph of the Franco forces, I was summoned home, ostensibly for consultation, but really, as Cordell Hull says in his memoirs, "to leave our hands free to recognize the Franco regime."

My sympathy had been wholly with the legal, constitutional, democratic government of Spain. The nonintervention trickery, cynically dishonest, was supplemented by us with our embargo denying the Spanish government, which we recognized, its right under international law to buy arms and ammunition to defend it-self. My government stood militantly behind this embargo, thus placing us in collaboration with the Axis in one of the moves in its campaign to wipe out democracy in Europe. President Truman in his memoirs apologizes for having voted in the Senate for the em-bargo and concedes that our policy contributed to the overthrow of the Spanish Republic; and Sumner Welles has written that our Spanish policy is a black blot on our record as a democracy. I never abandoned hope that the embargo would be lifted. I wrote President Roosevelt that, however good our intention was in adopt-ing the embargo, events had proven beyond any possible question that we were collaborating with the aggressor nations, Hitler's

Germany and Mussolini's Italy. His reply came not in a letter but in a speech a little later when he said that while our intent originally was good, the effect had been to align ourselves with the aggressor nations.

But the fall of Barcelona was fatal to Spanish democracy. A famous foreign correspondent of an American paper, stationed in Paris, telephoned me at St.-Jean-de-Luz one day that a "distinguished Frenchman" would like to see me confidentially, that he was going for the weekend to Lyons and would like me to drive there quietly to see him. He left no doubt in my mind that the "distinguished Frenchman" was Herriot, who had staunchly supported the Spanish Republic throughout. But Barcelona fell; and the next day the correspondent phoned that the man I was to meet had become discouraged and thought it best to wait a while to see what would happen next.

It was while seated in the lounge of the *Queen Mary* on March 28 listening to the radio news that I heard of the capitulation of the republican army in Madrid. Thus the fall of Spain's capital, the city that Franco with the aid of the military forces of Hitler and Mussolini could not take for almost three years, finally was achieved, in part through the "nonintervention" of the democracies.

CHAPTER XIX

The Rooseveltian Years

WHEN I LEFT for Spain in 1933, twenty years and a little more were to intervene before my definite return to the United States to live. But, though far removed from the American scene, I was intimately acquainted with political activities at home through letters from men high in the councils of the Democratic Party and the nation. Jim Farley wrote me very frequently and fully, with complete frankness, analyzing the conditions in the country as a whole and in different states, and these letters throw a vivid light on events important in the political history of those dramatic years. Letters and conversations with Roosevelt furnish an explanation of some motives and events that may be of interest to the historians of the future.

I did not return on leave from Spain until the early summer of 1935, when, on board the Italian liner *Conti Grandi,* we sailed from Gibraltar. I had hoped for a quiet vacation with relaxation among personal friends, aloof from politics and politicians, but even before I landed I knew I was doomed to disappointment. One day on the boat I was startled by the wireless bringing the news that the Supreme Court had held the NRA unconstitutional. This was one of the major organizations on which Roosevelt had depended for the rehabilitation of the economy of the country. The action of the Court seemed to cut the ground from beneath much of what he had done and planned, and it threatened all the other measures he had employed.

When we reached New York the country was fairly boiling with political controversy, for a Presidential election was but one year in the future. The President, who a year before had been hailed as the savior of the nation, had already become in most fashionable and wealthy circles "that man." I recalled that two years before, when I congratulated Roosevelt on the enthusiastic public acclaim of his work of rehabilitation, he had said that he was "always a pessimist" and had asked, "How long will it last?" It had not lasted long.

There was no possibility of rest and relaxation in New York. Three days after landing we went to Washington, where the beautiful home of Walter Schoellkopf, first secretary of the embassy in Madrid, had been placed at our disposition, but, aside from the hours passed in this house, I was to find Washington more exhausting than New York, and partisan rancor more intense, more fanatical, almost pathological.

I called at once on Cordell Hull, who received me as an old friend. This tall, slender statesman with a truly beautiful face had always impressed me as a superior person. Soft-voiced and meticulously careful in his utterances, he had never spoken in the House without extensive research and much thought, and though he lacked the more conspicuous qualities of an orator, his speeches were of such caliber that his colleagues read them in the *Record* with profit. In this respect he resembled Edmund Burke, whose orations in the House of Commons often found the benches empty, but whose great speeches were studied with admiration by members who found his delivery dull. Hull was the statesman's statesman. Had he been nominated for President in 1924, the year his party deliberately committed suicide at the national convention in New York, he might have been elected. His one obsession was his desire for an easy flow of goods from one country to another, unhampered by artificial barriers set up by selfish interests. Unhappily, just when he became Secretary of State, a post in which he hoped to accomplish something, the totalitarian states, extremely nationalistic, began to take over the control of commerce, and then came the war. But for twelve years, the longest tenure in American history, he was to win international renown by his wise direction in international affairs with very few mistakes.

Having known him for years, I had always been aware that this even-tempered, modest gentleman was capable of expressing himself with vigor, but I was astonished at this meeting by the richness of his vocabulary of profanity. It was just after the close of the controversy with one of his subordinates. I gathered the impression that he had become convinced that this assistant, who had been close to Roosevelt in the campaign of 1932, had set out to usurp his functions as head of the State Department. That day he was bitter over the treatment accorded him at the London Economic Conference, where, naturally, he was the head of the American delegation. He spoke in scathing terms of the arrival in London of his subordinate in an airplane, "with much beating of drums," with a view to scrapping Hull's policy in the conference. He felt the impression had been created that his assistant had arrived to supersede his chief. The result was Roosevelt's acceptance of the assistant's resignation.

Hull had also been annoyed by his experience in the Pan-American conference in Montevideo. He had in mind radical changes in our South American policies which were to culminate in the Good Neighbor policy, but he had been sent without actual authority to break new ground. When he reached the conference and found that much was expected of him, he telegraphed the President for authority to act. A reply being delayed, he telegraphed again, but the answer was discouraging. This aroused the fighting spirit of the Tennessean, and he sent a sizzling telegram: "If we do not stand for this, for God's sake what do we stand for?" He was then given a free hand, with the fine results that followed.

Then, too, that day he was not wholly enamored of the so-called brain trust. He seemed distinctly sour, clearly a bit impatient with the experts. "Experts are all right," he said. "I've used them many times. But I use them to collect facts and material, not to bring me a program of their own for my signature.

"But you should see the President at once," he said finally. I had expected to postpone the call at the White House for a day or so, but he made an engagement for me at four o'clock that day. I had an appointment at the Spanish embassy a little earlier, and it was with difficulty that I reached the White House at four, to find Roosevelt in conference with his advisers on the NRA decision.

When at length I was admitted, I found Roosevelt alone at his desk. He threw back his head, burst into a hearty laugh and exclaimed, "God, I'm glad you're back!"—which was soon to be explained by the burden of work that was put upon me. I commented on his healthy appearance, and Marvin McIntyre, his secretary, who was there at the moment, said, "Yes, and without benefit of clergy." Roosevelt smiled a bit sheepishly. The joke referred to his failure to attend church with regularity.

But soon the jovial mood passed, and he became serious. I wrote down that night what he said about the Supreme Court decision and the almost incredible bitterness of the reactionary element against him.

"The people have not been in control of this country since the Civil War," he said. "First the railroads were in the saddle, and then the industrialists, and then the big bankers took control of industry and the railroads. For long now the bankers have had the people by the throat." Bitterly he said that two years earlier the bankers had been on their knees before him, volunteering to do anything he asked. Now they were opposing everything he did—now that he had saved them from a crash in the spring of 1933.

Turning to the NRA decision, he said that members of the United States Chamber of Commerce who had denounced the NRA up to the time of the decision had gone to him asking that it not be scrapped entirely, and offering voluntarily to go on with it. "I said to them, 'Very well, I've said that you're practical men. Here are six hundred industries of one type. Suppose five hundred live up to the rules voluntarily, and a hundred do not. As practical men, tell me if the five hundred can go on following the rule if one hundred do not.'"

He paused a moment thoughtfully and then laughed. "It's amusing how little some really intelligent big-moneyed men know of the country and the spirit of the people and the times," he said. He referred to a visit from a great industrialist, who had called to point out the way to prosperity; his suggestion was to give the signal to the great corporations to go full speed ahead, doing as they pleased.

A few days later I had lunch with Roosevelt alone outside his office, facing the lawn. Having been caught in a traffic jam, I was two or three minutes late, and I found him at the table with a rather cold expression on his face. He accepted my explanation and apology rather grimly, I thought. The old gaiety was not apparent this time. He talked freely and at length on the approaching election of 1936, predicting a bitter fight, with the press largely in opposition. "We shall scarcely have a single metropolitan paper with us," he said.

And again he went back to the NRA decision. I told him I had heard that Justice Brandeis, who had decided against the NRA, to the surprise of many, had expressed the hope that the President would not be discouraged. I suggested that Brandeis was a liberal and his friend.

"Ah, yes, he is," he said. "But once he wrote a book against monopoly and the concentration of great economic power, contending that the resulting problems were too big for one man to handle. That's in his mind. He feels the same about the NRA."

After lunch I noticed with surprise that his hand shook when he lighted his cigarette. That evening at a garden party at the home of the three Misses Patton I met Dan Roper, the Secretary of Commerce, and, commenting on Roosevelt's nervousness, asked if it was something new. "Yes," Roper replied, "just since the Supreme Court decision."

The next day I had lunch with Vice-President Garner in his office in the Capitol. He was eating raw onions. "I'm the only member of the Senate permitted to eat them," he said with a bad-boy grin. He was still loyal to the Administration, but I got the impression that he, a stout conservative, was becoming restless.

Roosevelt had said, when I lunched with him, that he wished me to arrange to return for the campaign the next year. Dan Roper, an old friend, also invited me to lunch with him, in his office in the enormous building that housed his Commerce Department, and when I did he urged me to resign and return to write political articles for the National Committee. I have since seen a reference to this plan, on which I had not been consulted, in the published diary of Harold L. Ickes, then Secretary of the Interior. Even before this, Cordell Hull had written me that Roosevelt had some work to do that he thought I could do better than any other person; the suggestion had been sugarcoated with an extremely flattering offer of future preferment.

During this hectic home leave I did promise James A. Farley, in a conference at the national headquarters, to write a weekly article for the committee and to return after the convention to participate in the speaking campaign. In truth I had my reservations to return home in August 1936 for two months on the stump when the outbreak of civil war in Spain necessitated a cancellation. While eager to help my party, I doubted the propriety of a diplomat's taking an active part in a political campaign, and I still think it improper.

Happily Ed Flynn, party leader in the Bronx, who was then vacationing in St.-Jean-de-Luz, had tea with us at our villa in Fuenterrabia and agreed that it would be the height of impropriety for me to leave my post under the circumstances. Later Roosevelt wrote me that I was "absolutely right about not coming home at this juncture."

It was evident that the fight to prevent Roosevelt's re-election would be one of extreme bitterness. From Flynn I learned of the incredible hatred of the President in high social circles. The Bronx leader had attended a dinner at a fashionable summer resort near New York, where, though the guests all knew of his close personal and political relations with Roosevelt, he had to listen to the most venomous personal abuse of the head of the nation. At length Flynn had risen and proposed a toast: "To the President of the United States." Few responded, none of the women, the latter being more violent than the men. I recalled the attitude of these circles toward Roosevelt before his election. He was then a prime favorite among them and was considered quite sound. Did he not belong to an old and aristocratic family? Was not J. P. Morgan a friend of his mother and occasionally a guest at her home? But when he announced his program to restore government to the people they turned upon him with the bitterness with which the same element had blackguarded Jefferson for the same reason. Both were denounced as "traitors to their class."

The vacation of 1935 turned into a nightmare. Political and social engagements made relaxation impossible. In a dark little room in the Metropolitan Club in Washington, supplied by Farley with a typewriter, I sat for hours pounding out articles and speeches. This was all the more maddening because I had written the first draft of *Jefferson in Power* in Madrid and had planned to comb the newspapers of the period of 1801–1809 for the final rewriting. By engaging a stenographer and by hurrying to the Astor Library in New York between engagements, I managed to go through the papers, but when I went on board ship for the return to Spain I was in a state of exhaustion.

I was not to see America again throughout the almost three years of the Spanish Civil War—not until March 1939, when I was summoned home for "consultation."

The real reason for my being called back then was, as I have indicated and as Cordell Hull would say frankly later, to leave Washington free to recognize the Franco regime. England and France had already accorded it recognition and there was some uneasiness and impatience over our delay. I had been openly in sympathy with the Loyalists' fight for the preservation of their democracy. My preference for the legal government was based on political, not personal, grounds. Officially I had followed our line of neutrality between the two sides, and it was on the request of the Francoists that I undertook to negotiate the first exchange of military prisoners, and succeeded. I was on personally friendly terms with many people on the Franco side as well as on the side of the Republic and had often helped rebel officers in humanitarian matters, as in getting medicine to relatives in Barcelona, where the remedies could not be found. Nevertheless it would be clearly out of the question from every point of view for me to continue as ambassador after the Franco government was recognized by Washington.

I left taking with me memories of a beautiful land and a charming and gallant people whom I liked regardless of political ideologies. Vivid in my memory are the old dusty villages, the palaces and the old country houses, the beauty of the Andalusian landscape, the Castilian plains and the green Basque coast, the Prado and its treasures, the harvest fields with their primitive methods, the gypsies in the dance, the flamenco singing from the balconies in Seville, the warmth of the people, and their courage. These memories help to soften the tragic memories of a terrible and bitter war.

At quarantine fifteen or more reporters met the ship and poured into my stateroom. I could not talk with them until I had reported to the President and the State Department, but I left them in no doubt about my own position. I went immediately to Washington, prepared to see the President that night, but in a telephone conversation he suggested that it would be best for me to see the State Department first. I had abundant reasons to know that he had not been entirely comfortable with the policy we were following.

I saw Roosevelt the next day, not in the executive offices but in his study in the White House. He looked grim and unhappy, showing none of the exuberance with which he ordinarily greeted an old acquaintance after an absence.

His first words to me were, "We've made a mistake. You've been right all along."

Startled, I made no reply, and he went on: "I can see no reason to hurry about the recognition of the new regime. We'll let them stew in their juice for a while."

That night I went to the home of Key Pittman, chairman of the Senate Foreign Relations Committee and author of the embargo. I had known him personally and politically for a long time, and we were the best of friends. He was alone. The moment I entered, he walked over to a table to get a cigarette and, glancing back over his shoulder, said, "I'm afraid we made a mistake about Spain. It seemed to me in the beginning that if we could exclude all outside interference and let the Spaniards work out their own problem it would be a wise thing. But our embargo didn't keep out the armed forces of Hitler and Mussolini."

This, coming on top of what the President had said that day, seemed tragic to me. But Pittman was the best of company, I was fond of him, and so we sat and talked until dawn. It was the last time I was to see him.

At a reception given for me by Senator Guffey, Sol Bloom, chairman of the House Committee on Foreign Affairs, asked me to appear before his committee and give it my impressions of Spain. I was surprised when George S. Messersmith, Assistant Secretary of State, standing beside me, urged me to accept. I talked to the committee for an hour, making my position plain, speaking with the utmost frankness and answering every question but one—whether we should recognize the new pro-fascist government. I replied that this was up to the President and the State Department. From the tone of the meeting and the reception of my remarks I got the distinct impression that Roosevelt and Pittman were not alone in concluding that our Spanish policy had been a blunder.

In my conversation with Cordell Hull I got no such reaction, for he clearly preferred not to discuss the Spanish situation at all. However, I found Sumner Welles, the Under Secretary, reflecting the feeling of the President. He too saw no reason to hurry the formal recognition of the new regime in Spain. The President, who had gone to Warm Springs, had left instructions that nothing be done about Spain in his absence, but this I did not know until later. Since it was crystal clear that we had decided on recognition, I could see no point in remaining in Washington, as Roosevelt had requested, and he was in Georgia. I knew that one of Ambassador William C. Bullitt's young men from our Paris embassy had been sent to arrange the recognition on Franco's own terms—which was done.

When Welles asked my opinion on recognition I told him that if it were not for our nationals' investments in Spain that might be confiscated I never would accord it, but that since the investments were there I would accord recognition on certain conditions: that the dictator give positive assurances regarding American invest-ments, and that he pledge himself to stop the "liquidation" of Spanish republicans, liberals and labor leaders.

Welles replied that these pledges had been made, though Hull in his memoirs says that Franco refused to make any promises. If any promises were given, not a single one was redeemed. Colonel Behn, head of the telephone company, was refused permission to enter Spain for a long time, and Mr. Caldwell, the manager in Madrid, was long excluded from the company's property, and soon the company found it more comfortable to sell the property, which had been a gold mine until then. The National City Bank was speedily bowed out of the country.

That there may have been some doubt about the authenticity of the assurances Welles says were given and Hull says were not seemed probable when Welles expressed the wish that I would not go to Madrid to collect my belongings. When I voiced my surprise that we were giving our blessing to a regime so barbarous that the American ambassador would enter the country at his peril, I was told that it was the Italians who were feared. I reminded him that on Franco's request I had acted in the exchange of military pris-oners and secured the release of many Italian pilots, and that the Italian ambassador had written me a warm letter of appreciation. I suggested that I could probably count on a *salvo conducto* from the Italian embassy, but Welles looked reproachful and said noth-ing. There really was nothing to say.

I had a significant conversation with Roosevelt in July when I made my farewell call before returning to Europe to wind up my affairs. I had found party leaders all agog over whether the President would be a candidate for a third term in 1940. Two members of the Cabinet had told me that they had been unable to get an inkling of his intentions, but that they thought I might. My engagement at the White House was for twelve-fifteen, but a delegation of labor leaders was conferring with him on WPA, and they found their host so agreeable that they lingered on, despite the frantic efforts of General Watson to shoo them off. At length they emerged, laughing and happy.

It was a blistery hot July day, the anniversary of the fall of the Bastille. I found the President without coat or vest, looking cool, comfortable, unruffled, and with color in his cheeks. It seemed that constant battling for eight years had given a certain grimness to his expression, making him look considerably like Andrew Jackson, his hero.

When he asked what I had heard since my return I audaciously replied that I had heard much speculation on whether he had finished his speech of acceptance. He seemed startled at first by the effrontery of the approach, but then he smiled, shrugged his heavy shoulders as if to brush my reply aside, and plunged into a serious discussion of the suggestion in about these words, as I recorded them in my diary that day:

"You and I, Claude, are interested in the Democratic Party, and it's not good for a party to revolve around any one man. That leads to disintegration. Take the case of the Liberal Party in England, whose disintegration is, in my mind, one of the tragedies in English history. It won in the election of 1906 under Campbell-Bannerman, and then in the election of 1910 under Asquith. It had several able leaders—Asquith, Lloyd George, Edward Grey. Then came the coalition under Lloyd George, and by 1920 it had become a one-man party. In the election that year Lloyd George said, 'I am the party.' That began the disintegration. Principles became subordinated to personalities." The expression and the tone were those of absolute sincerity. "I don't want that to happen to the Democratic Party," he added.

To draw him out, I suggested that in his case it was not so much the man as the man's principles and policies, and that no one could be nominated and elected on the Democratic ticket who was not a

New Dealer. And, I said, among the men not politically shelfworn who were truly in accord with Roosevelt's policies, it seemed impossible to find anyone with enough political background and personal appeal to party workers.

Here Roosevelt interrupted. "But Bob Jackson [Robert H. Jackson, then Solicitor General] is an ideal man for the Presidency —though the boys don't cotton to him."

I then said that the continuation of the Roosevelt policies might therefore force a third nomination. As to the third-term prejudice, I suggested that it had always been conceded that in case of a crisis, such as war, the tradition would not be a bar to a third term.

To this Roosevelt agreed, and then he said something that I was to recall less than two months later. He said that under existing conditions no one knew when war might come. I concluded that he had this in mind as the determining factor in his case.

"Suppose," he said, "a world war should break out in September."

And it did. I have since thought that had there been no war he would not have accepted a third nomination.

I then added that war changes all rules because it means a crisis, but that war does not necessarily mean a conflict with arms. I suggested that at home we were in the midst of a war to save democracy by making it function for the general good, and this too was a crisis.

I thought that Roosevelt showed by his manner and expression that the course of the conversation was not displeasing, but he interrupted here to say that Cordell Hull would make a good candidate because of his immense popularity. In the Presidency he thought that "Cordell might be swamped by details" and "buried under papers," since he was not so good an executive as he was a thinker, but that he could "surround himself with assistants to look after details." I admitted Hull's great popularity among thoughtful people, but wondered if this extended to the mass. Roosevelt thought it did.

Then he said, "Cordell with his fine mind and character and beautiful face would make an appeal. He would not be a militant campaigner, but we could nominate a running mate to stir up the animals."

At this point he was interrupted by a messenger from the State Department who announced that Hull would be over in a few minutes with his statement repealing the embargo against Spain in the Neutrality Act, and inquiring how much time Roosevelt would require.

"Is it written and typed?" he asked.

"Yes."

"Well, that's the message. I can do my part in ten minutes."

This made me positively ill. First a stern refusal to sell arms to a legally constituted, democratic government to defend itself against Nazi and fascist armed forces from Germany and Italy, and now the lifting of the embargo instantly so that we could sell arms to Franco to stock the arsenals for a fascist army against the democratic aspirations of the Spanish people. It seemed sad to me.

As I was leaving, Roosevelt smiled and said, "Well, keep your ear to the ground."

I left with the feeling that there would be a war and that Roosevelt would accept a third nomination.

A day later I saw Cordell Hull, who said he had discouraged the Tennessee Democrats from launching a movement for his nomination, since it would embarrass him in his work on foreign affairs. He said he expected to be asked at his press conference if he favored a third term, for other members of the Cabinet had declared themselves in favor. He did not indicate what his reply would be, though his loyalty to Roosevelt was as unquestioned as Roosevelt's loyalty to him. He looked well and cool despite the heat. He talked a bit about the unfortunate cleavage between Roosevelt and Farley with which the cloakrooms and drawing rooms were buzzing. He said he was very fond of Farley, "as everyone is who knows him," but that he was afraid things had gone too far to restore the old relations.

A few days after this I spent an hour with Farley in his office in the national headquarters at the Biltmore in New York, and he discussed his relations with the President fully and frankly. The substance of it was that in some way he must have lost the President's confidence, since Roosevelt did not consult him as formerly. He said he had been intensely loyal to him and he could not understand the change. Whenever he tried to get Roosevelt's attitude on the nomination the next year, the subject invariably was changed. He was thinking at the time of resigning from the Cabinet, and he asked my opinion. I urged him to do nothing of the sort. "You have the confidence, appreciation and affection of all the party workers down to the precincts, and your resignation would be misinterpreted," I said. He then said he would remain in the Cabinet until after the next convention.

With our recognition of the Franco government in Spain, I thought my adventure in diplomacy at an end. I declined one offered post, but finally, on the personal request of President Roosevelt, I agreed to go as ambassador to Chile. It seemed remote from the war I had predicted as inevitable, and I was eager for the sake of my family to get out of the poisonous atmosphere of hate. I knew of the charm of Chile and that it was a functioning democracy, the one most deeply rooted in tradition in all South America. Late in August 1939 we sailed on the Grace Line ship *Santa Maria* for Valparaiso.

I was not to see Washington again until September 1943, when I flew from Chile to be with Foreign Minister Fernández on his official visit to the United States. The capital was then literally a madhouse because of the war. But for the kindness of a friend who lent me an apartment at the Shoreham, it would have been difficult to find hotel accommodations. To enter the State Department, I, though an ambassador, had to present a special printed permit at the door, and I could not leave without again showing the permit to the guard.

Within a few days of my arrival I had my first meeting with President Roosevelt, which extended more than an hour. I was shocked by his appearance as he sat at his desk. He looked years older than when I had seen him last. His face was deeply lined, his complexion gray; there were dark circles under his eyes and he seemed utterly weary. He talked with his old animation, but he appeared to be forcing himself.

His first words, spoken with a smile, were, "Are you broke?" referring to the disastrous effect of war taxes on diplomatic salaries when there was no possible way of reducing the cost of maintaining an embassy. He was not in a happy mood, and he spoke with bitterness about the sniping of the newspapers, "especially the columnists." Factual news was published fairly in the news columns, but "some columnists are wholly unscrupulous," he said.

Turning to politics and the approaching election of 1944, he said, "The Republicans are split three ways. The most popular of their candidates is Willkie, but that's with the people, not with the party leaders and workers, who are against him. Dewey is just a prosecuting attorney without any vision or conception of international affairs. The fight between them may become so bitter that to get harmony the Republican convention, like that of 1920, may turn to a dark horse and nominate Bricker, a competent man with no striking ability, whose sole claim to attention is that as governor of Ohio he has reduced the cost of government, but this can be said of other governors."

Such was his reasoning in September 1943.

Commenting on the frequent changes of Ministry in Chile due to the multiplicity of political parties, which made unstable coalitions necessary, he said, "I told Churchill that in the reorganization in France there should not be more than two parties. If more, there should be a run-off election between the two highest at the polls so that the government in power can have a clear mandate."

A few days later I saw him again, at a reception for Fernández on the upper floor of the White House. He was seated on a sofa when the company, mostly Senators and Congressmen, filed into the room and shook hands. He said they could have tea, "but if you prefer whiskey and soda you'll find it yonder on the table," and most of the company moved instantly to the table. Roosevelt seated Fernández on the sofa beside him and they conversed in French a long time. As we were leaving, I told him that I was going to New York and would see Farley, and that if I heard anything of interest I would let him know. "I wish you would," he said.

I did see Farley, for whom I had a real affection. I was primarily interested in ending the gossip that he would bolt the ticket if Roosevelt was nominated for the fourth time, and in ascertaining what could be expected from him in the campaign.

When I saw Roosevelt on my return he greeted me with the question "What about your mission?" Momentarily I was puzzled, assuming he had reference to my mission in Chile. "I mean your mission in New York," he added.

I told him of my long conversation with Farley and that he had said he thought Roosevelt still liked him.

An expression of satisfaction flashed over his face. "I've always been fond of Jim," he said.

I then told him that Farley could not get over the Mead-Bennett fight for the gubernatorial nomination in New York, but the President made no comment. I also told him that Farley felt hurt that he had not been asked to undertake any war work. As for the coming election, I said that Farley did not know precisely what he would do in 1944 and would wait a while before deciding, but that he might resign the state chairmanship in New York and retire from politics. However, he believed in party regularity and would never support a Republican nominee against Roosevelt. I quoted him as saying, "I'll never forget listening to Al Smith on the radio making his speech for Landon in 1936. It seemed so unnatural that it made me physically sick."

Roosevelt listened intently, and when I suggested that should he send for his old friend the latter undoubtedly would come, he asked my opinion of a plan that he had in mind, or that may have just occurred to him. Governor Lehman, who had been director of the Relief and Rehabilitation Commission, was being transferred to another post and he had in mind asking Farley to take the position vacated by Lehman. I urged him to do so. I learned much later that Farley was not summoned to the White House by Roosevelt. But he would be one of the few invited to the services in the East Room when the President died, for none had been more intimately identified with Roosevelt's first nomination and his election in 1932 and 1936.

The conversation shifted to reminiscences, inspired by my saying that Governor Cox had just telephoned me that he was writing his memoirs.

"Good," exclaimed Roosevelt, brightening. "Tell him for me that he must write the story, never yet made public, of our call on Woodrow Wilson after the San Francisco convention in 1920." This was the convention that had nominated Cox for President, with Roosevelt as his running mate. The big question then had been whether to support the League of Nations. As he told the story:

"After the convention I stopped off in Dayton to see Cox. I told

299

him that we were damned if we did and damned if we didn't; that if we made a fight for the League of Nations we would probably be defeated, and if we didn't we would be accused of cowardice and charged with disloyalty to the Administration. Cox said, 'Well, we're going to see President Wilson early next week and we can postpone a decision until then.'

"I went with Cox to Washington, where we were greeted by a great crowd at the station, and we drove directly to the White House. We were asked to wait for fifteen minutes, as they were taking the President to the veranda looking out on the grounds. When we came in sight of the veranda we saw Wilson in a wheel chair. He had a shawl thrown over his shoulder to conceal his left arm, which was then paralyzed. Cox gasped and in an undertone said to me, 'My God, he is in a bad condition!'

"We went up to the wheel chair and Cox greeted him. Wilson, who seemed very weak, said in a voice scarcely audible, 'I'm glad to see you. I'm very glad to see you.'

"I had noticed that there were tears in Cox's eyes when we first caught sight of Wilson, and now, emotionally, he said, 'Mr. President, we're going to be a million per cent with your Administration, and that means for the League of Nations.'

"Wilson replied in a feeble voice, 'I'm grateful, I'm very grateful.'

"We left him very soon and again I noticed tears in Cox's eyes."

At this point, Roosevelt straightened in his chair and bent over his desk.

"We came directly to this room where we sit, and Cox sat down at this table"—and Roosevelt put his two hands on the table—"and asked Tumulty for a pencil and paper, and right here, on this table"—slapping the table—"he wrote the statement that made the League of Nations the paramount issue in the campaign."

This story, all the more dramatic and historic coming from one of the two greatest Presidents since Lincoln about another, seemed to me thrilling. Had I foreseen then that the speaker, like his great predecessor, would be stricken and die while on duty in the service of the nation and humanity, it would have seemed even more dramatic.

That day Roosevelt looked rested, the lines in his face had smoothed out, his complexion was good—in striking contrast to his worn and weary appearance a short time before. When I made this observation to a friend, he said that when I first saw Roosevelt after my arrival from Chile, Churchill had just left the White House after a visit of some days. Roosevelt usually retired reasonably early, but it was impossible to get Churchill to bed before two or three in the morning. While Churchill slept late, Roosevelt wakened early. While Churchill took a short nap during the day, this was impossible for Roosevelt. Thus, I was told, Roosevelt for days had averaged but a few hours' sleep at night.

It was during this visit of Churchill's that Roosevelt, wishing to see him, went to his room, knocked and, on being told to enter, opened the door to find the great Englishman stark naked because of the terrible heat. Roosevelt apologized and started to back out. "No, come on in," called the Prime Minister. "I have told you time and again that the British Empire has nothing to conceal."

More worn and aged was Cordell Hull that summer of 1943. When I went to see him he seemed a very old man and utterly weary. Never before in twenty years had I seen him when he had not spoken with emphasis and at some length, but that day there was no vigor in his conversation, and he talked little. I saw him again when I drove to the airport to meet Fernández. I found Hull waiting in his car and joined him there. Again he seemed old and tired. Referring to the resignation of Sumner Welles, he said there had been only minor differences between them as to policy. At the dinner he gave for Fernández at the Carlton he said but little and was clearly eager to cut the evening short.

Later I accompanied Fernández to his conference with Hull in the latter's office. While Fernández was giving him his impressions of his visits to several American republics en route to Washington, Hull listened intently, with a pleasant smile, but he said little himself. I was not surprised when, in little more than a year, his health broke down completely and he suffered the agony of abandoning his high station before the conclusion of the war and the formation of the plans for future peace.

Two years intervened before I saw him again—when I accompanied President Juan Antonio Ríos of Chile on his official visit to the United States and took him to call on Hull in his apartment at Wardman Court. As we stepped out of the elevator we found the old statesman waiting for us in the hall. He showed the good effect of his long rest. His complexion was good and his manner mellow, and, always handsome, he had never been more so.

His mind was still active on international problems, and he seemed particularly concerned over our rapidly increasing annoyance with Russia because of her obstructive and delaying actions. "We must remember," he said, "that for a quarter of a century Russia has had little practice in international negotiations, and that suspicions growing out of that quarter of a century cannot be blotted out instantly. We must be patient and not permit ourselves to become ruffled. If we cannot get an agreement now, drop it and take it up six months later, or a year later, but under no circumstances must we break with Russia. The peace of the world is involved in a final understanding with her."

During the next year and a half I was continuously at my post in Chile, but during this period I received numerous personal letters from Roosevelt. These astounded me in view of the terrible burdens of war that pressed upon him. Toward the close I noticed an increasing shakiness in his signature, but the old virility was in everything he wrote, and some of his letters sparkled with humor.

He wrote me just before he left on the fatal trip to Yalta, the journey which, together with the unprecedentedly bitter fight in the election of 1944, unquestionably hastened his end.

On the evening of April 12, 1945, I was called to the telephone at the embassy residence just as some guests were leaving. It was my friend Father Weigel, an American priest who lectured at the Catholic University in Santiago. He expressed his sorrow and placed himself at my service. When I inquired the meaning of the offer, he merely said, "The President." I was still in the dark.

"The President is dead," he said.

"What President?" I asked, thinking it might be the President of Chile.

"President Roosevelt," he said. He had heard it by radio. A few minutes later it was officially confirmed.

It seemed to me that a sustaining pillar of a trembling world had fallen.

Immediately a stream of Chilean officials, ambassadors, senators and personal friends began pouring into the house. This continued for several days. Never in Chilean history had the death of any foreigner so touched the emotions of the people; they knew that Roosevelt had been their friend. Cardinal Caro called at once to offer the cathedral for a memorial service, something without precedent, since the dead President was not of the Catholic faith. The presidents of the Senate and the Chamber of Deputies came to announce that memorial services would be held in the two chambers and to invite me and the embassy staff to seats on the floor. In both houses very fine tributes were paid by the spokesmen of all political parties. But even more impressive to me were the delegations of workers who came from the factories in their work clothes to express their sympathy; and still more touching the delegations of small schoolchildren bearing flowers.

The greatest human being I had ever known, and one of the greatest in all our time, had passed into history.

CHAPTER XX

My Fourteen Years in Chile

My hope for a period of rest and relaxation after Spain in an atmosphere of serenity amidst the beauty of Chile was dashed when, within a day after our arrival, war was declared in Europe, and South America became a diplomatic battlefield. At once I found myself back where I had been, fighting against the Nazis, and immediately after the end of the war the Communists took up where the Nazis left off. My antagonists during this long period were totalitarians of both the right and the left, but Chile as a whole was soundly democratic.

These controversies in no way diminished the entrancing beauty of the country and the charm of the people or my admiration for their democratic institutions. Santiago, the capital, with nearly a million and a half population, is beautiful because nature made it so. Always in the distance looms the matchless Cordillera de los Andes, standing sentinel. In the winter, when snow seldom falls in the city, the snow-capped mountains glistening in the sun are beautiful beyond comparison. Breathtaking in their beauty are the sunsets on these majestic heights.

The business section of the city resembles that of any large town in the United States. I found it much busier and more hectic than Madrid. The residential section had moved away from the turmoil of the center to where tree-lined streets gave charm and quiet. Most of the houses in this section, architecturally individualistic, are set back in spacious grounds colorful with flowers—which are abundant in Chile—and shut off from the street by walls of shrubbery. In most places the visitor rings the bell at the locked gate to get entrance to the grounds. The American embassy residence, home of our ambassadors since 1922, is rather palatial and faces the Parque Forestal, a miniature Bois in the middle of the town. One looks in vain for imposing colonial buildings, so cherished in Peru. The one official colonial building in Santiago is the Casa de la Moneda, designed by the famous architect Joaquín Tosca after Somerset House in London. It is a solid structure occupying a full city block, with an entrance through grilled gates where soldiers stand sentinel as before Buckingham Palace. The many rooms are furnished with taste and some elegance, but, since the windows look out on noisy commercial streets, it feels like a public building rather than a home, though officially it is the residence of the presidents of Chile. The Foreign Office, occupying a third of the building, is entered through the Plaza Bulnes. This structure, along with the Municipal Theater, the Club de la Unión and the big hotels, dominates the center of Santiago.

Much of the artistic activity of the city centers in the Municipal Theater. I was to find that the Chileans are enthusiastic and discriminating music lovers. I heard concerts and recitals and saw many ballets and plays in this huge theater, and it was always packed to the top gallery with crowds which included students and the poor. French theatrical companies with brilliant artists appeared frequently. I saw the famous Italian actress Grammatica and her company in the plays of D'Annunzio, Barrie and Pirandello, and Margarita Xirgu, the celebrated Spanish actress, then in exile, in plays of Shakespeare, Benavente and García Lorca. I was always impressed by the reaction of the audience, which was more restrained than in many other Latin American countries. Perfect silence was maintained during the performance. If it was outstanding the ovation was tremendous, if just good the enthusiasm was more controlled, if bad it was still received with good manners and a polite amount of applause.

Most impressive to me was the marked resemblance between Chile's institutional life and our own. Her democratic constitution is revered; the three co-ordinate branches of government, executive, legislative and judicial, are each independent. The differences from ours are rather minor ones. Unhappily, the multiplicity of political parties makes it impossible in a presidential election for any one party to get a clear majority, and this results in coalition governments which are often precarious and short-lived because of differences between the parties in the coalition. During my four-teen years there I dealt with seventeen foreign ministers, but almost all were men of judgment and capacity.

From the beginning of the Second World War, I found the great majority of the people true to their democratic traditions, in sympathy with the Allies and friendly toward the United States even before the attack on Pearl Harbor, though many of these pre-ferred a policy of official neutrality. Even so, the enormous re-sources in strategic material in the country were reserved for the United States from the beginning.

There was, however, a strong undercurrent of sympathy with Germany in influential circles, and this was natural. German skill, perseverance and resourcefulness had redeemed to cultivation the rich fertile section of the south. The large German colony, becom-ing prosperous on the land, expanded into industry, shipping and banking, and at the beginning of the war it owned the telephone system in the south and many newspapers. These Germans had married into Chilean families. A German officer had trained the Chilean Army for years, and the armed forces had adopted Ger-man equipment and methods; Chilean officers had been invited to Germany for special training; Chilean physicians and surgeons had studied in German hospitals and laboratories; German scholarships had been given to Chilean students, who had been received in Ger-many with warm hospitality. Many if not most of these Chileans had returned convinced that the Germans really were a master race with the highest degree of culture, and that the German Army was irresistible.

Still, most German-Chileans had not been impressed with the Nazi philosophy. But when Hitler fared forth winning bloodless victories during the period of appeasement, and when in the first year of the war his armies swept easily into country after country, many German-Chileans, from pride of race, were swept into sup-port of the Axis.

Though there was abundant evidence of a fifth column, I was puzzled to find that the mere suggestion of its existence was bit-terly rejected in government circles. Walking one day in a drizzle of rain with President Aguirre Cerda on the grounds of the sum-mer palace at Viña del Mar, I asked him if its activities were being followed, and I was surprised by the vehemence with which he denied its existence. He was an ardent democrat, an admirer of Roosevelt, and I was to conclude that the Chileans are prone to close their eyes to the more unpleasant realities. They are, moreover, a proud, patriotic people, very sensitive with regard to their sovereignty and quick to resent anything that might seem an attempt to impose our will and policy upon them.

At this time the embassy knew that German Nazis—not Chileans of German descent, but Germans trained in the Nazi school of espionage and sabotage—were active in Chile. Illogically, while stoutly denying the existence of danger, the government was secretly alarmed lest the copper and nitrate mines within shooting distance of the sea might be attacked. It was because of this fear that Aguirre Cerda gladly agreed to a joint meeting of the general staffs of the United States and Chile to make plans for a co-ordinated defense of the continent if attacked by the Nazis from Dakar. I presided at the preliminary meetings in these negotiations, which went off speedily and successfully. Our officers were delighted and President Roosevelt sent me a letter of congratulations. Later the War Department gave me a decoration in appreciation of what I had been able to do for the co-ordination of continental defense.

Such was the situation before the attack on Pearl Harbor. Five days before that treacherous attack, I learned that the Japanese ambassador called on the Chilean Foreign Minister, Rossetti, to say that war with the United States was inevitable and to ask refuge in Chile for Japanese nationals then in Panama. Two days before Pearl Harbor I was informed that the German ambassador had called to reinforce the Japanese request. Both requests were sharply denied, and orders were flashed to the Chilean consulate in Panama not to grant visas to the Japanese. This information I telegraphed immediately to Washington.

It had been agreed at the 1940 inter-American foreign ministers' conference in Havana that an attack on one American nation would be taken as an attack on all, but, unhappily, the Act of Havana had not yet been ratified by the Chilean Congress.

Just before the attack Aguirre Cerda died. A sincere democrat and an intellectual, he had based his thesis on the sentence "To govern is to educate." He was a modest man. I conversed with him while Jo Davidson was working on his bust, now in Washington, and he impressed me as almost embarrassed that so much genius was going into the preservation of his likeness. Throwing all his strength into his work, he had weakened under the strain. One day in his office in the summer palace he asked me, in wondering tones, how Roosevelt stood up under the pressure, and when I replied that he had no nerves and loved a fight, Aguirre Cerda took a long breath and shook his head. I knew then that he felt himself sinking under the strain.

His death threw the country into a presidential election, stoutly contested on both sides, though on a dignified plane, and Juan Antonio Ríos was elected. Meanwhile the Acting President did not feel free to take any decisive action in the international field while heading a Ministry of mere transition. Nothing could be done between Aguirre Cerda's death and the election of Ríos, and two months would intervene before he could take office. We could only mark time.

Ernesto Barros Jarpa, a distinguished lawyer, a personal friend of mine and a friend of the United States, who became the new Foreign Minister, was opposed to an immediate rupture with the Axis on the ground that it would accomplish nothing and would make more difficult the transmission of war material from Chile to the United States. I made my fight for it with the proper officials behind closed doors. I offered no public criticism of Chile's position, gave out no interviews, made no speeches and certainly made no threats. Meanwhile there were disagreements within the government circles on rupture, and public opinion, now mobilized, was parading with bands and banners demanding immediate action. The Ministry resigned, and when Barros Jarpa was succeeded by Joaquín Fernández it was understood that rupture was near.

During the interval I saw President Ríos many times and was assured that preparations were in progress for breaking diplomatic relations with the Axis. Public opinion, he thought, had to be prepared. Because of the long debate on rupture extending from the banker to the taxi driver, I am convinced that in Chile there was a clearer understanding of the significance of the war than in any other country of the continent, and the goal was reached in perilous times without deviating one hairbreadth from the democratic process and without a violation of the Chilean constitution.

Through this long period of preparation I was constantly

attacked in the pro-Nazi press. In the final issue of a Nazi paper the day before the rupture I was honored with a full-page open letter giving me the role of villain behind the scenes. Later, when the Nazi press went out with the departure of the German embassy, recourse was had to a chain of mimeographed letters bearing the names of historic patriots and sent through the mails, and in these I continued to be the pet aversion. One of these is especially choice as an illustration of the poverty of ideas behind the propaganda, and I submit an excerpt from it to lighten these pages:

There is a man who refused to fulfill the desires of Ambassador Bowers, and this man of honor was expelled on the following day from the Army.

Who selects those who make the expensive trips to New York with the nation's money? Bowers.

Who benefits by the tyrannical and arbitrary black list which has left thousands of Chileans without work and in hunger? Bowers.

Who controls and censors the organs of the press and radio? Bowers.

Who is feared and obeyed by some of our government people, parliamentarian groups and many political leaders? Bowers.

To whom do we owe Department 50 [the secret service] and the institutions outside the law, a shame to the nation and typical of colonies or subjugated people? Bowers.

Who ordered the obligatory shipment of meat and other articles of prime necessity to the United States, leaving our own people in hunger? Bowers.

Such was the tone of the attacks, which were, of course, without a scintilla of truth. Their absurdity deprived them of any effect on public opinion.

During this period I formed a very high opinion of President Juan Antonio Ríos. His regime covered the critical years of the Second World War, and history will give him credit for having piloted the country safely and with dignity through perilous times without compromising its democratic institutions or violating its constitution. Cancer claimed him as a victim soon after the victory, and another presidential election was necessary.

In a spirited campaign Gabriel González Videla was elected to succeed him. I knew him to be a convinced democrat, but in a closely contested campaign he had the support of the Communists in the Popular Front, and it was these who gave him his plurality.

After his election and before his inauguration he told me that this placed him under an obligation to put three Communists in his Ministry. The reaction abroad was naturally bad, and for a few months the effect on his administration was not good. When he found that these ministers were using their offices to undermine his administration, to create social disorders and to encourage illegal strikes, he turned upon them with indignation and put them out.

The Chilean Communists had strength beyond their numbers. They followed the party line religiously and unanimously. They maintained perfect discipline. They felt no embarrassment in completely reversing their position overnight on orders from Moscow. Unlike the members of other political parties, they worked incessantly. They followed their leader without question. "Theirs not to reason why." Through their infiltration into labor unions they often imposed their will by threats. But the secret of their strength was in the fact that in close elections their votes could sometimes determine the result, and the politicians of non-Communist parties were sometimes prone to cultivate them for their support.

In the early stages of the war, before Hitler swept into Russia, they were venomously hostile to the United States. During this period it was impossible to differentiate between the propaganda of the Nazis and that of the Communists. But the moment Hitler turned on Russia the party became a militant supporter of the United States. This continued until the end of the war, when they again adopted the old Nazi slogans as their own. Thence onward as long as I was in Chile they concentrated their hate on the United States, and one late afternoon they threw stones through the windows of my house. When, to prevent a repetition of this offense, the government stationed *carabineros* about the grounds of our summer house in the little town of Villa Alemana, the Communist paper dubbed me "the Viceroy of Chile."

González Videla, having expelled the Communists from his government, had now become their pet aversion. A coal strike at Lota, prepared along subversive revolutionary lines, gravely threatening the economic life of the nation, came as a challenge. Convinced that the Communists' orders from Moscow reached them through a Yugoslav general who mysteriously appeared about this time, González Videla broke diplomatic relations with Yugoslavia and

followed at once with the expulsion of the new Russian ambassador and the Czech minister. Relations with Bulgaria, Romania and
Albania were severed, a Law for the Defense of Democracy was
enacted, and throughout the greater part of González Videla's
regime he waged open war with the Communists.

Thus during my fourteen years in Chile I was engaged in war-
fare with both the Nazis and the Communists. To a Jeffersonian
democrat nothing could have been more agreeable.

I have never known a lovelier land than Chile, with its towering
Andes that are always in view, with the incomparable beauty of its
famous lakes, with its rivers teeming with fish, with its charming
coast line, its skiing fields and its delightful countryside. But living
as a diplomat in Chile is not without its problems. Its social activities are a bit terrifying to a diplomat past forty. The Chileans are
famous for hospitality, and there is no "season" for entertaining,
which goes on without intermission throughout the year. Luncheons began at one and continued until three; dinners scheduled for
nine or nine-thirty seldom found the guests at table earlier than ten-
thirty, and, with liqueurs, coffee and cigars later, they seldom broke
up before twelve-thirty or one at the earliest. Cocktail parties were
innumerable, and attendance at many of them was almost obligatory diplomatically. Unlike cocktail parties at home, where one
may drop in for a few minutes for a cocktail and canapés, in Chile
to leave under an hour usually calls for an apology or explanation.
The receptions at embassies and legations, literally packed with
people, are often an abomination but unescapable.

When the hot months came, we sought relief outside the capital.
We spent three summer vacations in Viña del Mar, a small city of
great charm by the sea, but here one met the same people one had
dined with in Santiago, and the social game continued with even
greater zest. To escape this we spent several summers at Zapallar, a
quiet resort and one of the most beautiful I know anywhere, where
the air is fragrant with the odors of the sea and the neighboring
woods. However, we had to abandon this delightful spot, since
communication facilities with the capital were all but nil. Seven
summers found us on the edge of small cities on the road from Viña
del Mar to the historic old town of Quillota: two in a comfortable
modern house with ample grounds at Limache, two at Quilpué,

which is noted for its pure healing air, and three at Villa Alemana, where we had large grounds enclosed by a high brick wall and abounding in fruit, apples, oranges, lemons, figs, almonds, peaches and pomegranates, and with a grape arbor, very wide and in length equivalent to more than a city block, bearing huge luscious grapes. We literally lived throughout the day in the shade of this arbor.

The entertainment of visitors is a part, and usually a pleasant part, of the duties of those in the foreign service. In Chile our list of visitors was long. Admiral Richard Byrd stayed with us at the embassy for several days en route home from the Antarctic. Cardinal Dougherty of Philadelphia came, to be warmly received and to find a boyish delight in his ride from the station to the hotel in an old ornate state coach drawn by four horses, with mounted *carabineros* riding in the rear and on either side; in the darker days of the war Henry Wallace, Vice-President of the United States, made an official visit on which he rendered great service and was received with enthusiasm. Later President Herbert Hoover appeared on an official mission. I thought him mellowed by the years and in fine fettle. On my insistence, Eleanor Roosevelt came as special ambassador for the inauguration of President Ibañez, went through five incredibly crowded days of continuous ovations from thousands packing the streets, and achieved a personal triumph surely unequaled by any man we have sent to a coronation or inauguration. North American bankers, industrialists, educators came in a long procession. All these visits entailed luncheons, dinners, receptions. An impressive number of distinguished Europeans also appeared. Lord Willingdon, erstwhile Viceroy of India, headed a numerous company of bankers and industrialists from England; Hore-Belisha, the able Liberal leader and War Secretary, and Sir Samuel Hoare (then Lord Templewood), the Conservative, made short visits, as did the vice-president of the Italian Senate and the Italian Under Minister of Foreign Affairs. Among literary men of distinction were André Maurois, the brilliant French biographer, and Philip Guedalla, the English historian and biographer of Palmerston. One was never bored in Santiago.

In my memories of Chile two men who were my friends stand out most vividly.

Arturo Alessandri Palma had twice been President of the Republic, and soon after my arrival he was elected to the Senate, which
named him its president. He continued to preside over the Senate
until his death, when he was more than eighty years old. His-
torically more significant were his constructive achievements in
social legislation, in which Chile led South America. These measures sponsored and pressed by Alessandri have not been much disturbed since. More than any other one man, he was the architect of
Chile's thoroughly democratic constitution. A consummate politician, a master of all the tricks of politics, he could be an oppor-
tunist until fundamental democratic principles were involved, and
then he was as immovable as Gibraltar. I have never known a man
of more colorful personality. He was tempestuous at times and
easily moved to anger, but as easily to regret. Belligerent, always
ready for combat, with his finger on the trigger, he sometimes let
his quick temper lead him into bitter phrases and devastating char-
acterizations of his political foes, all the more deadly because of his
partiality for fighting words. In early life he had been dubbed "the
Lion," and he was still a lion in his old age.

Short in stature, his shoulders a bit rounded from bending over
the table, with a roughhewn puckish face exuding a zest for life,
Alessandri captivated the multitude. Whenever he appeared and
there was a crowd, he was cheered. Once at a fashionable wedding
when, as *padrino* for the bridegroom, I was waiting at the church
door for the bride, I was startled by loud cheering and assumed the
bride had arrived, though this reception would have been without
precedent. Then I noticed Don Arturo approaching, pounding the
pavement with his heavy stick, and knew he had been the object
of the strange demonstration. I saw him many times on his walks in
the Parque Forestal across from the embassy residence, always
accompanied by a huge man, his secretary, and an enormous Great
Dane dog that was devoted to him. I never was entirely comfortable
in his apartment with this dog stretched quietly on the floor and
never taking its eyes from me. Once when I urged Alessandri to
accept an invitation for a mission to the United States he said in all
seriousness, "No, no. The dog is too old to travel."

I have delightful memories of the hours I spent in his modest
apartment. Time was never wasted in his presence. The old fighter,
seated in his easy chair, with a light rug over his knees in cool

weather, was as entertaining as a comedian. His conversation was vivacious, sparkling with wit and humor, sometimes acidic with irony or sarcasm, and always politically wise. We occasionally differed in politics, but without the slightest cooling in our personal relations. In reminiscent mood he was especially delightful.

He died as he would have preferred. He had dismissed his car and gone for a walk, and, feeling ill, he stopped at the house of a friend and asked the servant for a glass of water. As she left for the water he took up a book, and on her return he was dead with the book clasped in his hand. I went immediately to his house. The narrow winding street in front was literally packed with a silent multitude, and Pepe, our Spanish chauffeur, had difficulty in getting my car to the door, even with the aid of the police. This tribute was from the heart.

His diary, when published, will uncover many secrets of Chilean history over a long period of years. I have never known a more exhilarating man.

Another cherished friend was José María Caro, who became cardinal primate during my Chilean days. His slight, frail-appearing frame seemed scarcely strong enough to sustain his spirit. He was in his mid-seventies when I first knew him, and when I left he was in his eighty-sixth year and still constantly active. Never, with the single exception of Cardinal Gibbons, have I seen a cleric who seemed so much a spiritual force, so much the symbol of a soul, with so much inherent goodness and, despite his exalted rank, so much humility. His origin was humble, and this no doubt explains in part his intimate understanding of the poor and lowly. No one in Chile was so generally loved in all circles regardless of creed.

Habitually sweet and gentle in his manner, he could be firm and stern when the occasion called. Once when he had withstood pressure to do something he instinctively knew would have had an unfavorable reaction, and his position was vindicated by events, he chuckled and said, "It was not for nothing I was born a *huaso* [cowboy]." I was very fond of this truly good and great cleric and had him frequently at my table. So often that one day when accompanying me to the dining room he looked up at me with twinkling eyes and asked facetiously, "Is this more Yankee propaganda?" I had the honor to speak in behalf of the diplomatic corps when forty thousand people assembled in the stadium to pay tribute to him on the sixtieth anniversary of his induction into the priesthood.

When, as a young priest, he had been told by the doctors that he had less than a year to live because he had tuberculosis, he had gone about his parish duties as though pushing death aside. In his eighties he was twice stricken with pneumonia; the second time, when he was eighty-five, his death seemed certain, but soon he was traveling over the country again on his official duties. He was my friend throughout the fourteen years of my tenure, and when I made my farewell call upon him he gave me a silver medallion bearing his likeness.

Despite my diplomatic duties and the social activities connected with them, I found time to write by avoiding golf and bridge. In my study in the embassy residence I wrote *Young Jefferson*, the third book of my trilogy on Jefferson, and *Pierre Vergniaud: Voice of the French Revolution*.

Vergniaud had fascinated me ever since I read Lamartine's *History of the Girondins* as a boy. He impressed me as the classic orator of the French Revolution and as the noblest figure among the leaders—not only because of his rare eloquence, which is literature and comparable with that of Cicero, but because he alone among the five most conspicuous leaders championed and died for democratic principles. During the most lurid and dramatic years of the Revolution, 1791–93, he was concededly the most brilliant figure in the tribune, but, more than that, he was intellectually honest and sane and humanitarian. Mirabeau and Danton were tainted with corruption, Robespierre encouraged the Terror, and Marat—perhaps an anarchist, perhaps insane, but certainly bloodthirsty and hysterical—gloried in it; yet American historians have written biographies of these men and ignored the one man who worked and died for the principles Americans espoused. This seemed all the more remarkable to me because during the French Revolution the speeches of Vergniaud were more frequently quoted in the American press than those of any other.

I decided to fill the void. I had been gathering material on Vergniaud for years, and in intensive research I uncovered manuscript material that had escaped the notice of the historians. The American reviewers did not seem to recognize this material as new, but the scholarly reviewer for the London *Times* thought it important. On my desk is a small bronze bust of Vergniaud copied from one in the possession of his family and inscribed to me by them in the bronze.

During almost eight of my fourteen years in Chile Harry S Truman was President of the United States. Previous to his administration I had enjoyed no such personal relations with him as I had with President Roosevelt. I had met him for a fleeting moment in 1932 when I spoke at a party banquet in Kansas City and he was toastmaster. He had been elected to the Senate after I had gone to Spain. When, after he succeeded to the White House, I met him at a dinner there, I was captivated by his infectious smile, his natural and gracious manner, his simplicity and utter lack of pose.

Entering the White House unexpectedly through the door of tragedy, he accepted his responsibilities with both daring and humility. He had the all too rare capacity to make decisions and assume responsibility. He had one other supreme equipment for the Presidency—he was a politician, he knew the common man. It seemed to me during his first term that there was almost a conspiracy to belittle him. Even the leaders of his own party seemed to accept the predictions of the metropolitan press and the commentators that he would be defeated in 1948. In the convention that nominated him in 1948, Sam Rayburn, pointing to his really fine record of achievement, asked the delegates if they were not proud of it, and then indignantly shouted, "Then in God's name why don't you act like it?"

But Truman was a fighter and, almost unaided by his party, he went into the campaign alone and with supreme confidence. A month before the election the press was already inclined to speculate on the personnel of his opponent's Cabinet, and Truman smiled. Through the New York *Times* I followed his speeches and their reception. The first week I was surprised; the second week I thought after all he had a chance; the third week I was certain of his election if he had a little more time. He did not need it. I had said I thought if he had enough time he would win, and on the morning after Election Day I gained a not entirely deserved reputation in Chile for political prophecy. In a letter I received from Truman immediately afterward I found him free from bitterness or resentment, but jubilant over the discomfiture of his foes.

For some years I corresponded with him, and in all his letters he was without bitterness. When General MacArthur returned to Washington after the President had dismissed him from his command in the Army, following futile efforts to persuade him to work in harness, Truman was so far from pettiness that he ordered government offices closed that the employees might pack the streets and cheer the hero of the Philippines. Very few men would have been capable of that act.

When President González Videla of Chile made an official visit to the United States and was a guest at Blair House, where the Trumans were living while the White House was undergoing repairs, the visitor was startled and delighted with Truman's informality and simplicity. That night President Truman sat down at the piano and played Mozart and Chopin, his daughter Margaret sang, the Chilean visitor laughingly placed a Chilean manta over Truman's shoulders, and the evening passed with informal chat and laughter. The next day the Chilean said to me, "Last night I found one of the most delightful human beings I have ever seen."

I am proud that I served for twenty years on pleasant terms with two great Presidents, and one of them was Truman.

Before the inauguration of President Eisenhower I tendered my resignation, and, being a personal or political appointee of Roosevelt, I expected an immediate acceptance. I heard nothing from Washington for seven months, but in August my resignation was accepted in a letter from the President:

August 3, 1953

DEAR AMBASSADOR:—

I am accepting your resignation as Ambassador to the Republic of Chile and as Representative of the United States on the Economic Commission for Latin America and of the Economic and Social Commission of the United States, to be effective September first.

You are to be congratulated on your distinguished record as American Chief of Mission to two important countries. This includes six years as Ambassador to Spain during a difficult period, and an extraordinarily long tenure in your present post since 1939.

With appreciation of your effective representation and good wishes for the future,

Sincerely,
DWIGHT D. EISENHOWER

Also much appreciated by me was a letter from Sumner Welles, then in retirement after a most distinguished career as Under Secretary of State. No man in Washington understood so perfectly or sympathetically the problems of Latin America, and no one was so familiar with the personnel and the psychology of the various nations. I therefore have some pride in this letter.

Bar Harbor, Maine
August 8, 1953

MY DEAR MR. AMBASSADOR:
I cannot let pass the announcement of your retirement as Ambassador to Chile without sending you these lines to let you know how deeply I regret this news. You have served with the utmost distinction during these last fourteen years as our Ambassador in Chile, and your services have been of immense value, and never more so than during these latter years when our inter-American relations seem to have been regarded as of such minor significance in Washington. It was a great personal satisfaction to me to have had the privilege of cooperating with you in the past.

Please accept my warmest remembrance and every good wish for the years to come.

Yours very sincerely,
SUMNER WELLES

Had there been no other commendation, this alone would have been compensation enough for years of labor in a field not too much appreciated by the American people. I had served under three American Presidents, Roosevelt, Truman and Eisenhower; and under four Chilean Presidents, Aguirre Cerda, Juan Antonio Ríos, Gabriel González Videla and Carlos Ibañez, all of them my friends.

I was not prepared for the Chilean reaction to my recall. For a month the Chilean newspapers contained editorials and special articles and letters in commendation of my work, and we were exhausted by almost daily farewell luncheons and dinners for more than a month. Those that were distinctly Chilean impressed me most. I was greatly moved by the Chilean luncheon at the Club de la Unión sponsored by Cardinal Caro, the president of the Senate and the Chief Justice of the Supreme Court, and attended by the leaders of all political parties but the Communist, and by the professional, industrial, commercial and cultural circles. An old friend, Ernesto Barros Jarpa, spoke for the assembly. Oscar Fenner, the Foreign Minister, gave a farewell luncheon at the Cousiño Palace that was attended by seventeen former ministers of foreign affairs with whom I had been officially associated. My colleagues gave the traditional luncheon at the Unión, where another friend, Hugo Pena, ambassador from Uruguay, presented to us a handsome silver plate bearing the signatures of all the chiefs of missions. President Ibañez gave me a farewell luncheon in the Moneda.

Like all who know it, I shall always carry Chile in my heart.

CHAPTER XXI

Postscript

The manuscript of my father's book ends here. The last chapter had not been written and to take its place I give some extracts from his diary telling about the years after his return to the United States.

—PATRICIA BOWERS

Washington, September 30, 1953

We landed in New York from the *Santa Cecilia* after a pleasant voyage with the exception of one night just beyond Buenaventura when we ran into the most violent thunder and lightning storm I have ever seen. The day after our arrival we came to Washington. I met scores of old political friends and former associates. . . . Today I had half an hour with John Foster Dulles, Secretary of State, and was surprised by the cordiality of his reception and his praise of my diplomatic career. He asked about Spain and my forthcoming book and said it should be published. . . . Tonight we came back to New York, arriving at midnight.

New York, October 1, 1953

Schuster of Simon and Schuster, and Barnes, formerly foreign editor of the *Herald Tribune*, spent two hours with me on my Spanish memoirs.

October 8, 1953

Called on Freda Kirchwey at the *Nation*, and then to the studio of Luis Quintanilla, the Spanish painter and republican, on Eighth Street, two flights up. He painted my portrait in 1933 for an exhibition planned in New York by Ernest Hemingway. At the time Janet Speirs, a very beautiful girl, was my secretary. The two were married in New York three years later. Luis showed me portraits of writers Hemingway, Dos Passos, Nathan, Miss Parker, Carl Van Doren and others—all excellent, especially Van Doren's.

October 26, 1953

Got to Memphis last night and put up at the Peabody Hotel. This morning a number of men called, most of them with copies of my book for an inscription. At noon had lunch with some delightful people at the Tennessee Club. In the afternoon General Wooten, my military attaché in Chile when I first went there, called. At seven o'clock gave my lecture on Jefferson and Civil Liberties at the State College. It was raining briskly but the attendance was large and the principal of a high school in Kentucky drove with four students a hundred and fifty miles to hear the lecture and told a reporter, "It was worth it." I like to think it, but I doubt it. At the close Professor Mitchell, head of the history department, had some people in for me at his house.

October 27, 1953

I dreaded today, since I had to lecture in the morning, in the afternoon and again in the evening. Lectured on Polk in the morning, on Jackson as the creator of party government in the afternoon and on Jackson's administration in the evening. Large audiences and prolonged applause at the close of each. Had dinner with President Smith at his home in the evening.

October 28, 1953

This morning Professor James W. Silver, head of the history department in the University of Mississippi, came to drive me to Oxford and the university—an eighty-five-mile drive. It is through rolling country over a perfect road. We lunched well at the Mansion in Oxford and then on to the university, where I was lodged at the Alumni Hotel. At three o'clock I had a conference on history. I sat and smoked and talked and answered questions. At night I delivered my lecture on Jefferson. Afterward went to the home of one of the professors, where several of them assembled with their wives. Stayed late.

November 11, 1953—Visit with Truman

The increasing hysteria of the McCarthy crowd in summoning Truman before the committee is without precedent. Truman was out when I arrived, but I had a long chat with Mrs. Truman, who looks well and happy, and I enjoyed her sense of humor in talking about protocol. Margaret came in, slender and in blue. . . . Truman breezed in, looking youthful, buoyant, confident. We chatted for about forty minutes. He seemed pleased when I congratulated him on his speech last night at New York University in which he attacked the hysteria of the times and of the un-American proceedings. He ascribes the bitter attacks on him to his Labor Day speech and his speech in St. Louis.

Of Admiral Leahy he spoke warmly. But he said when plans were being made about the atomic bomb Leahy told him, "The damn thing will not go off." When soon afterward it did go off he said he never reminded Leahy of his pessimism.

November 17, 1953

Today I had luncheon at the New York *Times*, the guest of Arthur Hays Sulzberger. I did not have any intimation that it was to be a birthday surprise for me—four days ahead of time! Nor did I know until they brought in a cake with one candle—a generous gesture. Among the guests were Turner Catledge, Anne O'Hare McCormick, the famous *Times* writer on international affairs, Cyrus Sulzberger, the international correspondent, Ben Fine, the education editor, and Theodore Fred Kuper. A very pleasant affair. There were differences of opinion on Truman's speech, but none as to the absurdity of the charge of disloyalty. I noticed that the staff did not hesitate to disagree with the publisher—that men are intellectually free on the greatest paper in the world.

November 23, 1953

This evening on television I saw and heard President Eisenhower. He seemed thinner in the face than before he became President, and he looked far from happy. Indeed, he seemed downright mad. He spoke of the Americanism he knew as a boy in a little town in Kansas and then said an American citizen has a right to his opinion and he need not fear to express it in the presence of the most powerful. And when he said that a man accused of a crime has a right to face his accuser who cannot hide in shadows he was apparently aiming at McCarthyism and taking a slam at his Attorney General who made the atrocious charge against Truman. . . . He did not smile during the speech and he seemed in deadly earnest. If he can muster the confidence and courage to actually take command and take a stand against pro-fascist proceedings he will have the country behind him. He is not an inspiring speaker, but his earnestness tonight was impressive.

December 5, 1953

This afternoon met Gabriela Mistral, the Chilean poetess who won the Nobel Prize for Literature a few years ago. She had not been in Chile during my fourteen years there. She was made a permanent Chilean consul and has resided in different countries, and I had not seen her, though she said this evening that we had met in Spain—she was stationed in Madrid just before the war there. I had understood that she was in poor health and I had pictured her as very old and frail, but her appearance and manner this evening gave no such impression. She wore a blue checked suit. Her iron-gray hair was given a boyish cut. Her eyes and voice denoted perfect health. She speaks her mind, uses sarcasm often, and has her likes and dislikes strongly developed. I mentioned a certain woman in Santiago. She smiled and chuckled. "I left Chile to get away from her," she said. She talked with animation, very amusing during the three hours I was there.

Victoria Kent, the Spanish deputy, was also there. When I went to Spain she was a very interesting member of Azaña's party in the Cortes. She could not have been thirty and had the animation and charm of a brilliant woman. I have often wondered what became of her and was delighted to see her. She is just as brilliant and interesting, and the twenty years have been kind to her.

Indianapolis, December 12, 1953

Arrived in Indianapolis at 8:50 this morning and was met at the station by Evans Woolen of the Fletcher Trust Company, whose father had been my good friend. The old station, which I had not seen for thirty-five years, has scarcely changed since in my boyhood I saw President Harrison and his Cabinet emerging in couples for the funeral of the President's wife. After registering at the Claypool, I was driven about town by Woolen, through the northern region, country in my youth and now built up with pretentious houses, and out to old Fairview Park, now the large campus of Butler University. After I returned to the hotel an old friend of school days called, and in the midst of our chat the phone rang and a woman announced that she and her sister, whose brother was a friend of mine more than fifty-five years ago and died half a century ago, would like to see me. They amazed me by showing me two pictures I had given their brother—one of me when about thirteen years old and the other a picture of myself and a friend taken in Lebanon sixty-three years ago. I was holding a campaign picture of Blaine and my friend one of Harrison. We had differed on which the Republicans should nominate in 1892. I would have given much for this picture but the woman seemed so pleased to have them that I did not have the heart to ask for it.

At 12:30 came the luncheon of the Indiana Historical Society, where I was to speak on "History's Warning Finger." It was a slanting attack on the McCarthyism and cowardice of these days and a warning that our freedoms are fading. The speech was cheered at length at the close and many came up to say that we need more such plain speaking. I was persuaded to stay for the Indiana Pioneers dinner in the evening.

New York, December 27, 1953

Spent an hour and a half with Eduardo Irarrazaval in his apartment at the Gotham this morning. He is en route back to Chile after four months in Paris. Most of our conversation was on conditions in Chile. . . . He thinks our flirtation with Perón most dangerous and that if we take Perón to our bosom all South American countries will adopt Peronism and we lose any influence we may have. He returns to Chile in a few days. As Minister of Foreign Affairs, the last under González Videla, he impressed me as a man of great integrity and vision and our relations were warm and understanding throughout.

January 24, 1954

Attended a luncheon in honor of Theodore Fred Kuper. There were three hundred men and women at the tables. Before we went in, Ben Fine, education editor of the *Times*, came to me to ask if I would speak briefly about my old friend Kuper and I was glad to do it. The lunch was an impressive tribute to the man I have described as having "a genius for friendship."

April 4, 1954

Took the five o'clock train to Washington, where I speak at the Women's National Democratic Club tomorrow. Twenty years ago I spoke a number of times before the club when Daisy Harriman, since minister to Norway, was president. She now has a charming house in Georgetown and her dinners are unusual. The guests, after dinner, remain at the table in general conversation. Tonight she had an interesting group including Justice Black of the Supreme Court, Senator Jackson, Senator Moody, and Mowrer, the brilliant press correspondent. I was seated between Justice Black and the charming and brilliant wife of Senator Douglas. Justice Black, who is partial to my books on American political history, amazed me by praising my *Vergniaud* as a book all Americans should read. Senator Jackson, who is on the McCarthy committee, was given rough treatment because of the naming of Sears as counsel for the committee in the controversy between McCarthy and the Army when Sears is a militant advocate of McCarthyism. . . . Jackson is an attractive young man and took all the ribbing in good part. I was told that Washington is torn wide open on McCarthyism. Mrs. Harriman and Alice Roosevelt were close friends years ago and are still friends of a sort, though not as before. Alice is a McCarthyite and her group is of this persuasion.

April 5, 1954

Up late and in my room until 12:30—the hour for the luncheon at the club. . . . At the speakers' table was Senator Fulbright, a brilliant fellow. Mrs. Woodrow Wilson, who very seldom goes out now, appeared today. I had not seen her since 1935, when we were luncheon guests at her house. Had a long talk with her.

The speech seemed to go off with a bang. It was a strong attack on the un-American antidemocratic trend under McCarthyism. Was given an ovation at the close until I had to get up and bow. The women asked that copies be printed and Senator Fulbright took my copy and will try to get it in the *Congressional Record*. It was such a vigorous speech that I doubt if he succeeds.

May 20, 1954

I went to Louise Crane's to meet José Antonio Aguirre, the President of the Basques. He looks even younger than when I last saw him in the embassy in Santiago. I sat with him at the buffet dinner and he told the amazing story of his escape during the war to Germany, where he posed as a Panamanian physician and remained undetected for months until he crossed over into Belgium. Norman Thomas was there and he expressed appreciation for the editorial I wrote on Debs at his death. He is tall, slender, white-haired. Very agreeable.

May 26, 1954

Lunch at the Century today with Joe Barnes. Present: Barnes, Geoffrey Parsons, chief editorial writer of the *Herald Tribune*, an old and much-cherished friend, Vincent Sheean, the writer, and William L. Shirer, correspondent in Berlin just before the war. All warmly sympathetic toward my position in, and book on, Spain. I have never had such an interesting conversational session. We sat down at one and left at four.

July 8, 1954

Tonight we went with Colonel Hartfield, Fannie Hurst, the novelist, Helen Wessel and others to Jones Beach to see scenes from *Arabian Nights*, presented by Guy Lombardo. We had dinner at the South Shore Terrace. The audience faces the narrow strip of water and the Emperor's palace and much of the spectacle is on and under the water. The night was cool and the smell of the sea invigorating. I enjoyed talking with Fanny Hurst, who is a great woman as well as a successful novelist.

She told me about her first meeting with Dreiser. She had just ventured into the hurricane of New York from the more conventional life of St. Louis, her home. Having a wish to write and publish, she went to see Dreiser in his offices at some women's magazine. "I found him with his foot on a shoeshine stand and a boy busy blackening and shining his shoes, and that made a great impression on me," she said. When she explained that she wished to write something for his magazine he grunted and for a moment was silent. Then he said, "Come to my apartment in the morning and I'll see what I can do." This rather alarmed her. Dreiser had a reputation that made a visit to his apartment seem a gamble with virtue. But she went. He lived then in the apartment on Eleventh Street with which I was familiar. Apparently his intentions were honorable and he ended by inviting her to submit a story.

October 20, 1954

This afternoon we took Chavela Edwards to the Village to the studio of Luis Quintanilla, and since Luis was captivated with her beauty and enthusiasm and she with his courtliness and art, more than two hours passed pleasantly. Luis displayed his work, many pictures of fruits and flowers which I had not known he painted. Then the portraits. Those of literary celebrities were amusing. He had asked them what they would have liked to be and thus he painted them and most were fantastic. Dorothy Parker had wanted to be a homebody, so he produced a picture of a lady with her face but in a pose she had never known—a plain woman at her knitting. Luis proudly brought out her letter to him, a very witty one.

October 22, 1954

Dinner tonight with Allan Nevins of Columbia University at the Faculty Club. Again we had Abraham Flexner, the distinguished educator and writer. After dinner we went to the library building for Nevins' seminar, walking all over the lot, climbing stairs, and Flexner told me that he is eighty-eight years old! Amazing, since his mind is alert and young. The students are working on their final thesis and Nevins gave us an interesting talk on his excursion to Boston to look over the papers of the Adams family.

October 23, 1954

Sybil and I had dinner with Eleanor Roosevelt at her town house on 62nd Street, though we had difficulty getting in. The bell, rung three times, brought no result. The window in the basement was open and Sybil appealed to the cook. Finally Mrs. Roosevelt appeared, laughing. We found three other guests, an Indian and his wife and an old family friend who was an early law partner of Roosevelt. We dined at a table in the living room, Mrs. Roosevelt doing the serving. Soup, delicious ham, a salad, cheese and ice cream with angel food cake. Mrs. Roosevelt never looked better—is much better-looking than she used to be. We talked some politics, especially New York politics. On international affairs she was very acute and interesting. She foresees a grave problem when atomic energy is applied to industry and a machine can do the work of fifty men. Will it mean great unemployment? Or if work hours are reduced to almost nothing, will these millions loaf—and unless they find some way to employ themselves, will they not degenerate? She had no solution.

October 27, 1954

This morning I spoke as a United States delegate to the Congress of All the American Republics, which is part of Columbia University's bicentennial celebration. I had prepared to discuss all the freedoms, but I delivered only the parts on popular education, academic freedom and something no one else has touched upon, freedom from want, and I proposed a Marshall Plan for South America. I was surprised by the warmth of my greeting when introduced and was astonished by the reaction to the speech, since every succeeding speaker referred to it and Eduardo Santos, the brilliant journalist and former President of Colombia, in the course of a good and eloquent speech based on mine, referred to my speech a number of times. I was congratulated by many, including Ricardo Alfaro, former President of Panama. A young man introduced himself as the son of Secretary of State Dulles—a fine-looking and most agreeable chap.

April 27, 1955

Last night went to Washington by train to meet Colonel Hartfield and party coming in the morning by plane for a drive to Charlottesville for my lecture on the Bill of Rights at the University of Virginia. In our party were Hartfield, Mr. Brown, lawyer for the New York Telephone Company, Judge Walter of the New York Supreme Court and Mr. Watson, eighty-six years old, who graduated from the University of Virginia Law School in 1894. The drive through Virginia was a delight, the day bright, the pastures green and dogwood in blossom. We had lunch at Culpeper and reached Charlottesville about three o'clock and went to the charming Farmington Country Club, where we stayed. The house was designed by Jefferson. The surroundings beautiful, the rooms pretty and the food excellent. At six o'clock we went to the home of the Dean of the Law School for a buffet dinner. The lecture was in a large hall of the university, which was filled. My lecture— plain speaking on the defiance of the Bill of Rights today—ended with a long ovation. We returned to the club and had drinks and talk until midnight. I was awakened in the morning by the rapturous singing of birds—an experience I have not had for years. On the morning of Thursday we drove to Monticello and Ashlawn, lunched at the club and drove back to Washington. My party barely caught the plane for New York and I went in search of a hotel.

May 8, 1955

Agustín Edwards of Chile came to see me this afternoon. He, like all intelligent Chileans, is alarmed by the desperate state of Chile's economy and finances. The dollar has reached the appalling figure of one to 435 pesos and when I went to Chile in 1939 it was one to 35. The conditions are just made for chaos and Perónists and Communists. Some drastic economic and financial reforms are imperative, but were any Chilean to undertake them, politics, jealousies and suspicions would intervene to defeat them. Edwards has the go-ahead sign from President Ibañez to negotiate with the Klein organization of economic experts, who put Peru's house in order, to take over the task in Chile. The President's consent is the best proof that conditions are desperate.

June 22, 1955

Lloyd Paul Stryker, foremost trial lawyer and author of two or three fine biographies, died yesterday after a stroke. He wrote me about *The Tragic Era* when it came out, but I did not meet him personally until a few months ago at a small luncheon. His defense of Alger Hiss was masterful and he hung the jury. Hiss must have been an ass to take another lawyer in the second trial. Stryker told me that the excuse of Hiss was that a fair trial was impossible in New York, that he would try for a change of venue to New England and he thought it advisable to get a New England lawyer. Stryker did not believe Hiss guilty. When he went to him the lawyer asked, "Are you guilty? That I must know," and Hiss denied guilt. Stryker was a genius as a trial lawyer. He was dramatic. He was devastating in cross-examination and he was brilliant. No one in my time has been so great as a trial lawyer except Max Steuer, whom I also knew, but Steuer was not the orator that Stryker was.

328

September 5, 1955

Patricia Costello, an old friend in Santiago, where her Cuban husband was with the U.N., came to call today. A remarkably attractive and bright woman. She tells an amusing story about Hemingway, who lives in Cuba. She was introduced at a cocktail party and told him that it was an enormous pleasure—and he beamed. That she liked his book *The Old Man and the Sea*—and he beamed. And then she asked him if it was autobiographical, and to her amazement he turned his back upon her. When I suggested that the Old Man was old and in the last stage of decrepitude and he resented the implication that he was the Old Man, she said it was true; that he later told a friend of hers that she had been beastly rude to him. "She asked if the story was autobiographical," he said.

October 28, 1955

Spent almost two hours with Bernard Baruch at his home this afternoon. He had been a good friend from my arrival in New York in 1923, but I had not seen him since my return from Chile. He is now eighty-four years old and still active. I found him looking in good health though he has been hard of hearing for some years. He seated me close to him, directly facing him to hear better. Much talk about long dead days. His hostility to Truman is hot as ever, but his enthusiasm for Stevenson is promising. I could not determine what he thinks of Jimmy Byrnes's queer actions during the last few years.

He thinks the new face we have put on at home is in contempt of morals and common sense, observing that civilizations are wrecked from within, as in the case of Rome. Baruch brought in Scotch and soda and cigars, though he himself does not drink until after five and he had cut down on his smoking. A delightful afternoon.

November 4, 1955

Attended Mayor Wagner's luncheon for President Castillo Armas of Guatemala at the Waldorf. While in the lobby waiting to go up I ran into General Crittenberger for an exchange of news. Met many old friends during the cocktail period and after the luncheon. As we were leaving found myself close to Cardinal Spellman, to whom I was introduced. Since we occupy the opposite poles on Franco I expected some coldness. He astonished me with his cordiality and said I am a master of the English language, and I wondered if he based it on *My Mission to Spain*.

329

November 16, 1955

My entire day at the Manhattan Club. After lunch Colonel Hartfield stayed to go over with me the request that I act as chairman of the committee to raise money for the improvement of Woodrow Wilson's birthplace and the purchase of some adjoining property belonging to the place where Wilson was born.

December 8, 1955

Recently I agreed to serve on the committee supporting Adlai E. Stevenson for the Presidential nomination and today I attended a dinner for one hundred people interested, on the roof of the Pierre. Ran into Eddie Miller, who so long was Under Secretary of State for South America, and chatted with him. Also with Marshall Field, who presided, and Ambassador Ellsworth Bunker, who was in Argentina, one man who did not kowtow to Perón.

February 7, 1956

Attended a meeting of the Committee for Stevenson for the West Side of this town from Greenwich Village to 120th Street. I have had the chairmanship wished upon me and while I have made it clear that I am not an organizer, they say others will do that and I am to deal solely in policies.

April 3, 1956

Called by appointment on President Truman this morning. Looking in the pink of condition, his eyes sparkling, complexion pink, his voice vibrant, he gave me a warm greeting. Mrs. Truman was in the room looking more happy than in the White House, also looking young. She admitted she is happier as it is. The President was working out his itinerary for his European trip next month with my old friend Woodward, once Chief of Protocol and later ambassador to Canada. He is to accompany Truman. They are visiting England, France, Belgium, Holland and Italy.

He had written me that there are too many men posing in the Senate and the House as Democrats who ought to be seated across the aisle with the Republicans they serve. He expanded on this theme this morning. He says the Truman Library for the housing of all his papers is progressing. He has arranged for an office there for himself as long as he lives after the library has been given to the Nation. Commenting on the importance of the Presidential papers, I told him that Charles Evans Hughes had told me Mrs. Harding had gone to the White House immediately after Harding's death and destroyed all his papers. This interested Truman, who had not known it. He had tried to see the Harding papers and could not find them.

I suspect he is making his European journey, lasting until the eve of the Democratic Convention, to avoid complications and his involvement.

Lexington, Kentucky, May 21, 1956

Arrived in Lexington about nine this morning. Until dark the train journey was delightful because of the vivid greenery and the woods. Holman Hamilton met me at the station and took me to the Lafayette Hotel. After lunch he drove me about town and I thought Lexington fascinating and beautiful, rich in historical association. Impressive to me the large number of fine old Georgian mansions a century and more old. I had not realized that Jefferson Davis had attended college here before going to West Point until a three-story brick residence painted white was pointed out to me as his lodging place. Nor did I realize that Mrs. Lincoln had her education here till I was shown the large brick house that was a girls' school when she was a student here.

At six-thirty back to the Lafayette Hotel—to the Gold Room, where I spoke for an hour on the aftermath of the Civil War. This was on the program of the Civil War Roundtable. The speech went off well and will be published. After the lecture a dozen very congenial men took me to the attractive home of Holman Hamilton, where we ate, drank and swapped stories until late.

August 16, 1956

Saw the convention on television more completely than if I had been in it. Candidates for President were nominated. The best speech made by Senator Kennedy of Massachusetts, who nominated Stevenson.

November 17, 1956

Yesterday went by train to Princeton to speak at a dinner arranged by Professor Monroe, of the Woodrow Wilson School of International Studies at the university, on how to remove the barriers to understanding between the Latin Americans and the North Americans. I was met at the station, put up at the Princeton Inn, and immediately driven to the Nassau Tavern for cocktails before dinner there. At the cocktail party I found Hallet Johnson, my counselor in Madrid. He is living in Princeton in the former house of the late university president. Also there was Dr. Whittaker from Pennsylvania University. . . . The dinner was excellent. Dr. Whittaker presided and made a generous introduction. My speech went over satisfactorily. . . .

January 4, 1957

Eduardo Irarrazaval, who was González Videla's last Foreign Minister and who has been here undergoing an eye operation, phoned me yesterday and I had an interesting visit with him for an hour and a half at the Gotham Hotel. Our chat ranged over old incidents when I was ambassador. He is pessimistic over the fate of the Klein plan to put Chile on its economic and financial feet. The Minister of Economy in office at first was completely in accord with the Klein plan, but intrigue entered in and the Minister was removed. All this, together with the approaching congressional elections there, adds to the confusion. It was a pleasure to see this very able, courageous, honest man with whom I had the most perfect relations.

January 5, 1957

This evening González Videla, President of Chile from 1946 to 1952, and his wife came to call. He looks chipper and happy and his beautiful wife never was more attractive. They say that the cost of living in Chile is so high they marvel how the poor can eat. He says the political parties that lost public confidence, making easy the election of Ibañez, have by no means recovered that confidence, but he took exception to my suggestion that with parties out dictators come in, by saying the Chileans are democratic and would not tolerate a dictatorship. The fine housing projects so wonderfully sponsored by Mrs. González Videla, she tells me, are making no progress because of increased costs. . . . He brought me a photograph of himself in his Presidential regalia, flatteringly inscribed. Marie, the cook, who usually serves us dinner at 6:30, did not get away until 8:30.

February 28, 1957

Had a very interesting visitor for three hours this afternoon—Doris Dana, the companion and friend of Gabriela Mistral, who died recently, making Miss Dana her executor. She had been with Gabriela Mistral in

Rome and Mexico, and here Gabriela lived in Miss Dana's house on Long Island. She corrected not a few myths. I knew that Chile had made the poetess a consul for life with permission to choose her own posts, but I did not know that Chile at first overlooked the matter of salary until Unamuno, the Spanish philosopher, made an open protest. I had assumed the press story that she chose Gabriela for a name because of her admiration for D'Annunzio was true, but the story was not true and she hated D'Annunzio.

I was told that her biography will be written by the brilliant Chilean literary critic, Hernán Díaz Arrieta, who signs his criticisms "Alone." He was a great friend of Gabriela Mistral and in Rome stayed for two months with her and Miss Dana.

When the Nobel Prize money came the poetess wished most of it allotted to charity, with a good part for the village of her birth, where most of the people were miserably poor, but in the distribution the village was left out and got only a few dolls for children. This distressed her and she told Miss Dana she wished to be buried in this remote village. "If they got no money they at least shall have my bones."

Miss Dana leaves for Chile in April. She said there is an enormous amount of unpublished manuscript, including a long poem, descriptive and philosophic, about Chile and its towns and cities. Unhappily she did not like Santiago and this appears in the poem. She never felt comfortable there and rather feared it. She preferred the provinces.

April 7, 1957

Went to New Haven to take part in a panel discussion before the John Dewey Society of Yale University. Since everyone is traveling today I was unable to get a place in the chair car and went in the day coach, which was crowded. I was to be met at the station, but after making myself conspicuous to attract the attention of anyone looking for me, without effect, I got Yale by phone and learned that the affair was to be in Dwight Hall. Called a taxi and went to Dwight. There I found the pleasant young man who missed me at the station and found the affair was at one-thirty instead of one. My young friend took me to a restaurant for lunch. . . . I spoke first on the panel. . . . Well received. Professor Harper followed. Meanwhile Mr. Gerhard Seger, the German-born journalist now living here, was lost en route. He appeared just in time and he followed my line exactly. Then questions from the students, keen, wise, penetrating questions that promise well for the oncoming generation. . . . The John Dewey Society is doing a fine job on the young men at Yale. I was deeply impressed by them.

May 28, 1957

This evening went to Columbia University for a reception for Eduardo Santos, former President of Colombia and editor of a great newspaper at Bogotá. He went into exile when the dictatorship took over and stole his paper, and now with the victory for democracy in the overthrow of the dictator he is on his way back. I recalled to him the dinner I gave in Santiago in his honor on the night of the 1944 election here, since he had expressed a wish to get the returns on American soil.

[*My father's last book*, Chile Through Embassy Windows, *did not appear until February 1958, a month after his death. However, a Spanish translation was published in Chile in July 1957. My father loved Chile and said so, and the Chileans deluged him with letters of appreciation. A street in the capital was named for him, and a foundation to help poor students was set up by Chileans and given his name. The University of Chile invited him to come to Santiago as a guest and to give a lecture in the Hall of Honor of the university. My father was delighted and deeply touched. He hoped to be able to accept the invitation to go to Chile later in the year, but his health did not permit his making the trip. He died on January 21, 1958, at the age of seventy-nine. A little over a year before, on his birthday, he wrote the following in his diary.*]

November 20, 1956

Seventy-eight years ago in the little Quaker town of Westfield in Hamilton County, Indiana, I was born into a home sorely stricken by the death of my idolized four-year-old sister just one week before. I am afraid there was no hilarious celebration over my advent. The seventy-eight years since have had many lights and shadows. Happily I enjoyed the lights and never mourned over the shadows. The world on which I opened my eyes then passed long ago. . . . Two terrible wars have been fought in those years and ancient monarchical dynasties have fallen and out of Russia has come Communism. . . . And now, with the hydrogen bomb ready to demolish cities like New York and London and to exterminate the human race, it is not stupid to conclude that we are not moving forward, for the new Dark Age casts a shadow on the happiness of man.

334

My health is good—exceedingly good for my age, though fifty-five years ago I could not get life insurance. I sit at my typewriter writing books, articles and speeches as forty years ago, and I get just as much thrill out of my work now as I did then.

Index

Heitman Ed

Due May 31

ILL

Strachey, Lytton, 104
Stryker, Lloyd Paul, 328
Sullivan, Mark, 149, 150
Sulzberger, Arthur Hays, 322
Sulzberger, Cyrus, 322
Sulzer, William, 188, 189
Swope, Gerard, 216
Swope, Herbert Bayard, 106, 108, 216, 252

Taft, William Howard, 68, 211–212
Taggart organization, 46
Taggart, T., 47, 64, 113
Tagore (Hindu poet), 223
Tammany Hall, 113, 141, 177, 182, 187, 230
Tanner, Corporal, 10
Tarkington, Booth, 14, 161
Taylor, Deems, 166
Teapot Dome scandal, 71, 119
Tedeschini, Cardinal, 270–271
Terre Haute, Indiana, 48, 49–51, 56, 59, 153, 168
Terre Haute *Gazette*, 48, 50
Terre Haute House, 50
Terre Haute *Star*, 50, 57
Terre Haute *Tribune*, 50
Thomas, Norman, 325
Thomas Jefferson Memorial Foundation, 133
Thompson, Genevieve, 202
Thompson, Richard W., 49
Thurman, Allen G., 8
Tilden, Samuel J., 251
Titan, The, 156, 169
Toledo, Spain, 273-274
Tomlinson's Hall (Indianapolis), 13, 14, 19, 44, 45, 47
Tosca, Joaquín, 305
Tragic Era, The, 127, 141, 152, 176, 181, 192, 208–210, 217, 220, 249
Trinity Church, 134
Trout, Dave, 3–4
Truman, Harry S, 192, 283, 316–317, 321–322, 330
Truman, Mrs. Harry S, 321, 330

Truman, Margaret, 317
Tucker, Henry St. George, 239
Tumulty, Joe, 94, 124
Turmoil, The, 161
Turpie, David, 32–33
Turtle, The, 15–16
Twelve Men, 156

Unamuno, 278
Uncle Tom's Cabin, 53
Underwood, Oscar W., 113, 122
United Mine Workers, 76
United States Chamber of Commerce, 288
Untermyer, Samuel, 75–76

Van Buren, Martin, 67, 250
Van Doren, Carl, 152, 166, 219
Van Doren, Mark, 166
Vanderlip, Frank, 259
Vergniaud, 324
Villa Alemana, Chile, 310
Viña del Mar, Chile, 311
Virginia, University of, 134, 135, 192
Virginia Resolution, 126
Viviani, René, 130, 131
von Welczeck, Count, 271
Voorhees, Daniel W., 8, 49

Wadsworth, James W., 144–147
Wagner, Harr, 30–31
Wagner, Robert F., 145–148, 181, 186, 187, 189, 190, 232, 249, 252, 253
Walker, James, 144, 241, 244
Wallace, Henry, 198, 312
Wallace, Lew, 22
Walsh, Frank, 166
Walsh, Thomas J., 70, 119, 134, 180, 185, 204, 239, 244
Warburg, Felix, 134, 135, 136
Warner Brothers, 127, 128, 129
Warrum, Henry, 37–38, 47
Washington, D. C., 66–90

INDEX

Wassermann, Jakob, 166
Watson, James, 211
Watterson, Henry, 108
Webster, Daniel, 66, 68
Weigel, Father, 302
Welles, Sumner, 283, 292, 293, 301, 318
Westfield, Indiana, 1, 334
What Price Glory?, 110
Wheeler, Burt, 239
When Knighthood Was in Flower, 25
While Rome Burns, 109
White, William Allen, 251
Whitestown, Indiana, 2, 11, 45
Wickersham, George, 216
Williams, Dixon, 112
Williams, John Sharp, 69–70, 74
Willkie, Wendell, 298
Wilson, Woodrow, 69, 79, 86–89, 92–93, 94, 95, 96, 101, 107, 121, 122,

125, 130–132, 134–135, 144, 151–152, 212–215, 230, 299
Wilson, Mrs. Woodrow, 125, 131, 193, 194, 325
Women's National Democratic Club, 225, 324
Woollcott, Alexander, 109
Woodward, William E., 165
Woolen, Evans, 323
World to Win, A, 250
World's Illusion, The, 166
Wylie, Elinor, 165

Yale University, 333–334
Yeats, William Butler, 256–257
Young Jefferson, 315

Zamora, Alcala, 267–268, 270
Zangwill, Israel, 83
Zapallar, Chile, 311
Zuloaga, Ignacio, 281–282